Anitsalagi Elohi Anehi

Anitsalagi Elohi Anehi

STORIES AND
TEACHINGS
OF THE
NATURAL WORLD

Christopher B. Teuton and Hastings Shade

WITH LORETTA SHADE AND LARRY SHADE

ILLUSTRATED BY MARYBETH TIMOTHY

Cherokee Earth Dwellers

University of Washington Press • Seattle

Cherokee Earth Dwellers was made possible in part by generous gifts from Jill and Joseph McKinstry and from the Hugh and Jane Ferguson Foundation.

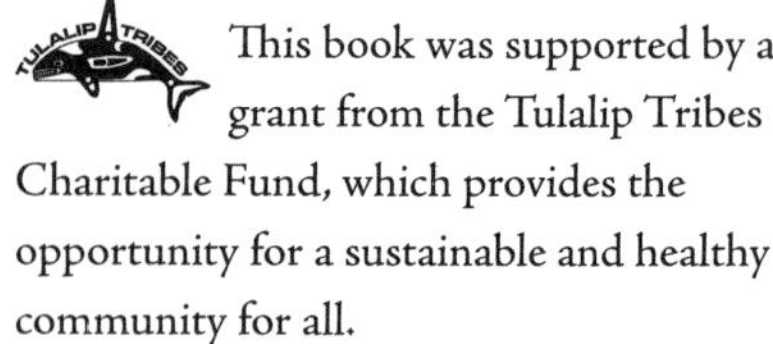

This book was supported by a grant from the Tulalip Tribes Charitable Fund, which provides the opportunity for a sustainable and healthy community for all.

Design by Mindy Basinger Hill
Composed in 11.5/15pt Adobe Jenson Pro

27 26 25 6 5 4

Printed and bound in the United States of America

UNIVERSITY OF WASHINGTON PRESS
uwapress.uw.edu

LIBRARY OF CONGRESS CATALOGING-IN-PUBLICATION DATA
Names: Teuton, Christopher B., author. | Shade, Hastings, 1941–2010, author. | Timothy, MaryBeth, illustrator.
Title: Anitsalagi elohi anehi = Cherokee Earth dwellers : stories and teachings of the natural world / Christopher B. Teuton and Hastings Shade ; with Loretta Shade and Larry Shade ; illustrated by MaryBeth Timothy.
Other titles: Cherokee Earth dwellers
Description: Seattle : University of Washington Press, [2023]. | Includes bibliographical references and index.
Identifiers: LCCN 2021043732 (print) | LCCN 2021043733 (ebook) | ISBN 9780295750163 (hardcover) | ISBN 9780295750187 (paperback) | ISBN 9780295750194 (ebook)
Subjects: LCSH: Cherokee philosophy. | Nature—Folklore. | Cherokee language—Vocabulary. | Cherokee Indians—Social life and customs.
Classification: LCC E99.C5 T345 2022 (print) | LCC E99.C5 (ebook) | DDC 975.004/97557—dc23/eng/20211012
LC record available at https://lccn.loc.gov/2021043732
LC ebook record available at https://lccn.loc.gov/2021043733

∞ This paper meets the requirements of ANSI/NISO Z39.48-1992 (Permanence of Paper).

FOR LORETTA SHADE • 1946–2021

Contents

Note on Pronunciation and Presentation of Cherokee

A is not A as in fate but A as in far. An *ah* sound.

E is not E as in eat but E as in hey. An *eh* sound.

I is not I as in ice but I as in police. An *ee* sound.

O is as pronounced in English, but throaty and from back of the throat. An *oh* sound.

U is not U as in run but U as in blues. An *oo* sound.

The V is sounded as *uh* as in uh-huh.

The TS- consonant is sounded as *j* as in jug. Most other Cherokee consonants sound similar to those used in English.

The first occurrence of each Cherokee word is italicized and followed by a translation in parentheses.

Although often not customary in Cherokee language spelling, for the sake of readability we capitalize proper nouns—names of people, places, and organizations.

ᎠᏂᏣᎳᎩᎡ ᎶᎯ ᎠᏁᎯ ✦ *Anitsalagi Elohi Anehi*

Introduction

Duyukdv

OPENING A STRAIGHT PATH

From outside the chapel you could hear their laughter. Before me sat a group of elderly women and men huddled around several hand-bound books with blue construction paper covers. The books were titled things like *Atsadi*, or Fish; *Itlugv ale Detlugv*, or Trees; and *Saluyi ale Inage ale Diganatla'i*, or Animals in the Woods, Forest, and Domesticated Animals. With deep intensity and delight they were flipping through the books, looking at page after page of names and stories of creatures of the natural world. They would look over at one another and point out a word or story, and say things like, "My dad used to tell this one." Or, "I still eat one of these berries every day. Good for the kidneys." And all the while, these Cherokee elders were speaking the Cherokee language. Their first language.

We had been brought together at the chapel of the Cherokee Heritage Center by Loretta Shade, esteemed Cherokee elder and fellow fluent speaker, to discuss a unique archive of names, stories, and teachings of the natural world compiled by her late husband, Hastings Shade, who passed on in 2010. Like Hastings and Loretta, these folks were raised at a time when the natural order was taught to Cherokee children, and they learned the names and stories of the world humans share with other creatures. Like the others who would come to contribute to our project, they had gatherered out of respect for Hastings Shade and to offer commentary on the lists of names and stories he compiled. Working with Loretta Shade and her son, Larry Shade, our aim was to create a book that portrays traditional ways of knowing the Cherokee natural world. Reflecting on this knowledge and the relationships it fosters, I came to learn, may lead one to find interconnection, balance, health, and maturity. Or, as Hastings would say, to learn to "stand in the middle": *ayetli gadoga* (he/she stands in the middle). Using Hastings' original title for one of his hand-bound collections, we called it *Cherokee Earth Dwellers.*

Cherokee Earth Dwellers represents what Hastings called a *sgadudv dvhdatlesv*, or a community that comes together as a whole to help one another. Hastings taught that there was perhaps nothing more characteristic of Cherokee culture than the impulse to share with one another and help another in need. This is what it means to be a *sgadug* (community). This book includes elders, cultural traditionalists, storytellers, artists, and students of Cherokee culture, family and friends alike, who in the spirit of this impulse have come together to contribute their memories, knowledge, artistry, and stories to bring Hastings' depiction of a living Cherokee cosmos to completion.

The core of this book are the teachings Hastings Shade shared, which include his own writings as well as collected stories and names for the Cherokee natural world that were passed along by other elders for him to share. A citizen of the Cherokee Nation, Shade was an honored elder, educator, cultural traditionalist, storyteller, and man of the woods. Chief Wilma Mankiller of the Cherokee Nation named Shade a Cherokee National Treasure in 1991 in recognition of his traditional knowledge. He served as deputy principal chief of the Cherokee Nation from 1999 to 2003.

Loretta Shade and Larry Shade represented the Hastings Shade family and his intent for his work throughout this project. Through oral interviews and consultation they reflected on Hastings' teachings and shared their own knowledge and stories of the Cherokee natural world. Before her passing in 2021, Loretta Shade was a deeply respected elder, cultural traditionalist, and teacher of the Cherokee language. Like her husband, she was raised with Cherokee as her first language and spoke, read, and wrote Cherokee. In recognition of her passionate commitment to teaching and perpetuating the Cherokee language since the 1970s, Loretta Shade was named a National Treasure by the Cherokee Nation in 2018. Like both his parents, Larry Shade is an educator and cultural traditionalist who continues his father's art of gig making. He has taught mathematics and science and coached several sports throughout his career, including at Sequoyah High School and the Cherokee Language Immersion school in Tahlequah, Oklahoma.

In addition to this core group of contributors, *Cherokee Earth Dwellers* includes interviews, stories, and commentary from invited friends of Hastings and Loretta Shade. All are well-known knowledge keepers. And though in humility they might say otherwise, I recognize each of them as elders. There is no set definition of "elder" in Cherokee community, though I have heard some say one needs to be a language speaker, raised traditionally, be respected, and carry wisdom to hold this title. I subscribe to Cherokee elder Sammy Still's definition, which is that being an elder does not necessarily mean one is old, but that one has lived a Cherokee life, gained wisdom, and shares that wisdom through teachings. As Cherokee Nation historian Julie Reed writes, elders are "historians, teachers, and healers" (2016, 8).

The late Sequoyah Guess was a citizen of the United Keetoowah Band of Cherokee Indians. A close friend and long-time collaborator of Hastings, Sequoyah was a beloved and renowned storyteller, novelist, filmmaker, and teacher of Cherokee, his first language. In addition to being a storyteller, snake handler, and reptile safety educator, Cherokee Nation citizen Woody Hansen is an ordained and practicing minister. Like Shade, Guess, and Hansen, Sammy Still is an original member of the Turtle Island Liars' Club. He is a proud practitioner of traditional Cherokee crafts as well as a noted photographer, journalist, and storyteller. Fellow Liars' Club member Choogie Kingfisher was honored as a Cherokee National Treasure in 2019 for his contributions as a cultural educator and storyteller. Dorothy Ice, a Cherokee Nation elder and fluent speaker, is recognized as a Cherokee National Treasure for her loom weaving. Cherokee Nation elder Rufus King is a retired pastor who, with his wife, Melvina King, is deeply committed to perpetuating the Cherokee language. Ryan Mackey is curriculum supervisor of the Cherokee Nation's Cherokee Language Master/Apprentice Program. A spiritual leader and traditional cultural practitioner, Mackey is a gifted storyteller. David Comingdeer was honored in 2014 as a Cherokee National Treasure for his stickball making. A recognized cultural traditionalist and spiritual leader, he is head chief of Echota-Tanasi Ceremonial Ground in Park Hill, Oklahoma.

I am a citizen of the Cherokee Nation and member of Echota-Tanasi Ceremonial Ground. A first-generation college graduate, in 2003 I earned a Ph.D. from the University of Wisconsin–Madison. I am currently professor of American Indian Studies at the University of Washington–Seattle, where I teach courses on Indigenous oral and written literatures. I was honored to learn from and collaborate with Hastings Shade, Sammy Still, Sequoyah Guess, and Woody Hansen in the creation of a collection and study of Cherokee storytelling and teachings, titled *Cherokee Stories of the Turtle Island Liars' Club* (Teuton 2012).

The teachings shared in *Cherokee Earth Dwellers* are made all the more urgent by the endangered health of the Cherokee language. In northeastern Oklahoma, home to the Cherokee Nation (CN) and United Keetoowah Band of Cherokee Indians (UKB), there may be fewer than two thousand fluent first-language speakers of Cherokee. There are approximately two hundred fluent first-language speakers of Cherokee on the Eastern Band of Cherokee Indians (EBCI) reservation in western North Carolina. Beginning in the eighteenth century, Cherokee society has endured a persistent and often coercive "shift" to English from Cherokee as the common language of community. This "language shift," as linguists call it, arose within the context of Anglo-American settler colonization of Cherokee people and their territory. Through warfare, disease, forced displacement, intermarriage, and the necessary adoption of Euro-American economic and social institutions for survival, Cherokee society transformed in the nineteenth century. While complex lines of division were often fluid within families and communities, Cherokee society divided roughly between those acculturating to Anglo-American culture as a means of survival and those who chose to continue their ancestral traditions. The use of either English or Cherokee language often demarcated those lines. Through the first half of the twentieth century, Cherokee-English bilingualism continued in many Cherokee families and communities. However, the eventual dominance of English in the workplace, schools, and social institutions increasingly limited the social domains of Cherokee to a language of family, kin, traditional ceremony, and Cherokee-language Christian churches. The number of fluent speakers began to dip precipitously when the intergenerational transmission of Cherokee language in the home began to wane.

Today Cherokee people and governments are actively decolonizing through their Cherokee language revitalization efforts. During the Tri-Council meeting of the three federally recognized Cherokee governments (CN, EBCI, and UKB) on June 27, 2019, a "state of emergency" was declared for the Cherokee language and a resolution was adopted calling for continuing development of tribal language revitalization programs (Brings Plenty 2019). In response to the potential loss of Cherokee as a spoken language, Cherokee governments are dedicating significant resources to teaching and revitalizing the Cherokee language. Both the EBCI and CN maintain Cherokee language immersion schools: ᎠᏤ ᎩᏚᏩ ᏧᎾᏕᎶᏆᏍᏗ (Atse Kituwah Tsunadeloquasdi), or New Kituwah Academy on the Qualla Boundary of the EBCI, and ᏣᎳᎩ ᏧᎾᏕᎶᏆᏍᏗ (Tsalagi Tsunadeloquasdi), or Cherokee Immersion School of the CN in Tahlequah, Oklahoma. The CN maintains a tribal language department that has worked with companies such as Apple, Google, and Microsoft to incorporate the Sequoyan script as a supported font. The CN also has an active Cherokee Language Master/Apprentice program and offers free online Cherokee language courses as well as free courses in partnership with Rogers State University Public Television.

In 2019, under the leadership of Principal Chief Chuck Hoskin Jr., the Cherokee Nation passed the Durbin Feeling Cherokee Language Preservation Act. Named in honor of Cherokee Nation linguist Durbin Feeling, the act allotted millions to renovate the former Cherokee Casino Tahlequah building into a language center and provide for its operation. Deputy Chief Bryan Warner explained the administration's rationale for this redoubling of financial investment: "The Cherokee language, I believe, is the soul of the Cherokee people. It is the source of our pride and strength as a tribe. That's why revitalizing the Cherokee language has become a priority of the utmost importance. The investments we are making in our language programs are meant not only to preserve the Cherokee language today, but to encourage us as Cherokee people to embrace our language and to use it for many generations into the future" ("Chief Hoskin" 2019). Cherokee language teaching in academia continues to be important to these language revitalization efforts. Northeastern State University in Tahlequah, Oklahoma, has an established Cherokee language curriculum, as do Western Carolina University, UNC-Chapel Hill, UNC-Asheville, the University of Oklahoma, and, most recently, the University of Arkansas.

Like other endangered Indigenous languages, Cherokee has suffered a diminishment of its lexicon. As the number of first-language speakers declines, so too do the number of words people know and use to describe their world. Adding further complexity, each community within the Cherokee Nation may speak Cherokee in slightly but noticeably different ways. Loretta Shade spoke a dialect of Cherokee unique to the Lost City–Hulbert area, which may include phrases, words, and pronunciations that differ from the Cherokee spoken in the communities of Briggs, Vian, or Kenwood. Lexicons having to do with one's vocation, such as being a farmer or business owner, or with one's interests, such as horse breeding or pottery making, are even further threatened. As an example, Loretta shared with me an image of a house upon which Hastings Shade had labeled in Cherokee all the structural parts of a home. From its roof and chimney to its rafters and studs, all construction parts were named in Cherokee. I took a picture of the diagram and texted it to David Comingdeer, who with his son, Spencer Comingdeer, is a home builder. "This is amazing!

Wado!" David texted me back in thanks. Loretta and I knew that as a student and speaker of the language, David would put the words to use. And that was Hastings' hope in documenting those words.

There was a time when some of those who contributed to *Cherokee Earth Dwellers* might not have done so. Among Cherokee people traditional knowledge is shared on a "need to know" basis, as Hastings would say. It remains customary for Cherokees to share their cultural knowledge mainly within their families and communities. However, among the fluent speakers and cultural traditionalists with whom I am familiar, the endangered state of the Cherokee language has generated a renewed drive to share and perpetuate traditional knowledge. As an example, esteemed Cherokee elder and spiritual leader Crosslin Fields Smith's 2018 book *Stand as One: Spiritual Teachings of Keetoowah, Awakening to the Original Truths* shares the "Original Truths" of the Keetoowah Society, a central Cherokee spiritual community. A guiding tenet of the book "stresses the lessons and teachings contained within the Original Truths are no longer the sole ownership of the Keetoowahs or Cherokees" (Martyn 2018). As Smith is quoted, "It is time for all to know" (Martyn 2018). Like Smith's work, *Cherokee Earth Dwellers* presents traditional knowledge while respecting Cherokee cultural boundaries, especially around specific details concerning ceremony and medicine.

Beginning in the 1970s, Hastings Shade recorded and documented Cherokee knowledge. He was aware that *dideyohvsdi* (teachings) of traditional knowledge taught to him by his grandfathers and relatives were at risk of not being known to others outside his family. Finding tremendous value and meaning in these teachings, in the spirit of sharing Hastings wrote down what he knew as well as knowledge entrusted to him by his elders. As *Cherokee Earth Dwellers* illustrates, Cherokee knowledge begins with the Cherokee language itself, which traditionalists like Hastings state was, along with fire, a direct gift to the Cherokee people from *Unetlvnv* (Creator, or "the one who provides or gives"). A legend tells that as long as Cherokee people speak to the ceremonial fire in Cherokee, it will not go out. If the language should die, so will Cherokee peoplehood.

In documenting more than six hundred Cherokee names of the natural world, Hastings Shade took a powerful stand for the continuing life of the Cherokee language. There is perhaps no more basic and fundamental use of language than as a tool to name our world. Naming extends our relationships in the world, giving our realities shape, form, and meaning. Through naming we relate to space. Through naming we position ourselves in time. Even today, the fluent speakers from the CN, UKB, and EBCI who make up the Cherokee Language Consortium create new Cherokee words at each of their quarterly meetings, continuing the process of naming our world. As Maori scholar Linda Tuhiwai Smith states, naming "is about retaining as much control over meanings as possible. . . . For communities there are realities which can only be found, as self-evident concepts, in the indigenous language; they can never be captured by another language" (Smith 2012, 159).

For thousands of years, deep and intimate observations, partnerships, and kinship with other creatures led to accepted names for the other creatures that inhabit the Cherokee world. In Cherokee language, one is named by others, not by one's self. When I say, "*Noyi dagwado'a,*" or "My name is Noyi," I am literally saying, "Noyi I am called (more than once/ repeatedly)." The prefix d- at the beginning of *dagwado'a* makes the verb distributive, or referring to multiple parts. One's name is a term for the multiplicity that comprises you as a person—someone with a body, a mind, a spirit, and other qualities, characteristics, and relations. Understood from the context of naming, Cherokee subjectivity is distributive, not singular. A foundational part of one's identity is determined by how others name—see, understand, and place—within the community of life the distributed self that is you. As you and your relations change, so you may acquire different or additional names. Knowledge of the Cherokee natural world became encoded through the process of naming and is often reflected in the names themselves.

Biologists use a German word, *umwelt,* meaning "the environment" or "world around," to describe the perceived world unique to a particular animal (Yoon 2009, 15). We know all animals have particular sensory and cognitive capacities that shape their view of reality. A bee finds its way back to its hive through the use of smell and landmarks. An eagle hunts with its sharp sight. This concept of umwelt also applies to humans. We humans all share similar sensory and cognitive capacities. But for us, it is our specific cultural differences created through relationships with place that shape our unique ways of defining, engaging, and understanding our umwelt, our perceived world. As Carol Kaesuk Yoon explains, "The umwelt is more than just a view of the living world. It is and always has been a view of the reality around us, the context in which we understand who we are" (Yoon 2009, 18). In Cherokee thought, definitions of reality trace back to Cherokee language and traditional dideyohvsdi shared by elders. Knowledge and understanding of the natural world and our relations with other creatures are foundational to those teachings.

As storyteller Sequoyah Guess would say each time he began an animal story, "*Ilvhiyu tsigesv nigada inage anehi tsalagi tsaniwonisgv*": in the great forever that was, all the forest dwellers spoke Cherokee. This was how his grandma, Maggie Turtle, would begin her stories. And, no doubt, she learned this lesson from her elders; Cherokee traditions hold that all creatures once spoke Cherokee. The problem, as Hastings Shade would say, is that we have forgotten how to *listen*. In fact, Hastings held that everything that moves is alive and that one may speak with anything that is alive. As we now know, all matter is, at the subatomic level, moving energy. From clouds to birds, oceans to quarks, within this most expansive Cherokee view of the umwelt we exist in a living, communicative world. Deep experiential knowledge of this world led to a recognition of shared characteristics, as well as differences, among creatures that live together in specific spaces. Starting at the macro level and working its way down to finer orders of division, the Cherokee worldview begins with a three-tiered cosmos: *Galvladi*, or the Sky World; *Elohi*, or the Middle World; and *Elohi Hawinadidla*, or the Under World. Broadly, the creatures in these three worlds share characteristics defined by being of the sky, of the earth, or of the waters. Yet they are in constant relationship both with other worlds as well as other creatures with whom they share life. Cultural teachings about these creatures, including their names, stories, and places in which they live and interact with us, together define the contours of a living Cherokee natural order. Even for elders such as Hastings who spent a lifetime in the outdoors, learning about the Cherokee natural world and natural order was a continuing process.

As the contributors to *Cherokee Earth Dwellers* demonstrate, families, communities, and individuals have their own unique experiences, stories, and relationships with the creatures of the natural world. Our relationships with the Cherokee world are evolving, never static. There is always more to learn from the other life-forms in our world as well as from each other. In fact, one common thread through stories of the natural world is the wonder and mystery that are ever present in our engagement with other creatures, who may share characteristics with their fellow species members but who are also, in the end, individuals like each of us.

Learning Cherokee names for the natural world is no substitute for fluency in the language or experiential knowledge of the outdoors. However, the stories, reflections, and commentary in *Cherokee Earth Dwellers* demonstrate that knowing names and understanding the meaning behind them may offer a foundation from which to build an awareness of the relations that compose Cherokee views of the world; to nurture those relations one's self; and to continue the process of asserting Cherokee self-determination as a sovereign people. Learning animal names and the stories that shape our living knowledge of the Cherokee world may enable one to understand the place of a person within a traditional Cherokee view of the natural order. In Hastings' terms, one may learn to "stand in the middle." It was in recognition of the way Cherokee reality is grounded in an understanding of the natural world that Hastings began collecting names and stories of Galvladi, Elohi, and Elohi Hawinadidla.

Hastings Shade was trusted by other elders. And they would share their knowledge with him. For this reason, he would often carry a pocket notebook with him when he met with his elders and would write down stories and teachings they shared. Dating back to the 1970s when he first began this archive of Cherokee knowledge, he eventually organized his collection into several volumes of beings: Birds, Animals, Insects, Fish, Reptiles and Amphibians, Plants, Edible Plants, and Trees. His intent was to compile these lists of animal names and stories with accompanying pictures so that the animals could be identified. But with his other duties and art interests, as well as with the complication of creating images for each creature, Hastings never completed the project.

The first vision Loretta Shade and Larry Shade had for our book was a dictionary of names. When Hastings began the collection in the 1970s, the immediate concern was to record names for the natural world; even at that time, widespread knowledge of that world was limited. Still, there were many more thousands of Cherokee speakers, and more people had grown up in rural settings where traditional Cherokee visions of the natural world are more common. A dictionary of animal and plant names would have been a welcome supplement to existing cultural knowledge. Speaking with Loretta and Larry, however, it became clear that Hastings' collection assumed his readers would have a baseline cultural understanding of traditional Cherokee views of reality. Within such a context, the complexity and richness of his archive of creature names and stories would come alive. Without that knowledge, however, the archive might appear simply as word lists. Hastings' great hope for the collection was that it would invigorate relationships with the natural world and instill a renewed appreciation and reverence for the Cherokee language. Given that impulse, we agreed the book needed explanations and commentary from other elders and cultural traditionalists as well as a guiding writerly voice to present and explore the conceptual world within which a traditional Cherokee vision of the natural world may be understood in its richness.

It is in the spirit of that intent that the contributors to *Cherokee Earth Dwellers* participate in the book and that I, as a scholar and student of Hastings Shade, also have a voice in the text.

When I collaborated with Hastings, he shared with me his writings and said, "Use any of 'em you want." Years later, Loretta Shade shared with me Hastings' books of animal and plant names, as well as other miscellaneous writings, both as a source of knowledge and for publication in *Cherokee Earth Dwellers*. Starting with these materials and my own recordings of Hastings, Loretta and I talked about the Cherokee worldview Hastings had grown up within and the teachings he shared. In the course of our work together, it became clear that much of the knowledge that Hastings shared was also known by Loretta. They each brought to their union the knowledge, traditions, and the ways of speaking Cherokee language from the communities where they grew up. While each had individual areas of specialized knowledge, in the course of their lives together what they knew became family knowledge. Though it was Loretta and the family's wish that *Cherokee Earth Dwellers* center Hastings Shade's work in recording and documenting Cherokee teachings and language, this book is also a reflection of the deep cultural knowledge of Loretta Shade. Loretta had been a partner throughout the project, continuing Hastings' and her own life's work to perpetuate Cherokee language and culture. Like many others, I am honored to have called her my elder and teacher.

From 2015 to 2021, Loretta, Larry and I met together, talked on the phone, emailed, and texted one another about the teachings in *Cherokee Earth Dwellers*. We recorded conversations with elders and storytellers at a variety of locations, including Loretta's home in Hulbert, at the Town Branch restaurant in Tahlequah, and even in the conference room at the local Holiday Inn Express. A significant number of conversations were recorded at the chapel on the Cherokee Heritage Center grounds in Park Hill, Oklahoma. The Heritage Center was a central location to meet. But more than that, the tranquility of its setting and the history of both the chapel and the Heritage Center grounds are conducive to the sharing of teachings. Now densely covered with oaks, pecans, sycamores, and bois d'arc trees, the Heritage Center grounds were once the home of the Cherokee Male Seminary. Since the 1960s the Heritage Center has been a site of knowledge sharing and the perpetuation of Cherokee culture. As such, the Heritage Center and Ho-Chee-Nee Trail of Tears Chapel were ideal places in which to reflect upon and record stories of the Cherokee natural world.

Cherokee Earth Dwellers presents stories and knowledge of the Cherokee natural world of both ancient origin and recent occurrence. The past, present, and future are alive and in conversation within these teachings; that is a facet of their power. Whether recognizable as oral history, myth, legend, family stories, or personal experience narratives, the teachings shared in *Cherokee Earth Dwellers* are considered "traditional," but not in an unchanging way, as some might think when considering that word. For Cherokees, what is "tradition" and "traditional" is not simply what was known and practiced in the past. Instead, as Cherokee scholar Clint Carroll states, the term *tradition* "is a shorthand and accessible (if imperfect) way to communicate concepts, behaviors, practices, ethics, and values that are grounded in cultural forms and identities of a people" (Carroll 2015, ix). Cherokee tradition is living cultural knowledge that continues to be shared intergenerationally; it grows and changes within Cherokee community and is in turn defined by community. Cherokee traditions are diverse and understood in slightly different ways between Cherokee communities. Some communities may share a similar story or teaching, but each may tell it in their own way. There is good reason for this. Choogie Kingfisher's grandfather explained to him once why Cherokee knowledge is shared collectively: "That way, you'll *need* each other. No matter what you go through, you're always going to need each other."

Cherokee Earth Dwellers represents traditional Cherokee teachings as shared by Hastings Shade, Loretta Shade, Larry Shade, and esteemed contributors to the book. Passed through families and among friends and teachers, these teachings are threads of a great web of Cherokee knowledge of the natural world. They are shared in the spirit of *gadugi*, the Cherokee value of people working together for the benefit of all.

Cherokee Earth Dwellers presents dideyohvsdi in a variety of forms—conversations, interviews, personal reflections, stories, names, elder sayings, and illustrations. While each form of expression has unique qualities, they share an epistemological framework tied to the grammatical structure of the Cherokee language. Cherokee ways of knowing place primary importance on firsthand experience and trust. In Cherokee language, if one did not witness an event oneself, then a reportative suffix (*-e'i*) is used to denote that the event recounts as-told-to knowledge. No matter how mundane or everyday, experiences that were not witnessed firsthand are described with this reportative suffix. Even if one trusts a teller completely and is affirming the teller's account, the reportative suffix is used. When a speaker shares a secondhand account with another person, the burden of considering what is true and what is false falls on that subsequent listener. Consequently, Cherokee ways of knowing are deeply bound in relations, trust, personal experience, and personal judgment. One may only affirm as true what one has experienced firsthand or what one has learned from a trusted source. This view of what is knowable, what is real, is illustrated in Cherokee views of storytelling.

Two sets of terms for "story" and "storyteller" signal different degrees of engagement with as-told-to knowledge. *Kanohesgi* is a term for "storyteller," or "one who gives an account of an occurrence." *Kanoheda* means "an account," or "a story." The related word *adanohedi* means "what is told," or "an accounting of an event." Together, these terms might be used to describe historical narratives or personal accounts that express a sense of being told by individuals who personally experienced events. For example, a personal account of the Trail of Tears found in a history book may be described as kanoheda. Even so, in retelling that firsthand account a Cherokee speaker would still use the reportative suffix in speaking of it because the speaker was not there to witness the events personally.

The other Cherokee word for "storyteller" is *gayegogi*, which literally means "liar." Rather than a derogatory term, the use of *gayegogi* for "storyteller" traces back once again to Cherokee grammar and cultural perspectives on what may be considered true. Unlike kanoheda, gayegogi stories by definition highlight the boundaries of explanation and common experience. Myths, legends, and historical stories outside of memory are all inherently gayegogi stories because none of us witnessed them firsthand. Contemporary tales that stretch the imagination also fall into this category. In Cherokee thought, whether or not we believe such stories depends upon two factors: trust in the truthfulness of the words of the *aniyegogi* (liars, or storytellers) and the validation of personal experience. Gayegogi stories are passed down by word of mouth from elder to child, person to person, most often in families but also in community settings. If one trusts one's elders or aniyegogi as telling the truth, there is no reason to doubt a story's veracity. However, even when considering the words of respected elders, Cherokee grammar and epistemology prioritize an individual's unique perspective, experiences, and freedom to decide what is real and what is not. One may trust in the words and experiences of one's relations or dismiss what one hears as untrue.

Ironically, the freedom to choose what is true or false may better position a person to be open to stories that offer a more expansive view of reality than what one has yet personally experienced. Cherokee epistemology grounds truth at a more foundational, interrelational level in trust and personal experience. As Cherokee linguist Ben Frey of the EBCI explains, when a gayegogi shares a lie it is as if the storyteller says, "Here's a story.

It's entirely possible, even understandable for you not to believe it. And yet I'm going to tell it anyway. For good reasons." It is then up to us to listen to the story, discern its meanings, and consider what those reasons may be. Perhaps kanoheda may be understood as margin stories, or stories at the periphery of Cherokee epistemology that, while reliant on trust, personal experience, and judgment, do not stretch the boundaries of conventional Cherokee thought. The stories of the gayegogi, however, stand at both the center and the very limits of Cherokee worldview. These stories ask us to trust others and lead us to explore the limits of our personal experiences and thought. They compel us to reflect on how we might understand the world differently if we were to accept as *duyukdv* (true or straight) what elders and our other relations say, and what we likewise may not be able to verify or explain.

In my experience, people commonly enjoy hearing, reading, and revisiting in conversation the teachings of gayegogi stories and other dideyohvsdi through their own personal experiences of similar events. This process of reflecting on traditional stories and teachings and their cultural truths in relation to personal, contemporary experience is a core aspect of gayegoga discourse and, as such, of the narrative structure of *Cherokee Earth Dwellers*. Perhaps just as important as the epistemological implications of gayegoga discourse are the social bonds that are formed and renewed when reflecting together on stories and teachings. In the sharing of stories, teachings, and experiences, interpersonal trust may be established. In turn, a more expansive web of relations and realities may be opened for individuals and the community as a whole. In this way, reflecting on the words of the aniyegogi and insights of dideyohvsdi remain relevant, deep founts of knowledge, renewal, and transformation for Cherokee individuals and communities.

Through conversations, stories, and writings, *Cherokee Earth Dwellers* models the way Cherokee people are continuing students of Cherokee culture. Like Hastings Shade, Loretta Shade, and the other contributors to this book, I stand in awe of Cherokee cultural traditions and the guidance they offer one to "stand in the middle" and how they lead one to health, maturity, and meaning. Unlike most contributors, however, I grew up outside traditional Cherokee culture. At the same time, my status as a fellow Cherokee, friend, kinsman, researcher, listener, and student of the elders and cultural traditionalists presented in *Cherokee Earth Dwellers* positions me as a guide for the reader who, like myself, seeks a greater understanding of Cherokee lifeways. As explained by Loretta Shade, her family's educational goals for this project were to share this knowledge with the full range of Cherokee and non-Cherokee readers, from traditionally raised Cherokee who are fluent in the language to non-Cherokee readers who wish to learn about Cherokee worldviews. With these goals in mind, I become both a stand-in for the interested reader as well as a guide, posing questions, presenting contextual information, and telling stories that I hope will prove generative.

Loretta Shade, Larry Shade, and I collaborated throughout the process of writing *Cherokee Earth Dwellers*. We discussed at length the legacy of Hastings' writings and teachings, and how he wished them to be passed on to future generations. We decided whom to invite to participate in the book, how to organize the text, and what themes and ideas should be highlighted. In this way, *Cherokee Earth Dwellers* models the deeply collaborative, community-driven, and community-centered focus of decolonial Indigenous research methodologies. Our intention was to push back against narratives of loss that often shape works on Indigenous traditional knowledges and language revitalization. *Cherokee Earth Dwellers* demonstrates that traditional teachings about the body, mind, spirit, and natural world articulate complex epistemologies of self-determination that, when put into practice, may enable people and communities to create wellness. Community values such as consensus in governance, respect for all life, and gender equity are reflected in story. These teachings are shared not out of nostalgia for the past but, as Cutcha Risling Baldy states, "to demonstrate how these epistemologies are also modern philosophies of decolonization that can build Indigenous futures" (Risling Baldy 2018, 8).

When it came to recording reflections on Hastings and his archive, a similar focus on centering community knowledge was followed. I would push record on my digital recorder and the conversation would take on a life of its own. I present these conversations and stories in order to showcase the artistry of Cherokee storytelling and depth of Cherokee teachings, as well as the beauty of Cherokee voices, in both Cherokee and English. Orally recorded stories I denote as "told by" the storyteller, while those that were written and edited I denote as "by" the author.

The chapters of *Cherokee Earth Dwellers* are composed of juxtaposed narratives, conversations, stories, teachings, and creature names. This organization is modeled on Cherokee storytelling. Stories are heard or read in the context of each other, with little direct explanation of how the themes or ideas explored within them are connected. Instead, listeners and readers are invited to find meaning across what may at first appear as gaps of connection or understanding. This interpretive methodology respects an individual's unique perspective and standpoint. At the same time, there are patterns of Cherokee thought one may follow across the stories and conversations in *Cherokee Earth Dwellers*, especially as they apply to specific creatures and spaces in the natural world. In this way, there is a necessary tension in the book between individual interpretation and cultural teachings; each of us must find our own perspectives in relation to the teachings.

Cherokee history and teachings tell us the homelands of the Cherokee people, what today people in Oklahoma still call *tsalag uweti*, or the "old Cherokee country," are the mountains and valleys of the Southern Appalachians. Archaeology confirms that Indigenous peoples have lived in that region for well over 11,000 years. It remains unclear exactly when the people now known as *Anitsalagi* or *Anikituwagi*, the Cherokee people or, using the traditional name for ourselves in the Cherokee language, the people of Keetoowah, became a distinct people and settled along the rivers and streams of Appalachia in autonomous towns of two hundred or more people. The Cherokee language split from other Iroquoian languages 3,500 years ago, and Cherokee prehistory tells that we settled in the Smoky Mountains after a generations-long migration. But before and long after their first encounter with a European, the Spaniard Hernando de Soto and his conquistadors in 1540, the Cherokee were the largest and most powerful Indigenous nation in the Southeast. Cherokee territory was vast, covering over 81 million acres of mountains, valleys, and agricultural fields in what are now northern South Carolina, western North Carolina and Virginia, eastern Tennessee, and northern Alabama and Georgia. A common language, clans, kinship system, and culture tied Cherokee people together in relationships across these incomparable lands and waters.

When citizens of the Cherokee Nation were forcibly relocated from their homelands to Indian Territory in 1838–39, the US federal government assaulted not only their sovereignty as a self-governing nation but their very notion of themselves as a community of relatives, whose extended family included not just their fellow human beings but the lands, waters, creatures, and spirits with whom they had shared life. A pattern of continual loss of traditional territory due to European and Anglo-American settler colonialism began in the late seventeenth century with the signing of the first treaties with Europeans. With nearly every subsequent treaty, the Cherokee lost more of their traditional homelands. Fed up with the relentless pursuit of their lands, some Cherokee moved west in the late eighteenth century, settling first in *Aniwasasi* (Osage) territory in what is now Missouri and then later moving into what is now western Arkansas. These "old settlers," as they are called, found the Ozark Plateau region familiar, similar to their homelands. Their presence was not welcomed by the Aniwasasi and led to decades of armed conflicts between them, a direct aftershock of Cherokee lands having been colonized in the east.

The Cherokee settlements in the Ozarks and, later, west on the adjacent prairie plains of the Cherokee Nation, were certainly less lush and ecologically diverse than the Southern Appalachians. The Great Smoky Mountains are one of the oldest mountain ranges in the world. Over their 200 to 300 million years of existence an incredibly diverse ecosystem developed that rivals or surpasses other temperate-zone areas on the planet. There are more native tree species (105) in the Smokies than in all of Europe. There are over 1,300 native vascular plant species. Over 31 species of salamanders are found there—the world's most diverse population. In reestablishing themselves in traditional Aniwasasi territory in the west, the Cherokee were required to adapt their umwelt to a new environment. While a substantial amount of the flora and fauna on the Ozark Plateau and prairie plains were familiar, there were new creatures with whom to establish relations as well as missing relatives.

The names and teachings of the Cherokee natural world explored in *Cherokee Earth Dwellers* consist mainly of those creatures found on the Cherokee Nation reservation in northeastern Oklahoma. The Cherokee names for the natural world spoken by citizens of the Eastern Band of Cherokee Indians, located in the traditional Cherokee homelands in far western North Carolina, may differ from those names and teachings in the West because the flora, fauna, lands, water, and sky are not the same. They are different relations. However, Loretta Shade tells that many of the Cherokee names for the natural world are shared between Cherokee peoples from the Eastern Band of Cherokee Indians and those Cherokee speakers in the West. Over time, pronunciations for the words may have changed. The knowledge of animal and plant relatives, as well as knowledge of the spirits that live in the natural world, came along with the Cherokee people when they traveled west to what is now Cherokee Nation territory in Oklahoma. Stories did, too. But over time, living along the watersheds and tributaries of the Neosho, Verdigris, Illinois, and Arkansas Rivers, Cherokees established relations with this place.

It was always the intention of the Shades that *Cherokee Earth Dwellers* serve as a teaching tool and guide for reconnecting with the natural world. The book's illustrations are a key component of this mission. Acclaimed Cherokee Nation visual artist MaryBeth Timothy provides pen-and-ink illustrations of creatures selected by Loretta Shade for their importance to Cherokee tradition. Readers are encouraged to use these illustrations to identify creatures and to reflect upon the unique ways we may visualize story and our other-than-human relations. In this way, *Cherokee Earth Dwellers* may facilitate what Cherokee Nation scholar Jeff Kanohalidoh Corntassel calls "everyday acts of resurgence" (Corntassel et al. 2018, 98). Identifying, naming, and knowing stories of the creatures with whom we share our world may strengthen our relationships with one another and our homelands. By using the language in this small, everyday way, together we may change the ways settler colonialism has weakened our cultural traditions and, in so doing, distanced us from the natural world and our relations with it.

Among the most important relations in my world as a researcher and writer are those with other Cherokee and Cherokee Studies scholars. Cherokee intellectualism continues within the oral tradition, but Cherokee culture is fortunate to have deep sources of knowledge in historical and contemporary written works as well. Among other primary sources, Jack F. and Anna G. Kilpatrick's *Friends of Thunder: Folktales of the Oklahoma Cherokees* (1964) was important to me for its model of how other Cherokee scholars have engaged the ethnographic process. The classic *Myths of the Cherokee* (Mooney 1900) was also an important reference. Often cited as "James Mooney's *Myths of the Cherokee*," in returning to this work I marveled that Eastern Band elders *Ayu'ini* (Swimmer) and *Itagunahi* (John Ax) alone contributed well over 80 percent of the stories and teachings in the book. I find inspiration in the work of these two elders and others who had the vision to understand the power of print to carry on Cherokee knowledge to future generations.

I am honored to count as my colleagues many contemporary scholars of Cherokee history, language, literature, politics, sociology, environmental studies, and law. Members of the active and growing ᏗᎦᏓᏤᎵᎢ, or *Digadatseli'i* (We Belong to Each Other), the Cherokee Citizen-Scholars Society, are committed to research and publishing that upholds the inherent political and intellectual sovereignty of the Cherokee Nation, Eastern Band of Cherokee Indians, and United Keetoowah Band of Cherokee Indians. I am proud to be a member. Among the many thinkers, both Cherokee and non-Cherokee, whose writings and conversation have influenced *Cherokee Earth Dwellers*, Ben Frey, Clint Carroll, Benny Smith, Crosslin Fields Smith, Robert J. Conley, Charles Hudson, Jeff Corntassel, Julie L. Reed, Barbara R. Duncan, John C. Standingdeer Jr., Theda Perdue, George E. Lankford, Heidi M. Altman, Rennard Strickland, Wendell Cochran,

Richard Foreman, Levi B. Gritts, Thomas N. Belt, and Durbin Feeling have been particularly important.

Cherokee Earth Dwellers consists of four chapters. *Sagwu* (One), *Ayetli Hidogesdi* ("You Will Stand in the Middle"), introduces Hastings Shade's teachings and contributor reflections about "standing in the middle," a way of being physically, spiritually, socially, and morally centered and in relationship within the Cherokee natural world. *Tali* (Two), *Elohi* (The Middle World), presents the creatures and forces that inhabit the Cherokee middle world. This chapter recounts origin stories of earth, fire, and of the Cherokee people as well as names for animals, plants, and natural features found on this world of solid earth upon which we humans seek balance between the opposing energies of sky and water. *Jo'i* (Three), *Galvladi* (The Sky World), presents names and stories of the creatures and forces that inhabit the air and sky. The many stories about birds are the focus of this chapter as well as the forces of the air, including wind, thunder, and lightning. Perhaps more than any other facet of the Cherokee cosmos, the Sky World is connected with communication and messages. *Nvgi* (Four), *Elohi Hawinadidla* (The Under World), recounts stories of the creatures and forces that live underground and under water. The Under World is a mysterious source of life, transformation, and emotion largely obscured from human vision; we see very little of it and may enter it only for short periods of time. All things underground and under water are associated with the Under World, including fish, snakes, and insects.

One afternoon as we worked together on *Cherokee Earth Dwellers*, Loretta said she was proud of me and what we were creating together. And she said Hastings was proud of me and our work, too. In these few words, Loretta confirmed her and Hastings' teachings as well as those of the elders who had come before them. Over and over, those teachings say the Cherokee world is holistic, interconnected, and infused with everlasting spirit. In the course of our writing *Cherokee Earth Dwellers*, beloved elders and friends have passed on. But their spirits and teachings continue. It is Hastings and Loretta Shade's hope that this collection will enable us to reflect on the interrelated nature of the Cherokee world. These names, stories, and reflections introduce Cherokee values and how those values may help us establish dynamic balances in a world that is alive and infused with energy. By reflecting on dideyohvsdi and remembering the names and stories of the creatures with whom we share life, our world becomes filled with relations. Upon opening a straight and true path of duyukdv, we may come to "stand in the middle."

Sagwu ✦ One

Ayetli Hidogesdi

"YOU WILL STAND IN THE MIDDLE"

Cherokee Earth Dwellers

On a warm July afternoon in 2014, I sat in the Branch restaurant in Tahlequah, Oklahoma, capital of the Cherokee Nation, waiting to meet Loretta Shade and Larry Shade about a book project. Loretta and I had met years before when her late husband, the renowned Cherokee Nation elder and political leader Hastings Shade, and I collaborated on a book of traditional stories titled *Cherokee Stories of the Turtle Island Liars' Club*. I knew she was a deeply respected elder in her own right, a treasured teacher of the Cherokee language since the 1970s. Hastings had also talked about his son, Larry, the high school coach and teacher, but we had never met. A sedan pulled up to the restaurant. Loretta entered carrying a plastic grocery bag and was with a man bearing a striking resemblance to Hastings, only younger and bigger than the elder I knew. Larry must have recognized the expression on my face. "Yes, I know I look a lot like him," he said as we shook hands. He sounded like Hastings, too, with a gentle, deep voice. Loretta was as I remembered her: small, with medium-length curly brown hair, glasses, and a kind, friendly, straightforward manner. We sat down to glasses of iced tea and Loretta placed on the table the plastic grocery bag she had been carrying. Inside, covered in pale blue construction paper and bound with rusty binder clips, were catalogs of Cherokee names for creatures of the natural world that Hastings had assembled before his passing. Eight in all, the catalogs were titled Birds, Animals, Insects, Fish, Reptiles and Amphibians, Plants, Edible Plants, and Trees. The dog-eared booklets appeared unassuming.

"When did Hastings begin writing down these names for the natural world?" I asked as I thumbed through the collections.

"The 1970s," Loretta said.

"He always carried a little notepad with him," Larry said. "He would write any ol' thing that he would hear from the elders in the community. He used to say, 'I gotta meet with so-and-so today, they're supposed to have something for me. Or show me something.'"

"A lot of times I went with him," Loretta said. "And it was very warm meeting and sharing knowledge with that person. You'd just relate to whatever they were talking about and you'd think, 'Well, this person grew up just like me.' You know? And a lot of times, Hastings would say, 'So-and-so' learned from his grandpa.' He'd say, 'We're going to compare what our grandpas knew.' Or grandmas. And that was really good," Loretta said and paused. "Hastings was a lifelong student of Cherokee culture."

Loretta explained the significance and scope of Hastings' life as a word collector. Making his rounds as a woodsman and teacher, Hastings filled pocket-sized notebooks with words, teachings, and knowledge he was raised with and that were shared with him by other Cherokee elders. Later he transcribed the words and stories from these notebooks and created collections of teachings and his catalogs of earth's creatures. Working slowly and diligently, Hastings cataloged more than six hundred names and stories of the creatures in the Cherokee natural world. Together with all those who shared knowledge with him, Hastings Shade had gathered the largest collection of Cherokee names for and teachings of the natural world in existence.

Now Loretta and her family wished to share Hastings' collected works to contribute to Cherokee cultural and linguistic revitalization. They had approached me as a writer because Hastings grew to trust me during our collaboration on *Cherokee Stories of the Turtle Island Liars' Club*. "It was always Hastings' intention to publish this work and share it with future generations," Loretta said. "Hastings saw himself as fighting to keep Cherokee culture alive." I remembered what his friend Sequoyah Guess once wrote of him: "His weapon is his knowledge and his opponent is the future threatening to drive Cherokee heritage into obscurity." Making Hastings' work accessible to a wide audience of readers would continue his legacy of teaching language, culture, and history for generations to come.

The Cherokee lifeways that Hastings' elders shared with him are rooted in teachings about our place as human beings within a living and interrelated natural world, Loretta explained. Passed down through *tsunilosv* (culture, or "what they have passed on"), these teachings instill values and practices that enable people to live in a balanced, healthful way in relation to ourselves and to others. To understand this way of life fully, Hastings said, one would need to be born into it. "There are subjects that are not allowed to be discussed and others that shouldn't be because they are of the family and not for the public," he once wrote. But in his cultural revitalization work, Hastings shared the broad outlines of a reflective practice, or way of being, focused on living in accord with Cherokee values to establish *tohi* (peace or flow) in body, mind, and spirit. To live with tohi, Hastings said, is to "stand in the middle": *ayetli tsidoga*, or "I stand in the middle." This, I understood, was a vision of a life lived well, a "good life" as taught to him by elders. His cultural and linguistic revitalization work all centered on the goal of teaching and perpetuating this Cherokee way of life.

With humility and gratitude I accepted the responsibility and gift Loretta and her family presented me to weave Hastings' archive of names, stories, and teachings into a book. I would need their guidance, as well as the guidance and wisdom of other elders and knowledge keepers, to portray the vision of the Cherokee cosmos Hastings shared. We agreed to work together to this end. That meeting was the origin of *Cherokee Earth Dwellers*. The next day I traveled back to my home in Seattle, Washington, the bag of Hastings' name books guarded on my lap and my head full of questions. What are the characteristics and patterns of the Cherokee natural world Hastings was taught? What is our role as human beings in the Cherokee cosmos? Why is it important to know the creatures with whom we share this world? And what does it mean to "stand in the middle?"

This chapter of *Cherokee Earth Dwellers* explores the reflective practice Hastings called "standing in the middle," a way of relating to the center or middle (*ayetli*) within ourselves and maintaining balance in the modern world through living in tohi of body, mind, and spirit. These teachings present a model of how to understand and navigate the forces and tensions that shape the Cherokee cosmos, finding our place within them through healthful relationships with our fellow creatures. As Hastings and Loretta shared, this way of being has been passed down in stories, teachings, and symbols for generations. It depends, I came to understand, on a continuing critical process learned and practiced over one's life.

Hastings Shade, or Ulasgvhi

One spring day in the early 2000s, my good friend Sequoyah Guess and I met Hastings Shade at the old United Keetoowah Band casino in Tahlequah. They were close friends, and Sequoyah considered Hastings his "immediate elder." We spent the afternoon sitting next to each other playing slots and talking. When it was time to leave, Hastings said he wanted to show me something and we walked to his car. In his early sixties at the time, Hastings was of medium height and build, with straight black hair parted on the side, a moustache, and goatee. Though physically gentle and unassuming, there was a calm strength and intensity in Hastings' presence. He opened the trunk and showed me a beautiful handmade bow. "It's for sale," he said in his deep voice. Though I could not really afford it, I also knew it was a rare opportunity to purchase one of Hastings Shade's treasured bows. I paid him cash for the bow and he passed twenty dollars to Sequoyah. "You see?" he said, his dark eyes smiling behind his amber-colored glasses. "We all win." That lesson in sharing—art, knowledge, money—stays with me. Even in that small exchange, Hastings was sharing and distributing knowledge and tradition, helping everyone out. There are ways for us all to win if we support one another. It was a lesson in *gadugi*—a Cherokee value in which people come together to help one another. That was one of many lessons I came to learn from him.

Hastings Shade was former deputy principal chief of the Cherokee Nation and an honored elder, teacher, husband, father, kinsman, and friend. A full blood, he was raised traditionally with Cherokee as his first language. He had one grandfather for fifteen years and the other for thirty-nine years. And in his time together with Charley Smith, Albert Shade, and other family elders he was taught Cherokee arts and lifeways grounded in knowledge of the natural world. He was a carver, master bowmaker, and hand-forged gigs for fishing. In 1991, he was honored as a National Treasure by the Cherokee Nation for his work reviving the game of Cherokee marbles. Hastings was a founding member of the Turtle Island Liars' Club, a group formed in the 1990s consisting of renowned Cherokee storytellers and traditionalists. In classes and youth-elder camps he shared these arts and his knowledge with others through demonstrations, story, and writings. And in this way, throughout his life as a teacher and artist, he bridged the Cherokee past and present with the goal of perpetuating Cherokee culture and traditions. As Larry Shade once said, "My father was a remarkable man—even to me, his son."

I once asked Hastings how he'd like to be introduced. "Traditional," he answered. He was born in 1941 and raised within a Cherokee-speaking household where family life revolved around learning Cherokee teachings from one's elders and living that knowledge in one's daily practices. Hastings said, "I just listened to the elders. Learned from the elders what I know. Always, the elders used to tell me a long time ago, you know, 'Why would I lie to you? Because when I ain't here anymore it won't make any difference. So, why would I lie to you?' I always remembered that, and when they would tell me something I take it as the truth" (Teuton 2012, 23).

His greatest wealth of knowledge and experience was in the teachings of plants, animals, and life in the *inage'i* (the wild or forest). He was at home in the woods and spent much of his life hunting, fishing, and gathering medicine. Even as he aged and developed a heart condition, Hastings told me he would continue to go out to the forest for as long as he was able; that was what he was taught to do, and I understood he had relationships that must continue with the creatures of the woods.

Larry Shade recalled how his father had initiated him into becoming attuned to the natural world:

> We would walk into the woods going huntin' and you could hear the animals and the wind. Leaves rustling. I didn't realize until I got a little older, but as we walked through there he was teaching me to listen. He would just lift his hand and say, 'Stop.' And he would say, "Do you hear the birds?" And I said, "I don't hear any birds." And that's when he'd say, "Listen, there's something in here." That's when I got accustomed to listening to the blue jays, especially. Blue jays are one of the birds of nature where if anything is not normal in their area, they're going to let you know. So that's how I learned to listen for blue jays as I hunted. When you walked into their area they would let the other animals know. And if you were there a lot then they would get used to you. That was one of the ways we hunted. Not to mention that Hastings could smell a deer probably three or four hundred yards away.

Hastings and I had spent time talking about teachings of the natural world and about learning to listen to it. I was fortunate to have recorded those conversations. But it was through exploring his writings, the names and stories of the creatures of our cosmos, as well as the reflections of his family and friends on his life and works, that I came to a deeper understanding of the lifeways he wished to perpetuate, what he saw as threatening those ways of life, and how they may lead one to "stand in the middle."

ᎠᏴᏫᏯ

ᏔᎵ ᎡᎶᎯ ᏕᏥᏁᎳ
ᎠᏎᏍᏗ ᏌᏊ ᎠᏅᏓᏙ
ᎠᏁᎦᏴᎵ ᎬᏲᎲᎤ
ᏚᏳᎦᏛ ᏯᏣᎵᏍᏙᏗ ᏱᎩ
ᏥᎾᎾᎢ ᎠᎦᏙᏗ ᏥᎠᏘᏍᎬᎢ
ᏘᏥᎦᏙᎳ ᎡᎵᏊ ᏱᏓᎩᎵᏓᏍᏓ
ᏔᎵ ᎡᎶᎯ ᏕᏥᏁᎳ
ᎠᏎᏍᏗ ᎠᏅᏓᏙ ᏙᎯ ᏄᏏᎾ.

ᏱᎵᏍᎦᏂ ᏧᏓᏣᏗ

INDIAN

I live in two worlds
But my spirit is one
My forefathers taught me
That true I may be
To see with my heart
'Cause my eyes may deceive
I live in two worlds
But my spirit is relieved.

1976.
H. Shade

Chris Teuton, or Noyi

Some months into my work on *Cherokee Earth Dwellers,* I began to question if I was the right person to co-author this book. "Who am I to weave together Hastings' writings and teachings?" I asked myself. I thought the book might need me to be someone I am not. I then remembered a teaching Hastings shared with me. He showed me a Cherokee shell gorget design with two interlocking rectangular loops. The loops represent different life paths, he explained. We are connected, but distinct. Each of us is unique. Our upbringing, our perspectives, our beliefs are different, yet we are in relationship. And that diversity in life is important for our community to thrive. Remembering his teaching helped me regain trust in myself and in the path before me.

Over time, in thinking with Hastings' works and in my conversations with Loretta, Larry, and others, my role in *Cherokee Earth Dwellers* became clear. In the sgadug (community) of this book, you will encounter elders, cultural traditionalists, storytellers, and artists, all with their unique perspectives to share on the Cherokee natural world. I present Hastings Shade's living archive of writings and remembered teachings with enough cultural context to begin to understand its richness and complexity. Like you, I bring my own perspectives, interests, and experiences to thinking with this work. Through sharing my process of relating to these writings and teachings I hope to model a method of learning in relationship with story and the natural world that Hastings and other elders have shared with me.

As I continued my journey with this book, I felt a longing in me. Hastings' call not just to think about but to feel and act on teachings made me realize I was divided. Like many Cherokee folks, I knew the names and some stories of the creatures we see daily. But if I was honest with myself, I did not truly know those creatures as my relations. As a Cherokee Studies scholar I had read widely on traditional views of the natural world and of the Cherokee cosmos. But that knowledge too often did not shape my daily interactions. Elders had shared their knowledge and teachings with me. While I heard them, I knew somehow I had not fully listened. Despite what I had learned about Cherokee teachings of the natural world, there remained a divide inside me between what I had been told and what I knew, between what I felt and what I lived. Learning with Hastings' collections set me on a journey toward closing that division, making these teachings part of my daily life.

When I returned decades ago to the Cherokee community and the lands and waters we call home, I was a young man seeking my roots. I am a citizen of the Cherokee Nation, but I was born and raised by my Cherokee mother mostly away from Cherokee country. When I look back at my life, I marvel at the twists and turns that led me to reconnect with kin, forge lifelong friendships, learn with elders, and join a spiritual community. There continues to be guidance in these twists and turns. It is a testament to the generous, loving spirit of the Cherokee people that through friendships and the wisdom of our traditions I found my roots. My children have been raised with them.

One of the greatest honors of my life was collaborating with the Turtle Island Liars' Club, a group of traditionalists that included Hastings Shade, Sammy Still, Sequoyah Guess, and Woody Hansen, to publish *Cherokee Stories of the Turtle Island Liars' Club*, a book exploring the power and pur-

ABILITY TO DO THINGS
by Hastings Shade

All Indians have the ability to be creative—to do something, even though some say, "I can't do anything." The ability to do things was given to them by the Great Spirit—before a different culture was introduced to them. Those who say "I can't" have depended on a different culture to lead them around. If we don't try to do things on our own that we were given the ability to do, we will lose that ability.

pose of Cherokee stories and storytelling traditions. I now experience myself in relation to my kin and ancestors as a citizen of the Cherokee Nation, a member of Echota-Tanasi Ceremonial Ground, and a Cherokee community member whose life's work as a professor of American Indian Studies keeps him from living in the Cherokee Nation but not separate from Cherokee life.

Like many of you, I spend time in the outdoors and deeply value my relationships with particular places and creatures. But I am not a person of the woods as Hastings was. I do not know the sky, lands, and waters of northeastern Oklahoma, much less our Smoky Mountain homelands, as well as many do. I did not grow up learning the names and stories of many of our plant and animal relatives. I am not a fluent speaker of the Cherokee language. But I hope you share with me an openness to teachings about the Cherokee world, its life forms, and the ways we relate to them. I hope you feel as Hastings, Loretta, Larry, and the others in this book do that the time is now for us to recommit to understanding and experiencing ourselves as members of an interrelated living world.

Loretta Shade, or Losi

My first interactions with Loretta Shade I found a bit intimidating. In her late sixties, she struck me as friendly but no-nonsense—not unlike other powerful Cherokee women I know. Once, many years ago, when Hastings and I were recording stories in his car, she came out to the vehicle and knocked on the window. Hastings rolled it down. Without a word, she passed us two hot dogs and walked away. Part of that gravitas comes with the territory of being a renowned elder and matriarch of a family, as Loretta surely was. Over time, however, I came to know Loretta as a deeply kind, knowledgeable, and generous person committed to sharing Hastings' and her own legacy of work with the Cherokee world. She was one among a talented family of female Cherokee leaders. An elder among a network of elders and traditionalists, Loretta herself was honored in 2018 as a National Treasure by the Cherokee Nation for her decades of work teaching the Cherokee language. Her self-effacing demeanor belied her own deep knowledge of Cherokee tradition shared among family and friends, accumulated over a lifetime. In our discussions of Hastings' work, with good humor and care, Loretta shared her own knowledge of the Cherokee natural world.

One spring afternoon Loretta and I sat with our friend Sequoyah Guess in the Cherokee Heritage Center chapel and began recording the interviews for this book.

"So, I start out with my name?" Loretta asked.

"Yes," I said.

"My name is Loretta Shade. I'm from the Lost City community at Hulbert, Oklahoma. And I was raised there on land that was allotted to my grandmother, Emily Dreadfulwater. My mom and dad's names were Margie and Rufus Henson. There's five of us girls in the family and one brother. And I was married to Hastings Shade, who was former deputy chief of Cherokee Nation. And we raised three boys and have three grandchildren, two boys and a girl, and I have step-grandchildren. And we were raised cultural. Traditional. We were raised with all the customs of the Cherokee way, and not only the Cherokee way but other tribes that were around us with children that were raised like us. Cherokee language is my first language. I spoke Cherokee when I started school, but I don't remember when I started speaking English. My teacher would allow me to go home with her so she could teach me some more words in English. I thought it was 'cause I was her favorite student," Loretta said and smiled. "But she was also teaching me how to play piano, which was really neat."

"The stories that we were told are stories that we have carried on. Hastings has written down a lot of them, and we did a lot of Cherokee curriculum. He taught in the community. He also taught in universities, like Connors State, Rogers State, and Bacone College. And I taught at Northeastern State University for eighteen years and out in the community for about fifteen years. And Cherokee customs have been a big part of our lives. It was just a way of life. It's not something that we learned as a life experience. But it was our culture. And we were taught history, and you lived the history. My grandmothers and grandpas and uncles and aunts all spoke Cherokee. If you didn't speak Cherokee to them, they wouldn't listen to you," she said and laughed.

"Were you taught much about the natural world when you were growing up?" I asked.

"We were taught about the plants. Edible plants. We were taught about the animals and why they are called the names they have. Why they have that name in Cherokee. The reptiles and amphibians. Why they are there. And they taught us about the insects and the trees. There's many, many ways to say different names of the natural world. The earth, the air, or the wind. Fire. They're all related. They're a part of the world that we live in. And Hastings and I always talked about the Sky World, the Middle World, the Under World. The seven levels of heaven. And the four directions and the other directions, what they mean and why they are associated with certain colors. That's just how we grew up. And that's how we raised the kids and the grandkids. If you asked 'em what parts of the crawdads are edible, they would know. They would know how to cook it. And also there's parts of the crawdad that are used for medicine.

"Like Grandma used to say, 'Everything out there that's growin' has a value. Just like us.' She said, 'We have values. And we want y'all to grow up to know these things so you won't be out there lost.' Or be lookin' for your identity. And she said that's what young people are doin' nowadays. They don't know who they are, they don't know where they came from. And to reach this certain type of goal in your life, she said, 'Everybody can be successful if they just go about it the right way.' Her biggest teaching was stay away from alcohol and drugs—*adayvsdesdisgi*, or things that harm your mind. These are the worst things that can happen to your life. It's true. All those people that drink or do drugs, there's somethin' wrong with 'em now. They wouldn't *listen* to anybody. And she would say, 'Well one of these days they're gonna' regret that they did that.' And I always told mom, 'Grandma was right.'"

FOREIGN SUBSTANCE ✦ *by Hastings Shade*

ᎣᏍᏓ ᏂᎨᏒᎾ ᎢᎦᏙᏗ
ᎮᏍᏗ ᎪᎱᏍᏗ ᏧᏥᎩᏍᎨᏍᏗ ᎠᎴ ᎣᏍᏗᎮᏍᏗ,
ᎠᏓᏲᏍᏓᏁ ᎣᏍᏗ ᎠᏰᎵᎢᏚᏗ ᎠᎴ ᎠᏓᏔᏗᏍᏗ.
ᎢᎦᏓ ᏥᎩ ᎢᎩᏲᏍᏓᏁᎨ ᎣᏍᏓ ᎢᎦᏓᏅᏝᏗᎢ—
ᎪᎱᏍᏓ ᏂᏚᎵᏍᎬᎾ ᏂᎦᎵᏍᏔᏂᎨ.
ᏂᎦᎥ ᏥᎩ ᎤᏁᏝᏅᎯ ᎤᏬᏢᏅ ᎣᏍᏓ ᎢᎩᏙᏗ, ᏴᎾ
ᏩᏮᏁᏄ— ᎤᏲ ᏥᏄᏩᏁᏔ, ᎣᏍᏓ ᎨᏒᎢ . . .

Do not take anything into your body
that can alter your ability to reason
and to think things out.
Some things make us react without
thinking of the consequences.

Again, the Creator made all things
to be used good—

Man has made the good things bad.

Larry Shade, or Gvhnohvlegv

When I met Larry Shade I was taken by how he possessed an active, intense energy that reminded me of his father. He was always glad to meet and share memories of Hastings and his teachings, but Larry's time was precious and he was always on the go. Like Hastings, he is a doer. A teacher, coach, and family man, Larry lives a full life working with Cherokee youth and, in his own ways, carrying on the legacy of his father and the elders who share knowledge with him.

"My name is Larry Shade. My Cherokee name is *Gvhnohvlegv*, which was given to me by my *eduda* (grandfather). I'm the eldest of three boys, born and raised in the Cherokee culture by my blood parents Loretta and Hastings Shade, who made sure we understood the Cherokee culture and history, and that we practice it today as it was done centuries ago.

I have always been a resident of the community of Lost City in Cherokee County in Oklahoma. I went to school at the now-closed K through eighth grade Lost City Elementary School and went to Hulbert High School. I attended Northeastern State University, where I received my B.S. in education. I have taught mathematics, science, and coached several sports throughout my career.

I was taught to respect and live by the Cherokee way of life, and it is that way of life that I enjoy sharing. We lived not far from Fourteen-Mile Creek in Cherokee County. I'm a third-generation gig maker. I hand-forge crawdad and fish gigs, as my father and grandfather did for many years. Many a fish sacrificed themselves for our table fare!

I understand the medicines, the ceremonies, and the cultural food. And why they are important to keeping our traditions alive.

What I love the most is the stories. How these stories teach us morals. How to use and treat the environment for our daily use. What I try to understand is how these stories relate past, present, and future.

My fondest memories are when I was a young child going out for visits with my parents. They often helped community members during their time of need. This is when I remember the stories that were told by the elders in the Cherokee language. How they grew up in the Cherokee way of life. And the adversities they faced and events that they got to witness personally. How what we call myth and legends were a way of life for them. What plants were used for medicines. Witnessed seeing mythical beings such as Little People and creatures that we often talk about but seldom see today. Listening to strange stories that relate to unbelievable happenings

AN ENCOUNTER WITH *TSISDETSI* (*Mouse*) • *Told by Larry Shade*

In conversations concerning Cherokee teachings, Larry often offered examples from his own life experiences. In this way he showed me that "standing in the middle" is an everyday practice of reflecting on one's experiences in relation to the teachings one has learned. This story of the mouse is just such an example.

"You know, one of the coaches I coach with is very traditional. He grew up that way. Several years ago I helped him for two years. Our goal was to coach the kids to the state championships. We were at regionals and the girls were out warming up, getting ready to play. He said, 'Coach, let's head to the locker room and talk about our game.' We opened the doors and were walking in when all of a sudden we hear a noise above us, and a mouse rolls off the ceiling ductwork, and it lands and it's dead. And he went, 'I wonder what that means?' Then, 'Well, it's a good sign.' I said, 'I don't know. We'll see.' But the whole time after that we're thinking about what happened and why it happened. A while later, the girls came in and we got ready for the game. And as we're leaving to walk out to the court, there was this little bitty mouse on the floor. I don't know where it came from. And I said, 'Leave her alone.' The other coach said, 'Hmph. Kind of a re-birth, ain't it?' And I said, 'Well, actually that might be a good sign.' And we beat the other team that night and went to the state championship. That was just a little bitty thing, you know? But nature talks to us. We just don't listen anymore."

or events. How certain people in our community had Cherokee abilities and healing methods that we no longer see today.

This is my mission: to keep our past alive through these stories that our elders so personally treasured.

I'm only a bridge to the past to what these people knew and shared. I personally get to practice with my family what it means to be *aniyvwiya* (Cherokee, or American Indian)."

Nvgi sudetiyvsadisv ditlilostanv (Four Seasons Diagram)

Hastings wrote poems, short reflections, and stories from his life. He also wrote stories of animals, of the cultural values attached to certain creatures, and descriptions of Cherokee customs. But without the tools to understand these teachings in a Cherokee cultural context, some readers might miss the complexity of thought and depth of the ways of knowing

Nvgi sudetiyvsadisv ditlilostanv (Four seasons diagram)

that Hastings passed on. This was a concern of his. In a preface to one of his collections, he wrote, "To those of you not raised in the traditional ways of the 'Indian,' as we are mistakenly called, these writings may be amusing to you. For others, it will stir something deep down inside of you. For the traditional people it will open your mind to the stories you heard growing up."

One day while studying Hastings' writings I found a diagram he had created depicting the Four Seasons, Four Directions, Seven Clans, Seven Important Things in the World, and Five Basic Colors used in Cherokee tradition. The diagram is a circle with interconnected levels and divisions identifying some key characteristics of Cherokee worldview. It offers a way of visualizing the interconnected patterns of Cherokee tradition, each part a piece of a larger whole. Working from the outermost circle toward the center, one encounters the directions, the cycle of the year, and earth's creatures. At the unity of the center, there is fire, symbolized by the color yellow.

As Hastings would be the first to note, this diagram is but a model of some key aspects of Cherokee life and teachings. But in finding this diagram, I was reminded to start slowly, with basic knowledge, as that is the foundation of one's orientation. When you study it, focus not only on what is represented in the diagram but even more on the web of relationships that tie all these things and ideas together. It is in these connections that the patterns of Cherokee thinking, values, and worldview emerge.

And so, with this cyclical diagram to orient our journey, and with Hastings' works and Loretta's reflections as a guide, we may explore the role of teachings, storytelling, and critical reflection in orienting one's self toward *ayetli* (the center or middle).

Dideyohvsdi (Teachings)

Hastings often reflected on teaching and learning from within a Cherokee cultural context. He recognized, Loretta explained to me, that since fewer and fewer people spoke Cherokee and had been raised traditionally, he had to explain and translate the methods of teaching and learning he used and that his elders taught him. The perpetuation of Cherokee culture depends not only on *what* is taught, but *how* it is taught. The processes of teaching and learning go hand in hand; we become teachers by first learning how to learn.

Loretta and Larry shared that Hastings modeled a form of teaching learned from his grandfather, Charley Smith. When out hunting, his grandpa would encourage Hastings to be aware of his surroundings, watch the behavior of the creatures, and listen to the sounds. He introduced Hastings to the names of plants and explained what symptoms they treat. Hastings needed to listen to his grandpa and observe what he pointed out; sometimes he was shown a plant medicine only once, told its name and what it treated. If he missed that opportunity, it did not come again. "Grandpa would say, '*Nitsadulihv'i tsadetlosgwasdi. Tla yidetlosgwasdi.*' That is, 'If you want to learn, you'll learn. If you don't want to learn, you won't learn,'" Loretta said.

Dorothy Ice, a Cherokee elder and Cherokee National Treasure for loom weaving, had a similar learning experience with traditional teachings. "They took us out," she said. "Walking. Fishing. They took us out into the woods. They would stop and say, 'Remember what this is.' They'd say, 'I'm going to tell you one time. You better learn it. If you don't, you won't know it. You better listen.' You know? They took us out. And that's all I remember. My parents. Grandparents. Uncles." Once knowledge was taught and learned, then it belonged to that person. It became part of that person and one was expected to use that knowledge.

It may seem strict to share knowledge with a person only once and expect it to be remembered. But there is reasoning behind this approach. Shared through demonstration and spoken words passed from person to person, Cherokee teachings are alive. Some teachings have been passed down since time immemorial, tracing back to when an animal or plant relative shared knowledge with a person. "Teachings are not simply information," Loretta said. They are about relationality and responsibility. Knowledge, like everything else in the Cherokee cosmos, exists in living relationships. To be taught tradition means a person develops a relationship with a teacher, teaching, the knowledge it conveys, and with creatures themselves.

Whether or not a teaching is remembered and becomes part of a person depends on who that person is and the individual's natural inclinations, talents, and abilities. Sequoyah Guess's grandma, Maggie Turtle, shared medicine teachings with him. "She would take me along into the forest, and she would point out plants and say what they are for, but it never seemed to connect in my mind," he said. Instead, her animal stories and the different voices she used for each creature captured his imagination and became part of him. He did not learn medicine but became a storyteller and shared those teachings. Similarly, Loretta recounted growing up with elders who would observe people and their inclinations to a calling. "You don't say anything to them when they are little, but you just pay attention. 'See, that one's going to be a carpenter.' And they noticed this when the babies were born. They looked at their hands. They looked at their feet. Mainly to make sure they had all their fingers and toes!" Loretta said and laughed. "But that's how they told, 'Oh, this one's gonna be seamstress. She already has the sewing hands.'" A child's inclinations would be observed and nurtured with teachings.

If a teaching sticks and is learned, it becomes part of a person. But with that relationship comes the responsibility of using the teaching and sharing it. Loretta, Larry, and I spoke of this approach to teaching that Hastings was taught and passed along:

"He would say, 'This is a teaching.' He would never say, 'I'm a teacher.' He would say, 'This is a teaching. I want to make sure you remember this,'" Larry said.

"Another one was, 'I want you to know,'" Loretta said. "And you use it."

"'You need to know, and don't forget it,'" Larry said.

"He taught you something, you use it," Loretta said. "Hastings said, 'One of these days kids aren't gonna have anybody telling them our traditions and our customs. They're not gonna know.' He said, 'Somebody's got to lead this.' That was his intent."

In his writings, presentations, and work with youth and elder teaching camps, Hastings taught through demonstration and story. When teaching how to make gigs or carve bows, he would demonstrate a skill, show a person how to perform it, then coach the person through until the skill was learned. Then the skill belonged to that person. But with the practice of storytelling, the teaching method was subtle.

Hastings' goal in his writings was to share traditional teachings to offer people direction, a map of sorts to understand the values that shape a traditional Cherokee understanding of duyukdv, what is straight or true. But Cherokee education is not coercive or mandatory. Once the stories are shared, it is up to each of us to decide how we will relate to them or not.

Traditional stories are teaching tools, Hastings would say. They may entertain, but they are not strictly for entertainment; they teach Cherokee values. Those values shape the patterns of one's mind, how one thinks and behaves. I once asked Hastings if the stories he told should be explained for people to understand their meaning or to just present them and allow people to understand them in their own ways. "Just let them ride," he told me. As each person is unique, everyone will learn different things from a story, make different connections to their lives and their experiences, and find different meanings. Once learned, a story will change with a person over time as one develops a relationship with the story. It was his hope that the lessons in these teachings would ultimately enable people to make choices about how they want to live. One may learn to "stand in the middle" with Cherokee teachings. Or one may choose another path. The key, Hastings said, is to first learn to listen. To the story. And to one's self.

Elohi, Galvladi, ale Elohi Hawinadidla (Earth, Sky World, and the Under World)

Hadlv gedoha? Where am I? Before a person stands in a place, I reasoned, you need to know where you are. So I asked Loretta to tell me about the Cherokee cosmos. Our universe has three layers, three "worlds" in Cherokee thought, Loretta explained. There is *Galvladi* (Gah-luh-lah-dee), the Sky World that extends up from the earth to the heavens; *Elohi* (Eh-loh-hee), the Middle World of land; and *Elohi Hawinadidla* (Eh-loh-hee Hah-wee-nah-dee-dlah), the Under World below the surface of earth's lands and waters. The Cherokee cosmos is an ordered universe, each world with its own creatures who are uniquely adapted to the forces and energies of their place, endowed with gifts and characteristics that give each creature dignity and purpose in life. All creatures in the three worlds are living, sentient, and unique, with their own families, peoples, stories, and ways of being.

Hastings once explained to me that balance and interconnection are fundamental to Cherokee cosmology. While distinct, each world and its creatures are in constant, dynamic relationship; this is what Hastings meant by balance. Creatures of the earth, sky, and underworld do not exist in isolation but thrive through interacting, cooperating, and living through each other in cycles of life and death.

We come to know ourselves by observing and learning from one another. This was a key reason, Loretta explained, that Hastings recorded the names of beings in *Unetlvnv uwotlvnv* (oo-neh-tluh-nuh oo-woh-tluh-nuh), what Creator made, or "nature". We humans have a place in this ordered and forever changing cosmos, but it can only be understood in context. Traditionally, a child would learn of the role of human beings in the world by being taught the names, stories, and customs of the other creatures with whom we share life. This was how Loretta and Hastings were raised. For those of us who did not learn this growing up, we can still learn of our relations and our place. And we begin that process by learning about where we live.

Hadlv tegv? Where are you from? *Elohi digegv.* I am from *Elohi. Elohi gedoha.* I am on *Elohi. Ayv Elohi gehi.* I am an earth dweller.

Na Ayetli ale Galaquogi Winiduyugodv ale Hisgi Ulsuwid (The Center, Seven Directions, and Five Colors)

Hastings often talked to me about the idea of the center, or *ayetli.* And when he talked about ayetli he would identify this spatial orientation with his hands. "You want to be right here," he said, his hands chest-high, palms facing each other, fingers pointing forward. "Not here," he said, moving his hands to the left. "Not here," he said, moving his hands to the right. "But right here." At the time, I felt I understood what he meant. A person should be in a good place within one's self. Right in the middle. Centered. But in the course of my studying his writings and talking with Loretta, the symbolism of ayetli grew richer in meaning.

In traditional Cherokee thought, Hastings shared in his writings, life's whole journey may be oriented through directions, colors, and seasons. Yes, we are physical creatures who understand ourselves in terms of space and time. But we are also spiritual beings who grow in awareness over time and continue after our physical forms grow old. There is no death of the spirit in Cherokee thought, Hastings explained. You just continue on your journey, learning and experiencing. Two journeys, one physical and the other spiritual, are intertwined and inseparable. Knowing these orientations, symbols, and where one stands in relation to them is key in recognizing patterns of the natural order as understood in Cherokee terms.

Cherokee teachings map seven directions according to the path of the physical sun and our own place in relation to it. The opposed directions symbolize interdependent oppositions that together define a whole. The East (*dikalvgv*) is white, peace. "Every day the sun comes up, it's a *new beginning*," Hastings wrote. "White is pure." North (*tsuyvtlv*) is blue, a place of cold, defeat. West (*wudeligv*) is black, the place where the sun goes down, death. South (*tsuganawv*) is red and warm, a place of friendship and power. Ayetli is yellow and symbolizes *atsila* (fire), which Cherokee tradition says was a direct gift from *Unetlvnv* (Creator, or "the one who provides or gives"). Nature, Mother Earth, "the provider of all things" for life on Elohi, is symbolized by the color brown, and the immortal spirit by gray, a color symbolizing messengers. For each of us, there is also a place above us (*galvladidla*) and below us (*eladidla*). Knowing where we are in mind, body, and spirit within these seven directions and five basic colors orients us in the world.

As there are seven directions that position us in space, there are four seasons of life that orient us in time. Spring represents birth, when everything awakens. Summer represents adult life, when things mature, age, ripen. Fall is the elder time of life, when everything begins to wilt, become old and brittle, gets tired and sleepy. Winter represents death, when everything goes to sleep, dies.

The symbol of ayetli at the heart of the four directions holds special meaning in Cherokee tradition. "The center is where the gift that was given to the Cherokee by the Creator exists. This is the fire," Hastings wrote. "It is yellow to symbolize fire, and as long as the fire burns there will always be Cherokees. One thing we as Indian People have to realize, the fire only understands the Cherokee language, or Native languages."

An elder teaching regularly heard is that as long as we speak to the fire in Cherokee it will not go out, and as long as terrapins sing around the fire we will have the fire to use. To some, this is a reference to the songs sung in Cherokee by men at the stomp dance, as well as to the turtle shell rattles worn by women as they create the rhythm of the dance at the grounds. Since time immemorial, the fire has tied us to Unetlvnv, and it is through prayerful song and the smoke of the fire that we commune with our source. Though Cherokees practice a variety of religions today, this reverence for fire continues.

Just what does the center mean? Cherokee teachings circle around the fire, but all of us must answer this question for ourselves. As I thought with Hastings' words and my own experiences, I reflected on Unetlvnv, that which created this thing called life. I began to feel more deeply how my life and the turn of seasons are entwined in relationships with the sun and fire, gifts that warm us, offer light, and enable life to exist on Elohi. And with that orientation, I turned back to Hastings' teachings and Cherokee storytelling for guidance.

Gayegogesdi (Storytelling)

Gayegogesdi. Storytelling. Visit with Cherokees and you will hear stories. You may hear a simple story of what someone saw that day and how it brought to mind a past event. You may hear a story about a family member. Or a place. You might even hear a traditional story, such as a teaching that was shared with an elder when growing up. It may be a story with animals as characters. Or what some might call mythical creatures. Or even plants. No matter what kind of story is told, it is likely to have some wit and humor in it—either in its telling or in the reflections about it afterwards. And after the story is told, if it is the kind of story that warrants more discussion, you may hear a conversation about what the story means to a person, how it connects with other events people have experienced firsthand or have heard about, and how it is similar to or different from other stories folks know. If you are in a group, some may speak and others may keep their own counsel. It is understood that every person is entitled to one's own relationship with the story. After a while someone may tell another story, and so the conversation, laughter, and teachings roll on. This is how I was taught Cherokee storytelling works. Storytelling weaves the past, present, and speculative future together through narrative teachings and individual interpretations within a community context of traditional knowledge.

Storytelling and stories remain central to Cherokee culture not because Cherokees simply love telling and listening to stories. They remain central because in Cherokee thought, our world still depends on the meaning each of us finds in the stories we hear, tell, and read. Traditionally, it is up to each and every one of us to decide with our own minds what is real and true, or false and unreal in the stories we encounter. Though social pressures may exist to see the world in certain ways and carry on traditions, Cherokee ways of knowing emphasize our individual freedom as human beings to decide for ourselves what we choose to believe as true or false in the way we see and live our lives. Each generation encounters Cherokee tradition anew. This understanding of reality and truth is expressed in Cherokee language and grammar.

Gayegogi, the common term for "storyteller" used by Hastings Shade and other fluent Cherokee speakers, highlights a tension between personal experience and communal knowledge. *Gayegogi* is a cultural pun that means "he/she is lying," or "liar." Rather than a negative term for a teller of untruths, the meaning of *gayegogi* as "storyteller" relates directly to the primary importance Cherokee language places on personal experience in determining what is real or true. In Cherokee language, experiences not witnessed firsthand are recounted with a reportative verb ending (*e'i*), which signals that the speaker does not have firsthand knowledge of the event. Passed down orally from generation to generation, myths, legends, and historical stories outside of living memory may all be "lies"; none of us has firsthand experience of these. At the same time, such stories and remembered experiences are the foundation of Cherokee culture and knowledge that has been passed down orally and in other ways since time immemorial. How can these two aspects of gayegogesdi tradition coexist?

The Cherokee word for "true," *duyukdv*, is related to the word for "straight," *tsiyukdi*. Another related word for "true" or "truly" is *udohiyu*, which contains within it the word *tohi* (peace, harmony, and wellness). There is an association in word and concept with truth being straight, as if it may lead one in unobstructed, flowing movement like the path of a river down a mountain. In fact, Loretta explained, duyukdv is a Cherokee term for the straight path of a moral and ethical life, one that is lived harmoniously, peacefully, flowing, and well in both one's self and in the world. What is "true" in this sense relates to living a good life in tohi. What is "false" leads away from it to disharmony, conflict, and illness.

Hastings once told me that there was no deviation in the traditional teachings and stories passed down to him by his elders. They are not false. "We still depend on stories," Hastings would say. They teach Cherokee values and how to live ethically in a living cosmos. The teachings they express would lead one on a true—a straight—path. Still, in using the pun "lie" for a traditional story that is presented as straight and true, Cherokee storytelling acknowledges the challenge we all face in accepting another's experience of life as true, especially when some stories may be hard to believe. No matter where we receive our teachings—from textbooks to elders—what we experience and, ultimately, live through our actions as true and false is up to each of us.

Traditional stories and teachings that stretch the imagination and our everyday notions of what is real or reflective of actual experience challenge us to consider what we mean by truth. Some people are satisfied to interpret such stories of talking animals or spirit beings as simply metaphorical. But no matter how much they stretched the imagination, Hastings and Loretta shared elder stories as expressive of what is true in the Cherokee way. "Try it yourself, if you don't believe me," Hastings would say of their teachings. I believe he understood that as we all wish to have our own experiences and unique perspectives honored, we need to extend that respect to others. Through gayegogesdi, we create a community of listeners, thinkers, and tellers. We explore and shape our shared world and reality. And, at the same time, in the midst of the laughter and goodwill, expressions of duyukdv and of tohi take form. In this way, stories transform us.

KANANESGI AMAYI ALE ATSILA
(*Water Spider and Fire*) ◆ *by Noyi Teuton*

For Cherokees, a people of the fire, there is perhaps no more important teaching than the story of the gift of fire. Hastings would often tell this story and reflect on how Kananesgi Amayi, Water Spider, is a teacher. By observing her, Cherokees learned how to make pottery and how to fire it. And they learned how to weave. To contain things. Though smaller than other creatures, Kananesgi Amayi used the abilities Creator gave her to acquire the gift of fire for human beings. As Hastings would say, fire was a gift, but we all had to work for it. I tell a version of this story I learned from him.

Ilvhiyu tsigesv nigada inage anehi tsalagi itsaniwonisgv. In the great forever that was, all the forest dwellers spoke Cherokee. When Elohi was new, ours was a dark and cold world. All the creatures we know today were there at that time, placed on Elohi by *Unetlvnv* (Creator). And it is told that all the creatures were white, except for *aniyvwiya* (American Indians). All creatures talked and listened to one another. And they cared about one another as kin.

The *inage anehi* (forest dwellers or animals) saw their human relatives shivering in the cold and darkness. Aniyvwiya needed something to keep them warm. And so the forest dwellers came together to help them.

Kananesgi amayi ale atsila (Water Spider and fire)

The creatures knew of *atsila* (fire). They had heard Unetlvnv tell *Ayvdagwalosgi* (Thunder) to set fire to a sycamore tree on an island. Unetlvnv had set aside this gift of fire for whomever could learn how to carry fire from the tree and bring it safely across the waters to the mainland. Get the fire, and it would be theirs to use. And so *Anagalisgi* (Lightning) had struck the sycamore tree, and it burned and smoked on the island.

All the animals, birds, insects, and reptiles came together in council. It was decided that one of them would have to get the fire for aniyvwiya. *Yona* (Bear) stepped forward and said, "Let me go first." And so the largest and strongest animal was chosen for this task. With his white coat on he walked into the water, lifted his head, and began to move his legs. This was when bear learned to swim. He got to the island and approached the burning sycamore with its smoldering trunk and smoky, hollowed-out top. He circled the tree and thought about how he could carry the fire back across the water. But whenever he got close to it, fire would scorch his fur. The first couple of times his fur turned shades of yellow. Each time he approached the fire, his fur got darker. After many tries his fur had turned black. Bear failed to get the fire, but this is how the bears got different shades of color.

Yona swam back from the island. "I tried to grab fire from the tree, but it was too hot. It scorched my fur," he said to the council of animals, who looked at him in his new dark coat. The inage anehi would need to choose another creature to carry the fire. As they were discussing who should be next, little Water Spider, *Kananesgi Amayi,* stepped forward. "Give me a chance," she said. "Let me try!" But the animals all smiled and said she was too small. They chose another creature.

One after the next, many forest dwellers tried to get the fire. And all of them lost their white color. The blue racer crawled straight for the fire and had his skin scorched on contact. The Black Snake tried something different and went to the top of the tree. But, stunned by the heat and smoke, she fell into the charred sycamore and turned black. Black Racer scorched not only her skin but her eyes as well. This is why all snakes shed their skin today.

Each time someone failed to get fire, Kananesgi Amayi said, "Let me try!" But they always said she was too small.

Anitsisqua (birds) tried to help aniyvwiya as well. *Kholvn* (Raven), *Koga* (Crow), and *Squalisdi* (Blackbird) all had their white feathers turned black from the heat and smoke. The feathers on the head of *Suli* (Buzzard) burned off, and he even lost his ability to smell, which is why he eats dead and rotten things.

Wahu'i (Screech Owl) tried to approach the fire carefully. It flew to a limb above the sycamore, leaned over, and looked down into the tree. But right at that moment the fire flamed up and burned his eyes. Screech Owl's eyes are still red. He comes out at night because he can't see well in the daylight. *Digalisquali* (Long-eared Owl) also tried to look into the tree. Fire burned rings around her eyes. The stripes in the rings where she rubbed her feathers putting out the fire remain in her eyes today.

All inage anehi got their color trying to get the fire. And each one has its own story.

But when all had failed, the council finally gave little Kananesgi Amayi her chance.

Kananesgi Amayi lived near the water, and she had watched *Digulidisgi* (Dirt Dauber) make little balls of mud and carry them back to build his nest. She found a mud ball he had dropped. She took that ball and shaped it with her many hands into a small clay pot with a lid. She tied the

Yona (bear)

pot to her back with her web and set off across the water to the island.

At this time she didn't go under water, but being so small she just glided over it.

When Kananesgi Amayi got to the burning sycamore tree, she found Thunder had sent a group of giants, the *Aniatsila,* or Fire People, down to guard the fire. From the efforts of all the other animals, Unetlvnv must have thought someone who hadn't earned the fire might try to steal it. Aniatsila guarded the fire and could instantly sense when any fire was missing.

Kananesgi Amayi watched the Fire People walk around the fire guarding it. She worried that they might step on her. She ran a little ways, then hid. Ran a little ways, then hid. And that's just what spiders do today.

When she reached the burning tree she took the clay pot off her back and put a small ember from the fire inside it. She strapped the pot back on her back with her web and set off for the water. The Aniatsila immediately sensed an ember was missing and started to circle the tree looking for it.

Kananesgi Amayi continued to run a little ways, and hide. Run a little ways, and hide. The Aniatsila didn't see her, but they were getting closer and closer. She ran and hid all the way to the edge of the water. If they caught her the Aniatsila might take the fire away from her, so Kananesgi Amayi dove into the water and hid. The Fire People could not follow her there and thought the fire was surely out. But the hot ember inside Kananesgi's pot had baked the clay and made the pot waterproof. She swam across the water and gave Cherokee people this first fire, which they buried for safekeeping. Unetlvnv gave Water Spider the ability to live under water, which is where she hides her egg sac to this day.

Hastings taught that this first fire continues to burn, tended through the generations by protectors of this sacred flame. When people want to thank Unetlvnv, they dance around the eternal fire burning today at Cherokee stomp grounds. And we commune with atsila whenever we sit, look into her flames, watch, and listen. Water Spider is honored not only for risking her life to gift us fire but for teaching us how to make pottery and fire it. She is honored and revered as she was in the ancient past, with Cherokee artists continuing the tradition of depicting her beautiful designs and her image. As Hastings said, you don't have to be big to accomplish great things.

Fire and the Language

Sequoyah Guess and I were driving one winter afternoon from Oaks to Hulbert to visit Loretta. The cold, overcast weather, coupled with the dry fields and shady forest lands put us both in a quiet, contemplative mood. A beloved and renowned storyteller, novelist, filmmaker, and teacher of Cherokee, his first language, Sequoyah often accompanied and assisted

Hastings in his cultural work. He now continued that calling with Loretta and me. I had been thinking a lot about the story of Water Spider and the Fire. I had heard Hastings and others tell this story about how Water Spider stole fire from the Fire People and gave humans this gift. It is arguably the best-known traditional Cherokee story. One regularly sees the image of Kananesgi Amayi in Cherokee arts and crafts, on shop signs and T-shirts. People are proud of having Spider as our teacher. And for good reason. Through her gifts, humans were able to thrive and prosper. She taught us selfless generosity, ingenuity, and that everyone matters and has the ability to contribute to the community. These remain core Cherokee values.

Hastings would often talk about how the Cherokee language was a direct gift from Unetlvnv. These two gifts, the Cherokee language and fire, Hastings and other elders speak of as cornerstones of Cherokee peoplehood. If we lose either, according to prophecy, we will no longer be Cherokee. They did not say we would not exist as human beings but that we would lose our unique identity as Cherokees.

As a member of Echota-Tanasi Ceremonial Ground, I am proud to have a relationship with *Agayulage*, Old Woman, the fire at the stomp grounds. Each Green Corn celebration, with joy and anticipation, we take out the old fire and with it all our animosities and grievances gathered over the past year. With the calling forth of a new fire, we cleanse ourselves as a community and begin anew—just like the corn. We speak to the fire in Cherokee, and terrapin shells sing throughout the night. This is one relationship I have with fire.

I asked Sequoyah if he had considered other meanings for the fire that Kananesgi Amayi gave to the Cherokee. There was much to reflect on in the story. The spirit of gadugi exemplified by the animals who came together to help humans. The gift of fire presented as a test of worthiness by Unetlvnv. The reason why the colors of the animals were shaped by fire. I understood that the gift of fire meant warmth and survival in a dark and cold world. But I had been thinking that of all the animals, only water spider was able to use a tool—her small clay pot—to accomplish her task. In bringing us fire, she taught us not only to use a tool but to use our minds to survive. "Do you think the fire represents consciousness?" I asked Sequoyah. "Yeah," he said. "She brought not only heat, but light. The fire is an expression of Creator, but it's also in us."

I often think back to that conversation when I tell the story of Kananesgi Amayi. And I remain amazed at the wisdom of the story. In it, all parts of the Cherokee world are represented: sky, earth, underworld, animals, plants, humans, and the giving spirit that binds us all. It is a story with teachings about how to live ethically in our living world. It is also a story with teachings about how to relate to ourselves. Who among us has not had to cross waters and reach that center of ourselves where the fire of our spirit awaits? If we are fortunate, each of us may find or rediscover that fire inside ourselves that gives our life purpose and meaning. My friend Ben Frey tells me the Cherokee word for meaning or purpose, *gadvgv'i*, means "it's sticking into the center." Perhaps it is through the weakest parts of ourselves that we find our greatest strengths, our abilities to stick to the center and become whole, real people.

Anigehya ale Anisgaya (Woman and Man)

When Loretta and I explored the teachings about tohi and duyukdv with which she and Hastings were raised, I was reminded of an aspect of Cherokee worldview so fundamental to Cherokee peoplehood that it was often passed over in our discussions: the role of gender in Cherokee society. There are no markers of gender in Cherokee grammar, but different genders are recognized in Cherokee language and society. The word for woman is *agehya* and the word for man is *asgaya*. There are words for old woman, *agayulage*, and old man, *utvsonv*, as well as words for boys and girls of different ages. Relatives are also identified by their gender. These terms reflect not only the specificity of Cherokee language, Loretta said, but the place of people in a matrilineal Cherokee society shaped by people's roles and responsibilities to one another.

Historically, Cherokee life was shaped by the matrilineal clan structure. Cherokee Nation citizen and historian Julie Reed uses the term *osdv iyunvnehi*, translated as the "continual act of perpetuating positive well-being for the community," to describe how Cherokee society existed up to around 1800 (Reed 2016, 5). Cherokee community wellness depended "on matrilineal descent, matrilocal dwellings, egalitarian relations among all members of society, gadugi, and a commitment to communal landholdings to sustain everyone" (6). A person's descent was traced through one's mother—not the father—as one's clan identity passed from mother to child. And to be Cherokee, one had to be a member of a Cherokee clan. For this reason, there were no orphans in Cherokee society. Cherokee women also controlled their own homes, and if a marriage should end, the man returned to live with his own mother's clan (Reed 2016, 6). Land was held in common, and labor on the land was valued equally in assuring survival (7). Whether hunting, fishing, or farming, men, women, elders, and children all worked for the prosperity of the community, with the health and support of families as the central concern. As Reed writes, "Cherokee people did not view individual want as a failure to the individual in need; it was a failure of the entire community at the micro level and clan networks at a macro level to respond to the need as required by gadugi and the rules of kinship" (Reed 2016, 6).

As Loretta, Hastings, and the other contributors to *Cherokee Earth Dwellers* teach, Cherokee oral tradition recognizes women as central to Cherokee life. Gender equality and gender balance within community are fundamental to "standing in the middle" and living a life in tohi and duyukdv. This egalitarian view of Cherokee community wherein everyone has a contribution to make, regardless of age or gender, is reflected in stories such as *Kananesgi Amayi ale Atsila*, where the female water spider is the only creature who can bring fire to the people. Cherokee origins as a people trace back not to men but to women. Star Woman, *Ulisigi*, is the one who brought the Cherokee people to *Elohi*. *Nvdo iga ehi*, the sun, is a woman in Cherokee cosmology. The sacred fire is *Agayulage*, Old Woman. And Mother Earth, Hastings said, is a woman as well.

Patriarchy and paternalism came to the Cherokee with settler colonialism, which disrupted matrilineal descent, the Cherokee clan structure, and eventually the communal landholdings that provided for Cherokee prosperity. In spite of colonialism, Cherokees today continue to recognize and celebrate the centrality of women in Cherokee life. Over time, in reflecting on the teachings shared in *Cherokee Earth Dwellers*, I came to understand that disruptions to tohi in Cherokee community have often been gendered, with oral traditional stories of men or women not treating each other as equals. Often in these same stories, we are presented lessons on how to regain balance and once again "stand in the middle." The story of "The Crooked-Faced Boy" at the end of this chapter offers such an example. In this way, oral traditions offer lessons on how to maintain balance in community as well as how to confront the gender inequity that came with settler colonialism and continues to disrupt relations across the Cherokee cosmos.

Decolonial Teachings

Hastings Shade knew Cherokee history. He wrote of how our sovereignty as a nation was upheld by our numerous treaties with England and the United States. He also wrote of how those treaties were repeatedly violated. He wrote of our forced removal to Indian Territory in 1838–39 on the "Trail where they cried," as well as how our sovereign Cherokee Nation government was disbanded by the Curtis Act of 1898, only to rise from the ashes in the 1970s. As deputy principal chief of the Cherokee Nation, Hastings was aware that our identity as a people had been under constant attack by an American government and society that sought to assimilate the Cherokee into the mainstream through its laws, education system, technologies, and economic system. Hastings' answer to settler colonialism was to perpetuate the teachings he believed are at the core of Cherokee peoplehood.

I spoke to Loretta about the deep concern she and Hastings had regarding changes to Cherokee culture. She shared with me one of his reflections. Hastings wrote, "We have come to depend on another's customs, another's way of life. We are just now realizing that if we are to survive as Indians we will have to maintain our Indian way of living. With the loss of language, you also lose your customs and traditions. We are now in a struggle to maintain our identity." While it has always been important for Cherokees to adapt to survive in a changing world, the challenge, as Hastings saw it, was to interact and learn with other cultures while retaining a sense of Cherokee identity. For Hastings, Cherokee oral traditional teachings about our understanding of the Cherokee cosmos and the natural world provide the foundation of Cherokee identity.

As I worked my way through his writings, I saw time and again Hastings offering warnings of immediate threats to the different aspects of our selves. Each of us is a being with a body, mind, and spirit that comprise our whole self. Hastings' way of thinking about the whole person reminded me of another elder's writings. In his book *Stand as One*, Cherokee Nation elder Crosslin Smith writes that in the traditional Cherokee view he was taught, there are three parts to every person: body, mind, and spirit (Smith 2018, ix). Just as Hastings expressed, in order to be a complete person, one living with tohi, one needs to bring together these parts of one's self. Our minds, bodies, and spirits are impacted by things and forces that pull us away from wellness. The threats may take any number of forms. They may be cultural, as when the influence of the dominant culture eclipses

Cherokee values and teachings. Or they may be physical threats, like drugs and alcohol. Perhaps the greatest threat is to our relationship with spirit. Each of us is a unique being with inherent dignity, purpose, and destiny. A role to play in community, just like water spider. We find meaning and belonging in our relationships with our fellow creatures, but when these bonds are weakened, we lose this ability to feel compassion and connection with one another. We lose the ability to create community.

UK'TAN AND AWOHALI • *by Hastings Shade*

Hastings rarely interpreted traditional stories, but sometimes he did so to show how a story may help one understand the present. Uk'tan, a powerful and deadly creature born of the sun's jealousy of the moon, was once a man. It has the body of a great snake, the antlers of a deer, and can fly, though it is usually encountered in waters. The Eagle represents knowledge and foresight in Cherokee teachings.

Long ago there was a battle between *Uk'tan*, or Flying Dragon, and *Awohali*, or Eagle.

The battle lasted for many generations, but the Uk'tan never defeated Awohali. Just about the time Uk'tan would start to get the best of Awohali, the Awohali would fly higher and higher, until at last Uk'tan fell back to earth—defeated.

The Uk'tan represents the white culture and Awohali represents Indian culture. The Uk'tan couldn't compete with Awohali's ability to fly high—his ability to adapt.

This is why the eagle is known to fly the highest of any bird to this day. The ability to adapt represents the Indian's ability to use the white man's language and teaching to his own good. The dragon falling represents the white culture's inability to adapt to the Indian culture.

The Indian can live in the white man's culture. This is demonstrated by how most all Indians can speak and understand the white language, and only a few whites can speak or understand the Indian language and culture.

At the time the Flying Dragon fell was when the Indians began to learn to read and understand the white language.

Uk'tan ale Awohali
(Uk'tan and Eagle)

But in spite of all these threats, there was hope—*utugi igvsv* (hope for us all)—because the strength and wisdom of Cherokee teachings remain. In this time period, when the earth's creatures are dying off in unprecedented numbers and Mother Earth's climate is changing, Hastings saw Cherokee traditions as a path toward the center and a sustainable, healthy way of living. In many of his writings he identified a modern threat in terms that arise out of Cherokee tradition. In this way, he showed that while the characters in stories may change, the energies and tensions in our world remain the same. The work of seeking tohi, striving for balance, and standing in the middle continues.

Tohi Oyelv (Peaceful Body)

Hastings' teachings about "standing in the middle" circle around a sense of wellness that includes one's body, mind, and spirit. Cherokee storytelling explores the importance of traditional teachings on the "mind"—the values, ways of knowing, and ways of acting in the world shaped by these teachings. But I wanted to understand the body better in relation to a Cherokee sense of wellness that Hastings explored in his writings. I drove to Loretta's home in Lost City one fall afternoon and we talked about health, wellness, illness, and a traditional understanding of the body in the teachings Hastings shared.

"What is the word for 'healthy body' or 'well body' in the language?" I asked Loretta.

"*Tohi oyelv*," Loretta replied. "That means 'peaceful body.'"

Loretta showed me a chart of the Cherokee body that Hastings had created in the Cherokee language. It was his goal, she explained, to have the body chart in Cherokee Nation health clinics to aid not only fluent speakers of the language but also those who wanted to understand Cherokee words for the body and for conditions that may arise within it. It is used that way today. Loretta explained that Hastings had put a lot of effort into creating the body chart and was proud of the knowledge it shared. In its creation and usage, the chart brings together Hastings' twin goals of sharing Cherokee culture and perpetuating it through everyday practice.

Hastings' "Cherokee Words for Body Parts" provides names for head, heart, liver, tendons, and kneecap—about ninety-nine in all—all that most people will ever need to know in order to describe one's own physical structure. But on the right side of the body diagram he includes a list of "Diseases and Other Things"—*vhyugi ale soi tsudanelvda*—that may affect a body. Some conditions appear physical in nature, such as aneurysm, broken bone, and fever. These are both unfortunate and common physical ailments that one might expect to befall a person in the course of life, such as a burn, rash, bruise, or arthritis. I could see a snapshot of some of the most common conditions a person might experience when in need of medicine. The chart has terms for fell off, slipped, and frostbite. But I found it curious that Hastings also chose to name common expressions of the body in its normal state of physicality: he lists words for standing, walking, kneeling, squatting, and jumping. Yawning. Listening. Talking. Shouting. Dream. Why were these descriptions included in an anatomy chart of parts of the body?

It was only when Loretta encouraged me to consider Hastings' chart as a whole, with its names for parts of the body, physical actions, and feelings one might experience in illness and in health, that some of its meaning in a Cherokee cultural context became clear to me. While the chart names the Cherokee body and describes how it may be impacted by illness and harm, it is not an anatomy chart. It is a model of Cherokee embodiment. It names parts of the body and describes illness within a Cherokee understanding of health and wellness of one's whole being. In tohi oyelv, the spiritual dimension of our physical self is understood through the term tohi. A healthy body is one at peace and in harmony within itself and with its surroundings. The emotional life of our bodies, minds, and indeed our spirits is acknowledged in Hastings' chart. He includes the words for crying, laughing, talking, listening, and feeling depressed. These are terms we use to describe the health not just of our bodies but of our whole selves.

Cherokee Nation elder Tom Belt and his co-author Heidi M. Altman write of tohi as the "neutral state of being from which illness is a departure" (Altman and Belt 2009, 12). According to Belt and Altman, tohi in the Cherokee worldview is "the proper or normal state of the world," while "*oshi* or *osi*" is the "normal state or neutral state of the individual" (13). The words *osi* and *osda* are related and commonly understood as meaning "good." Cherokees greet each other and say, "*Osiyo*," or "*Osigwutsu?*" which are commonly translated as, "Hello" and "Are you still good?" In fact, fluent speakers understand these greetings as referring to "one's state of being" as normal, neutral, and peaceful, in keeping with tohi (17). To say "*Osiyo*" means "all is normal presently," while to say *osda* means things are normal right now (17). The concepts of tohi, osi, and osda are not understood in terms of good and bad, but in the orientation of a person and community toward peace, neutrality, and ayetli—the middle or center (17).

In a traditional understanding of Cherokee health and wellness, Loretta helped me understand, illness and disease are those things that move one away from one's center. Cherokee medicine understands disease as the disruption of tohi. The word for disease, *vhyugi* or *ahyugi*, Belt and Altman define as "an angry or resentful entity that comes to visit" (Altman and Belt 2009, 20). To this day traditional Cherokee notions of health, wellness, and medicine hold that the nature of one's well-being relates to whether one is in tohi or, through one's own thoughts and actions or the malignant work of others, one's harmonious state of being has been disrupted (Lefler and Belt 2022, 12–13).

Hastings once told me that in Cherokee thought, we are born, mature, age, and then we die. But the spirit continues; it never dies. The body will

INDIAN LAW: KINDNESS-HONESTY-SHARING ✦ *by Hastings Shade*

Hastings often shared elder teachings in brief, seemingly straightforward explanations of Cherokee morals and customs. He said he was not the type of "liar" to embellish a story for the sake of artistry. His concern was getting across the teaching.

Very simple—hard to do—because of the different culture being taught to us.

Through the white culture—only know how to own, to possess, to have dominance over.

This is not the Indian way—the Indian way is kindness to everyone, no matter who-color-race-religion.

Honest—to speak the truth no matter what. Lying cannot make you live longer—but can cause great pain somewhere in your life. Lying has gained many things for people. What they don't know is—you cannot take these things with you when you die—they only leave their family behind to pay for these things—only create more problems.

There was a time that the Indians didn't lie—there was no need to, this was learned from a foreign culture—a person cannot lie to a true Indian.

Sharing—Indians believe in sharing whatever they have—material and spiritual things. Indians didn't believe in owning land, because they believe they were put here by the Great Spirit to take care of the land that was known to them as Mother Earth—this is why they were willing to share the land with the foreigners when they first arrived.

Share by teaching—
Share by giving—
Share by being honest.

naturally age, becoming damaged and frail. That is natural. But if the spirit becomes sickened through losing one's spiritual balance in relation to the living world, one's total health as a person is jeopardized. I now understood why terms like Drugs, Nightmare, and Insane are on Hastings' body chart. He warned of the dangers of one's temper, and of the need to be vigilant for the signs of evil, or *usonv'i*, of places and people that are out of balance. The sound of a chain. Red eyes. Such things may draw us away from living in tohi. Hastings wrote of Cherokee values in teachings about kindness, honesty, and sharing. He shared knowledge of the ways in which we may cleanse ourselves spiritually, and the places wherein we may grow and build strength in tohi. In all these teachings, he showed how the body, mind, and spirit are one in Cherokee worldview.

TEMPER ✦ *by Hastings Shade*

Learn to control your temper, and you can do anything you want to.
Be a master of your temper.
Temper is an enemy to our minds—
It is not one of the emotions that Creator gave us—
He gave us a loving spirit.
Having a temper causes us to hurt the ones we are to love—
By word and action.

MODERN-DAY LIVING ✦ *by Hastings Shade*

Why we have so many Indian children who are dropouts and drug users:

The children have a hard time with two cultures. If they are taught the Indian ways and culture at home to begin with, they would understand and it would make it easier for them to adapt to the white culture.

Kids are not taught at home anymore. We leave the teaching to other people who are not of the same culture. This culture is totally alien to the Indian ways.

Again, we as parents send our kids into a different culture to be taught without having taught them their own culture.

This makes it very difficult for them to adapt.

ᎾᏃ ᎰᎩᏍᏆᏂᎪᎯᏍᎪ
(*Why Do We Wonder?*)

Ꮟ ᎠᏂᏲᏁᎦ ᎾᏂᎷᎬᎾ ᎰᎨᏒ—ᎠᏂᏴᏫᏯ ᏚᏳᎪᏛ ᎤᎾᎸᎢ—Ꮭ ᎤᏂᏍᏆᏂᎪᎯᏍᏗ ᏲᎨᏎᎢ ᎤᎾᎸ ᏚᏳᎦᏛ ᎨᏒᎢ—

ᏃᏊ ᎠᏂᏲᏁᎦ ᏧᏂᎷᏨ ᏄᏓᎴ ᎤᎾᎴᏅᎲ ᏓᎾᏕᏲᎲᏍᎬ—ᎤᎾᎴᏅᎲ ᎠᏂᏴᏫᏯ ᎠᏂᏍᏆᏂᎪᏍᎬ, ᎠᏂᏲᏁᎦ ᏓᎾᏕᏲᎲᏍᎬ ᎤᏂᎩᏎᎢ ᏚᏳᎦᏛ ᏓᎾᏕᏲᎲᏍᎦ ᎤᏁᎵᏎ—

ᎤᏦᏎᏙᏗ ᏄᎾᎵᏍᏓᏁᎸ, ᎢᎬᏂᏏᏍᎩ ᎨᏣ ᎠᏂᏰᎸᏍᎬ ᏄᏓᎴ ᏓᎾᏕᏲᎲᏍᎬᎢ—ᏍᏊᏍᏙᎡ ᎢᏳᏩᎦᏘ ᎨᎦᎰᏍᎪᏁᎸᎢ, ᎾᏏ ᏫᏃᏢᏓ ᏓᏌᎯᏍᏛ ᎠᎴ ᎦᎾᏗᏅᏗ, ᎦᏙᎢ ᎠᎴ ᏂᎦᎵᏍᏗᎾᏣᏍᏗ ᎤᎾᏕᎵᏍᎬ—ᎠᏲᏁᎦ—

ᎾᏍᏊ ᎠᏲᏁᎦᎰᎩ Ꮭ ᎨᏣ ᏑᎵᏍᎪ ᎤᏣᏍᏌ ᎢᏳᏪᏗ ᎠᎴ ᎤᏣᏍᏌ ᏧᏬᏪᎳᏅ, ᎠᎴ ᎤᏣᏍᏌ ᎤᏬᏂᏓ—ᏍᏊᏍᏙᎡ ᏓᏝᎠ ᏗᎪᏪᎵ ᏧᏃᎵᏅ ᏚᏳᎦᏛ ᏕᎪᏪᎳ—

ᏃᏉᎰᎩ ᎠᏂᏴᏫᏯ ᎠᎾᎴᏂ ᎠᏃᎵᎬ ᏚᏳᎦᏛ ᎨᏒᎢ—ᎾᏏ ᏓᎾᏕᎶᏆᎢ ᏲᏁᎦ ᏣᏪᏓ ᎠᎴ ᏧᏬᏪᎳᏅᎢ—

ᏚᏳᎩᏛ ᏂᎪᎸ ᎠᎬᏯᏗᎳ ᏓᏝᏒᎢ ᎠᏂᏲᏁᎦᏍᏛ ᏗᎳ ᏧᏂᎪᎵᎡᏗ ᎠᎴ ᏧᏃᏟᏍᏗ ᎤᏅᏍᏌ ᎤᏂᏬᏂᏓ ᎠᎴ ᏧᏃᏪᎳᏅᎢ—ᏚᏳᎦᏛ ᏂᏕᎬᎾ—

WHY DO WE WONDER?
By Hastings Shade

Before the Europeans came, Indians knew the truth and didn't have to wonder what the truth was.

We wonder now because we took for truth what the Europeans taught.

We have been confused because we have trusted a different type of teaching and have been lied to many, many times—through treaties and deals.

Even now some of the Europeans are beginning to see the truth—even though it is written in their own language on many, many papers. The truth has been before them all this time—all they had to do is read and understand their own language.

They are the ones who wrote these truths.

The Indians are now beginning to learn the truth again by learning to understand the Europeans' words.

Unetlvnv Uwotlvnv (What Creator Made)

Hastings' twin concerns with perpetuating Cherokee traditional knowledge and with calling attention to the threats to those ways of knowing are reflected in his meditations on nature. We are to live in harmony with nature. Nature is our source of knowledge and reflects the order of the cosmos. When one lives in harmony with nature, tohi is there: peace, respect, reciprocal relationships, and a calmness of spirit. At the same time, this way of viewing nature is under threat by those who would buy, sell, and trade our world. Though I understood Hastings' concerns, I still felt something was lost in translation with the word "nature."

ᎤᏐᏅᎯ ᎡᏙᎲᎢ (*Presence of Evil*)

ᎠᎾᎦᏴᎵ ᎤᏂᏃᎮᏓ—ᎤᎾᏓᏚᎡᏓ ᏯᎾᏛᏚᎾ ᎩᎶ ᏥᎦᎾᏏᏁᎪ ᎦᏙᎯ ᎪᎱᏍᏗ ᎤᏐᏅᎯ ᎡᏙᎨᎢ

ᎪᎱᏍᏗ ᎤᏴᏍᏗ ᏳᎶᎾᎡᏥᏟ—ᏓᎶᏂᎨ ᎤᏴᏍᏗ ᏳᏍᏗ, ᎾᏍᏉ ᎪᎱᏍᏗ ᎤᏐᏅᎯ ᎡᏙᎨᎢ.

ᎪᎱᏍᏗ ᏯᎪᎯ ᏗᎩᏅᎯ ᎨᏐᎢ ᏗᏫᏂ—ᎠᏨᏍᏗ ᎾᏓᏘᏍᏓᏁᎳ—ᎾᏍᏉ ᎤᏐᏅᎯ ᎨᏐᎢ. ᎢᎬᏂᏏᏍᎩ Ꮎ ᏗᎩᎦᎨ ᏗᏂᏫᏂ Ꮭ ᎤᏁᎳᏅ ᎤᏬᏢᏅ ᏱᎨᏐᎢ.

ᎢᎦᏓ ᎢᎾᏓ ᎠᏁᎭ ᏗᏂᎦᏙᎳ ᎩᎦᎨ ᏚᎦᎳᏍᏗᏍᎪ ᎠᏨᏍᏗ ᏱᏓᏘᏍᏓᏁᎳ—ᎠᏎᏍᎩᏂ Ꮭ ᏙᏳ ᏗᎩᎦᎨ ᏱᏓᏂᏫᎾ.

ᎤᏐᏅᎯ ᎤᎵᏏᎬ ᎤᏗᏍᏆᎶᏣᏚᎠ—ᏙᎯᏳ ᏚᏳᎦᏛ ᏯᎪᎯ Ꮭ ᎾᎥ ᎡᏙᎲ ᏱᏚᏣᏚᎵ ᏤᏓᏍᏗᎢ—ᏍᎩᏃᎾᏳᏍᏗ ᏂᏚᏓᏧᏅᏓ ᏧᏤᏟᏗ ᏥᏚᎦᏗᎨ.

PRESENCE OF EVIL
by Hastings Shade

The elders say that when you hear a chain that sounds like it is being pulled across the ground, it usually means there is something evil around—

And if you smell something that smells really bad—has an odor of sulfur—usually means there is something evil around—

And if you see something that has red eyes, it usually means something evil, because red eyes do not occur in nature—

Certain types of snakes have red eyes that shine red when you shine a light on them—

Evil hides in darkness—does not like to be revealed for what it truly is—

If people could see evil in its true form, they would stay away from it—that is why it uses all kinds of disguises.

When Loretta and I started our work on *Cherokee Earth Dwellers,* I had many questions about the Cherokee natural world. "How is 'nature' understood in Cherokee worldview?" I asked. My mind was focused on words, concepts, and categories. I wanted to understand better—so that I could explain to readers—how the three worlds of Cherokee cosmology work together. I wanted to know how the creatures of the natural world were categorized. And to start, I wanted to know how "nature" is understood from traditional Cherokee perspectives.

After Loretta and I spoke with other elders about the natural world, I realized that for Cherokee traditionalists, the natural world is not an

NATURE • *by Hastings Shade*

Indians believed they were to live in harmony with nature—they couldn't understand how the white culture wanted to own the land, to control it, to change it, and to use it and be masters of it.

Indians believed that the air, water, and land could not be bought, sold, or traded—that they were a part of it, and they were to live with them and not control or change them—nature was the source of knowledge, the natural order of things.

Indians believed that when you live with nature, all other things will fall into place. Harmony with nature and spirituality is necessary to good health.

Modern medicine is just beginning to recognize this—some hospitals are hiring medicine men to teach the traditional Indian methods of treating the sick—although much of the traditional medicines cannot be developed.

The elders know that the different culture will use this as a tool to make money when this is not what they were taught when the medicine was given to them.

abstraction that can easily fit into a category. Folks know certain plants or animals or fish. They garden or hunt. They work with medicines. People have different levels of knowledge or specialties in these areas of practice, depending on their inclinations, their experiences, and what they have learned from others and the creatures with whom they interact. I learned that in a traditional Cherokee understanding as expressed by Hastings and shared by Loretta and other elders with whom I spoke, the natural world is understood through our individual relations with the beings with whom we share life. When I spoke with elders on their views of "nature," they would tell stories about the ways they had lived growing up. They talked about the animals they hunted and the gardens their families grew. They talked about the medicines that came from our plant relatives and how they continued to relate to those medicines. They knew *Unetlvnv uwotlvnv*, what Creator made, not by the abstract term "nature" but by their lived relationships with their environments and the stories and teachings that had been passed down to them about the living world. It was the loss of these *relationships* that Hastings lamented in his writings. But he offered hope in the form of Cherokee teachings and practices we may learn that acknowledge, sustain, and create relationships.

TAKE CARE OF HER AND SHE WILL TAKE CARE OF YOU ✦ *by Hastings Shade*

Some of the stories, myths, and legends are also prophecies. The elders knew what was ahead for the tribe, but a lot of time they couldn't come right out and tell us. They couldn't say, this is what's going to happen, or you might see this in your lifetime. So they told them in story form, just like their elders told them. A lot of time we heard the stories and didn't really know what they meant until it happened. Then we would say, "So this is what they were trying to tell us."

Just like the natural disasters we are experiencing today. The hurricanes, tornadoes, floods, fires, earthquakes, landslides, and drought that are happening on Mother Earth.

Our elders say, we as Native people were put here on Mother Earth to take care of her. If we do not do what we were put here to do, she is going to turn on us one of these days. We are seeing that now.

Fires that destroy whole forests and homes, changing peoples' lives. Hurricanes and floods that ravage towns, communities, and the countryside. Tornadoes and earthquakes that level whole towns and buildings. Landslides that cover towns and homes, killing thousands of people. All of this we are seeing today. We were told, take care of Mother Earth. Take care of her and she will take care of you, they would say.

For instance, my grandmother told me one time, "One of these days you are going to be buying your drinking water." I didn't really think about what she had said until one day I stopped and got me a bottle of water to drink. Then I thought about what she had said. "So this is what she meant by telling me that." No longer could I lie down by a spring and let the water sing to me as I got a cool drink. If I could hear the song today it would probably be a mournful song because the water is no longer fit to drink.

We throw trash into gullies, hollows, and ditches. When it rains it washes everything into our streams and pollutes the water that we come in contact with. Then Mother Nature carries it back up into the sky and causes it to rain back down on us, our own creation: pollution.

The rain is no longer pure, the snow is no longer white, and the air is no longer clear. We have done this. We have no one else to blame.

We as human beings have caused all of this by not doing what we were put here to do: To keep Mother Earth clean and to take care of her.

WHAT THE ELDERS SAY ABOUT NOWADAYS ✦ *by Hastings Shade*

We have become dependent on machines—everything we think about doing is metal—*talugisgi*.

We think about going somewhere, we ride in a car—a machine.

We think about cooking—we cook on a metal stove. When we used to use wood to cook on an open fire that was alive, food was better.

Our water comes from a machine. When we want water we turn on a faucet, which is metal. Water is pumped through a metal pipe or something that has no feelings. We used to drink from a spring, we could hear the water sing to us—water was good.

Even the medicines that we use are made by machines.

When we used to gather by hand and feel and talk to the live plants—the medicines were good.

METAL HAS NO FEELING

And to make this metal we have stripped Mother Earth—
And dug holes in her.

This is our Mother—
This is why we are paying for the shape we are in.

We are sick with many diseases—

The air is no longer good—
The water is bad—
The trees and animals and plants are dying—

All these things and more are happening because of our disrespect for our Mother Earth and each other

Greed has blinded us—we no longer see with our hearts—we no longer hear the plants and animals talking to us—our world is filled with anger and the sound of machines.

We do not take time to communicate with nature—
Our Mother Earth grows old.

Sing the songs of our Mother Earth, and she will be young again.

A VESSEL FOR THE MESSENGER ✦ *by Hastings Shade*

While many of Hastings' writings warn of the ways we have become distant from the natural world, others such as his story of the pipe, the sweat lodge, and five different houses where we grow offer teachings on how we may cultivate a relationship with the center.

Ganvnowa, Pipe

When the Creator began to hand out the abilities to the different species he had created, he gave each one something special.

To the Birds the ability to fly and navigate when they migrate.

To the Animals, the ability to sense things, to survive.

The Fish, the ability to live underwater and provide food.

The Trees, the ability to create oxygen.

The Plants and Weeds, to feed the different species.

The Wind, to blow over Mother Earth.

The Fire, for heating and cooking.

Earth, the ability to sustain life, providing everything that is needed to survive.

The Rain, to provide water for everything.

The Moon, to let everyone know that the Creator does not go to sleep at night and to watch over the Women and Children.

The Sun, to help things grow and give light.

Then it was Man's time to receive his gift. The Birds said, "Let us trade Man our ability to fly for his gift." The Creator said, "No. You already have your gift." All the other species said, "We would like to trade Man our gifts for his." Again the Creator said, "No." Then he said to each one, "I will add one more gift to each of you, and that will be Medicine." This included all the Insects, Amphibians, and Reptiles. All Man has to do is learn how to ask for the Medicine and it will be given to him.

The special gift that Man received was *tsola*. Tobacco. Tobacco is a direct gift from the Creator. At one time it was good, but Man has made it bad.

At one time, tsola was used only for prayer. Then man began to use it for pleasure and to make money. That is why today it causes problems. Man has created that.

This is why the Pipe, *ganvnowa*, was created, so tsola would have a vessel to travel in. If you notice, smoke from tsola rises up. You can see it, then it's gone. When the Creator smells the smoke he knows Man wants to talk to him. And he will listen.

If you put tsola in a fire, sometimes the smoke will not rise. It will stay close to the ground. This is why direct fire is very seldom used to burn tobacco.

Wind, Fire, Earth, and Water were created to help all species that are here on *Elohi*. These four things that are here to help can take life in an instant. So each must be treated with respect.

ᎠᎵ ᎠᏓᏪᎶᏗᎢ ᎧᎳᏦᏕ (*Sweat Lodge*)

ᎠᎵ ᎠᏓᏪᎶᏗᎢ ᎧᎳᏦᏕ ᎤᎵᏍᎨᏗ ᎤᏂᏰᏄᏒᎢ ᎠᏂᏴᏫᏯ—ᏗᏙᎳᏤᎩ ᏴᎥᏗᏭ, ᎦᏅᎦᎴᏍᎪ ᎣᏓᏅᏛ ᎠᎴ ᎥᏰᏄᎢ—

ᎯᏍᎩ ᎢᎦᎢ ᎤᎵᏍᎨᏗ ᏧᏂᏰᏄ ᎪᎱᏍᏗ ᎤᎾᎢ ᏰᏛᎶᎳ—

ᏌᏉ.—ᎠᏥᎳ, ᏅᏯ ᏗᎦᏃᏬᏙᏗ,—ᏅᏓ ᎢᎦ ᎡᎯ ᏄᏝᏂᎬᎬ ᎠᎴ ᎤᏬᏢᏅᏅ ᎤᏁᏝᏅᎯ, ᏓᏟᎶᏍᏗᏓ—

ᏔᎵ.—ᏅᏯ, ᎢᎩᏥ, ᎡᎶᎯ, ᏓᏟᎶᏍᏗ—

ᏦᎢ.—ᎠᎹ, ᎦᏛᏅ ᏓᏓᏁᏟᏴᏏᎶᎬ, ᏓᏟᎶᏍᏗᏓ—

ᏅᎩ.—ᎤᏃᎴ, ᎢᎩᏥ, ᎡᎶᎯ, ᎦᏬᎳᏕᏍᎬ, ᏓᏟᎶᏍᏗᏓ—

ᎯᏍᎩ.—ᏧᎧᏒᏍᏗ, ᎦᏅᏏᏓᏍᏗ ᎠᏰᏟ ᎠᏂᏴᏫᏯ ᎠᎴ ᎤᏁᏝᏅᎯ ᎠᏁᎲᎢ, ᏓᏟᎶᏍᏗᏓ—

SWEAT LODGE ✦ *by Hastings Shade*

The Sweat Lodge is important to the Indian—when used properly it purifies the mind and body.

The five things that are important to the Indian are found here:

The Fire—that heats the stones represents the powers of creation and the sun.

The Rocks—represents our Mother Earth.

The Water—represents the change of our lives.

The Air—represents the breath of our Mother Earth.

The Smoke—is the messenger between the Indian and the Great Spirit.

ᎯᏍᎩ ᎣᏧᏓᎴ ᎧᎳᏦᏕ ᏕᏓᏛᏍᎬᎢ
(*Five Different Houses Where We Grow*)

ᏌᏬ ᎨᏒ—ᎦᏬᏂᎯᏍᏗ ᎧᎳᏦᏕ— ᎤᎾᎢ ᎢᏗᏃᎮᏍᎪ ᎪᎱᏍᏗ- ᎣᏍᏗ ᎨᏒ ᎠᎴ ᎤᏲᎢ—ᏂᎦᎥᏉ ᎨᏒ—ᏭᏢᏍᏗᏇ ᏱᏚᏙ—ᏱᎩᏬᏂᏌ, ᎤᎾᎢ ᎨᏐ ᎯᎠ ᎧᎳᏦᏕ—

ᏔᎵ ᎨᏒ—ᎠᎵᏍᎩᏍᏗ ᎧᎳᏦᏕ— ᎧᏘᏲ ᎠᎴ ᏧᎾᏉᎯᏍᏗ— ᎠᏎᏍᎦᏂ Ꮭ ᏲᏂᎦ ᏧᏂᏃᎩᏍᏗ ᏱᎨᏛᏓ-

ᏦᎢ ᎨᏒ—ᎠᏛᏓᏍᏙᏗ ᎧᎳᏦᏕ— ᎢᎦᏛᏓᏍᏙᏗ ᎪᎱᏍᏗ ᎨᎨᏲᎲᏍᎬ— ᎠᏂᎦᏴᎵ— ᎠᎴ ᏗᏂᏲᏟ— ᏂᎦᎳᏍᏗᏘᏬ ᎩᎶ ᏣᏚᎵ ᎤᏛᏓᏍᏙᏗ, ᏂᎯ ᎯᏬᏂᏍᎬ ᎠᎴ ᎠᏂᏬᏂᏍᎬ ᎢᏓᏕᎶᏆᏍᎪᎢ—

ᏅᎩ ᎨᏒ—ᏕᏓᏛᏍᎬ ᎧᎵᏦᏕ— ᎤᎾᎢ ᏕᏓᏛᏍᎪᎢ— ᏕᎦᏓᏘᏏᎥ ᎠᎦᏙᎯᏍᏗ— ᎠᎴ ᎠᎦᏔᎾᎢ.

ᎯᏍᎩ ᎨᏒ—ᎣᏍᏓ ᎠᏓᎳᏘᏍᏗ ᎧᎵᏦᏕ— ᎤᎾᎢ ᎣᏍᏓ ᎠᏓᎳᏘᏍᏗ ᎢᏗᎶᏘᏍᎪ— ᏕᎦᎦᏙᏍᏛ ᏕᎦᏓᏘᎾᎥ ᏓᎾᏛᏍᎬ— ᎠᏓᏕᏲᎢᏗ— ᎠᎴ ᎠᏓᎨᎢᏗ—

ᎯᎠ ᎯᏍᎩ ᎧᎳᏦᏕ ᏭᏄᏍᏗᏇ ᏱᏚᏙ— ᏱᏂᎦᏛᏁᎳ ᎤᎾᎢ ᎨᏐ ᎯᎠ ᎧᎳᏦᏕ—

FIVE DIFFERENT HOUSES WHERE WE GROW ✦ *by Hastings Shade*

#1 Talking House: Where you sit down and talk about things—anything—things that are good—things that are bad—this house can be anywhere we talk.

#2 Dancing House: Where ceremonies are held—dance grounds—but not to white man's music.

#3 Listening House: Where you can listen to what is being taught—elders—kids—anyone who wants to listen to you—or to them—where we learn.

#4 Growing House: House where we grow—family knowledge—wisdom.

#5 Pleasure House: Where we find pleasure—watching family—kids grow—giving—teaching—loving.

These houses can be anywhere we are when we experience these things.

THE CROOKED-FACED BOY ✦ *Told by wahde galisgewi*

When Loretta, Larry, and I discussed who their family would invite to contribute to Cherokee Earth Dwellers, wahde galisgewi immediately came to mind. Wahde became close friends with Hastings Shade and his family many years ago when they worked together for the Cherokee Nation. Also known by his English name, Ryan Mackey, wahde is a respected cultural traditionalist and spiritual leader who serves as administrator and curriculum supervisor of the Cherokee Nation's Cherokee Language Master Apprentice Program. With their deep commitment to Cherokee language and culture, Loretta Shade told me, Hastings and wahde would often meet and share their knowledge with each another. Loretta spoke to me with deep emotion when she remembered wahde singing a Cherokee spiritual song at Hastings' funeral.

After his passing, members of the Liars' Club and other friends of Hastings created the annual Hastings Shade Memorial Storytelling event. The community gathers each spring for a night of telling "lies" and sharing Cherokee cultural knowledge in community. One year wahde told a story that I return to often. The late elder Benny Smith had shared this story with me many years before. On behalf of Loretta Shade and her family, I asked wahde if we could share his telling of this story in Cherokee Earth Dwellers. He graciously agreed. I am grateful to wahde for contributing this story. And I am grateful to "The Crooked-Faced Boy" for its teachings about our natural world and what is truly beautiful.

"*Siyo nigadawa*," wahde said. He stood in front of the small audience seated in chairs facing him.

"*Siyo!*"

"*wahde galisgewi dagwado'a. itsvyeliilitsvhv tsitsilug kosahiyadidl.* I'm going to take off my 'Sequoyah' coat," wahde said, and folks laughed. He was wearing a trench coat similar to the ones Sequoyah Guess was known for wearing.

"Shoot. I don't know," wahde said, and paused a moment. "What story should I tell? Oh, I've got a long story. It's a good one, though. I tell it about once a week, so I ought to know it," he said, and folks chuckled again.

"*Igohiya tsigesv. Sagwu yiwakt.* Long time ago. They say that . . . our people have lived in four worlds." wahde paused.

"The first world is an island of giant turtles. We had to leave that world behind. They say the second world—*amayetli*—between the waters. It means between the waters. It also means an island. So people aren't really 100 percent sure where that is, exactly. It's possible it's down between the Pacific Ocean and the Gulf of Mexico. Somewhere in Central or South America, even. Other people say, 'No, it's up north.

Around the Great Lakes. Between those waters.' I don't know. But the third world, they call that *tsalag uweti*. And that's the old Cherokee place. We know where that's at. That's our homeland. And we're in the fourth world, today. Indian Territory. The State of Sequoyah. So, we're not promised a fifth world," wahde said and let the meaning of that statement sink in.

"They say this story took place in the second world, wherever that was. Between the waters. Maybe on a journey between the two worlds; I don't really know. But it was before we hit our homeland. They say that all the Indians were living the same way back then. They were all doing the same things. Back then, people were all farmers, and they lived in really large villages. Larger than the villages in the Southeast that we came from. Larger than our homeland's villages. You know, we might have had a couple hundred. Maxed out at less than a thousand in our villages. A long time ago, they say, in the second world, all those different tribes spoke different languages. They had different cultures. Different ways of doing things. But for this story, they said all those different Indians lived the same way. They all lived in huge villages. So big . . . that the gardens were inside the walls. So big . . . that the rivers ran through the middle of the village. They didn't have to leave the walls of that village for anything. That's how big the villages were. They were so big they never needed to go outside the walls. And there was a good reason for that. Everybody was really afraid to go outside of the walls because there were big, man-eating monsters outside the walls. That's what they say, you know?

"And that's how the story goes. That there were these huge, monstrous things outside the walls. So nobody wanted to leave or they would be taken.

"So, we were farmers. Most of our food came from the crops that we grew. Everything took place inside that village. And they had so many things growing in those garden spots that the wild animals would find their way inside the walls, and not only did we have enough produce growing in the gardens to help feed us, but there were so many wild animals getting into the village that we didn't have to go to the woods to hunt. We could hunt inside the village walls.

"Our people were . . . were very," wahde paused in thought, rubbing his hands together, "comforted."

"They were living a comfortable lifestyle, I should say. Really, they were *spoiled*. According to the story, they said that our people had become spoiled. Indian people had become spoiled. All these different tribes, their life had become so easy that they had a lot of free time. They didn't have to go hunting. They didn't have to build things. They didn't have to spend a whole lot of time doing anything for food because it was all right there. And they had so much . . . that they were taken care of. They had so much . . . they had excess.

"They could use that excess time to create beautiful works of art. Their pottery was beautiful. Their baskets were beautiful. The decorations on their walls, even the walls themselves were painted up with beautiful designs. They had so much time they perfected this ideal of 'beauty.' This ideal of 'art.' And they were happy about it. They were very, very happy. They were proud of themselves. They had such a high idea of what beauty was that when they went to their gardens to pick their food, they would only eat the very best of what grew. They would let the other stuff rot. They would only pick the very best food because only the very best, only the most beautiful was fit to be eaten. And when they would go into the same fields to hunt the wild animals that would come into the gardens, they would only choose the most perfect animals to eat. They would kill them all because they couldn't leave them in their corn fields. But they would only eat the very best of what wandered in there. They just let the rest go. So there was a lot of waste.

"They were so focused on this idea of beauty that . . . only beautiful people were allowed to get married. Only people of a certain height. Certain size. High cheek bones. Nice brown complexion. Long black hair. They had to look just a certain way. In fact, even the most beautiful of those that were allowed to get married, only those were the ones that were allowed to have kids. And the most beautiful of them, they were the leaders. They didn't choose the leaders because they were wise or smart or knowledgeable. They didn't choose them because they were kind and generous. They chose them because they were beautiful. And that was the criterion. That became the most important thing during this time period. The idea of beauty.

"Well, this one village in particular, they were very lucky. There was a beautiful young woman in this village. She was *beautiful*. They knew about her for miles around. And they knew that they were very lucky because one day she was going to be their leader. They weren't just lucky because she was beautiful physically, but she was beautiful on the inside, too. She was very intelligent. She was kind. She was generous. She was giving. So she was beautiful in every way, and they knew that one day she would make them a wonderful leader. But she wasn't old enough. Back then, you had to be of a certain age before they would let you do anything. You had to have your kids raised, or at least you had to have kids. And you were supposed to be married. And so they said, 'As soon as she has a husband and a baby, we're going to make her our next leader.' That's what they had decided. And so she looked all around and she finally found herself a husband. And he was just as good-looking as she was. But he was *stupid*," wahde said, and the audience laughed in surprise.

"You can't have everything, alright? But, you know, they didn't mind. She was smart. It was all gonna work out. And sometimes, they didn't always have enough animals inside the walls. Sometimes people would go out hunting. And one evening, that's what her young husband did. He left the walls of the village to go out hunting. And everybody warned him, 'There are terrible, giant, man-eating monsters outside the walls. And they'll *eat* you.' And he just said, 'Yeah. Sure. That's just what they tell people.' So he went outside the walls and I really don't know if he was eaten by a monster. But he didn't come back," wahde said and paused.

"He didn't come back, and everybody began to mourn. That young woman that was beautiful that was gonna be the leader, she began to mourn. And she was inconsolable. And the village, they loved her. She was already a beloved woman in that village. And they loved her and mourned with her. And just when she was about to give up hope for herself, she realized that she had put on some weight. She was actually with child. And so, when she realized that, she had some hope. She had some happiness. She realized there was a piece of her husband still alive. And the village was just as happy to celebrate that as she was. So as the days passed and she got rounder, she got more happy. As it began to get colder she got happier and happier. And it was in the late fall in the middle of the night, maybe early in the morning, when it was time for the baby to come. And they brought her into the center of town. All the elders gathered around. And . . . and the baby came. And all the elders held the baby up," wahde said and lifted his hands, "and they all went . . . *eww*!!" He made a face, and the audience laughed.

"You all have seen babies like that, right?" and everyone chuckled again. But then wahde turned serious. "Not like this baby. One of his eyes was higher than the other. His face was all . . . twisted and contorted. He was a crooked-faced baby. And they held that baby to the mom, and they said, 'You know what you have to do.'" Wahde paused.

"So, immediately she started crying. She took the baby in her arms, and she left the village and went outside into the darkness. Now, I don't know if she was supposed to leave the baby there. Or do something to the baby. But she knew that she couldn't come back inside the walls of that village with that crooked-faced baby. She went out into the darkness and she held that baby and she couldn't put him down. She looked at that baby, and she didn't care what his face looked like. She loved him. And . . . it got so dark in the middle of the night that maybe her mind was playing tricks on her . . . but she saw these shadows move. And they were big, and they were misshapen. And they would loom out of the darkness toward her, and she would just close her eyes and hold her baby. She wouldn't let him down for nothing. And she heard these noises. And these sounds. And she just knew something was coming to get her. As the night went on and the sun started to come up, the light started to come, and the darkness receded. She was left holding her baby.

She smiled down at her baby, and she loved him no matter what his face looked like. And that morning grew into day, and she held the baby. And the daytime grew into evening. And she held the baby even as it was getting dark. She remembered the night before and the sounds and the shadows . . . and the shapes. And she thought, 'I might not be here. Something might come and get me and my baby.' But she wasn't going to put that baby down for nothing. So she held that baby.

The sun went down and it got dark. Started getting cold. She was afraid. And it was everything that she had feared—all those shapes and those movements. Big, looming things. It was almost like they were approaching right up to her face. But nothing touched her and nothing bothered her. She was okay through the darkness of the night. She held on to that baby, and when the sun came up the next morning she was okay. And when she looked down at that baby and smiled and laughed, this time the baby looked up at her. And it smiled and laughed right back. And they say when that baby made that facial expression, it was considered fully human. And for her to leave the baby there . . . or kill it . . . would have been murder.

"So she took her baby back inside the walls of that village. And everybody knew what she had done. Everybody knew that she had waited until that baby made that facial expression to come back inside. And nobody spoke to her again," wahde said and paused. "Nobody looked at her. Nobody walked up to her. Nobody talked to her. They would see her coming and they would turn away from her. That's how they treated her for the rest of her life. And that's how they treated her crooked-faced baby.

"But that crooked-faced baby grew up to be a crooked-faced little boy. And the only person that would speak to him, look at him, approach him, was his mother. And she made it a point to show him how much she cared about him by how she treated him. When she approached him she always approached him with a big smile on her face and with her arms out like that," wahde said and stretched his arms out for a hug. "She was always having her arms out and a big smile on her face. And she did her best to make up for the mistreatment from all the other people."

"One day, he came to her and he said, 'You know, Mom. These people, they act like I'm not there. They talk about me right in front of me. They don't talk to me. They won't look at me, Mom, not like you do. They talk about me. And they say mean things. And they say mean things about you. They say things that are meant to hurt me.' He said, 'Is it true that they used to love you? Is it true that when they looked at you . . . they didn't see me? That, before I was here, you were going to be their leader? Is that true?' And she said, 'Yeah. That's true. But I don't care. I don't care what they say. I chose *you*. And no matter what, I'm not going to give you up. They can turn their backs on us all they want, but we belong to each other, and I'm not going to give up on you.' And he said, 'Mama, they would treat you right if I wasn't here. They would treat you how they're *supposed* to.' She said, 'I don't ever want to hear that again. Not one more time. I don't want to hear it.'

"And after a week, maybe two, she woke up really early one morning before the sun came up, and she was all alone. That little boy, that crooked-faced boy, decided to leave his mom hoping that her life would be better without him there.

"So he left early that morning. He went out into the woods. And he had heard the terrible stories about the monsters. He had never left the walls of that village; hardly anybody had. And so, as he walked out into the darkness he fully expected to be taken immediately and killed and eaten by one of these giant monsters. But it didn't happen. As he walked out into the darkness, he was walking blindly at first. But even before the sun started to come up he heard these sounds he'd never heard before. He had never heard morning birds. He had heard the night birds before, but he had never heard the birds in the morning. And when he heard those birds sing, he thought, 'This is beauty. This is what real beauty is.' And then when the sun did start to come up and he could see the colors of those birds, he was just struck by all the colors of their plumage. He saw the plants. It was fall, so there was still berries and bright colors. He saw all the beauty of the forest around him. And he was just completely astounded," wahde said and paused.

"He had never seen anything like that in all his life. And he thought to himself, 'I feel sorry for those people in the village. They think they know what beauty is. They think they know what art is. But they've never been outside the walls of that village. They haven't seen what I've seen.' And he just became more enraptured with the beautiful world around him. And when he stumbled across a spring-fed creek, he saw the water, he heard the sounds. Things that he had never seen before. Not even his own reflection in the water disturbed his happiness. And he thought to himself, 'The people in the village, they might not understand this beauty. But my mama would. I wish my mom could come and see this. Maybe if I could bring her out here into the woods and she would see this beauty, she would appreciate these things. And realize there aren't monsters out here. The monsters are the people in the village.' He thought, 'I'm going to go find my mom.'

"But he had become so disoriented while he was wandering in the woods and distracted by the beauty that when he tried to find his way back, he couldn't find his way. He was completely lost. And the sun had come up, the morning had stretched into the early afternoon and he was still wandering around looking for the village. And it got dark. Not just dark like a cloudy day. But *dark*. Darker than night. The entire forest was pitched in darkness. And it became deathly quiet. All the birds had quit singing. He heard no animals. He heard *nothing*. Even the wind had quit blowing it had gotten so quiet. And he sat there in the darkness. He couldn't see anything. But in the darkest part of the woods . . . the darkest part of the area around him . . . he could see movements. He could see motion. And as he waited, he heard this sound: DHUUM. DHUUM. DHUUM. DHUUM. Something out of that dark part of the woods was coming at him. And he looked closely and he could see it. Something big and misshapen. Monstrous. Coming out of the woods for him.

"And he thought, 'There's nothing I can do.' He had heard stories all his life about these monsters in the woods, how they would come and they would take you and they would eat you. They would rip you limb from limb. And even the sight of these monsters could cause someone to die of fright. And he knew there was nothing he could do. So he just curled up in a ball and he covered his head. And he waited for that monster to come and take him. And as he was curled up in a ball it just got louder. BOOM. BOOM. BOOM. BOOM. BOOM. And at the last minute he looked up at that monster and that monster had this snarl on his face," wahde said and curled his lip, arms raised above his head, looming over the child. "And that monster was reaching out toward him with both arms when that little crooked-faced boy looked up at the monster. . . . And he looked up at the monster and that boy held his arms out just like this," wahde said, reaching up as if for a hug, " . . . and he smiled."

"And that monster said, 'WHAT are you doing?'" The audience laughed at the break in the tension.

"'Don't you know I'm here to *eat you?* I could tear your arm off in front of your face and eat it right here. When people look at me they die of fright. But when you look at me you hold up your arms and smile? What's wrong with you?'

"And that little boy said, 'Well, I got confused. The only person in my entire life until right now, that has ever even approached me, much less with their arms open and with a smile on their face, has been my mother. When I saw you reaching for me with your arms out it reminded me of my mom. And when I saw your face, you looked so much like my reflection in the water . . . I knew somebody who looked like me, they weren't going to hurt me.'

"And they say that monster asked him, 'What's your name?' He said, 'I don't have a name. But they call me the crooked-faced boy. What's your name?' And that monster said, 'My name is detsadageyusesdi.' And when he said that, the forest opened up. Like stomp dance song or hymn. Good beats. Good music. They say that all the birds, they started to sing. All the animals, they started to sing. The lights came back on. And everything was good. Everything was good.

"And that boy looked at the monster and he said, 'Are you still gonna eat me?'

"And he said, 'No. No, I'm not going to eat you. But there are bigger, badder, uglier monsters in the woods than me. Maybe if we travel together they'll leave you alone.'

"So as those two walked through the woods, that little boy's stomach started to rumble. And that monster pointed at some of the plants growing near the creek.

"He said, 'You know, if you dig up those plants, those roots, that's food.'

"'Really?' the boy said.

"'These plants over here, you can eat the shoots off of it in the springtime. Right now they're not so good. But over here, these plants growing in the water, they're kind of hot, but you can eat those just as they are.'

"'You know all about these plants.'

"And that monster said, 'Yeah. I live in the woods!' This is my Walmart you know," wahde said, and we all chuckled.

"'That's beauty,' the crooked-faced boy said. 'That's beautiful. What you know is beautiful. I wish all the people in the village knew what you knew. I wish they had that beautiful knowledge that you have.'

"And they say that monster thought for a minute. And he kind of stepped back and he said, 'That's true. But those people in the village, they gave up on us. They threw us away. They wouldn't understand. Don't waste your time thinking about them.'

"And that little boy didn't say anything else. They just went down the road.

"It was maybe a week or two later, maybe a month at most, and that monster and that boy were traveling along and suddenly the forest got dark again. It was the middle of the daytime. But it got darker than night. Every sound was silenced. No sound of the wind. Everything was quiet and still. They heard no animal noises. No bug noises. No birds. Completely dark and quiet. When that little boy looked around, there was no monster standing by his side. He was alone in the darkness. But not too far away, in the darkest part of the woods, he could see motion coming toward him. Something huge and hideous. And distorted and monstrous. It was looming in the darkness coming his way. And he could hear it: DHUUM. DHUUM. DHUUM. DHUUM. Like Jurassic Park, for all you older folks," wahde said, and we smiled.

"That's how he felt. He just curled up in a ball and he covered his head and he waited to die and you heard that DHUUM DHUUM DHUUM DHUUM. That big monster was coming out of the woods at him. And at the last minute he looked up, and he saw that monster reaching out like this," wahde said and snarled his lip, reaching down with his arms open wide.

"And . . . and that boy reached up and smiled," wahde said and paused.

"And that monster said, 'WHAT ON EARTH ARE YOU DOING? I'm here to EAT you. Don't you know that when other monsters look at me they flee in terror? And when people look at me they die of a heart attack. I could swallow you whole. I'm big and I'm fierce, but you look at me and you SMILE? And raise your arms like I'm supposed to hug you?'

"And that crooked-faced boy said, 'I'm sorry. The only person in my life until just the other day that has ever come at me with their arms open and with anything resembling a smile on their face is my mother. Nobody's even looked at me or faced me. Nobody's held their arms out to me. Nobody's spoken to me. And when I saw you coming toward me like that, your face looked so much like mine that I knew you weren't going to hurt me.' That monster stopped for a second and he said, 'What do they call you? What's your name?' He said, 'I don't have a name. They just call me the crooked-faced boy. What's your name?' And that monster said, 'My name is detsadalvquodesdi.'

"And at that point the forest opened up. The birds they started singing. The animals started singing. The bugs started singing. The sun came out. It was like . . . beautiful music. Good beats. And they say at that point everything was good.

"The boy said, 'Are you going to eat me, Mr. Monster?'

"And the monster said, 'No, I'm not going to eat you.' And when he looked around, that other monster came out of hiding, and those two monsters started visiting and they started walking together and they said, 'Maybe if we travel together the other monsters will leave us alone. Nobody will bother us. And as they started visiting, that crooked-faced boy said, 'I'm hungry. Let's eat something.' And he started talking about those roots, and the new monster, he said, 'That plant. That's good food, but it's also medicine. If you use those leaves off of that, if you have a fever or something, that helps cool you down. Over here, the bark off this tree, that helps with muscle aches.' And he started pointing out all these different things. And that crooked-faced boy said, 'That's beautiful. That knowledge you have, that medicine you have, it's beauty. That's what real beauty is. Those people in the village, they think they know beauty but they don't. I wish the people in the village knew what you guys knew. I wish we could go back and teach 'em.'

"That new monster said, 'No. Those people threw us away. They don't understand. It's better that you just forget all about 'em.'

"Well, this happened again and again and again. Every so often, the forest would get dark and everything would get still and a monster would come to eat him and . . . he would hug 'em!" wahde said, and we laughed.

"And all these monsters, they came out of the woods and they had names like ditsadasdelisgi itsehesdi. Detsadanvgalawosgesdi. Detsadatliyvsesdi. Ulisgedi detsadayelvsesdi. They had all these names. And there were a dozen or two. And, at some point, they would reveal their name to him, and the forest would brighten and everything would be okay. This happened again and again and again. Till there was just a gang of monsters and one crooked-faced little boy. Wandering around in the woods.

"And the boy said, 'Do each of you guys know something special about the forest?' And they all did. They all knew. Knowledge. Medicine. They all had something beautiful that they knew.

"And he said, 'We need to go back to the villages and teach these people this stuff. We need to go back to those villages and teach them.'

"And they said, 'No! If we went to those villages they would try to kill us, or they would run away screaming in terror. A big old bunch of monsters coming to town to teach you about things. . . . That's not going to work.'

"And he said, 'My spirit says different.' He said, 'Let's fast and pray for seven days and seven nights. And if we all have the same dreams . . . maybe we can do it.'

"And they said, 'Sure. We'll do that.' But on the first night they all dreamed the same thing. They all dreamed about *atsina*—a cedar tree. And how its needles or leaves can be burned on hot coals to make a pleasing aroma. Pleasing for Unetlvnv. Cleaning their area, their environment, their bodies, their spirits. How to use it to help themselves with. They all dreamed the same dream.

"And on the second night they all dreamed about the four directions. Igadasdeldodi nvgi duyukdv. That's what they were for. Four directions to help yourself with. And the teachings from those four directions. And on the third night they had a dream of a little *ogana*, a little groundhog. And he had this hole, and they all went inside this hole, and there were these hot rocks in there. And that ogana poured this liquid medicine on the hot rocks and they started to sweat out their sickness. They started to clean themselves.

"Each night they all shared the same dream. Until on the seventh night they all woke up and they said, 'Let's go teach.' And that's what they did. They started going from village to village to village to village. And at first it was just like they had feared. When they would go to town, the people would scatter. They would scatter to the four directions. Some of the Indians went up to the northeast, to the mountains; to the northwest to the rainforests; to the southwest to the deserts; to the southeast to the swamps.

"They scattered in all those directions.

"But there were always some who stayed behind to listen. And for those who stayed behind, those were the people they taught. For those who scattered to the four directions, they say that's how come Indians are all over the United States. You can go anywhere and there are Indians. It's a little harder to find 'em now. But they're scattered all over the United States. And in every tribe that you go to, we have different languages, different cultures, completely different ways of life. Completely different people. But we share some things in common. Some spiritual things. Some spiritual teachings. And they say that's the reason. It's because those wise ones came around from village to village. And they helped make sure that we really understood that medicine was beauty and that beauty was medicine. And that's a long story, but it's one story. And I'll cede the floor to the next person. *Wado*!"

Standing in the Middle

When I listen for the story's teachings, I think our world today is not so different from that of the villagers in "The Crooked-Faced Boy." Like them, we too often elevate our own creations over nature's beauty all around us. In our quest for safety, comfort, and escape from the fear we create, we use our technology to divide ourselves and wall ourselves off from Unetlvnv uwotlvnv. And in doing so, we sever our relations with our relatives and create inequities and imbalances that not only cost us tohi of our bodies, minds, and spirits but threaten our survival.

Elder teachings hold that in order to stand in the middle, one needs a united body, mind, and spirit. A healthy body—tohi oyelv—means living harmoniously, peacefully with others, without the dominance of anger or disruptive feelings clouding judgment. One may cultivate wellness by avoiding things and forces that disrupt health, like drugs and alcohol. Teachings shared through story—*gayegoga*—help us understand and imagine how to live in tohi, even as forces in the world try to push us off our center. As Hastings said, the storytelling tradition remains the source of Cherokee *dideyohvsdi* (teachings). Finally, we nurture the *adanta* (spirit or soul) through cultivating our relations. Our *sgadug* (community) is made up of all living things. When we recognize through our actions and intentions that we are all related, all dependent on one another, we strengthen our spirits.

Cherokee teachings do not glorify the strongest, most powerful creatures. We tell of Water Spider. We tell of the crooked-faced boy. We tell stories about all types, but we reserve a special place for those with good hearts. Those who are humble. Those who think of others. Those who do not ask for anything in return but serve their community with the talents and abilities they have. The small, the forgotten, the ignored, those too often considered different. The community is not whole until we all participate in the ways we are able.

I once told the story of the crooked-faced boy to a friend. The story stayed in his mind. One day he asked me about something that was troubling him. When the boy returned with the monsters to teach his village of their knowledge of the forest, he said, did the boy find his mother? I like to think the boy found her. But his mother and her love were with him throughout his journey. In greeting those "monsters" with love, he transforms them from man-eaters into teachers. And when he learns the teachings of the forest and comes to know true beauty, he connects to the source of his mother's love in Mother Earth and the natural world.

It was the hope of Hastings Shade, Loretta Shade, their family, and contributors to *Cherokee Earth Dwellers* that elder teachings of the Cherokee natural world may provide future generations with lessons on how to "stand in the middle" like that crooked-faced boy and his mother. To face our fears of that which we do not know, to connect with nature, and to come to see true beauty in an interconnected, sentient, and living world. And, finally, to share that knowledge with one another.

The knowledge shared in this book is but a portion of a Cherokee way of life that lives wherever Cherokees gather and share stories and teachings. With that humble acknowledgment, it is time to enter the Cherokee cosmos and, like that little boy, meet our fellow creatures, learn their names, and share some of their stories that teach us how to be human, how to find tohi in body, mind, and spirit. How to "stand in the middle." *Ayetli hidogesdi.*

Tali ✦ Two

Elohi

THE MIDDLE WORLD

"*Elohi*," Loretta said. "That's the world. One thing that's always there, I don't care what it is—even an everyday thing. The spirit world is always there. You have to be in tune with the spirit. If not, then it's useless. That's what Grandma always taught us, and Grandpa, too." We were talking about the three-tiered Cherokee cosmos that includes the Sky World above us, the Under World below the earth and waters, and the world of land upon which we creatures of Elohi live. I had heard Hastings and other elders speak many times of Elohi as a living place filled with creatures and forces that communicate with one another and have mutually dependent relationships. This view of a living, connected world is not a matter of belief but of experience, Loretta explained. Cherokees of different faiths may practice different forms of worship, but there is perhaps no more universal teaching in Cherokee culture than the understanding that the cosmos is infused with living, spiritual energy. How is spirit expressed in nature? How does this knowledge inform our values? What is the nature of Elohi? What forces shape it and those who live here? What are our responsibilities to Elohi as human beings? These are questions, Loretta explained, that we have long asked. The teachings concerning our place on Elohi were learned from and are continually experienced through our engagement with other creatures.

As Loretta and I talked, I thought about Hastings' discussion of "standing in the middle" and of how tohi in body, mind, and spirit are all dependent on knowing how to live well on Elohi. For all Cherokees in the not so distant past, and continuing today for many who grew up traditionally, understanding the Cherokee natural world through the creatures that inhabit it, their names, their stories, and how they relate to one another and to us was essential to finding balance, interconnection, maturity, and health. We human beings do not make our homes in the sky or under the waters—at least not yet. While we have relationships with those other places, other "worlds" in Cherokee thought, and depend on them to live, we are fundamentally creatures of *gada*—soil, earth, land. We are born on land, and we live our lives tethered to the earthen surface of this planet. Elohi is our middle, and it is upon Elohi that we human beings learn to stand.

In Cherokee mythology Elohi is the Middle World. Our world is created when the life forms and energies from the ordered, defined Sky World meet the chaotic, dynamic Under World. *Doyunisi,* little Water Beetle, dives down from Sky World deep into the waters of the Under World to bring a fleck of mud to the surface. When it hits the air, the mud spreads and creates a new space for life, uniquely itself but also a bridge that connects sky and waters. On the lands of Elohi creatures of both earlier worlds interact, overlap, and change as they negotiate delicate balances of respect, reciprocity, and interconnection required for tohi to flourish in this dynamic place. Shaped by both order and chaos, Elohi is characterized by growth and the constant striving for a dynamic balance of forces. Just as each of us has a center inside ourselves, Elohi is the center for all of us: the middle world revolving around the fire, our sun. On these learning grounds, we work toward tohi as we live together.

This chapter on Elohi presents names, stories, and reflections on the creatures and forces that inhabit the Cherokee Middle World. It tells of beginnings and an evolving ethics among creatures. Together, these teachings cross time to weave a continuing story in which we humans strive to live in harmony with other creatures in a cosmos defined by opposing energies and impulses. In this dance of continuing life and death, Elohi connects the Sky World to the Under World, the bridge—*asvtlv*—linking the two together. Hastings gathered and wished to share these names, stories, and teachings because actions have consequences in the Cherokee worldview. Our plant and animal relatives as well as other forces of life and destruction, elders teach, have real power over our lives as humans. Through understanding the natural order and one's place in relationships with other life forms on Elohi, one may establish tohi within one's self. And when we do this as community through teachings, we may create healthful patterns in which all may flourish.

THE SEARCH FOR ELOHI ✦ *by Noyi Teuton*

The story of Elohi begins with the creatures of the Sky World searching for a new home, a place to grow. Though Hastings and the other elders I spoke with for Cherokee Earth Dwellers *often referenced parts of this story, none of them told the whole story to me. I put the parts together and retell it here. Among the many important details and teachings in this story, there is one that stands out for us: humans were not here when Elohi began. We came later and had to find our place in this middle world.*

Ilvhiyu tsigesv nigada inage anehi tsalagi tsaniwonisgv. In the great forever that was, all the forest dwellers spoke Cherokee. And in that ancient time, what we know now as Elohi, the Middle World of *gada ale nvya*—dirt and rock—was all covered with water. The ancient animals lived in *Galvladi*, the Sky World, on the dome-shaped back of a giant turtle. *Yona* (Bear), *Tsisdu* (Rabbit), *Dlameha* (Bat), and all the other people that we know were there at that time. But, elders tell, the inage anehi were much larger than they are now, and they were not yet fully formed by their actions into the creatures we know today.

The families of beings grew and grew in Galvladi, and it became so crowded that some even fell off the sides of the giant turtle's back. A council was called to decide what should be done. The animals were curious about the water world far below Galvladi, which stretched as far as anyone could see. They decided the water world should be searched for dry land upon which the people could live. Bird after bird flew from Galvladi and searched far and wide, but no land could be found. It was then decided to send in the water animals to dive below the waters in search of earth. Strong, powerful swimmers who could hold

Anigidui

And so the story of human beings does not begin with the creation of Elohi, Hastings once explained to me. But like the creatures of the Sky World that first inhabited Elohi, human beings came from the stars. Our origins begin in the star constellation *Galaquogi Dinadalv*, the Seven Sisters, known in Western culture as the Pleiades. A story is told that one of the sisters, Star Woman, felt sorry for how the people were being treated there. So she gathered them up and brought them to Elohi. When she landed on Elohi, her body opened up and human beings stepped out. When Star Woman returned home she was punished by her sisters and hidden behind a cloud of dust. For this reason she is called *Ulisigi*, the Dark One. On a clear night you can see her six sisters, but Ulisigi remains dim behind her veil.

their breath for a long time were chosen first, but one after another each came back from the deep gasping for breath. None of them could reach the bottom. All the while, *Doyunisi*, the little water beetle known as Beaver's Grandma, kept saying, "Let me try!" Finally, Doyunisi had her turn. She dived into the waters and was gone so long that the other creatures feared her dead. It took all her strength and courage, but Doyunisi reached the bottom and returned to the surface with a little speck of mud. As soon as that mud hit air, it began to spread out in all directions.

After the people had waited some time, they asked *Suli* (Giant Buzzard) to fly down from Galvladi and see if the land had dried and was ready for them to live on. Suli flew all over the world in his search. And as he got tired, Suli flew lower and lower toward the earth. Suli got so low that his wings touched the earth and made valleys. And when they went up, Suli's wings made mountains. Suli flew back to Galvladi in exhaustion and announced, "Elohi is still muddy. It's not dry yet." And so the people waited some more.

Kolvn (Raven) was asked to check and see if the land was ready for the animals. Kolvn flew from Galvladi and was gone a long time. The people waited anxiously for any news. Finally, word spread of Kolvn's return and the people gathered at the edge of the giant turtle's shell to watch for Kolvn. At first Kolvn was just a speck far below, but as they got closer the people could see something dangling from Kolvn's beak. "It's a branch!" someone in the crowd said. The people now knew Kolvn had found dry land, and with the knowledge that Elohi was ready for them to live upon, they cheered Kolvn's return.

Hastings told of another star home of ancestors of the Cherokee. In a different part of the night sky there is a seven-pointed star, *Galaquogi Digosdayi Noquisi*. It is from this star, elders said, that sons of Unetlvnv came down to live with women of Elohi. The children of these unions were powerful people, Hastings said, as they had knowledge of the forces in the cosmos. They became the medicine people. Some practiced good medicine, others bad, but through their knowledge, words, and actions they could do wondrous things like influence the weather, heal, or harm. To this day the seven-pointed star is a symbol of the Cherokee. And the number seven may be found throughout Cherokee culture, from the seven clans to the seven directions.

Elders say the original name for the Cherokee was *Anigidui*, the Coming to the Top or Coming Out People. Though today the name "Cherokee" is commonly used, it is not of Cherokee language origin and likely comes from either a Choctaw-derived word for "cave dwellers" or the Creek word *chilokee*, which means "people who speak a different language." Cherokees also use the term *aniyvwiya* to refer to themselves. Translated as meaning the "real people" or "principal people," *aniyvwiya* is a term for American Indians, the principal or most prevalent people Cherokees encountered in the past. It is from Anigidui, Hastings said, that the name *Keetoowah* is derived. Hastings had described the meaning of Keetoowah to me as related to *giduninugo*—or coming out, like the bud of a plant does when it grows out from the earth. Cherokees began as hunters and gatherers but in ancient times created villages and became growers with permanent farms. Unetlvnv named the people Keetoowah as they came up from the ground, Hastings said. *Kituwah* is the name of the ancient Cherokee mother village site along *Daksiyi* ("Turtle Place," or the Tuckaseegee River) west of Cherokee, North Carolina.

One summer afternoon at his home in Lost City, I spoke with Hastings, Sequoyah Guess, and Woody Hansen, our friend and a fellow member of the Turtle Island Liars' Club, about the origin of the Keetowah people and their name. Hastings had been doing some metal work earlier in the day. As the rain began to fall we took shelter under the roof of his outdoor shop, the summer bugs playing a symphony for us.

"The Cherokees have been around for a long time," Hastings said. "When the people actually came here, the big animals were here. We have names for some of the extinct animals and birds. The wooly mammoth, modern-day elephant, and the butterfly all have the same name, *kamama*. Is it because of the shape of the ears on the mammoth and the elephant and the wing of the butterfly? Looking at them head on, they all have the same shape and outline. The elders say the *Tlanuwa* and *Siniqua* were big enough to carry off small children and small animals. So, you know, that put them underground. Then, as the big animals began to disappear, the people began to come out of the ground. That's how come we know the big animals were here."

In his list of animals, Hastings had included some of these ancient, long-extinct creatures once known to the Keetoowah. They remain known today through their names in the Cherokee language:

Giant hawk or falcon is *Tlanuwa*

Pterodactyl is *Siniqua*

Giant bison is *Yanasi equa*

Saber-tooth tiger is *Sahoni*

Giant lizard is *Tiyohali equa*

Giant sloth is *Doya equa*

Wooly mammoth is *Kamama*

Hastings, Woody, and Sequoyah reflected on the meaning behind knowing these names and teachings from the ancient past.

"The elders say these creatures were not killed but were only run off. They say they will return one of these days to get our children again. I wonder what form they will take this time?"

As Hastings spoke, I thought about the recent threats to humanity in the form of animal viruses. Hastings' reflection reminded me that in Cherokee thought, spirit is enduring but the physical form may change.

"The Bible is a parallel to the beliefs of the Native people, or Indigenous, you know," Hastings continued. "Because in our stories we've been here a long time. Ages. We know the names of the ancient, ancient ones. The old ones. Mastodons. Thunder lizards."

"Saber-tooth," Woody said.

"We know the names of 'em. Ten thousand, twenty thousand, thirty thousand, fifty thousand years."

"But, you know, does the time frame really matter?" Woody said. "It does to some, and they really focus on it, but then they lose focus on everything else," Woody said.

"Yeah," Hastings nodded.

"The thing is, some entity created the world and through time created us. Here we are today. For our grandkids, our great-grandkids, the same factors will still be there."

"So, we've been here for a while," Hastings looked at me and said, "And if we don't lose our language, we're going to be here a little bit longer."

"Mmhm," Sequoyah said.

I had heard other stories of Cherokee origins. Like the story of "The Crooked-Faced Boy" told by Ryan Mackey, these accounts of the ancient past provide teachings to consider. Hastings and other elders teach that Cherokees knew other homelands long before settling in what is now Oklahoma. In the migration story "Journey of the Four Directions," Hastings told how a long time ago the Cherokee lived on an island surrounded by undrinkable water. Was it salt water? Was it brackish water? The story

I heard does not say. The Cherokee thrived there, but one day the island began to shake and fire burst forth from its mountains. That home was lost, and some tell that the reason the people had to leave was for disrespecting the giant turtles that lived there. The Cherokee left that home and began a long migration to the cold lands of the north. The people stopped and settled along the way, meeting and sharing knowledge with other peoples. But some continued north until they reached a place called "where the white mountain moves." That was not a good place to stay, they say, and so from there they headed east, eventually finding their home along the rivers and in the rich valleys of what is now called the Smoky Mountain region.

There are differing accounts in Cherokee community of where human beings originated, how we became a people, and where we have lived. Some say we were created from clay. Others say we came from the sky. And some will wonder what is the "true" or the "real" story, the factual, verifiable history of how the Cherokee came to be as a people. But as Hastings, Loretta, and

HOW HUMANS WERE CREATED • *by Hastings Shade*

The Creator created four colors of humans: Red—Black—White—Yellow—and put them on four different islands on the place that is called Mother Earth.

Only the White has left his island and went to take the islands of the other three colors. The White did not heed the Creator and stay where he was put; instead he left the place where he was supposed to stay and imposed his desires on the other three colors.

The Red color is the only one that has stayed close to his Creator and tried to do as the Creator instructed him to do and that is to take care of his mother the earth, from which he was created.

The White began to take the land and began to unclothe the Mother Earth and tear her apart by digging and stripping the land. This made it difficult to care for her.

This is one of the things that the other three colors cannot understand—taking more than is needed to live.

The Red Man says that right now the Mother Earth is crying out for help.

But it may be too late to save her.

other elders say, stories are really teachings; they are all true inasmuch as they carry the wisdom and experiences of the past to the present.

To Keep Balance or Destroy It

"I understand where human beings come from," I said to Loretta, "but I'm wondering what kind of role or power we have in the world. Often it seems like we're out of place and destroying what we touch. I've heard human beings are in the position of trying to keep some kind of balance in the world," I said and paused. "Is that our role or responsibility?"

"Human beings can keep balance and they can destroy it," Loretta said. "Just like our use of mushrooms. If you take the root of the mushroom, it won't grow again. And if you don't thank them when you get them in the fall or spring, they're gonna move. Things move if you don't thank them. When you get a plant to eat or use it for medicine, you say in the language, 'This is what I want you to do.' Or 'Thank you for doing this, taking care of this person.' That's how you keep it there. If you pull the mushroom out, you're taking its life. And if you cut it, you're leaving the roots to stay. In another season it'll be back up. And we've seen that so many times."

Loretta's teaching reminded me of what Cherokee elder Tom Belt and his co-author, Heidi M. Altman, wrote about human beings in Cherokee cosmology. In a living spiritual world populated by animals and plants that existed before them, humans must learn to fit into this sgadug by observing the laws of nature passed down through oral tradition (Altman and Belt 2009, 13–14). When behaving and living in tohi, one creates the context for good actions to flow (14). When wrongs are committed, they inevitably lead to bad consequences, even if in the distant future (14). In Cherokee thought, actions toward others always have consequences, from good to bad; we are forever in the role of balancing. Fortunately, Cherokee oral tradition offers lessons on how to strive for tohi and how to make amends should one stray from the straight path. In the teaching Hastings shared about the creation of humans I saw that our characteristics as distinct peoples were defined by our relationships with particular places and stewardship over those lands.

Word Collector

One day over lunch in Tahlequah, Loretta and Larry explained to me the intention behind Hastings' collecting and writing down the names of creatures and their stories. I knew readers would be curious as to why he had spent decades visiting with other elders recording creature names and stories of the Cherokee natural world.

"His general idea was just to let people know that there were Cherokee words for those animals and that they were not supposed to die out," Larry said.

Even back in the 1970s, Loretta explained, there was an urgent need to teach Cherokee language and perpetuate the cultural traditions shared in the language. She and Hastings belonged to what could be one of the last generations of first-language Cherokee speakers. Witnessing the younger generations speaking English as their first language, Hastings understood the urgency to document and share Cherokee knowledge and traditions in the Cherokee language. Though much of his life was spent sharing Cherokee culture orally through classes and youth-elder camps, he also understood the power of the written word to carry on teachings that had been passed down over generations. It was for this reason that we collaborated on writing *Cherokee Stories of the Turtle Island Liars' Club.* He was committed to seeing these teachings carry on, Loretta said, no matter the format.

"What was his vision for these collections of creature names?" I asked Loretta.

"This material is for teaching. For people to *learn*," she said. "This book will help people who don't know their heritage. Don't know their identity. This will show them how close the Cherokee are to nature. And how they still depend on one another."

Larry and I nodded.

"And especially now with climate change," I said. "There's research that shows communities who lose their heritage languages also lose their relationships to the environments they live within. They lose that sense of valuing nature because they don't see themselves as related to it."

"Yes," Loretta said. "I feel like—and I don't know if other elders do, too—that plants and trees are dying because of climate change. Decaying."

"Was Hastings' vision for the collection that folks would learn not just the names of the creatures, but begin to relate to them once again?"

"Yes," Loretta said. She gestured to the Northeastern State University campus, just across Town Branch Creek. "All the trees on this campus have a Cherokee name. Like redbud. *Gagogi*. And dogwood. *Kanvsita*. But most students can't name them."

"But if you know the name of a tree or an animal and the story that its name tells, that's the start of a relationship with that creature."

"Yes!" Loretta said. "That's why these names need to be learned."

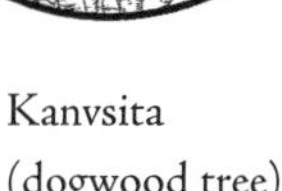

Kanvsita (dogwood tree)

Later that evening I visited with Sequoyah Guess and continued the discussion of the power of names, naming, and the reasons why Hastings dedicated himself as a word collector. He was a good person to ask, as Sequoyah often accompanied and assisted Hastings in his cultural work. "Sequoyah has pretty much been with Hastings from the beginning when they started making cultural materials," Larry Shade told me once. "He'd think of something, or Sequoyah would think of something, and they'd write it down."

Speaking of *Cherokee Earth Dwellers*, Sequoyah said, "When it's all together, it will be a great resource to have as a book. People who are out of touch with their culture will at least have a . . . starting point. They'll be able to ask, 'Hey, tell me about this tree.' Or animal. Or plant. And then grow from there." Listening to Sequoyah I was reminded of Hastings telling me that tradition was like a chair. It is meant to be useful. It has purpose. If it's only to be preserved and not used, you might as well throw the chair in the river. That was his motivation for collecting and sharing these words and teachings. They are to be learned and used by future generations.

Names

Hastings, Loretta, and other elders tell that, along with fire, the Cherokee language is a direct gift from Unetlvnv. Teachings say that Cherokee peoplehood is rooted to the ancestral language used to communicate, as well as to the fire that connects the people to their spiritual source. It is through the Cherokee language that Cherokee people first created a shared reality, complete with words that gave shape and meaning to their experiences, relationships, thoughts, and imaginations. And the most primal function of language is to name the world.

People ask, "*Gado usdi detsado'a?*" What is your name? And the question, "*Hiyoligis . . . ?*" Do you know so-and-so? And with these two simple questions Cherokee language speakers and learners forge connections. We learn what we are called, who our families are. We find out if we have mutual friends or relatives. We place one another in a shared world of previously unknown or newly created connections and relationships. I wanted to understand Cherokee naming practices better, and so Loretta and I reached out to other elders and cultural traditionalists to learn more.

On a bright spring morning Loretta and I sat in the chapel at the Cherokee Heritage Center with Cherokee elders Dorothy Ice, Melvina King, and Rufus King. We were looking over Hastings' books of Cherokee creature names and talking about the ways Cherokee naming creates relationships and connects us to the natural world around us.

"Is the process of naming important to Cherokees?" I asked.

"It was back when we were growing up," Melvina King said. Her husband, the retired pastor Rufus King, was looking through Hastings' collection of names.

"Naming the kids. That was important," Melvina continued. "Because they used to give you something, if they named you. That was the tradition a long time ago. If somebody named you, they would give you something. Now some of our kids don't have Cherokee names."

"Sometimes a person will call and say, 'Can you name my child and give a Cherokee name to my child?'" Loretta said. "I say, 'Well, do you have one picked out? Did you have a favorite aunt or uncle or grandma or grandpa you want to name 'em?' 'No.' 'Well, what do you want to call 'em? It's always 'Rising Moon' or . . ."

"'Crazy Horse,'" Dorothy Ice said.

"Running Deer," Loretta added. They all were chuckling now.

"And mostly," Melvina said, "it's not like that. You can't choose a name like that one. You just give 'em your aunt's name or whatever, ain't it?"

"Now they do it," Dorothy Ice said. "Used to, when an Indian built a house he had a door facing east."

"Yeah, yeah," Melvina nodded. "East door."

"That was medicine," Dorothy said. "And when a child was born, they'd take that baby and face it east. And named it. Give it a name. Whoever chose it. Give it a name and sing a song. That was the name that they gave. A lot of times, my father would go to that door. The first thing he seen would be that baby's name."

"That would be the name," Melvina King nodded.

One afternoon a few days later, I sat with my friend David Comingdeer at his home in Adair County, north of Stilwell, to speak with him about his observations on Cherokee naming practices. A well-known Cherokee cultural traditionalist, David is also chief of Echota-Tanasi Ceremonial Ground in Park Hill, Oklahoma, where my family and I are members. Many years ago, David and the other leaders of the grounds gifted me a name that I accepted as a member of Echota-Tanasi. I knew that as a person of the woods who worked as a wildland firefighter for the Cherokee Nation for over twenty years, David had a deep reverence for both the natural world and Cherokee knowledge of it. We talked about Hastings' collection of names and the importance of names to Cherokee culture.

"How are the names of creatures of the natural world important to our understanding of them in a Cherokee way?" I asked.

"The names that our ancestors have given to the world around us, the plants, animals, everything, it's not just a word. It's not just a sound that you make. It's actually telling a story of that animal. It may be describing a characteristic of it. Of the plants, too. And the trees. The names in Cherokee have a *meaning* and *describe* what that plant is or even what it does or even what it looks like. It's gonna describe it in some way, in most cases. And our animals especially. You've got animal names that literally describe something very specific about that creature or what it does.

"You know, we didn't even know what a horse was before the Spaniards brought horses over. But we observed that animal. We observed how the Spaniards used that animal, and then we adopted that animal into our life and it became a sacred part of who we are. The horse. But what is a horse? It carries stuff. It's a load bearer. So, when our ancestors saw it and they observed this animal they hadn't seen before, they named it *sogwil*. *Sogwili*. You know, 'the one that carries the burden on its back.' *Gasogwihldi*. It's describing what that horse does, and that's how beautiful our language is. It tells you a story just by saying the name of the creature."

"What is at stake in sharing the names Hastings collected and in learning them?"

"Anything that we can pass along and can perpetuate with our own tribe, we *must* do it. There's no external force that can come in and preserve and protect and perpetuate and defend our culture. We have to do it from within. The only way we can perish is from within, and the only way we can flourish is from within. And so, if we have an opportunity to capture and save and perpetuate information like what Hastings did, we must do it. We have a duty to do that. And we owe it to our grandchildren to pass along that legacy."

Cherokee naming practices have changed over time, but what remains constant is the power of the name. We are named by others to honor and continue the memory of our loved ones, or to forge a relationship between us and the world we encountered the day of our birth. We are named by others for how they see us. We may grow into new names and out of old ones. And just as we come to know our human relations through their names, we know and form relations with the other-than-human world through our names for our fellow creatures. Deep and intimate observations, partnerships, and kinship with other creatures led to names for the creatures that inhabit the Cherokee world. Over time, this knowledge of the natural world and our place in it—the natural order—has been encoded in words that define, categorize, and place us and our fellow creatures in relationships within time and space. Whether descriptive or expressive, Cherokee names tell stories. And in knowing those names and tying those stories together, Cherokee names portray the rich, interconnected, enstoried sgadug of the three-tiered cosmos.

"Are there things expressed in Cherokee names for plant and animal relations that don't come across in English?" I asked Loretta once.

"The names are not that meaningful in English," she said and chuckled. "They're not that . . . touching. Just put it that way."

The Creatures of Mother Earth

My work on *Cherokee Earth Dwellers* led me to biological taxonomy, that human tradition of naming and categorizing life forms into groups by their physical and behavioral similarities and differences. Most of us were taught as children the eight-level hierarchical system of taxonomy that charts back to Carolus Linnaeus, the Swedish taxonomist who invented this way of grouping life forms used to this day. Domain is the largest category, then there are kingdom, phylum, class, order, family, genus, and finally species. The invention of Linnaeus's system of taxonomy in the early eighteenth century was revolutionary because it offered the Western world a unified system for grouping and naming the world's creatures. Before then, different cultures used their own "folk taxonomies," or ways they grouped creatures according to how they understood and related to them. The stories and teachings they had of them. Linnaean taxonomy focused on physical similarities and differences between creatures, a universalizing approach that ignored the unique ways different peoples related to the creatures of their world. That was good for science, which is focused on measurement, but it came at the cost of diminishing other ways of knowing.

Taxonomy is now based on cladistics, which means it organizes creatures not just by their physical characteristics but also by their phylogeny, or how they evolved. As an educated teacher, Hastings was certainly aware of taxonomy, but he decided to group Cherokee creatures and their names in eight catalogs: Animals, Plants, Edible Plants, Trees, Insects, Birds, Fish, and Reptiles and Amphibians. I wondered why Hastings had chosen the specific categories he used for his creature name books and whether or not they related to traditional Cherokee ways of ordering the living world.

Loretta explained to me that Hastings classified creatures based on where they live, what they look like, and how they behave. There are creatures we encounter every day, which include human beings, plants, and animals. Human beings, *aniyvwi*, are of Elohi and are distinct from other creatures. Considered neither better nor worse than animals and plants, aniyvwi once were considered distinct because we walk on two legs and eat different foods than other creatures. The different foods animals ate distinguished them from one another. There are three divisions of animals: four-footed creatures, which are of Elohi; birds, which are of the Galvladi; and fish, insects, reptiles, and amphibians, which are of Elohi Hawinadidla. Of the four-footed creatures, there are those who live in the inage and those that are *diganatli* (domesticated). Diganatli such as farm animals have different relationships with humans than do wild animals, which live independent of us. Though Cherokees have many types of relationships with plants as food, medicine, and sources of heat and shelter, plants are considered one general category.

As the story of "The Search for Elohi" tells, the prototypes of the creatures we see on earth today originally came from the Sky World, that place of order and perfect forms. They came down to Elohi seeking room to grow and spread out, and in doing so they were shaped into different creatures through their experiences. It was during what has been called the ancient time, or *ilvhiyu tsigesv*, the "great forever that was," that creatures were transformed by their actions. For example, the story of *Kananesgi Amayi ale Atsila* tells of how the appearances of animals were changed in attempting to acquire fire for our benefit. There are many traditional stories that take place in the ancient time when the nature and appearance of creatures were in flux and adapting as they learned to live together and negotiated new balances in this three-tiered cosmos. But just as in Linnaeus's original taxonomy, Cherokee tradition presents an ordered, created world where every creature has its rightful, purposeful place in the whole.

Although the Cherokee cosmos and its creatures are interdependent and interrelated, there are also borders that traditional teachings, cultural customs, and ceremony acknowledge and respect. Each of the three worlds is naturally distinct, but thresholds between worlds, such as the edge of waters or the smoke rising from fire, are settings that Cherokee tradition recognizes as having transformative power. The going to water ceremony, for example, is performed on the edge of water at dawn or dusk. And the smoke from fire carries prayers to Unetlvnv. While the known laws of each particular world may be understood and navigable, in those in-between places there are transformative possibilities for connection, as well as dangers. *Dikanowadvsdi*, the Cherokee word for "law," contains the word *nvwoti* (medicine) within it. As Cherokee linguist Ben Frey explained to me, the concept of law in a Cherokee context is not about oppressive prohibition but about keeping one safe. *Dikanowadvsdi* means something like "do this and it will be medicine to you." This understanding of borders, thresholds, and law applies to creatures as well.

As long as creatures stay within their rightful places and perform their particular roles, all is well and ordered. The trouble is, Cherokees long ago recognized that some life forms do not easily fit into stable categories. Hastings once told me that those beings that can move between different worlds have power. They can be small, such as the mole, a four-footed creature of Elohi that spends its life underground in Elohi Hawinadidla. They can be like the owl, a bird that hunts in the night, has eyes on the front of its head, and looks something like a man standing with his arms behind his back. Or like *inada* (snake), a creature that is hatched from an egg like a bird but is loathed by flyers, and that can climb trees, sleep underground, and swim. Like these others, inada is an anomalous creature worthy of regard for its power to move through different worlds, and thereby to relate to different creatures and environments. Stories and teachings of creatures like Kananesgi Amayi, Uk'tan, and other boundary-crossers are deep sources of contemplation and symbolism.

These boundary-crossing beings are not limited to animals and plants. Earth, air, fire, and water are all powerful elements. Spiritual beings from Cherokee mythology such as the Thunders, Spear Finger, Bigfoot (*Utan Tsulasgi*) and the *Nvnehi* are part of our cosmos as well. They are associated with particular worlds of the three-tiered cosmos and may interact with humans, but they are not subject to the same physical laws that shape our existence. They are *anidawehi*, beings super with wisdom. People are taught to be respectful of the places and creatures associated with these beings. As an example, Hastings told that elders said to leave the pure white animals and pure black animals alone. They belong to the Little People. And if you take what is theirs, they will come for you. Though Hastings included some of these beings in his lists of creature names, a lot of their stories are told on a "need-to-know" basis. That is, told to a specific person for a specific reason.

After Loretta shared her knowledge of the Cherokee cosmos and Cherokee taxonomy, I understood the system behind Hastings' organization of the creature name books. Hastings' taxonomy reflects a traditional way of ordering the world, with Animals, Birds, Plants, Insects, and Fish all having their own places. But as was typical of his approach, he wished to make these works practical as well, and so he created separate catalogs for Edible Plants, Trees, and Reptiles and Amphibians. Together Loretta and I sorted the creature lists into each of the worlds in which they belong, while sometimes acknowledging particular noteworthy boundary-crossing species featured in Cherokee tradition.

Some of the names in *Cherokee Earth Dwellers* are ancient and untranslatable, their meaning likely lost to time. Some names describe a creature's body or its behavior. Some names reference a story or encounter Cherokees had with a particular life form. Each entry is presented as Hastings documented it, often with his or Loretta's comments. Many creature names are published here for the first time.

As you read and learn these names, imagine yourself entering a new world, with new inhabitants you must get to know. Some will become your friends; others may harm you. Over deep stretches of time, some have come to symbolize important Cherokee values. In keeping with this spirit of discovery, we present the creature names within the context of "The Origin of Disease and Medicine," a foundational Cherokee story about the nature of our animal and plant relatives and their relationships with human beings. Hastings' teachings and other stories that follow explore how tohi in body, mind, and spirit depends upon knowing and learning to live in harmony with our relations.

Forest Dwellers

ᏌᎷᏱ ᎠᎴ ᎢᎾᎨ ᎠᎴ ᏗᎦᎾᏟ • saluyi ale inage ale diganatli (sah-loo-yee ah-leh ee-nah-geh ah-leh dee-gah-nah-tlee) • **forest dwellers and domesticated animals**

ᏏᏆ ᎤᏤᎢᏍᏗ ᎤᏯᏍᎦᏟ • siqua utseisdi uyasgatli (see-qwah oo-jeh-ee-sdee oo-yah-sgah-tlee) • **armadillo** • Name means: grinning hog with a shell

ᎣᎦᎾ ᎦᏙᎡᎯ • ogana gadoehi (oh-gah-nah gah-doh-eh-hee) • **badger** • Name means: groundhog that lives in the ground

ᏜᎺᎭ • dlameha (dlah-meh-hah) • **bat** • "Included with the animals because of scientific classification. The animals didn't want him at one time. The birds took him." H.S.

ᏲᎾ • yona (yoh-nah) • **bear** • *"In Cherokee tradition,* yona *symbolizes courage*—tsulitsvyasdi—ᏧᎵᏨᏯᏍᏗ.*" H.S.*

ᏲᎾ ᎬᎾᎨ • yona gvnage (yoh-nah guh-nah-geh) • **bear, black**

ᏲᎾ ᎡᏆ • yona equa (yoh-nah eh-gwah) • **bear, grizzly** • Name means: big bear

ᏲᎾ ᎤᏁᎦ • yona unega (yoh-nah oo-neh-gah) • **bear, polar** • Name means: white bear

ANIYONA (*Bears*)

"Bear is brother to the Cherokees," Hastings wrote. He also wrote of a clan of people, the *Anitsogo*, who long ago became the bears we know today. He wrote nothing more on this topic, and so I wondered about this connection.

There is a story of the Bear Clan told to the ethnologist James Mooney by *Ayu'ini* (Swimmer) and published in 1901 in *Myths of the Cherokee* by the Bureau of American Ethnology. Ayu'ini's story of the *Anitsaguhi* clan reminds me of the *Anitsogo*, the clan of people Hastings had been told became the bears. The meaning of Anitsogo is lost to us, Hastings claimed, but through the similar names of these clans and details of the story, the pieces of this story may align. "Bear helped provide meat for man," Loretta confirmed. "But he'd turn on man if you made him mad."

Hastings and Ayu'ini both sought to perpetuate Cherokee culture, and so I feel it fitting to bring them and these Cherokee traditions together across time and distance to share teachings about *yona*, human beings, and the fluidity of our nature.

THE BEAR CLAN ✦ *by Noyi Teuton*

Ayu'ini tells that long ago there was a Cherokee clan called the *Anitsaguhi*. In one family of this clan, there was a boy who sometimes would leave his home and walk up into the mountains to spend his day. Time went by, and the boy started to spend more and more of his days up in the mountains, staying away from home longer and longer until he would be gone from sunup to sundown, never eating his mother's food. The boy's parents became concerned. They talked to him about being gone so much, but it did no good. He kept spending his days off in the mountains. His parents then noticed other changes in him. Long brown hair was beginning to grow all over his body. And so they sat him down and his mother asked him, "Son, why is it that you want to be out in the *inage*? Don't you want to eat with your family at home?"

"I find lots to eat in the forest," the boy answered. "And I like it better than the corn and beans we have in our village. Soon, I'll go to live in the inage."

The boy's parents were alarmed at his words and asked him not to leave his family and community.

"It's better in the inage than here," the boy insisted. "And I am already changing by being out there so much. Soon, I won't be able to live here anymore. Why don't you all come with me? There is food for everyone out there, and you won't have to work for it as we do here. If you want to come with me, you will need to fast for seven days and then we'll head out."

The boy's parents talked to elders and leaders of their clan about what their son had said. The clan held a council and talked the matter through. They came to a decision. As one of the elders said, "In village life we must work for our food. Still, sometimes there is not enough food to go around. The boy says that in the inage there is always enough food, and we won't have to work for it. Let's go with him." And so, the clan members fasted for seven days. On the morning of the seventh day, the Anitsaguhi left their village and followed the boy into the mountains.

Word spread to other towns about the decision of the Anitsaguhi. They sent leaders to ask the members of the clan to not go live in the inage. But when the leaders arrived, they saw that the Anitsaguhi were already on their journey to the inage and, like the boy, had begun to change. Their bodies were covered with hair like other inage anehi. They had not eaten human food for seven days and their new nature was taking root. They would not return to a life in the village. They said, "We are going to the inage, to the *dodalv* (mountains) where we will always have enough food to eat. From now on, you may call us *Aniyona*. If you are ever hungry, you may come to the inage and call us. We will come from the mountains and share our flesh with you. You don't need to be afraid to kill us because we have plenty of food and will live on." Then, Ayu'ini told, the Aniyona taught the leaders the bear hunting songs to call them. When they finished their teachings, the Anitsaguhi walked on toward the forest and the leaders started their return to the villages. It is said that when the leaders looked back one last time to see their kin, they saw families of bears lumbering into the woods.

Doya
(beaver)

ᏙᏯ • doya (doh-yah) • **beaver** • *"In Cherokee tradition,* doya *symbolizes resourcefulness*—eliyadvdi—ᎡᎵᏯᏛᏗ." *H.S.*

ᎬᎮ • gvhe (guh-heh) • **bobcat**

ᏯᎠᏂᏏ • yaanisi (yah-ah-nee-see) • **buffalo**

ᎨᎻᎵ • gemili (geh-mee-lee) • **camel** • New name to the Cherokee. It's a sound-alike name.

ᏪᏌ • wesa (weh-sah) • **cat**

ᎩᏳᎦ • kiyuga (kee-yoo-gah) • **chipmunk** • "The chipmunk would not vote with the animals when they were giving mankind diseases, so the bear took a swipe at him as he ran off and scratched his back. You can still see the scratch marks on him to this day." H.S.

ᏧᏢᏕᏍᏗ • tsutlvdesdi (joo-tluh-deh-sdee) • **civet cat, or ringtail cat** • Name means: having stripes around it

ᏩᎦ • waga (wah-gah) • **cow** • Borrowed from the Spanish word for cow, *vaca.*

ᏩᏯ ᎤᏍᏗ • waya usdi (wah-yah oo-sdee) • **coyote** • Name means: little or small wolf. Also known as prairie wolf, or *waya agodi ehi* (wolf that lives on the prairie).

ᎠᏫ • awi (ah-wee) • **deer** • Old version of name is *kawi.* • *"In Cherokee tradition,* awi *symbolizes prudence*—geyatahi—ᎨᏯᏔᎯ." *H.S.*

ᎠᏫ ᎤᏁᎦ • awi unega (ah-wee oo-neh-gah) • **deer, white** • "All the animals that are white belong to the Little People. If you kill one of their animals they will get revenge. So be careful what you kill." H.S.

ᎩᏟ • gitli (gee-tlee) • **dog** • "The dog that the Indian knew came to the Indian himself. He told the Indian for a few kind words and some scraps, he would stand guard. If something dangerous was coming he would put himself between the Indian and danger. The first name for the dog ᎩᏟ ᏳᏍᏗ (gee-tlee yoo-sdee) means—canine-like." H.S.

ᎧᎹᎹ • kamama (kah-mah-mah) • **elephant** • Name means: butterfly, because of the shape of the ears

ᎠᏫ ᎡᏆ • awi equa (ah-wee eh-qwah) • **elk** • Name means: big deer

ᏧᏟ • tsutli (joo-tlee) • **fox** • A catchall name for fox.

ᎢᏃᎵ • inoli (ee-noh-lee) • **fox, black, or gray fox**

ᏧᏟ ᎩᎦᎨ • tsutli gigage (joo-tlee gee-gah-geh) • **fox, red**

ᎤᎦᏐᏣᏁᏓ • ugasotsaneda (oo-gah-soh-jah-neh-dah) • **goat** • Also called *tsugsquanagiti,* which means "puckered butthole."

ᏥᎦᏯ • tsigaya (jee-gah-yah) • **gopher**

ᎣᎦᎾ • ogana (oh-gah-nah) • **groundhog** • Name means: lives in the ground

ᏐᏈᎵ • soquili (soh-quee-lee) • **horse** • This is the name given sometime around De Soto's arrival. Name means: "draped over"

ᏥᏍᏚᎴᏂ • tsisduleni (jee-sdoo-leh-nee) • **jackrabbit** • Name means: all ears

ᏢᏓᏥ ᎤᏍᏆᎴᏂ • tlvdatsi usqualeni (tluh-dah-jee oo-sqwah-leh-nee) • **lion, African** • Name means: bushy head

ᎠᏫ ᎤᏍᏗ • awi usdi (ah-wee oo-sdee) • **Little Deer** • Name means: Little Deer • "This is the one that looks after the big deer. It's a mythical creature. Pure white and small as a fawn, the Little Deer exists but only the best hunter can see him." H.S.

ᏌᎶᎳ ᏗᎯᎯ • salola dihihi (sah-loh-lah dee-hee-hee) • **marten** • Name means: squirrel-killer. Once he starts chasing a squirrel, it very seldom gets away.

ᏒᎩ • svgi (suh-gee) • **mink** • Name means: it stinks, or *asvgi.* Also the name for the onion.

ᏘᏁᏆ • tinequa (tee-neh-gwah) • **mole** • Name means: big lice

ᎠᏓᎴᏍᎩᎢᏍᎩ • adalesgiisgi (ah-dah-leh-sgee-ee-sgee) • **monkey** • Name means: the grabber

ᏥᏍᏕᏥ • tsisdetsi (jee-sdeh-jee) • **mouse**

ᎧᏒᏂ • kasvni (kah-suh-nee) • **mouse, field**

ᏎᎵᎢᏍᏆ • seliisqua (se-lee-ee-sqwah) • **muskrat** • *"In Cherokee tradition,* seliisqua *symbolizes endurance*—adadvnidiyadodi—ᎠᏓᏛᏂᏗᏯᏙᏗ." *H.S.*

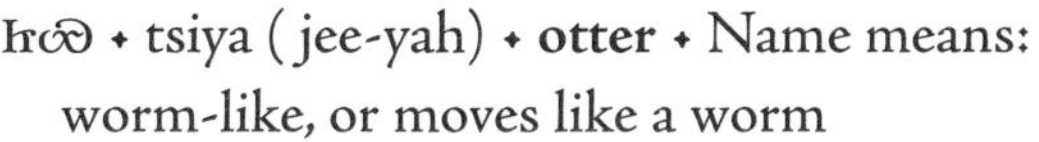

Seliisqua (muskrat)

ᏥᏯ • tsiya (jee-yah) • **otter** • Name means: worm-like, or moves like a worm

ᏢᏓᏥ • tlvdatsi (tluh-dah-jee) • **panther, or mountain lion** • *"In Cherokee tradition,* tlvdatsi *symbolizes strength*—utlinigidi—ᎤᏟᏂᎩᏗ." *H.S.*

ᏢᏓᏥ ᎬᎾᎨ ✦ tlvdatsi gvnage (tluh-dah-jee guh-nah-geh) ✦ **panther, black** ✦ Name means: black lion

ᏥᏍᏚ ✦ tsisdu (jee-sdoo) ✦ **rabbit**

ᎬᏟ ✦ kvtli (kuh-tlee) ✦ **raccoon** ✦ Name means: has a mask on

ᏆᏂᏈᏏ ✦ quaniquisi (qwah-ni-qwee-see) ✦ **rat** ✦ Name means: peach poop

ᎤᏃᏕᎾ ✦ unodena (oo-noh-deh-nah) ✦ **sheep** ✦ Name means: wooly

ᏔᎳᏍᎨᏫ ✦ talasgewi (tah-lah-sgeh-wee) ✦ **shrew** ✦ Name means: stomping his feet

ᏗᎵ or ᏗᎳ ✦ dili or dila (dee-lee or dee-lah) ✦ **skunk** ✦ "This is the animal that told the Creator he wanted to be left alone—so the Creator gave him the odor he has. Be careful what you ask for as you might get it." H.S.

ᏙᏯ ᎡᏆ ✦ doya equa (doh-yah eh-gwah) ✦ **sloth, giant** ✦ Name means: giant beaver

HOW THE RACCOON GOT HIS MASK AND RINGED TAIL ✦ *by Hastings Shade*

All the animals tried to get the fire for the people, even the Raccoon, *Kvtli*, tried.

When it became his turn to try to get the fire, he went to the tree where the fire was. There was a hole about halfway up the tree. He climbed to where the hole was and looked into the tree. About that time the fire flared up and the smoke covered his face and turned it black. He pulled his head out of the hole and began to wipe his eyes. As he did this he worked the black soot into his fur. Then he shook his head. When he done this, most of the soot came off his head except for where he had rubbed his eyes. That part stayed. This is why he has a mask on to this day and his fur has dark spots and streaks on it.

If you have ever been around Raccoon, you know he doesn't give up very easily. He turned around and stuck his tail into the hole. He thought he might be able to get some of the fire onto his tail and he could get the fire this way.

As he stuck his tail into the hole in the tree, the fire flared up again. When he felt the heat he pulled his tail out as fast as he could, but he wasn't fast enough. The fire had burnt black circles around his tail.

Today when you see him you can see he still has a mask on and you can see the rings around his tail.

He is also called the Ring-Tailed Raccoon. He got these things by trying to help the people get the fire.

ᏌᎶᎳ • salola (sah-loh-lah) • **squirrel** • A catchall name for squirrel.

ᏔᎳᏣ • talatsa (tah-lah-jah) • **squirrel, boomer, or red squirrel** • An Eastern Band Cherokee name

ᏕᏫ • dewi (deh-wee) • **squirrel, flying** • "Same as the bat. Because of scientific classification it has to be included with the animals but the birds took him also." H.S.

ᏌᎶᎳᏬᏗ • salolawodi (sah-loh-lah-woh-dee) • **squirrel, fox** • Name means: brown squirrel

ᏌᎶᎵᏯ • saloliya (sah-loh-lee-yah) • **squirrel, gray**

ᏢᏓᏥ ᏧᎶᏜᏗ • tlvdatsi julotlidi (tluh-dah-jee joo-loh-tlee-dee) • **tiger** • Name means: having stripes

ᏌᎰᏂ • sahoni (sah-hoh-nee) • **tiger, saber-tooth**

ᏥᏍᏕᏣ ᏓᎶᏂ • tsisdetsa daloni (jee-sdeh-jah dah-loh-nee) • **weasel** • Name means: yellow rat • *"In Cherokee tradition,* tsidetsa daloni *symbolizes judgment*—digugotanv—ᏗᎫᎪᏔᏅ." *H.S.*

ᏩᏯ • waya (wah-yah) • **wolf** • *"In Cherokee tradition,* waya *symbolizes guardianship*—ugasesdidega—ᎤᎦᏎᏍᏗᏕᎦ." *H.S.*

ᏐᏈᎵ ᏧᎶᎢᏍᏗ • soquili tsuloisdi (soh-qwee-lee joo-loh-ee-sdee) • **zebra** • Name means: horse with stripes

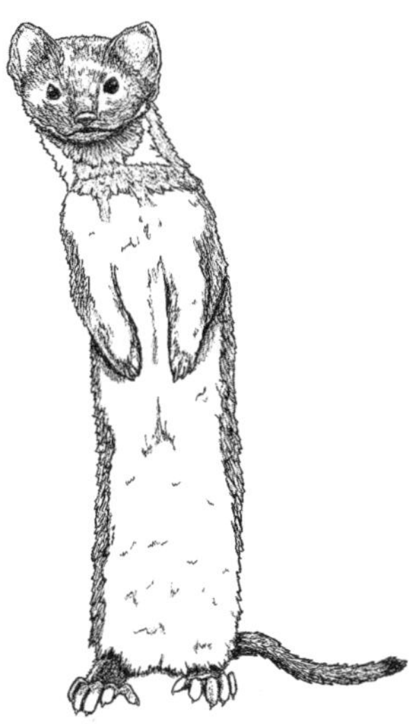

Tsisdetsa daloni (weasel)

Waya (wolf)

ADALENISGV VHYUGI ALE NVWOTI

(*The Origin of Disease and Medicine*) ✦ *by Noyi Teuton*

Cherokee oral tradition tells that human beings were latecomers to Elohi. The plants, animals, and other life forms were already here. Like other creatures, we had to test our boundaries, make mistakes, learn from our experiences, create relationships, and change our offending behaviors in order not just to survive but to live in tohi. This is an ongoing process.

"Originally," Loretta told me, "Unetlvnv sent the animals to provide medicine and food for human beings. But the humans abused them, and so they stopped." Without plant relatives defending us and giving us a second chance to learn from our mistakes, we would have perished. And without animals teaching us our place with vhyugi (disease), we would have destroyed more. I am grateful to elders for passing down this story which still has so much to teach us.

Ilvhiyu tsigesv nigada inage anehi tsalagi tsaniwonisgv. In the great forever that was, all the forest dwellers spoke Cherokee. All the creatures we know today were there at that time, placed on Elohi by *Unetlvnv*, the Creator. And it is told that all the creatures lived together in tohi and in friendship. But as time passed, human beings grew in number, creating villages and spreading all across Elohi. And as humans settled over more lands, the forest-dwelling animals who lived in those places were pushed out of their homelands and became cramped for space. Not only this, but humans had invented knives, blowguns, bows, spears, gigs, and hooks, which they used to hunt down and kill the forest dwellers for food, skins, and tools. All creatures, big and small, suffered because of the carelessness and disrespect of the humans. The forest dwellers decided to hold councils to discuss what had to be done to protect themselves from the humans.

The bears were the first to meet in council. At their council house in *Kuwahi* (Mulberry Place), Chief White Bear led the meeting. One after another, *aniyona* (bears) told of how humans had killed their friends. They had eaten their flesh and used their skins for clothing and warmth. After sharing their grievances, the bears decided unanimously to make war on the humans.

"What weapon do humans use to kill us?" asked a bear near the back of the council house.

"Bows and arrows!" answered all the witnesses. Others nodded in agreement.

"What are these made of?" a young bear asked.

"The bow is made of trees and the string of our own guts," answered a large old bear leaning in the doorway.

"Well, can we make our own bows and arrows?" the young bear asked after a pause.

One bear gathered a locust branch from the surrounding camp and another sacrificed himself for his kin and gave his innards for the bowstring. When the bow and arrow were made, a female bear stepped up to give it a try. She pointed the bow, aimed the arrow, and pulled the bowstring back. But when she let the arrow fly her long claws snagged the string. Her shot missed the mark. Seeing the problem, the bears cut her claws short. When she took her next shot, the bowstring pulled smoothly and the arrow flew straight to its mark. All the bears at the council nodded in approval.

With this success, other bears stepped forward to have their claws cut. Then White Bear, chief of the bears, stood and raised his paw high.

"We need our long claws to climb trees and dig," White Bear said with his deep voice. "*Unetlvnv,* the One Who Willed All Things to Be, has given us teeth and claws for our survival. If we cut our claws we may be able to shoot bows, but we'll all starve. And one of us has already given his life for the bowstring. These human weapons are not for us."

With these words the council ended. The bears made their way back to their homes in the forest. They had failed to find a plan to stop the increase and disrespect of humans.

The deer also held a council. Led by Little Deer, their chief, together they decided to inflict rheumatism—a painful disease of the joints and muscles—on any hunter who should kill one of them without first asking pardon for the offense. They sent word of their decision to a nearby village and also explained how to make amends when it was necessary to kill one of the deer people.

"From now on," Little Deer had announced at the deer council, "when a hunter wounds one of our kind he must offer a prayer asking pardon for taking our lives. I myself will run to the site of the killing and ask each spirit if it heard the hunter's prayer. And if the spirit has not, I will follow that hunter home by the blood drops of our relative. And I will strike the hunter down with disease." Since that time, hunters offer a prayer of pardon to the deer for killing it.

The fish and reptiles held a joint council and decided to attack the offending humans in their sleep. Dreams of snakes entwining their bodies and breathing in their faces, and of stinking, rotting fish would make humans lose their hunger, sicken, and die. Snake and fish dreams continue to this day.

Lastly, the birds, insects, and small animals gathered in council. Grubworm led the council, and it was decided that all should present their cases against humanity and then vote on whether or not to find humans guilty. Seven guilty votes would decide the verdict. Creature after creature stepped in front of the council fire and told of human cruelty and injustice.

"We must stop the increase of humans," *Walosi* (Toad) said to the council. "If we do not, they will become so numerous that there will be no place left on Elohi for us. They kick me and call me ugly and step on my back! Just look at the sores," he said and turned for all the council to see the spots on his skin. Walosi voted for death.

Tsisqua (Bird) was the second witness before the council. "They kill my kind, roast us in fire, and burn off all our feathers—even our feet!" Tsisqua voted for death.

One after another, each creature that stepped before the council told firsthand accounts of human disregard, disrespect, and violence. Only *Kiyuga* (Chipmunk) had anything positive to say about humans. "The humans don't trouble us. Maybe they leave us alone because we're so small. We vote against harming them," Kiyuga said and began to leave the council. Hearing these words, a visiting bear took a swipe at Kiyuga as he ran off and scratched its back. The marks remain there to this day.

When seven forest dwellers voted humans guilty, the verdict was decided. The council began its work of conjuring and naming new diseases—*vhyugi*. Creatures stepped forward to tell of the new sicknesses they had in mind. As they did so, a list was created. Upon hearing of each new sickness, Grubworm cheered and applauded from his place of leadership. Toward the end of the council, a voice from the back of the council house said, "Should not women sometimes die during their moon time?"

"*Wado*!" Grubworm said and stood up with enthusiasm. "It makes me happy that some humans will die, for they are so many that they walk all over me." He shook with silent laughter at this thought and fell over backwards. He tried to stand again but could not and had to wriggle away on his back, as Grubworm still does.

With forest dweller councils being held, the plants soon learned of the many sicknesses the animals planned for humans. Plants were friendly toward human beings, and so they decided to take pity on them. Each and every plant, including all the trees, shrubs, herbs, grasses, and even mosses, came to unanimous decision to provide humans with medicine for the diseases caused by the animals. And each plant solemnly pledged, "I will appear to help human beings when they call on me in need." And with their help and pledge, plants gave human beings not only food but also medicine. Each plant holds a gift of medicine it may share, should the spirit of the plant wish. And yet, even with this gift of medicine, illness remains with humans, as does the need to learn to respect our forest dweller relatives, and, indeed, all life.

ANINOHALIDOHI (*Hunters*) • *by Hastings Shade*

Hunters of long ago fasted for four days before they went on a hunting trip. This ensured a clean mind and body. After a kill was made, usually the liver or heart was eaten first. This signified that the animal lived on through the hunter.

When a hunter made a kill, he always said a chant and left some of the best meat at the site of kill, thus ensuring that the animal would never get scarce. They were taught to give back something that is the best.

As time went on, the Indian hunted without fasting; then if a kill was made, the hunter fasted.

It was a four-day fast for a deer kill and a seven-day fast for the bigger animals like bear, buffalo, and elk. Usually the first part of the animal that was eaten was the heart or liver roasted over an open flame so the spirit could leave the animal.

They believed that meat cooked in a pot hampered the free movement of the animal spirit, making for a hard hunt when they went out again. No part of the animal was wasted.

Animal Stories

Loretta and I were visiting with Sequoyah Guess when the conversation turned to animal stories. Like other Cherokee folks raised traditionally, Hastings, Loretta, and Sequoyah had grown up with these stories and understood them as teaching tools. I guessed that for some readers, stories featuring talking animals as characters might lead one to believe these lies are really for children. But just as Aesop's Fables of ancient Greek oral tradition were originally addressed to adults and explored the religious, social, political, and ethical life of the community, Cherokee stories of talking animals hold deep meaning that moves beyond simple allegories.

"It seems to me an important part of the storytelling tradition is that the animal stories mirror how people act toward one another, good and bad. Is that true?" I asked.

"Yeah, in most of the stories I tell there might be some kind of act or behavior by an animal which might be thought of as being mean or unkind to one another," Sequoyah answered. "But if you look at the overall message of the story, it's not. It's about a person being more in balance than the next person beside you, you know? I tell a story about Rabbit and Possum looking for wives. They grew up together and are best friends, but Rabbit is a trickster by nature, and he plays tricks on Possum throughout the story. And that's true with people. In Cherokee culture, you cut down or make fun of people you like. And they'll do the same to you, you know? And so, Rabbit plays tricks on Possum because he's a trickster but also because it's the way he grew up. Just like me and my friends. We're always makin' fun of each other, you know? So, there are underlying messages in all these stories about how we behave toward one another and about ourselves."

"When you tell these stories that your grandma taught you, are they *really* about the animals like Rabbit and Possum, or are they stand-ins for human characteristics? I'm wondering about how these stories relate to the actual animals we know," I said.

Sequoyah looked slightly surprised at the question and paused a moment in thought.

"Well, I've never really thought of the animals as not being . . . *beings*," he said and laughed. "I was taught and I've always thought of them being their own persons with their own natures. I've never thought of them as being part of *our* world. And hopefully, I tell these stories where not only are they seeing Rabbit and Possum but they're seeing people, too, in those situations. Because anything the animals go through we can learn from."

"So, if someone sees a rabbit after hearing your stories about Rabbit and Possum, they can think, 'That's Rabbit.'"

"Yeah, that's Rabbit. That's Rabbit. When I'm driving down the road and an animal is trying to cross it—a rabbit, deer, turtle, possum, armadillo, or raccoon—I try to miss 'em each time, not only because I don't want to end a life, but because I think, 'Well, they have a family at home.' And it's just like a human being. They have family. They have somebody that cares for 'em. Again, they're just like the plants, the fish, and the birds. They are their own person. I don't really think of 'em as being separate. It's just like they used to say, 'We're all in this together.' And that's not just humans, that's every living thing on this earth."

Plant Relatives

Just as animals have personhood, Loretta said, plants do as well. Hastings often spoke of how plants move and change in relation to weather, the seasons, and how they are treated by us. Take too much from it, and it may move. Neglect a relationship with a plant, it may leave as well. Just like animals, we know plants not in the abstract but through our continuing relationships with them.

The story of the origin of disease and medicine tells how plants have chosen to be friends to *aniyvwi* (human beings). They are providers of medicine (*nvwoti*), something with which to help yourself. And so it is through the gift of plants that we may work toward tohi. Elders say that each plant has a medicine to offer, should it wish to share of itself. "When you go out there to get plants, you thank them," Loretta said. "You pray over it. That's what you do. You pray, you ask for what you want it to do, or tell how it's gonna be used. Then you make sure you leave something when you take something. You give something back."

Plants

ᏚᏰᎬ • duyegv (doo-yeh-guh) • **plants** • Name means: something rooted up from the ground

ᎤᏓᏔᏅᎯ • udatanvhi (oo-dah-tah-nuh-hee) • **berry or fruit** • Name means: something grown on a tree or vine

ᎠᏂᏥᎸᏍᎩ • anitsilvsgi (ah-nee-jee-luh-s-gee) • **flowers** • "Flower" is *atsilvsg*.

ᎠᏥᎸᏍᎩ • ajilvsgi (ah-jee-luh-s-gee) • **flowering plant**

ᎤᎦᎶᎦ ✦ ugaloga (oo-gah-loh-gah) ✦ **leaf**

ᏧᎦᎶᎦ ✦ tsugaloga (joo-gah-loh-gah) ✦ **leaves**

ᎠᏰᎲᏍᏙᏗ ✦ ayehvsdodi (a-yeh-huh-s-doh-dee) ✦ **plant** ✦ Name means: putting it in the ground and letting it grow

ᎤᎿᏍᏕᏜ ✦ unasdedla (oo-nah-sdeh-dlah) ✦ **root**

ᎤᎧᏔ ✦ ukta (oo-k(a)-tah) ✦ **seed**

ᎤᏩᏱᏢ ✦ uwayihlv (oo-wah-yee-hluh) ✦ **sprout**

ᎠᏓᏫ ✦ adawi (ah-dah-wee) ✦ **Adam and Eve weed** ✦ Name means: Cherokee name for Adam

ᏔᏆᎵ ✦ taquali (tah-gwah-lee) ✦ **bear grass**

ᎤᏂᏍᏗᎸᏍᏗ ᎤᏔᎾ ✦ unisdilvsdi utana (oo-nee-sdee-luh-sdee oo-tah-nah) ✦ **big cockle burr** ✦ Name means: the big one that gets in your hair

ᎤᏛᏓᏍᏗ ✦ utvdasdi (oo-tuh-dah-sdee) ✦ **big ear weed** ✦ Name means: the one that listens

ᎤᏴᏍᏗ ✦ uyvsdi (oo-yuh-sdee) ✦ **bitterweed** ✦ Name means: bitter or sour

ᎠᏫᎠᎦᏔ ✦ awiagata (ah-wee-ah-gah-tah) ✦ **black-eyed susan** ✦ Name means: deer eye

ᏖᎾᏔᏁᏍᎩ ✦ tenatanesgi (teh-nah-tah-neh-sgee) ✦ **blackroot**

ᏔᏄᏄ ✦ tanunu (tah-noo-noo) ✦ **blazing star**

ᎩᏟ ᎤᏩᏔᎵ ✦ gitli uwatali (gee-tlee oo-wah-tah-lee) ✦ **bloodroot** ✦ Name means: dog's privates. Only a small amount is needed for red dye.

Gitli uwatali (bloodroot)

ᏕᏐᏆᎳᎦ ✦ desoqualaga (deh-soh-gwah-lah-gah) ✦ **blueberry**

ᎧᏁᏍᎦᏬᏗ ✦ kanesgawodi (kah-neh-sgah-woh-dee) ✦ **bluegrass**

ᏧᏣᏲᏍᏗ ✦ tsutsayosdi (joo-jah-yoh-sdee) ✦ **briars** ✦ Name means: sharp or can prick you

ᎬᏃᏌᏍᏗ ✦ gvnosasdi (guh-noh-sah-sdee ✦ **broom weed** ✦ Name means: broom

ᎬᏃᏌᏍᏗ ᏗᎪᏢᏙᏗ ✦ gvnosasdi digotlvtodi (guh-noh-sah-sdee dee-goh-tluh-toh-dee) ✦ **buckbrush,**

or Indian currant ✦ Name means: to make a broom with. Roots are used to make baskets. Also called *tsudanedla,* or stretched out.

ᎤᏲᏓᎵ ✦ uyodali (oo-yoh-dah-lee) ✦ **calamus**

ᏪᏌ ᎤᏂᎩᏍᏗ ✦ wesa unigisdi (weh-sah oo-nee-gee-sdee) ✦ **catnip** ✦ Name means: for the cats to eat

ᏪᏌ ᎦᏙᎦ ✦ wesa gatoga (weh-sah gah-toh-gah) ✦ **cattail**

ᎤᏂᏍᏗᎸᏍᏗ ✦ unisdilvsdi (oo-nee-sdee-luh-sdee) ✦ **cocklebur** ✦ Name means: gets in your hair

ᎤᏍᏗᏟ ✦ usditli (oo-sdee-tlee) ✦ **dandelion** ✦ Name means: has a crown

ᏬᎴᏓ ᎤᏁᏍᏓᎵ ᎤᏅᏌᏓ ✦ woleda unesdali unvsada (woh-leh-dah oo-neh-sdah-lee oo-nuh-sah-dah) ✦ **dewberry (small)** ✦ Name means: has ice around the ankles

ᎦᎾᏤᎢᏗ ✦ ganatseidi (gah-nah-jeh-ee-dee) ✦ **dipper gourd**

ᎤᏁᎦ ᎠᏔᏍᎩᏍᎩ ✦ unega atasgisgi (oo-neh-gah ah-tah-sgee-sgee) ✦ **dogbane** ✦ Name means: it explodes or pops white. Milk of the plant cures warts.

ᏲᎾ ᎤᏤᏍᏙ ✦ yona utsesdo (yoh-nah oo-jeh-sdoh) ✦ **fern** ✦ Name means: bear's pillow

ᎢᎾᏓ ᎦᏅᎦ ✦ inada ganvga (ee-nah-dah gahn-go) ✦ **fern, walking** ✦ Name means: snake tongue

ᏗᎵᏍᏆᎶᏍᏙᏗ ✦ dilisqualosdodi (dee-lee-sgwah-loh-sdoh-dee) ✦ **forget-me-not** ✦ Name means: to bump heads

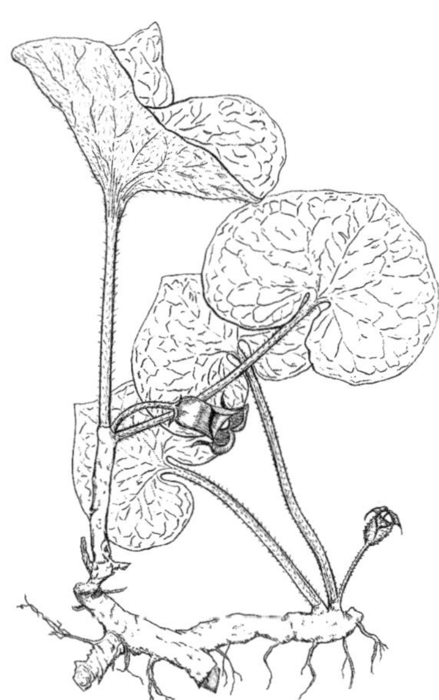

left
Gvnosasdi digotlvtodi (buckbrush)

right
Nuyugali didanesgi (wild ginger)

Odali galegi (ginseng)

ᏏᏆ ᎤᏂᎩᏍᏗ ✦ siqua unigisd (see-qwah oo-nee-gee-s-dee) ✦ **giant ragweed** ✦ Name means: hogweed

ᏄᏳᎦᎵ ᏗᏓᏁᏍᎩ ✦ nuyugali didanesgi (noo-yoo-gah-lee dee-dah-neh-sgee) ✦ **ginger, wild, or heart snakeroot** ✦ Name means: big stretch

ᎣᏓᎵ ᎦᎴᎩ ✦ odali galegi (oh-dah-lee gah-leh-gee) ✦ **ginseng** ✦ Name means: it climbs mountains

ᎦᏄᎸ ✦ ganulv (gah-noo-luh) ✦ **grass**

ᎧᏁᏍᎩ ᎢᏳᏍᏗ ✦ kanesg iyusdi (kah-neh-sgee ee-yoo-sdee) ✦ **greasegrass** ✦ Name means: like hay

ᏗᏅᏍᎩ ᏧᏔᎾ ✦ dinvsgi tsutana (dee-nuh-sgee joo-tah-nah) ✦ **greenbrier** ✦ Name means: big legs

ᎤᏅᏚᎯᏍᏓ ✦ unvduhisda (oo-nuh-doo-hee-sdah) ✦ **ground cherry**

ᏓᎶᏂ ✦ daloni (dah-loh-nee) ✦ **goldenrod** ✦ Good for the gall bladder.

ᏔᎳᏂ ✦ talani (tah-lah-nee) ✦ **gooseberry** ✦ This one you can eat.

Unesdali anvsatvsgi (Indian pipe stem)

ᎤᏯᎶᏘᏍᏗ ✦ uyalotisdi (oo-yah-loh-tee-sdee) ✦ **gooseberry, large** ✦ Do not eat this bigger one. ✦ Name means: swollen

ᎦᎸᏂ ✦ galvni (gah-luh-nee) ✦ **gourd plant**

ᎤᎾᏫᏳᏍᏗ ✦ unawiyusdi (oo-nah-wee-yoo-sdee) ✦ **heartleaf** ✦ Name means: like the heart

ᎤᏁᎩᏓ ✦ unegida (oo-neh-gee-dah) ✦ **hickory leaf**

ᏩᎴᎵ ᎤᏂᏣᎵᏍᏗ ✦ waleli unitsalisdi (wah-leh-lee oo-nee-jah-lee-sdee) ✦ **honeysuckle** ✦ Name means: what the hummingbirds suck on

ᏒᏍᏗ ✦ svsdi (suh-sdee) ✦ **horsemint**

ᏣᏃᏯ ✦ tsanoya (jah-noh-yah) ✦ **horsetail rush**

ᎤᏁᏍᏓᎵ ᎠᏅᏌᏛᏍᎩ ✦ unesdali anvsatvsgi (oo-neh-sdah-lee ah-nuh-sah-tuh-sgee) ✦ **Indian pipe stem, frostweed** ✦ Name means: ice for shackles

ᏧᏂᏍᏓᎸᏍᏗ ✦ tsunisdalvsdi (joo-nee-sdah-luh-sdee) ✦ **indigo, wild**

ᏧᏂᏍᏓᎸᏍᏗ ᏧᏔᏂ ✦ tsunisdalvsdi tsutani (joo-nee-sdah-luh-sdee joo-tah-nee) ✦ **indigo, wild (hairy)**

ᎧᏒᏂ ✦ kasvni (kah-suh-nee) ✦ **ironweed**

ᎤᎸᏗ ✦ ulvdi (oo-luh-dee) ✦ **ivy** ✦ Name means: climbed on

ᏩᎦ ᏧᏂᎯᎯ ✦ waga tsunihihi (wah-gah joo-nee-hee-hee) ✦ **larkspur** ✦ Name means: it kills cows

ᏚᏑᎩ ✦ dusugi (doo-soo-gee) ✦ **laurel**

ᎡᎵᎩ ✦ eligi (eh-lee-gee) ✦ **lichen**

ᎤᏂᏍᏇᏚᎩ ✦ unisquetugi (oo-nee-sqweh-too-gee) ✦ **mayapple** ✦ Name means: hats, for the shape of its leaves

ᎠᏔᏍᎩᏍᎩ ✦ atasgisgi (ah-tah-sgee-sgee) ✦ **milkweed** ✦ Name means: it explodes or it pops

ᎤᏥᏓᎵ ✦ utsidali (oo-jee-dah-lee) ✦ **mint**

ᎤᏓᏟ ✦ udatli (oo-dah-tlee) ✦ **mistletoe** ✦ Name means: together or gathered up

ᏄᎾ ᎠᎪᏗ ᎠᏁᎯ ✦ nuna agodi anehi (noo-nah ah-goh-dee ah-neh-hee) ✦ **mud potato** ✦ Name means: potatoes that live in the prairie

ᏦᎳᏳᏍᏗ ✦ tsolayusdi (joh-lah-yoo-sdee) ✦ **mullein** ✦ Name means: like tobacco

ᎠᏥᎳ ᏳᏍᏗ ✦ atsila yusdi (ah-jee-lah yoo-sdee) ✦ **mustard, wild** ✦ Name means: like fire

ᏥᏳᎦᎵ ✦ tsiyugali (jee-yoo-gah-lee) ✦ **New Jersey tea** ✦ Also known as *alisgali,* snakeroot, or redroot. ✦ *"In Cherokee tradition,* tsiyugali *symbolizes medicine*—nvwoti—ᏅᏬᏘ." *H.S.*

Tsiyugali (snakeroot)

ᎦᎾᏐᎳ ✦ ganasola (gah-nah-soh-lah) ✦ **parsnip**

ᎤᏩᎦ ✦ uwaga (oo-wah-gah) ✦ **passionflower**

ᏌᎷᏱᎦ ✦ saluyiga (sah-loo-yee-gah) ✦ **pepperbush**

ᏥᏍᏚᎦᎴ ✦ tsisdugale (jee-sdoo-gah-leh) ✦ **plantain leaf** ✦ Name means: rabbit ear

ᎣᎩᎾᎵ ✦ oginali (oh-gee-nah-lee) ✦ **poison ivy** ✦ Name means: my friend. ✦ An old teaching says if you make friends with this plant it will not bother you. "When you walk by this one," Loretta said, "spit on it four times and say, '*Tla sgiyusd yawaduli.*' 'That one I don't want.' It will leave you alone then."

ᏧᎬᏓᎶᏗ ✦ tsugvdalodi (joo-guh-dah-loh-dee) ✦ **polecat bush** ✦ Name means: striped

left
Selugwoya (rattlesnake master)

right
Diligalisgi gigage (redroot)

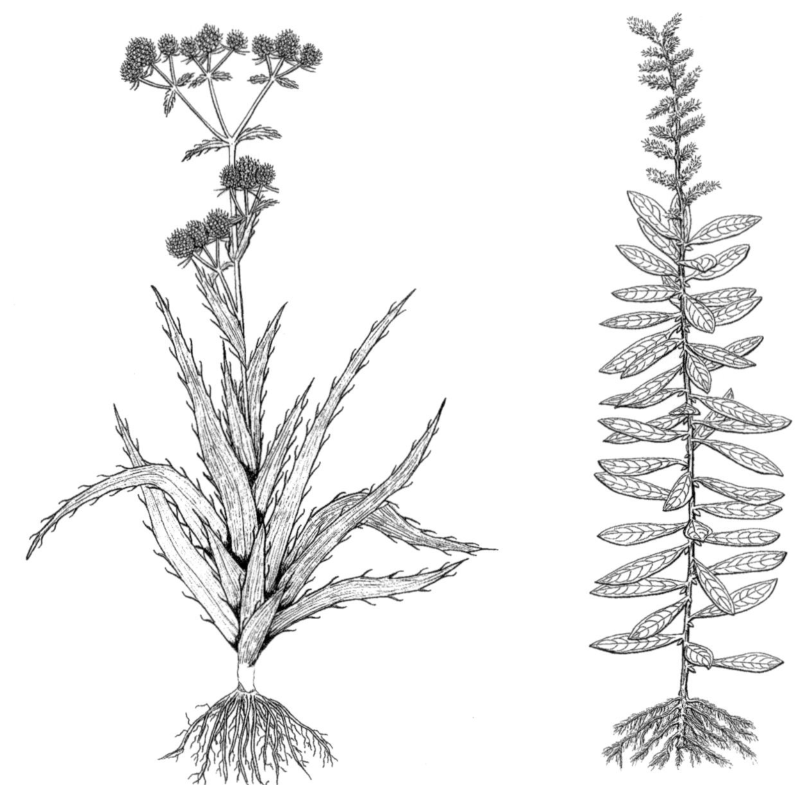

ᏗᎦ ᎠᏂᎩᎦᎨ ᎤᏥᎸ • gugu anigigage utsilv (goo-goo ah-nee-gee-gah-geh oo-jee-luh)• **Queen Anne's lace** • This is the plant you will find the little red chiggers on.

ᏎᎷᏉᏯ • selugwoya (seh-loo-gwoh-yah) • **rattlesnake master, button snakeroot**

ᏗᎵᎦᎵᏍᎩ ᎩᎦᎨ • diligalisgi gigage (dee-lee-gah-lee-sgee gee-gah-geh) • **redroot, dwarf prairie willow** • Name means: the red one that splits. Found on a hillside.

ᏛᎳᏑᎩ ᏣᏁᏆ • dvlasugi tsanequa (duh-lah-soo-gee jah-neh-gwah) • **rhododendron**

ᏛᎳᏑᎦ ᎤᏔᏂ • dvlasuga utani (duh-lah-soo-gah oo-tah-nee) • **rhododendron (pink)**

ᏛᎳᏑᎦ ᏧᎾᏍᏗᎢ • dvlasuga tsunasdii (duh-lah-soo-gah joo-na-sdee-ee) • **rhododendron (white)**

ᎠᎯᎢ • ahii (ah-hee-ee) • **river cane** • Used in many traditional arts.

ᏥᏍᏚ ᎤᏂᎩᏍᏗ • tsisdu unigisdi (jee-sdoo oo-nee-gee-sdee) • **rose, wild** • Name means: for the rabbits to eat

ᎧᏁᏍᎩ • kanesgi (kah-neh-sgee) • **sage grass** • Name means: hay

Gathering Medicine

Traditional medicine is gathered on the lands of Cherokee country from our plant relatives. Hastings grew up learning these teachings from his grandfathers. And like all forms of Cherokee knowledge, these teachings were grounded in relationship. Though Hastings rarely discussed medicinal practices publicly, the perpetuation of traditional knowledge and practices related to *nvwoti* was very important to him. Before his passing, Hastings was involved with the just-formed Cherokee Medicine Keepers, a group of "elder knowledge keepers" who share their land-based knowledge and stewardship practices with the goal of "*nvwoti asquangododi*—'to keep the medicine going'" (Carroll 2020, 155). This phrase, *nvwoti asquangododi*, explains environmental studies scholar and Cherokee Nation citizen Clint Carroll, "acknowledges the role that traditional medicine plays in maintaining Cherokees' relationships with the land" (155). One of the organizers of the Medicine Keepers, Carroll explains that the efficacy of medicine involves not just the plant properties but also the "faith and spirituality of the patient and healer" (155). In sharing and teaching about Cherokee plant knowledge, the inspiring work of the Medicine Keepers "revitalizes a way of life centered on spirituality and relationships to the land and cosmos" (155). One afternoon at the Cherokee Heritage Center, Hastings, Sequoyah Guess, and I discussed how private and state claims to property made it increasingly difficult to gather and maintain relationships with plants and the medicines they offer. The continuing work of the Cherokee Medicine Keepers is addressing this very problem.

"At one time we Cherokees were in eight states, you know? Most of our knowledge of plant life was in that eight-state area. Now, Eastern Band has, what, 50,000 acres? So they're pretty much confined to Qualla Boundary. And they rely on what plants they know in that area. So now, you know, the Cherokee Nation says, 'Okay. We got fourteen counties.' No. We don't have access to fourteen counties. We *live* in the fourteen counties."

"Those lands are not all Cherokee-owned," I said. "Since allotment, it's broken up mostly into individual parcels of private property."

"No. It's not all Cherokee-owned."

"It's a patchwork, right? But the fourteen counties are where we have tribal jurisdiction."

"Yeah. I could probably walk around here and pick up plants. But I can't step over that fence and get it. Now, if there was a plant over there I could steal it. But I would rather get it. I mean, ask somebody to get it. It's not good to steal."

"Mmhm."

"So, we're restricted to certain areas. We have only so many acres of Cherokee Nation tribal land."

"We are gatherers, by tradition," Sequoyah said. "We still gather. But, little by little, they're trying to take even that away from us because we can't go out and gather like we used to. Like, river cane. We just can't go out there and get it like we used to."

"You can't gather along the highway. If you see a plant along the highway, you can't stop and get it," Hastings said. "The State of Oklahoma says, 'No, you can't get it.' We can't go to our state parks and gather because state law says you can't gather. What's their excuse? 'Erosion.' The environment," Hastings said, ironically. "Now they're worried about erosion—a long time ago they didn't give a rat for whatever. Now this 'erosion' is a big deal."

"Even the land that I grew up on," Hastings continued. "There's now an owner of it who says, 'Yeah, you can go down there.' But the guy before him said, 'No. I don't want anybody on *my* place.' But the guy that owns it now said, 'You can go down there any time you want.' 'Cause I still go down there and visit, you know. Where I grew up. I'll walk down there. Walk down there and sit around down there. It's still home. Even though there's nothing there anymore. No house. But the feeling is still there. That's my home. That's where I grew up."

"Mmhm," I said, thinking of where I grew up in the mountains.

"Because it was a dirt floor," Hastings said and laughed. "And when you live on a dirt floor, you become part of Mother Earth. When I first went to talk to the guy that had it before, he said, 'No.' He didn't say it like that. He actually said, 'I don't want no S.O.B. on my land.' So. But this new owner, he said, 'Yeah, any time you want to go down there, just drive down in there.' He said, 'You don't have to tell me. Just go on down there.' So, I can live with people like that."

"Mmhm," I said.

"Because my land is open. I don't own a whole lot. But if you want to walk on it, it's up to you. All I ask is if you got a gun don't shoot toward the house," Hastings said and laughed. "But, just like that guy made a good point one day. He said, 'Man belong to Mother Earth. Mother Earth don't belong to man.' He said, 'One of these days Mother Earth ain't going to be buried unto you, you'll be buried unto her.' And that separates you."

WHEN YOU TAKE, LEAVE SOMETHING ✦ *by Hastings Shade*

When the Medicine Man gathered medicine, he would always leave something in its place. Indians believe that when you took something from nature, or Mother Earth, if you didn't leave something—then the food, medicine, etc. would get scarce and eventually fade away.

What was left could be any number of items ranging from a lock of hair, to a piece of clothing to spit. Usually the type of item that was gathered dictated what type of item was left.

ᏧᎾᏦᏍᏗ ✦ tsunatsosdi (joo-nah-joh-sdee) ✦ **sheep sorrel, or sour weed**

ᎤᏂᏍᏗᎸᏍᏗ ᏧᎾᏍᏗ ✦ unisdilvsdi tsunasdi (oo-nee-sdee-luh-sdee joo-nah-sdee) ✦ **silver burr ragweed**

ᏓᎶᏂᎨ ᎠᏥᎸᏍᎩ ✦ dalonige atsilvsgi (dah-loh-nee-geh ah-jee-luh-sgee) ✦ **small-flowered agrimony** ✦ Name means: yellow flower

ᎠᏖᏗᏍᎩ ✦ atedisgi (ah-teh-dee-sgee) ✦ **Solomon's seal** ✦ Name means: heats up

ᏌᎶᎵ ᎦᏙᎦ ✦ saloli gatoga (sah-loh-lee gah-toh-gah) ✦ **squirrel tail** ✦ Also known as yarrow.

ᎠᎾᏓᎩᎸᏍᎩ ✦ anadakilvsgi (ah-nah-dah-kee-luh-sgee) ✦ **sticktight** ✦ Name means: they jump or climb on you

ᏙᎴᏓ ✦ toleda (toh-leh-dah) ✦ **stinging nettle**

ᏒᏟ ✦ svtli (suh-tlee) ✦ **stinkweed**

ᏆᎶᎦ ✦ qualoga (gwah-loh-gah) ✦ **sumac**

ᏅᏓ ᏗᎧᏂ ✦ nvda dikani (nuh-dah dee-kah-nee)✦ **sunflower** ✦ Name means: it's looking at the sun

ᏅᏓ ᏗᎧᏂ ᎢᎾᎨ ᎡᎯ ✦ nvda dikani inage ehi (nuh-dah dee-kah-nee ee-nah-geh eh-hee) ✦ **sunflower, wild**

ᎤᎦᎾᏍᏓ ✦ uganasda (oo-gah-nah-sdah) ✦ **sweet Annie, sweet wormwood** ✦ Name means: sweet

ᎠᏂᏧᏣ ᎠᏂᏥᎸᏍᎩ ✦ anitsutsa anitsilvsgi (ah-nee-joo-jah ah-nee-gee-luh-sgee) ✦ **sweet William** ✦ Name means: boys that bloom

ᎪᎦ ᎦᏅᏍᎨ ✦ koga ganvsge (koh-gah gah-nuh-sgeh) ✦ **tansy** ✦ Name means: crow legs

ᏥᏥ ✦ tsi-tsi (jee-jee) ✦ **thistle** ✦ Same name as the sparrow hawk.

ᏦᎳ • tsola (joh-lah) • **tobacco** • "A direct gift from the Creator—just like the fire. When used as medicine you ask it and Creator for help." H.S.

ᎪᏍᎦᏓ • gosgada (goh-sgah-dah) • **tobacco, rabbit** • Name means: to smoke

ᏦᎳ ᎠᎦᏴᎵ • tsola agayvli (joh-lah ah-gah-yuh-lee) • **tobacco, wild**
Name means: old or ancient tobacco

ᏧᏩᏚᏂ ᏧᎳᎢ • tsuwaduni tsulai (joo-wah-doo-nee joo-lah-ee) • **vein weed** • Name means: having veins

ᏌᎪᏂᎨ ᎠᏥᎸᏍᎩ • sakonige atsilvsgi (sah-koh-nee-geh ah-jee-luh-sgee) • **Venus' looking glass** • Name means: it blooms blue

ᎦᎾᏑᏛᎶ • ganasudvlo (gah-nah-soo-duh-loh) • **witch hazel**

ᎧᏫ ᏳᏍᏗ • kawi yusdi (kah-wee yoo-sdee) • **yellow dock** • Name means: like coffee or like a deer (if using the old name for deer)

ᏧᏩᏙᎭ • tsuwatoha (joo-wah-toh-hah) • **yellow root** • Name means: to give out or to give some to each one

ᏓᎶᏂᎨ ᎠᏓᏅᏍᎩ • dalonige adanvsgi (dah-loh-nee-geh ah-dah-nuh-sgee) • **yellow sting** • Name means: yellow lying down. Version of stinging wood.

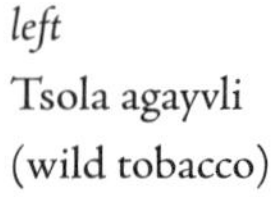

left
Tsola agayvli
(wild tobacco)

right
Kawi yusdi
(yellow dock)

TSOLA ALE AGAYULAGE (*Tobacco and the Old Woman*) ✦ *by Noyi Teuton*

I was talking on the phone one day to Jeff Corntassel, a Cherokee Nation scholar and my close friend, about my work on Cherokee Earth Dwellers when he reminded me of a traditional story of tsola, or tobacco. As Hastings and other elders tell, like atsila, tsola was a direct gift from Unetlvnv. We found it interesting to consider that atsila came from the Sky World through lightning as a gift to human beings, while tsola was a gift whose home was in the soil of Elohi. Jeff and I wondered if the old woman, agayulage, in this story of tsola is the fire itself, as these two gifts come together in ceremony, carrying our words and thoughts to Unetlvnv through smoke. We could see how she would so deeply miss tsola.

Ilvhiyu tsigesv nigada inage anehi tsalagi itsaniwonisgv. In the great forever that was, all the forest dwellers spoke Cherokee. And at that time, there was only one *tsola* plant that all the creatures shared, human beings and animals alike. One day the animals and human beings came to harvest tsola and found that *aniganuga*, white-fronted geese, had taken the plant for themselves as they flew south. All the peoples were suffering without tsola, and there was one *agayulage*, old woman, who became so weak and thin that the people said she would die without tsola to keep her alive.

The *inage anehi* (forest dwellers), *aniyvwiya* (human beings), and *anitsisqua* (birds) all got together for a big council to decide what to do, as was their custom. Many creatures volunteered to travel south and take back tsola from the aniganuga. The larger creatures went first, but the aniganuga guarded the plant and killed each creature before it could get to tsola. The many smaller creatures tried, but they too were defeated. *Tinequa* (Mole) thought to outsmart the aniganuga by digging underground and reaching tsola, but the aniganuga saw its tracks and one of them was waiting for Tinequa when it came out of the ground.

Waleli (Hummingbird) had been busy eating nectar and tiny insects as she does constantly to stay alive. But when she saw she could help, Waleli said, "Let me try! I can take back tsola from the aniganuga."

The other creatures worried about the tiny Waleli and looked away. Someone in the back said, "You're too small. Better to stay home and let another try."

"Let me try," Waleli said with confidence. "Give me a test. I'll *show* you I can do it."

The creatures looked at each other and nodded in agreement. One of them pointed out a plant in the *tloges* (field). "Show us how you'd get that," it said.

Next thing you know, Waleli was sitting right on top of that very plant. "That's fast," one of the creatures mumbled. An instant later, Waleli was back. All anyone had seen was a green blur.

"I'll get tsola just like that," Waleli said.

"*Hawa*," the creatures said. "Okay. We'll be here waiting for you."

In a flash, Waleli flew east. When she finally saw the tsola plant in the distance, she could tell the aniganuga were standing watch, looking out for any that would try to take tsola. But Waleli was so fast and so small that the aniganuga did not even see her coming. In an instant, she flew down to tsola and snipped off the top of the plant with leaves and seeds attached. A second later, Waleli was away from the aniganuga and out of harm's way as they still stared into the distance, looking tough.

The old woman, *agayulage*, was suffering and had fainted before Waleli returned. Some thought she might have died. They quickly put a spark to tsola and gently blew smoke into her nostrils. Agayulage opened her eyes and said, "Tsola!" She was alive again.

Kin and Clans

Hastings once explained to me that Cherokee ties with the natural world were so central to our identity as a people that Cherokee social organization and laws were defined by these relationships. The Cherokee system of kinship is rooted in the matrilineal clan structure. A child is born into the same clan as the mother, who in turn shares the same clan as her mother, and so on. Traditionally, Cherokee people do not marry within their own clan, as members of one's clan are kin and considered brothers and sisters. The child's closest relatives are members of the mother's family, kin through clan. In the past, if a person did not have a Cherokee mother one could be adopted as a Cherokee by being adopted into a clan, which was usually the Long Hair or Stranger Clan.

Up until the nineteenth century when the Cherokee Nation chose a new government modeled on the US Constitution and its legal system, clan identity and clan law shaped all facets of Cherokee life. In fact, one could not be Cherokee without being a member of a clan. One's clan defined one's kin and thereby one's place in society. Cherokee law was meted out and enforced through the clan system. If an infraction against a member of a clan was unresolved, it became an infraction against that person's whole clan and had to be balanced with justice against the offending individual or, in that person's stead, a member of the individual's clan. To maintain tohi, justice depended on balance between clans. But, under pressure to conform to settler American society, Cherokee governance changed, beginning a decline in the importance of matrilineal clan identity and its centrality to Cherokee social life.

In some Cherokee communities today, one's clan identity remains central to one's identity and belonging as a Cherokee person. Its continuing importance is perhaps most apparent at the stomp grounds, where members sit in arbors of the square grounds based on clan membership. Those men who do not have a clan sit under the Long Hair arbors at stomp dance ceremonies. Most important, though Cherokee governance has changed, the anitsalagi remain a matrilineal people and many folks know and continue to value their clan affiliation. For traditionalists such as Hastings and Loretta Shade and their family, matrilineal clan identity continues to shape how they define kinship.

Some scholars say the creature or elemental totem of a particular clan functioned mostly as a way to classify and distinguish the group from others, such as how the Denver Broncos and Oklahoma City Thunder work as names for sports teams. While members of a clan may have had an affiliation with its namesake, self-defining as a particular group gave that clan a unique identity. But Hastings told me that our relationships with our clans and the creatures with whom we affiliate ourselves as kin have deeper meaning.

Today Cherokees have seven clans, but elders told Hastings we once had many more. There is some disagreement about exactly how many clans we had. Some elders say fourteen, some twenty. Hastings created a list of the thirty-three clans his elders told him we once had. These clans were named for trees, plants, animals, and birds—creatures we shared our daily lives with, admired, and from which were gifted teachings. Clans also were named for the elements, including the wind and twister. A couple of the clans are named after ancient creatures, such as the saber-tooth tiger and Uk'tan, or winged serpent, clans.

Hastings explained to me that Cherokees saw themselves in their clan totems. Over time, through socialization, teachings, and relationships, they adopted the characteristics of their clans. They knew these creatures and shared an affinity with them, recognizing the diversity of human behavior and approaches to life through the varied ways other creatures behave and live. The tohi that creatures establish among themselves became a model for Cherokee people. The affiliation between humans and clans was so strong, Hastings told me, that some had the ability to transform themselves into their clan namesake. And some still have that ability today.

The list of thirty-three clans Hastings documented all existed in what he called the time of B.C. (Before Columbus). These clan names all contain the prefix *ani-* in front of the creature name, the plural form for living things commonly understood to represent "people." That is significant, because our clan affiliations united us through our mothers to the creatures of our worlds, expressing the deepest respect for our fellow life forms across our differences. "Women were given the Clans because they were the givers of life," Hastings wrote. Through our clans we defined kinship and belonging and demonstrated our understanding of law and tohi. Bringing these multiple clans, multiple peoples together, we became one people in harmony.

In the time of A.C. (After Contact), as Hastings would say, our clans consolidated into seven affiliations. I wonder if that consolidation happened because of colonialism and the change in Cherokee ways of life due to war, disease, the encroachment of settlers on our land, and our changing relationships with our fellow creatures. As Cherokees continue to assert our sovereignty as a people I wonder with some other folks if we may reinvigorate our clan system. That would depend, I imagine Hastings telling me, on reinvigorating our relationships with our fellow creatures. For some folks, those relationships continue.

MODERN CHEROKEE CLANS

1. Anitsisqua	1. Bird Clan
2. Aniwaya	2. Wolf Clan
3. Aniawi	3. Deer Clan
4. Anigodagewi	4. Wild Potato Clan
5. Anisahoni	5. Blue Clan
6. Aniwodi	6. Paint Clan
7. Anigilohi	7. Long Hair Clan

OLD CHEROKEE CLANS

8. Analitsadohvsgi	8. Priest Group
9. Aniugateni	9. Uk'tan Clan
10. Analisgusgi	10. Turtle Clan
11. Anitsogohi	11. Bear Clan
12. Anigiligeni	12. Nape of the Neck Clan
13. Aniugasuti	13. Rattlesnake Clan
14. Anikolani	14. Raven Clan (Became Bird Clan)
15. Anitawodi	15. Hawk Clan (Became Bird Clan)
16. Anitalitami	16. Wren Clan (Became Bird Clan)

17. Anitotsuwa	17. Redbird Clan (Became Bird Clan)
18. Anitsatloi	18. Kingfisher Clan (Became Bird Clan)
19. Aniwoya	19. Pigeon Clan (Became Bird Clan)
20. Aniguledinisgoni	20. Dove Clan (Became Bird Clan)
21. Anisahani	21. Saber-Tooth Tiger Clan (Became Blue Clan)
22. Aniyona	22. Bear Clan (Became Blue Clan)
23. Anikvtli	23. Raccoon Clan (Became Blue Clan)
24. Anigvhe	24. Wildcat Clan (Became Blue Clan)
25. Anitlvdatsi	25. Panther Clan (Became Blue Clan)
26. Anigiloi	26. Stranger Clan (Became Long Hair Clan)
27. Anigalohi	27. Hair Hanging Down Clan (Became Long Hair Clan)
28. Aniagaluga	28. Twister Clan (Became Long Hair Clan)
29. Aninole	29. Wind Clan (Became Long Hair Clan)
30. Anidinikewi	30. Blind Savanna Clan (Became Wild Potato Clan)
31. Anitsina	31. Cedar Tree Clan (Became Wild Potato Clan)
32. Anisdati	32. Holly Clan (Became Wild Potato Clan)
33. Aninvwoti	33. Medicine Clan (Became Paint Clan)

In his writings Hastings provided a summary of how all the B.C. clans became consolidated into seven clans A.C.:

> All the feathered ones became the Anitsisqua, Bird Clan. "The keepers of the birds. The messengers."
>
> All the hoofed ones became the Aniawi, Deer Clan. "The keepers of the deer. Known as the fast runners and hunters."
>
> All the ones with paws became the Aniwaya, Wolf Clan. "The largest clan. Most of the war chiefs came from this clan and were the only ones who could kill a wolf."
>
> All the ones with fangs and claws became the Anisahoni, Blue Clan. "Also known as the Panther Clan or Wildcat Clan. These were usually the builders and medicine people for the children."
>
> All the medicine people and teachers became the Aniwodi, Paint Clan.

The trees, plants, and earth people became the Anigodagewi, Wild Potato Clan. "Were known to dig wild potatoes to make flour for bread. And were the keepers of the land and Mother Earth."

All the people of the wind, twister, elements, and hair hanging down became the Anigilohi, Long Hair Clan. "Wore their hair fixed in different styles. The Peace Chief usually came from this clan and wore a white feather robe. The modern name is *agilo*, meaning Stranger Clan, as this was the clan for captives and adoptees into the tribe."

WHY INDIAN MEN SHOULD MARRY INDIAN WOMEN ✦ *by Hastings Shade*

When I was growing up, Indian men were always told to marry an Indian girl—this was to ensure that the children would always have a family.

When children were born they always took the mother's clan. The Cherokees have seven clans, and each clan member is considered a brother or sister. They were not allowed to marry within the same clan.

Women, on the other hand, were not told whom to marry—other than not into their own clan—because all children born would still have a family: the mother's clan. Men, now, were different—if they married a non-Indian—then the children were without a family, according to the Indians, being that non-Indians have no clans.

SEVEN PROPHECIES OF THE CHEROKEES ✦ *by Hastings Shade*

Prophetic teachings shared with him by his elders informed many of Hastings' perspectives. He summarizes some of these teachings below, which begin in the ancient past and take us right to the present.

1. A long journey toward the cold, or North as we know it
2. A white wave will cover the Cherokees
3. The Cherokees will move from their ancient homeland, some never to see it again
4. The Cherokees will cross a great river, or *yvwi ganvhida* (Long Person), to the West or where the sun goes down
5. The young Cherokees will leave their homes and tribe and come back having a hard time knowing who they are
6. The young ones will not or cannot hear their elders speaking to them
7. The Cherokees will again recognize the Fourteen Blood Lines

PROPHECY OF THE FOURTEEN GENERATIONS • *Told by Hastings Shade*

As Hastings considered it his duty to pass along the prophetic teachings of his elders, so Larry Shade shared with me an audio recording of Hastings speaking at a gathering where he explained the prophecy of the Fourteen Generations.

"One of the reasons I keep pushing the language, history, and culture is that . . . one of our legends says, once we recognize fourteen generations we're either going to lose what we have or we're going to gain it all back. Once we recognize fourteen generations we're either going to lose everything that we have as a nation—our language, history, and culture—or we're going to gain it all back. It's going to be up to us. How much effort we put into it. Again, a lot of our legends are learning things, learning experiences. Or teaching tools. So, in a sense, they're telling us that if we don't do what we're supposed to, we're going to lose our language. Our history and culture.

"This is fourteen generations. You got full, 3/4, half, 1/4, 1/8, 1/16, 1/32, 1/64, 1/128, 1/256, 1/512, 1/1024, 1/2048. And this right here—1/4096—was recognized by the Cherokee Nation on June 19, 1998. So we're in that period that our legend tells us. 1/4096. We're in that period of, if we don't do something about it, we are going to lose our language. We are going to lose our history. We are going to lose our culture. So, to us this is a big push.

"There are not very many speakers behind me. My generation probably has the most speakers. The generation behind us, there aren't that many. And I think you can probably count on your hands the generations behind that, the speakers. Because you're talking about the little ones. And that's where most of our concentration is going to be, our little ones. Because that's where our next speakers are going to come from. Fluent speakers. Don't get me wrong, everybody can learn that wants to. But our little ones are where the push is. And that's our concentration. We have to teach the little ones. 'Cause if we don't, that is our last effort. So this is the way it's broken down. Like I said, June 19, 1998, we recognize the fourteenth generation. So right now is a time we need to do something."

LAND ✦ *by Hastings Shade*

Indians couldn't understand the White Man's obsession to own land that he couldn't take with him when he died.

The Indian believes that he was put here on this earth to take care of the things that the Great Spirit has created. In return, the Great Spirit took care of him by providing him with food, clothing, medicine—through animals and herbs. And an Indian will usually take only what he can use and not waste anything.

The Indian believes the White Man was born without a heart of compassion and will attack his own brother for something he wants. The White Man sees only the things that can benefit himself, never a thought about others.

This can be seen today. Indians have wide visions and can see all around them. The White Man has narrow vision and only looks ahead at things that can benefit himself.

MINE ✦ *by Hastings Shade*

The place where I grew up was at the end of the road. Our house was the last house down that road. Even when I went into the military service in 1958 you could count the number of homes down that two-mile stretch of road on both hands and still have fingers left over. Now there are more than forty homes on that road. The road is blacktopped now.

I tell that because my grandma said, "One of these days you won't be able to walk on the place where you grew up. There will be a bunch of houses around here, and you won't even be welcomed here."

After my grandparents died, the land was sold. Different people bought the land and now I can't even go back to the place I was raised. The land is all posted.

One day I asked the man who had purchased the land if I could go to the old place where I grew up and visit the place. He said, "No. If I let you I would have to let everyone else on MY LAND." I wanted to tell him, "Man belongs to the land, land does not belong to man."

If you don't believe me, just wait. One of these days you will be buried in the land; the land will not be buried in you.

Grandma was right again. She knew what was going to happen.

Being in the World

Loretta and I sat with Sequoyah Guess one spring afternoon at the chapel at the Cherokee Heritage Center. As was customary when we would gather and talk about Hastings' collection of creature names and teachings about the natural world, our conversation flowed through interconnected topics, with teachings and personal insights shared along the way. That day we talked about the living earth and our modern experience of time.

"Grandma always used to tell me that everything in the world is alive," Sequoyah said. "Everything from rocks to the air. Everything. And you know how you can tell they're alive? She said, 'They all sing.' Everything in the world sings. And it wasn't too long ago that I was reading a science piece, and it said everything in existence vibrates and gives a hum. And I thought, 'That's what Grandma used to say.' I always say science is catching up with our teachings. And they are, you know?"

"Yes, it's comin' to pass," Loretta said. "Hastings and I used to talk about the prophecy that someday the world's gonna be covered by a giant spider web. At the time he thought it was telephone lines, but I told him it might be the World Wide Web. Giant spider web. And that was an old prophecy. Years ago some thought it was a crazy thing to predict, but it's come true."

"I remember Hastings saying everything that moves is alive. And you can talk to anything that's alive," I said. "Well, if you can talk to things and you're in communication, then you have to get along. You have to have relationship. Otherwise, you're just ignoring others. And that's rude, you know? That's not the way to engage the world."

"Well, people nowadays are too busy," Sequoyah responded. "They're going too fast. They don't have time just to look around, to *see* things. And that's one reason why nowadays you don't hear many stories anymore. Because people are too busy to go into the past. They don't have time to notice things happening. A long time ago they took their time."

"And they had time to think," Loretta added. "They had time to notice."

"Yeah, and they saw things happening. Today's world has just gotten so far away from being *in* the world. You know? Right now we're just part of the world. We're not *in* the world. Or it might be the other way. Maybe we're in the world but not *part* of the world. What I'm trying to say is that . . . we're all *one*. The world and people. Animals. Plants. The fish. Everything. We're all one. We're all *connected*. And once you start striving to be in balance with everything, then I believe that's when you really start becoming a human being. When you can keep that balance."

Loretta, Sequoyah, and I sat with his words for a few moments, then he continued.

"You know, people are too busy nowadays. They're too busy to live their lives. They're too busy trying to *stay alive*. And I think, if people would just slow down and start living—instead of just surviving—they would be much happier. There wouldn't be so much sickness. And people would start acting like people again. And caring for one another."

With those words, we returned to discussing Hastings' collection. His explanation of time and the cycle of months of the Cherokee year became part of our conversation, reminding us that the pace of our lives in tohi is set through Elohi's seasons of growth and rest.

TIME IS WITH US • *by Hastings Shade*

There is no word for time in the Indian language. The Native American or Indians always looked to Mother Nature to tell them when it was time to do certain things—like gathering food, material to make things, or seasonal changes.

The Europeans were the ones who introduced time when they arrived—they began to set time standards—like when to get up, what time to eat, when to start to work, and when to quit.

Indians believe if you cannot enjoy each day to its fullest, how can you enjoy life? You can't do this by watching a clock.

Indians believe that non-Indians are so dissatisfied with the present, and so concerned with the future, that they never really live in the present or enjoy it to its fullest.

European-Americans say, "My, how time flies."

The Mexicans say, "Time walks."

The Indians say, "Time is with us."

THE CHEROKEE ROSE ✦ *Told by Choogie Kingfisher*

In the spring of 2019 beloved storyteller Sequoyah Guess took ill. His condition worsened over several weeks until finally he was placed in hospice care. I came down from Seattle to visit with my dear friend and attend a benefit storytelling in his honor in the Sanctuary of the First Indian Baptist Church in Tahlequah, Oklahoma. The benefit was hosted by Pastor Dennis Sixkiller, organized by Woody Hansen and his family, and attended by many of Sequoyah's friends, family members, and fellow storytellers. Just the day before, my brother Sean and I had visited Sequoyah and his wife, Gina, while he was in hospice care in Fort Smith, Arkansas. We had wheeled him out to a window at the end of the hallway and visited. We talked and laughed, made plans for the future. And when it came time to go, he took my phone, looked out the window, and recorded a message for all to hear at the benefit storytelling. I played that message for his community the next day. And I recorded the event for Sequoyah to listen to the stories and words of his beloved friends and relatives as they took turns telling lies. The stories and reflections of that afternoon brought laughter and tears.

In my work on Cherokee Earth Dwellers, I have often thought back to a story about the Cherokee rose told by Choogie Kingfisher that spring afternoon. It was told not only to an audience but to a family member and fellow liar as he came to face his transition. In his rich baritone voice, Kingfisher shared this family story, by turns humorous and contemplative, that reflects on change and continuity. A master storyteller, Kingfisher was honored in 2019 as a Cherokee National Treasure for his work as a cultural educator and storyteller.

"I've been sitting back there listening and just reminiscing. Not even trying to formulate any type of story. I've told stories with Sequoyah many times. Been many places, been many miles. And like you said, I've known him since I was a kid. Grew up around him." Choogie paused.

"I didn't know what to expect coming here. I was really just going to sit back here and listen. And I've been having a blast just listening to everybody. I didn't plan on anything, you know. My one main goal tonight was to eat two bowls of chili," he said and the audience laughed.

"I done that. I done that. So I completed my *task*. But I can't talk about Sequoyah without talking about Hastings," Choogie said and paused. Folks in the audience murmured in agreement.

"You know, I grew up around all of them. So we were all family. I grew up around all of them and I'm glad to see that we all are Church people now. We weren't always like that. We weren't always like that." Members of the audience smiled knowingly.

"But I got a lot of love for Sequoyah. He's family. He's family to me. All these Liars' Club members I've been running around with, I'm the younger one of these three. I'm the *prettier* one as well." There were hoots from the audience. After a pause, he continued.

"I still don't know what story to tell. It's one of those things that . . . I just want to reminisce. You know, think about that bygone day that we don't see anymore.

"A long time ago, when my Grannie was living, there was an old house. And this old house used to sit up in a hollow, not too far from Rocky Ford Park. I remember it well because I was one of those kids that—I always got hurt. I was always the one in trouble. I was the *popular* one, let's just say that. I was the popular kid," Choogie said, and folks chuckled.

"Behind the house was a spring. But in the front yard, there was this rosebush.

"I don't know where this rosebush came from, but Grannie, she took care of it quite often. And, when my Aunt Pat moved and I would go visit Aunt Pat, I would notice that same type of rosebush. Hmm.

"'Where'd you get that at?' I asked my Aunt Pat.

"'Grannie gave it to me.'

"'Okay.'

"And at that time, I was a drifter, because we moved everywhere. Man, we've lived in Dry Creek down by Lake Eucha. We've lived up on the flats by Marble Field. Man, we've moved everywhere. And everywhere we moved, as I began to think about it, I remember seeing that rosebush.

"And so, one day I said to my Grannie, 'Grannie, wherever you are I always see this.'

"By that time Grannie had moved from that hollow to the other side of Batt Cemetery And right outside her door, there was that rosebush.

"I said, 'Grannie, how come everywhere you go I always see this?'

"So she sat me down. She said, 'Chooj, I don't know where this come from. But when I left home to go and make my own family, my mama gave me this flower.' And she said, 'Wherever you are, when you plant it and it flourishes, that's where you're supposed to be.'

"I was like, 'Cool. Well where did Grannie get it then?'

"She said, 'Her mama gave it to her.'

"I said, 'Where did it come from?'

"She said, 'Our family came from Georgia. That's as far as I know. And it came over that Trail of Tears with us. Every time they would stop, Grannie would plant that flower. And she would go on. She always wanted to go back to see if that plant ever grew.'

"And I wondered what kind of flower it was. So I became that investigator. That detective. And I found out it was that Cherokee rose. And, whenever we would move, Mom would take that flower, and she would take it with her.

"I never knew it, but Grannie always told her story. And she said, 'Wherever you plant this and it flourishes, that's where you *belong*.'

"This land we live on now, it's family land. Nobody owns it but us. We're blessed to have that. And when Grandpa wanted to move there, Mom, she was very skeptical. Because we were living down by Jay. We were living on Eucha. And Mom was very skeptical about moving all the way up toward Tahlequah. She said, 'What about my job?' Cause she was a teacher there at Jay. Dad, he was CHR for Jay Clinic. Wondering what he was going to do. But the opportunity came, and so we moved in 1976. We moved to Moody, Oklahoma. Established Kingfisher Acres.

"And mom took that plant and she planted it.

"First year, it didn't bloom. So she wondered.

"Mom began to take care of that land and she began to make a home place. And that following year, it bloomed. Not very big.

"The year after that, Mom continued to work on that place. And it grew bigger every time Mom would begin to work on the place.

"It used to be huge! And Mom would go out there. Summertime, she spent most of her days when she wasn't working on the place, sitting right there beside that rosebush.

"And I would hear her sing.

"I would hear her cry.

"I would hear her laugh.

"Grannie had already passed away by that time. My Grannie was a great influence on many people. Her funeral, just the viewing alone, took four hours. People came from all over the world to see my Grannie. And my Grannie lived in Rocky Ford, America. She touched many lives. And so I knew my mom missed her mama. I knew that's what that plant was. At least I thought I did.

"So one day I walked out to her and said, 'Mom, what is it about this plant? What is it about this rose?'

"She said, 'Son, a long time ago when I left home to make my own family, Grannie gave me this plant. And she told me, wherever I plant it and it flourishes, that's where I'm supposed to be. It's taken me years, but now this plant is growing. I know this is where I belong.' She said, 'I've been a Kingfisher longer than I've been a Tucker.' She said, 'This is where I belong.'

"I said, 'But what are you thinking about? Because I know what you're doing when you're singing.' I said, 'You're celebrating.' I said, 'But what is it when you begin to cry?' I said, 'I know you miss Grannie. But what is it?'

"She said, 'Son, a long time ago when she gave me this, Grannie said, "When I pass away, I will come back to you as a bumblebee. And I will take care of this flower."

"Mom said, 'Every time that bumblebee comes, I smile and I begin to cry, because I know that's Mom coming to take care of her flower. It's the same one—I can almost guarantee it—that comes to take care of this plant.'

"Mom said, 'Every once in a while, she'll bring somebody with her. I think it's Grannie. I *know* it's Grannie. And all those ladies, they'll be on those roses, taking out the nectar.'

"She said, 'I know it's them because of the way they talk.'

"I said, 'Talk?'

"She said, 'Yeah, when they were living none of them could take turns talking, they all talked at the same time.'" Choogie laughed, and the audience laughed with him.

"So whenever I go outside and I look at that rosebush, I remember that. And when that new bee comes, I know it's my mama coming to take care of that plant. I know it's my mama because that one bee is always the bossiest one," Choogie said, and we all laughed together.

"At least, that's what I thought about sharing with you guys today. *Wado*!"

THE CHEROKEE MONTHS OF THE YEAR ✦ *by Hastings Shade*

Though the names of the months of the year are well-known in Cherokee community, Hastings' descriptions of what the names actually mean remind us of how deeply the cycle of the Cherokee year is tied to careful observations of changes in the natural world through the seasons.

ᏏᏅᏓ ᏓᏓᏁᏟᏴᏏᏙᏌ ᏕᎾᎾᏮ ᎠᏂᏣᎳᎩ

ᎤᏃᎸᏔᏅ—ᎥᏥ ᏥᎦᏃᎯᎵᏙᎨᎢ

ᎧᎦᎵ—ᎤᏯᏮᎡ ᏧᏥᏍᏓᎷᎩᏍᎪ ᎠᎦᎵᏍᎬᎢ

ᎠᏅᏱ—ᏗᎦᎾᏝ ᎠᏧ ᎢᎾᎨ ᎠᏁᎯ ᏧᎾᏍᏗ ᏣᎾᏕᏌᏍᎪ

ᎧᏬᏂ—ᎤᏁᏍᏓᎳ ᏥᎬᎾᏬᏍᎪ ᎠᎮᎢ

ᎠᏅᏍᎬᏘ—ᏗᎦᎾᏝ ᎠᏧ ᎢᎾᎨ ᎠᏁᎯ ᏣᎾᏕᏯᎩᏍᎪ

ᏕᎭᎷᏯ—ᏥᏓᏗᎴᏌᏍᎪ

ᎧᏰᏉᏂ—ᎧᏄᎦᏟ ᎡᏆ ᎣᏂ

ᎦᎶᏂ—ᏥᏔᎩ ᏣᎾᏕᏯᎩᏍᎪᎢ

ᏚᎵᏍᏗ—ᎦᏄᎸ ᏥᎦᎵᏬᎪᎢ

ᏚᏂᏗ—ᏧᎦᎶᎦ ᏣᎾᏙᏍᎪᎢ

ᏅᏓᏕᏆ—ᎠᎹ ᏥᏕᎦᏔᏁᏍᏓᏔᏗᏍᏗᏍᎪ

ᎥᏍᎩᏱ—ᏕᎵᎬ ᏥᏓᏔᏍᎩᏍᎪᎢ

January ✦ *unolvtanv* ✦ ᎤᏃᎸᏔᏅ ✦ month of snow spirits in the wind.

February ✦ *kagali* ✦ ᎧᎦᎵ ✦ month of frost shining in the sun.

March ✦ *anvyi* ✦ ᎠᏅᏱ ✦ month when the young animals begin being born.

April ✦ *kawoni* ✦ ᎧᏬᏂ ✦ month of the melting of the ice on the waters.

May ✦ *anvskvti* ✦ ᎠᏅᏍᎬᏘ ✦ month when the animals begin to shed their winter coats.

June ✦ *dehaluya* ᏕᎭᎷᏯ ✦ month when the weather begins to get hot.

July ✦ *kayegwoni* ✦ ᎧᏰᏉᏂ ✦ month when the berries begin to get ripe.

August ✦ *galoni* ✦ ᎦᎶᏂ ✦ month when the birds shed their feathers.

September ✦ *dulisdi* ✦ ᏚᎵᏍᏗ ✦ month when the grasses begin to die.

October ✦ *dunidi* ✦ ᏚᏂᏗ ✦ month when the leaves begin to fall.

November ✦ *nvdadegwa* ✦ ᏅᏓᏕᏆ ✦ month when the waters begin to freeze.

December ✦ *vsgiyi* ✦ ᎥᏍᎩᏱ ✦ month when the trees begin to pop.

KANADI ALE SELU ✦ THE ORIGIN OF GAME AND CORN

by Noyi Teuton

The story of First Man and Corn Woman—Kanadi and Selu—is certainly known by Cherokee folks out west, but I personally have never heard it told. Hastings, Sequoyah, and I spoke of and referred to this story in our conversations. As an origin teaching, the story of Kanadi, Selu, and the Little Men has much to share about Cherokee ways of understanding the world. In honor of Ayu'ini (Swimmer), the Eastern Band of Cherokee Indians medicine man and cultural traditionalist who in the late 1880s shared with his friend, the ethnologist James Mooney, nearly 75 percent of the teachings collected and published in Myths of the Cherokee *(1900), I retell this story in his spirit of sharing.*

Ilvhiyu tsigesv, in the great forever that was, soon after Elohi was made, a hunter and his wife lived with their only child, a little boy, at Pilot Knob west of Cherokee on the Qualla Boundary. The man's name was *Kanadi*, the Lucky One, and the woman's name was *Selu*, or Corn Woman. The reason his name was Kanadi, Hastings once speculated, is that he was lucky in the hunt. But as the word *kanadi* also means smart, he could have been a smart hunter as well. Whenever Kanadi went out into the *saluyi*, or woods, he always came back with game. Selu would cut up the game and prepare it for their meal and wash it in the river near their home. Their little boy would play down by the river each day as children do, but one morning his parents thought they heard laughing and talking as if two boys were playing by the water. When their boy came home that night his parents asked him who he was laughing and playing with all day. "He calls himself my elder brother," the boy said. "He came out of the water. He says his mother was cruel to him and threw him into the river." With their little boy's explanation, his parents knew this new boy had come from the blood of the game *Selu* had washed away in the river water.

After that, the two boys played together each day. They were inseparable. But whenever Kanadi and Selu tried to see the new boy, he always went back into the water and disappeared. Finally, one evening Kanadi said to his son, "When you go down to the river tomorrow and the other boy comes out of the water, start a wrestling match with him. When you got a good hold of him, call us and we'll come meet him." The boy did as he was asked, and the next morning he challenged the boy to a wrestling match. Soon they were twisted up together. When the boy had a good hold of his playmate, he began hollering for his parents and they rushed down toward the river. As soon as the child saw Kanadi and Selu coming toward him, he yelled, "Let me go! Let me go!

You threw me away!" But his brother would not let him go. His parents grabbed the child and took him home. They kept the boy in their house until he became tame, but they say he was always wild, smart, and mischievous. Thereafter, he led his brother in all their tricky pursuits. After a while, his parents learned the boy was *adawehi*, or magical. They named him *Inage Utasvhi*: He-Who-Grew-Up-Wild.

Kanadi never failed to bring back a deer or some turkeys when he would go up into the mountains and hunt. So one day Wild Boy said to his brother, "I wonder where our father gets all that meat. Let's follow him next time and find out." So the next time Kanadi went out to hunt, the boys trailed after and followed him. They made their way up into the mountains, where they saw Kanadi approach the mouth of a cave with a huge boulder covering it. Kanadi slowly moved the rock aside. As soon as there was an opening, a big buck sprang out of the cave and stopped a short distance away. Kanadi calmly turned, notched an arrow, took aim, and felled the buck. He then picked the buck up and began walking home.

"Did you see that?!" Wild Boy shouted. "He keeps all the deer in that cave and whenever he wants meat he just opens it up, lets one out, and kills it." The boys took off for home and made it there before their father arrived back with his heavy load of deer meat.

A few days later, the boys headed up to Kanadi's cave in the mountains. When they got to the place they both put their backs against the heavy boulder and moved it just enough to make an opening. A deer sprang out suddenly. But just as they drew their bows to shoot it, another deer sprang out. Another one came right on its heels. Then another, and another. Deer kept coming out of the cave faster and faster, running off in every direction into the forest. And then the rabbits, raccoons, and all the other four-footed animals came running out of the cave in one big line. After the four-footed creatures, birds began flying out of the cave in one continuous flutter of feathers, wings, and songs. The birds were so thick they darkened the sky as a storm cloud. Their birdsong and flapping of wings echoed across the mountains. Kanadi heard what sounded like thunder and thought to himself, "What have my boys done now. I better go see what they're up to."

Kanadi followed the sound and headed up to the cave. There he found the boys standing silently by the mouth of the cave in stunned amazement at what had just happened. All the animals and birds were long gone. Kanadi was angry, but without saying a word he just walked into the cave and kicked the covers off four big jars. Swarms of mosquitoes, fleas, lice, gnats, bedbugs, and other biting insects flew from the jars and out of the mouth of the cave. The insects covered the boys and they screamed in fear and pain, slapping at the bugs that stung and bit them. Kanadi stood looking at the boys shaking his head until he felt they had learned their lesson. He slapped away the remaining bugs then sat the boys down.

"You two boys listen up," Kanadi said. "You always had plenty of food to eat, and you haven't had to work for it. When you were hungry, I came here and got meat for you and your mother would cook it. Now if you want to eat, you'll need to hunt all over the woods for game. And you may not find any. You go home now to your mother. I'll see if I can find something for us to eat."

When the boys got home they were tired and hungry, and so they asked Selu for something to eat. "We have no meat," Selu said, "but wait here and I'll find something for you." Selu took a basket and headed to the family's storehouse, which was built on poles high up off the ground to keep hungry animals out. Every day when Selu got ready to cook the family a meal she headed to the storehouse with a basket and would soon come back with it full of selu and *tuya* (beans). The boys had never been inside the storehouse, but now they wondered where all the corn and beans came from. "Let's go and see what she does," Wild Boy said. They climbed up the storehouse and removed a piece of clay from the logs so that they could peek in. They saw Selu standing in the middle of the storehouse with her basket in front of her on the floor. Leaning over the basket, she rubbed her stomach and the basket filled with big ears of corn. She then rubbed her armpits and beans flowed to the top. The boys looked at each other with amazement and said, "How can this be? Our mother is a *sgili* (witch, or ghost). If we eat any of her food it will poison us. We have to kill her."

When the boys came back into the house somberly, Selu knew their thoughts before they spoke.

"You are going to kill me then?" Selu said.

"Yes," the boys said, "You're a sgili."

Selu stopped making their meal and set her things aside. "You boys listen to me," Selu said. "When you have killed me, clear a big piece of dirt in front of our house. Take my body and drag it seven times around in a circle. Then drag my body again seven times around inside the first circle. You'll need to stay up all night and keep watch, but if you do, in the morning you will have corn to eat."

The boys then killed their mother with their clubs and cut off her head, setting it on the roof of their house facing west. "Look for your husband," they told her. They then cleared ground in front of their house, as Selu had instructed, but only seven small patches. This is why corn only grows in some places and not all around the world. Then they dragged Selu's body around in a circle. Wherever her blood spilled on the ground, corn sprouted. The brothers stayed up all night and watched their corn. In the morning it was full grown and ripe.

When Kanadi finally came home from the hunt the next day, he could not find his wife Selu. He found the brothers playing by the river and asked them, "Where is your mother?"

The boys looked at each other then said, "She was a witch, so we killed her. There's her head up on the top of the house."

When Kanadi heard these words and saw Selu's head, he became very angry. "I will stay with you no longer," he said and began walking east toward where the sun rises.

It is said that when Kanadi left and did not return, the boys went in search of him and found him still walking east. They then followed Kanadi toward the eastern edge of Elohi where the sun comes out each morning, facing many trials along the way. When the boys finally reached where the sky vault opens for the sun, they climbed through the gap at first light and up into the Sky World. There they found Kanadi and Selu. Their parents were glad to see them and said they could stay for a while. But after seven days they left for the Darkening Land on the western edge of Elohi where the sun goes down. The boys are still there and are known to the Cherokees as *Anisgaya Tsunvsdi*, the Little Men, or the Thunder Boys. To this day you can hear them talking to each other when thunder rolls across the skies.

Traditional Foods

While animals gifted the Cherokee *hawiya* (meat) and plants gifted *nvwoti* (medicine), it is through the gift of edible plants that human beings gained most of our daily sustenance. For most of our history, Cherokee people have been farmers and gardeners. While the hunt was traditionally associated with men, farming was a domain of women. These powerful associations are reflected in stories of First Man and First Woman told by the Eastern Band of Cherokee Indians medicine man Ayu'ini. Kanadi (First Man, or the Lucky One) is a hunter, while Selu is Corn Woman, the provider of all life-giving sustenance, maize, and beans. Since ancient times, Cherokees have understood that the essence of who we are is shaped by what we eat. Change one's foods, and you change one's nature. For this reason, Hastings said that he and his family still maintained their relationships with traditional foods by hunting, growing them, gathering them, and eating them. Of all the edible plants, it is likely selu with whom Cherokees most identify and whom they most revere. Selu's influence is all over Cherokee society and culture, from our family names to our art. And it is selu's growth cycle that sets a pattern of our ceremonial year in which we seek tohi, with the new corn, the Green Corn ceremony marking our traditional new year. But as with all things, selu exists within a community of other relations, including beans, squash, berries, and the other cultivated and gathered plants of the Cherokee table.

Edible Plants

ᏗᎦᏰᏍᏗ ᎠᎾᏛᏍᎩ ✦ digayesdi anadvsgi (dee-gah-yeh-sdee ah-nah-duh-sgee) ✦ **edible plants**

ᏒᎩᏘ ✦ svgiti (suh-gee-tee) ✦ **apples** ✦ Name means: it fell. *Svgta* is apple.

ᏒᎩᏘ ᎢᎾᎨ ᎡᎯ ✦ svgiti inage ehi (suh-gee-tee ee-nah-geh eh-hee) ✦ **apples, wild, or crabapples**

ᏚᏯ ✦ tuya (too-yah) ✦ **beans**

ᏚᏯ ᎠᏂᏤᎢ ✦ tuya anitsei (too-yah ah-nee-jeh-ee) ✦ **beans, green** ✦ Name means: green beans or new beans. Also called *tuya aninvhida*, or long beans.

ᏚᏯ ᎠᏂᎴᎩ ✦ tuya anilegi (too-yah ah-nee-leh-gee) ✦ **beans, pole** ✦ Name means: beans that climb

ᎤᏴᎭᏗ ✦ uyvhadi (oo-yuh-hah-dee) ✦ **bean vine**

ᎩᎦᎨ ᎠᏂᏢᏍᎩ • gigage anitlvsgi (gee-gah-geh ah-nee-tluh-sgee) • **beets** • Name means: red things that grow in the ground

ᎧᏂᎩ • kanigi (kah-nee-gee) • **blackhaw** • A raisin-like fruit from this tree is edible in the fall.

ᎧᏄᎦᏟ • kanugatli (kah-noo-gah-tli) • **blackberry** • Name means: may scratch you

ᏔᏆᎵ • taquali (tah-qwah-lee) • **bluebonnet**

ᏧᎦᎾᏕᎾ • tsuganadena (joo-gah-nah-deh-nah) • **cabbage** • Name means: having leaves or layered (*tsugadadi*). Also called *udasgewi*, or having a head.

Kanigi (blackhaw)

ᎤᏂᎵᎡᏍᎩ • uniliesgi (oo-nee-lee-eh-sgee) • **cactus**

ᎩᏔᏯ • gitaya (gee-tah-yah) • **cherry**

ᎤᎾᎩᏂ • unagini (oo-nah-gee-nee) • **chinkapin**

ᏎᏬ • selu (seh-loo) • **corn, or maize** • A gift from the Creator. Something that will take care of the Cherokees if they take care of it.

SELU • *by Hastings Shade*

One day, the Creator looked down and saw how the Cherokee were struggling and searching for food. So he came down and told the Cherokees, "I will give you something to take care of you if you will take care of it." He gave them corn.

It didn't look the way it does today. It was small and had very few kernels on it. Every so often the Creator would come down and check to see how the corn was growing. As the Cherokees kept watch over it, the corn continued to get bigger and bigger. This was how the Creator would check and make sure that the Cherokees were doing what he asked them to do.

The Cherokees did a good job of taking care of it, and now corn takes care of everyone, not only the Cherokees. Almost every product we see and use has corn in it.

All we have to do is what the Creator asks us to do, and he will take care of us.

ᎦᏃᎮᎾ • ganohena (gah-noh-heh-nah) • **corn, hominy**

ᎬᏍᏗ • kvsdi (kuh-sdee) • **corn, Indian**

ᏎᎷᏯ • seluya (seh-loo-yah) • **cornflower**

ᎦᎦᎹ • gagama (gah-gah-mah) • **cucumber**

ᏠᏏᏅᏓ • dlosinvda (dloh-see-nuh-dah) • **dewberry**

ᏒᎩ ᎤᏴᏍᏗ • svgi uyvsdi (suh-gee oo-yuh-sdee) • **garlic** • Name means: strong onion

ᎤᏂᏖᎸᎳᏗ • unitelvladi (oo-nee-teh-luh-lah-dee) • **grapes** • Name means: the ones hanging on

ᎢᏳᎩᏗ • iyugidi (ee-yoo-gee-dee) • **hazelnut** • A nut that looks similar to the acorn but does not have the tannic acid.

ᏥᏳᎦᎵ • tsiyugali (jee-yoo-gah-lee) • **hickory chicken**

ᏐᎯ • sohi (soh-hee) • **hickory nut**

ᎤᏥᎸ ᎤᏂᏴᏍᏗ • utsilv uniyvsdi (oo-jee-luh oo-nee-yuh-sdee) • **hot pepper** • Name means: flowers that are hot

ᎧᏩᏯ • kawaya (kah-wah-yah) • **huckleberry**

ᎪᎳᎬᏍᎩ • kolagvsgi (koh-lah-guh-sgee) • **huckleberry, big, or highbush huckleberry** • Name means: stem of plant being like a bone

ᎧᏄᏥ • kanutchi (kah-nuh-jee) • **kanutchi** • A drink made from hickory nuts.

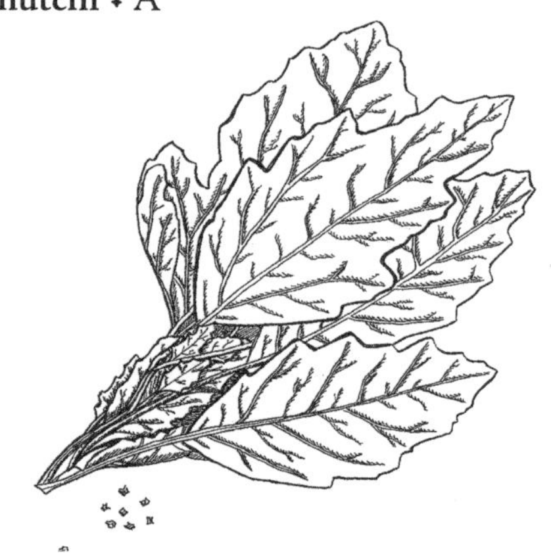

Advgi (lamb's quarters)

ᎠᏛᎩ • advgi (ah-duh-gee) • **lamb's quarters**

ᎤᏂᏍᏉᎵ • unisquoli (oo-nee-squo-lee) • **morel** • Name means: shaped like a stomach

ᎫᏩ • kuwa (koo-wah) • **mulberry**

ᎦᏫᏒᎩ • gawisvgi (gah-wee-suh-gee) • **mush melon, or musk-melon** • Name means: the one that stinks

Wisi (hen-of-the-woods mushroom)

ᎠᏫ ᏧᏲᏂ • awi tsuyoni (ah-wee joo-yoh-nee) • **mushroom, antler** • Name means: deer antlers

ᏫᏏ • wisi (wee-s(h)ee) • **mushroom, hen-of-the-woods** • Also called *unvjida*, the brain mushroom.

ᎤᎫᎫ • uguku (oo-goo-koo) • **mushroom, owl**

A RECIPE FOR ᎧᏅᏥ, *KANVTSI* ✦ *by Loretta Shade*

Hickory nuts were an important food source for the southeastern tribes, and *kanvtsi* is considered to be a real delicacy by the Cherokees in Oklahoma today.

The nuts are gathered in the fall and allowed to dry for a few weeks before the kanvtsi making begins. It is a simple process, but that does not necessarily mean that it is easy. Kanvtsi making takes some effort.

The hickory nuts are cracked, and the largest pieces of shell are removed either by shaking the pieces through a loosely woven basket or picking them out by hand.

A heavy log with one end hollowed out to a depth of several inches is placed on end, and the nuts, which still contain some shells, are put into the cavity and pounded with a long heavy stick with the end rounded to have the same contour, more or less, as the cavity in the log.

The nuts are pounded until they are of a consistency that can be formed into a ball that will hold its shape. Kanvtsi balls are usually about three inches in diameter and must be stored in a cold place. Today kanvtsi is usually preserved by freezing.

To prepare kanvtsi for the table, place a kanvtsi ball in a saucepan with about a quart of water and bring it to a boil to dissolve the ball. Allow the kanvtsi to simmer about ten minutes, and then pour it through a fine sieve. (A colander lined with cheese cloth works very well for this.) All the shells are left in the sieve. If you have the time and patience you can pick the larger bits of nut meat from the shells in the sieve and add them to the liquid kanvtsi.

The kanvtsi should be about as thick as light cream. Most traditional cooks will add about two cups of homemade hominy to a quart of kanvtsi. Some cooks prefer adding hominy grits to kanvtsi.

Such things as consistency and how much hominy or hominy grits to add are, of course, a matter of taste, as is the addition of salt. Most people like a bit of salt, and a few even add some sugar or honey.

Serve kanvtsi hot as a soup. The Cherokee people like to have kanvtsi to eat on any festive occasion.

Svgi inage ehi (wild onion)

ᎠᏂᏓᏫᏍᎦᎵ • anidawisgali (ah-nee-dah-wee-sgah-lee) • **mushroom, slick** • Name means: slick

ᎠᏥᎳ • atsila (ah-jee-la) • **mustard** • Name means: fire, because of its strong taste

ᏓᏆᏒᏂ ᎤᎵᏏ • daquasvni ulisi (dah-qwah-suh-nee oo-lee-see) • **mustard, wild** • Name means: turnip's grandmother

ᎤᏂᏍᎫᎦ • unisguga (oo-nee-sgoo-gah) • **oak ball**

ᎧᏫ ᎤᎵᏲᏗ • kawi uliyodi (kah-wee oo-lee-yoh-dee) • **okra** • Name means: crybaby coffee

ᏒᎩ • svgi (suh-gee) • **onion** • Name means: it smells

ᏒᎩ ᎢᎾᎨ ᎡᎯ • svgi inage ehi (suh-gee ee-nah-geh eh-hee) • **onion, wild** • Name means: onion that lives in the wild

ᏆᎾ • quanah (qwah-nah) • **peach**

ᏆᏀ ᏗᎵᎦᎵᏍᎩ • quanah dilgalisgi (qwah-nah deel-gah-lee-sgi) • **peach, Indian** • Name means: peach with a split vine. Also called *gilgalisgi*, or they split.

ᏗᎦᏛᏗ • digadvdi (dee-gah-duh-dee) • **pears** • Name means: measuring scale

ᏚᏳᏂᏍᏗ • tuyunisdi (too-yoo-nee-sdee) • **peas** • Name means: little beans

Dlayade (poke)

ᏐᎯ ᎠᏂᏅᎯᏓ • sohi aninvhida • soh-hee ah-nee-nuh-hee-dah • **pecan** • Name means: elongated nut

ᏌᎵ • sali (sah-lee) • **persimmon**

ᏆᏄᏂᏍᏗᎢ • quanunisdii (qwah-noo-nee-sdee-ee) • **plums** • Name means: peach-like or little peaches

ᏜᏯᏕ • dlayade (dlah-yah-deh) • **poke**

ᎤᏂᎾᏑᎩ • uninasugi (oo-nee-nah-soo-gee) • **possum grapes**

ᏄᎾ • nuna (noo-nah) • **potato**

ᏄᎾ ᎠᏂᏅᎯᏓ • nuna aninvhida (noo-nah ah-nee-nuh-hee-dah) • **potato, sweet** • Name means: long potato

ᎢᏯ • iya (ee-yah) • **pumpkin**

HOW THE ONION MADE IT RAIN ✦ *Told by Sequoyah Guess*

Loretta, Sequoyah Guess, and I were talking about the roles and responsibilities or Elohi's creatures, large and small, when a story came to Sequoyah's mind.

"One of the teachings I've seen throughout Hastings' collection is that every creature has a purpose," I said, "if it only will use its abilities."

"Well, it reminds me of the story of *svgi*, the onion. There was a big drought, and all the animals, fish, everything got together and said, 'Hey, we're gonna die unless it rains.' They all got together and tried to figure out a way to make it rain. And all this time, there was a small plant off to the side saying, 'Hey, I think I can make it rain.' But nobody listened to him. And finally Bear said, 'Okay. What's your plan?' And so, the plant had Eagle take her up into the sky and she told Eagle, 'When you see a cloud, dive into that cloud, and when we're in that cloud, squeeze me as hard as you can.' And they did that. And when they got back down to Elohi, there was a loud thunder clap and lightning and it started raining. Now it was that onion that made the clouds cry, you know? So that was a lesson I always caught from that one. No matter how small you are, you can still do great things and be a help to everybody. It don't matter your popularity. It don't matter your level of successfulness in business or politics or whatever. You still have the potential to do great things. Not just for yourself but for everybody."

"But what makes someone willing to help or to care about others?"

"That's part of being in balance," Sequoyah said. "Being a Cherokee is that you not only care for yourself, but you care about everybody else, too. And if you can do something that is a help to everybody, you should do it. And do it not because you're gonna get something out of it but because it's gonna help everybody."

"But just like in the story of Doyunisi when she dives down for the mud to form Elohi, or when Kananesgi Amayi gets fire for humans, all the big creatures don't think the small ones can do things. It seems like they have ideas about who should lead, and they don't want the small ones leading."

"Yeah. You see, the onion knew she needed help. She couldn't fly, but she knew who to call on to help her—Eagle. I think that is what makes a good leader. Somebody that knows their limitations and knows when to call for help to do things they know they can do."

"In a lot of the stories, it's the small ones that become leaders in spite of their limitations," I said.

"And I think that's always been true," Sequoyah said. "Those you don't think could lead or would lead are probably the best leaders because they're the ones that are gonna be thinking about the people and not just themselves."

"The best way," said Loretta.

ᎦᎳᏗᏍᎩ • galdisg (gahl-dee-sgee) • **radish, wild** • Tastes like cucumber
ᏒᏗᎳᎵ • svdiwali (suh-dee-wah-lee) • **raspberry**
ᏓᎵᏫ • daliwi (dah-lee-wee) • **rice** • "One story says that Tahlequah might have been named 'The Rice Place,' or 'Daliqua,' which is how it is pronounced in the Cherokee language." H.S.
ᎧᎾᏍᏔᏥ • kanastatsi (kah-nah-stah-jee) • **sassafras** • "Tea made from the root in the spring is a blood-cleansing tonic. In March it thins the blood. Any other time it thickens the blood." H.S.
ᏩᎫᎩ • wagugi (wah-goo-gee) • **squash**
ᎠᏂ • ani (ah-nee) • **strawberry**

THE ORIGIN OF *ANI* (STRAWBERRIES) • *by Noyi Teuton*

When the first *asgaya* (man) and first *agehya* (woman) were created, they lived happily together as husband and wife. But after a time they took each other for granted and began to quarrel. It was just little arguments at first, but then they really began to hurt each other's feelings. "I don't like the way he speaks to me or treats me," the first agehya thought. "He must not love me." And so the woman left the man and walked toward the sun in the east, seeking a new life. As soon as she had left, in his loneliness the man began to see all his bad behaviors toward agehya. He had been inconsiderate. Stubborn. Thoughtless. He began to see himself through his actions. And he grieved. He decided to follow agehya to apologize and, if possible, ask for a second chance. But the woman was too far ahead. She walked on. And she never looked back.

Sun saw the man walking after the woman. She could read his heart and knew he was sincere in his grief and shame over his behavior. Sun decided to take pity on man.

"First Man, I see you are grieving," Sun said to the husband.

Asgaya stopped, looked up, and said softly, "Yes, I am."

"Would you like to speak with the woman who was your wife?" Sun asked the man.

"Yes," he said. "Very much so."

"Then I will help you," Sun said.

"*Wado, nvdo iga ehi,*" asgaya said.

Sun shone its brightest rays down on Elohi and made a thick patch of *kawaya* (huckleberries), to ripen along the path where the woman walked. But instead of seeing them she passed on by, deep in thought and determined to reach the east, a new beginning. Farther down the path, Sun shone its rays again on a bunch of blackberries, and refreshed by the morning dew and Sun's rays the *kanugatli* grew ripe and juicy. But the woman did not stop to pick

ᎤᎦᎾᏍᏓ • uganasda (oo-gah-nah-sdah) • **sweet Annie, sweet wormwood** • Name means: sweet

ᎠᎾᏡᏓᎵᏍᎩ • anatlvdalisgi (ah-nah-tluh-dah-lee-sgee) • **sweet peas** • Name means: the ones that split

ᎤᏅᎫᎯᏍᏗ • unvguhisdi (oo-nuh-goo-hee-sdee) • **tomato** • Name means: they ooze. You're not supposed to eat it if you have an open sore. Also called *damatli*.

ᏓᏈᏒᏂ • daquisvni (dah-quee-suh-nee) • **turnip**

ᏚᏯᏳᏍᏗ • tuyayusdi (too-yah-yoo-sdee) • **turnip, Indian** • Name means: bean-like

them. She just kept on walking, determined to find her new home. Sun tried again and again to catch the woman's attention, but no matter what berry was placed in her path, she kept on walking. And she never looked back.

Sun realized it would take a special berry to make the woman pause. It would need to be beautiful. And the taste would need to remind the woman of love. And so Sun created a low green bush that the woman might see as she walked by with her eyes cast down in thought. And on this low bush she made grow large, heart-shaped, red berries.

At first, the woman did not see Sun's red berries, but as her eyes took them in she could not resist stopping and picking one to eat. She picked the first *ani* (strawberry) and ate it. It was the most delicious fruit she had ever tasted. She ate another, and another, and as she did so she began to think of her husband. She wished he could taste this fruit, too. She wanted to share this gift with him. The more ani she ate, the more the sweet taste made her aware that she missed her husband, for all his flaws.

For the first time in her journey, she turned and looked back west. There the man was in the distance, walking toward her with his head hanging down. And even at that distance, she could see the pain and remorse on his face she knew so well. She picked the ripest, juiciest ani as a gift for her husband and wrapped them in her dress. Then she turned and walked toward him.

And I imagine when they met each other on the path, the first asgaya told the first agehya how he felt about her. And that he was sorry for the way he had behaved toward her. And in return, she placed an ani in his mouth, a symbol of their love and a seal of her forgiveness, as Sun shone down upon them.

ᏎᏗ • sedi (seh-dee) • **walnut**

ᎠᏥᎳ ᎤᏚᎯ • atsila amayi uduhi (ah-jee-lah ah-mah-yee oo-doo-hee) • **watercress** • Name means: fire standing in the water

ᎬᎩᏍᏗ • gvgisdi (guh-gee-sdee) • **watermelon** • Name means: to eat as is

ᎤᏣᎴᏍᏗ • utsalesdi (oo-jah-leh-sdee) • **wheat** • Name means: sticky or gooey

"We're Made of Fire and Water"

When Loretta, Larry, and I discussed people I should speak with about Hastings' collection of names and stories of the natural world, David Comingdeer immediately came to mind. The Shades have long been friends with David, and he knew Hastings well from their time working together in service of the Cherokee Nation. I have known David for over twenty years as a friend and chief of Echota-Tanasi Ceremonial Ground. Like Hastings and the Shade family, David Comingdeer is a respected and knowledgeable Cherokee cultural traditionalist. He was named a National Treasure by the Cherokee Nation for his artistry in making and dedication to reviving the tradition of carving Cherokee stickball sticks.

For over twenty-six years David worked as a wildland firefighter for the Cherokee Nation. He served as supervisor for the Cherokee Fire Dancers, an elite American Indian firefighter unit deployed across Indian Country and the United States battling wildfires. With his many years of experience and knowledge of fire and forests, David was an ideal person to talk to about these important facets of the Cherokee world.

We sat at the dining room table of David's house north of Stilwell, Oklahoma, which he shared at the time with his adult son, Spencer Comingdeer. He and Spencer had recently renovated the house themselves. They had built a wide and deep front porch with a metal roof he had salvaged from a nearby farm. Inside, David had built the stone hearth around his wood stove and inserted within its mortar family mementos. Stickball sticks, books, pictures, and family heirlooms were arranged thoughtfully on the room's light blue walls. David's woodshop sat just past the front yard, adjacent to the pasture where he and Spencer had two horses. In the distance stood a grove of pines he had planted in neat rows years before for future harvest. Altogether, the Comingdeer homestead had an air of order, industriousness, and tohi.

"As a wildland firefighter, you've spent a good deal of your life in the woods. How did you come to choose that life in the forest?" I asked.

"Wow," David said and paused to think. "I think it chose me. I was always fascinated with our natural world around us. Water, rivers, the ocean. My natural environment. And, of course, the timber. You know, the mountains. Very appealing. Just draws me in. And when I was a young man, a teenager, someone who was involved in coordinating wildland fire personnel suggested to my mom that I might make a good firefighter. When I heard that I thought, 'Well that would be a great thing to try.' And I've loved it. I've done it for twenty-six years. I have fought fire in every state that could burn, except for Alaska and Hawaii. It's been a wonderful life for me, for my children, for my home. And I wouldn't have traded the experiences for anything. And the people that I've worked with, the fire personnel that I've worked with, are some of the most amazing people. Strong. Trustworthy. Very dutiful. Always helpful. A lot of initiative. We had to work as a team, and that's been a wonderful experience. A very unique group of people that fight wildland fires. There are actually very few of them in America. A lot of people get in it for a season or two, but your long career firefighters, there's very few of us. Those that stick with it for a long time. It's hard. It's hard, hot work. But it's been very rewarding."

"How did you first come to learn about the forest?"

"Well, as a boy, you know, we hunted. We were always out hunting. I hunted squirrels. And next to our home we had thousands of acres of forest. And that was my playground. Me and my dog. And my .410," David said and laughed. "And, you know, I started bringing squirrels home, so my dad said, 'Well, you gonna bring 'em home you're gonna eat 'em.' So I learned how to eat squirrel as a young man. Learned how to skin 'em, fix 'em, and cook 'em. And also fishin.' Lot of fishin.' Did a lot of that. But just being out in it. And cuttin' firewood with my dad when I was young, learnin' what kind of wood you used for firewood, what kind of wood you used to start a fire with, and what kind of woods could heat the house. What kind of woods are good to smoke meat. You know, there's a different use for all these different woods, and so I had to learn the species of woods. And then as I grew into manhood and became a firefighter, I learned different timber burns differently. Cedar burns different than an oak. Grass burns different than brush. So I learned how to recognize and identify certain species that existed in the wild land, in the backcountry where wildland fires occur. I had to learn the species of trees. I just learned everything I could about how wildfire reacts with certain types of timber. And that dictated how we suppressed certain fires. And what kind of tools we needed to put the fires out. How many people it was gonna take, what kind of equipment, do we need air support—all that depended on what the fuel type was like on the ground. Or in that timber. And so I was forced to learn that. And I embraced it. And I *have* learned."

"Were there folks who taught you Cherokee ideas about the natural world?"

"Well, you know, that comes through people like Hastings and other elders that I was very, very lucky and very fortunate to have spent time with. A lot of them have passed away now. I'm forty-five. So a lot of the guys I looked up to when I was nineteen or twenty years old, they're not here anymore. They've gone on. And the things that I've learned from my elders here in the area about our natural environment have to do with stick making or bow making. Firewood. What types of firewood are good. And what medicines are out there. Natural medicine that we use. And so I've had a very well-rounded experience in life, both as a profession and in a cultural community. And I'm familiar with everything around me. I grow trees. I've planted hundreds and hundreds of trees in my life here at home. And I grow several species of trees here for future use for my family. And also reforesting the land.

And I manage that land with fire, with controlled burning. So I just love to play with the land. I *love* working with and understanding the seasons. And I actually feel like I'm a part of it. Like I have made a difference. I don't own thousands of acres of my own, but I have helped to manage millions of acres that belong to us as a people, Americans and Cherokee Indians. And other tribes. I've worked on their tribal areas, too, managing wildfire, whether it be controlled burning or suppressing wildfires to protect them.

It's been a wonderful life. And most of the work that I've done, whether it be from a cultural or a professional side, *is* all outside. It's all in the woods. In the wild country. In the forest."

"Do your cultural knowledge and cultural ideas about the natural world come to bear on your professional work?"

"Absolutely. Absolutely. What we firefighters in this area have learned is that the native species that we depend on for medicine and for other cultural resources are all fire dependent. They need fire as much as they need rain. If you take the rain away, and you have a long drought, certain things can die off. They'll just die off. Well, if you take the fire away from these fire-dependent species, they also die off, because foreign invasive species come in and overcrowd them. Certain grasses, certain brush, even timber. We have foreign timber here that's not native here. And without the use of fire on the land, in a controlled manner, it's just as bad as not having water on the land. It kills our native species. So a healthy and very robust burn cycle is absolutely essential to maintain our native species, which are our medicines and our cultural resources here."

"Fire is so important to our people," I said. "Do you talk to folks about our cultural knowledge and use of fire?"

"Well, it can't be denied that as far as back as we look in our culture as a tribe—even back east when we existed in the land of our forefathers—fire and the use of fire were a part of the way we treated the land. I'm sure everybody knew about fire. You knew whether it be cooking, heating, you knew what kind of wood you used for this and that. But also treating *the land* with fire at the right time, to where your flames were calm and just cleaned the forest floor. Because we observed. We were a part of nature. When we were in our original tribal state and the tribal towns were intact. And we had no external forces disturbing us. Our people, our forefathers understood their place, and they knew that lightning came down from the sky and would set fire to the land. And our ancient ancestral people knew that the only way they could protect their tribal towns was to use fire to fight fire. They weren't willing to let a fire come through and burn up the town. They knew how to secure their area and burn away from the tribal town and keep wildfire off them. And so, over time, they learned to do controlled burns and to treat that land with fire. And not wait on the lightning. 'Cause if you wait too long . . . . And they knew this. And the US Forest Service is just figuring it out now. If you take fire out of the ecosystem for too long, you get a tremendous amount of fuel loading. And when it does come from the heavens and lighting strikes those mountains, and it does catch on fire—'cause it's always going to—you kill firefighters. The fires are so intense, and they not only kill the timber because of the fuel loading, but it makes it very, very difficult on the fire personnel to suppress those fires successfully and safely. It becomes very, very challenging. So the one thing that has occurred here in North America that has hurt our forest is the lack of fire. And our tribes knew that. And we used to use that a lot."

"Does that have to do with the idea of balance? Of having a balanced ecosystem?"

"Yeah. It's like I said, you know fire's a natural part of our environment, and most of our native species here are fire dependent because they grew to be in a fire environment. You know, even our native grasses, which are the healthiest for our cattle, are fire dependent. They're built to burn. They're built to burn, and then a rebirth of even stronger life comes after that. And, you know, the great buffalo herds in the West, those prairies were burned off by lightning or Native hands, which produced a bumper crop of high-protein native grasses for the buffalos. That's why we had millions and millions of buffalos. It could sustain life. Fire and rain sustain life on earth, and there is a balance there. You can't take either one of 'em out. You take fire out, you get overcrowding, you get disease, and then the forest tries to thin itself by decay. Or fire destroys it."

"It seems some people perceive fire as the enemy," I said.

"Well, that's what has been promoted since the 1940s. You know, 'wildfire's a demon.' It's a demon. There's been commercial posters out there, old commercials with Smokey Bear and what not, you know, 'This demon is comin' over the mountain. What are we gonna do?' I remember seeing this. And is rain a demon? Rain is life. Rain is the blood. The lifeblood of our environment and of us, our bodies. And fire is the same. We're made of fire and water. When we lose the fire, that's what they call death. When we lose that fire that's in us. It's in our heart, in our mind, and it's in our bloodstream. When that fire flickers out, we're gone. That human has passed away. And the earth does the same. It's the same. *It has to have that fire*. That lightning or the hand of man to manage that forest. That's what our ancestors did. They knew. They were part of it. They were as much a natural part of the environment as the lightning itself. Our tribes in their original state were just as much a part of the environment as lightning itself."

Middle World

When I reflect on the meaning of Elohi that the teachings of Hastings, Loretta, and other elders have shared with me, I come back to David Comingdeer's powerful statement that "we're made of fire and water." *Atsila*, fire from the Sky World, and water, *ama* from the Under World, shape our very being. Without either of these living elements we could not exist. And yet we do not live in fire and we do not live in water, but are of Elohi, this world of soil and rock upon which we stand. Along with the other creatures of Elohi, we are of the middle, *ayetli*, and strive to know better our home territory and our fellow creatures of this place so we may thrive together in tohi. At the same time, the creatures and forces of the other worlds are part of our lives as well. Our very bodies are made of the water in our cells, the minerals in our bones, and the sun-fed creatures we live upon.

Hastings often said that each of us will find different meanings in traditional teachings and stories. It is our responsibility to discover those teachings for ourselves. For me, living well on Elohi means valuing our human and other-than-human kin, recognizing all life as in community, sharing our existence, and working with one another for our mutual benefit. These values, I have come to experience, are important to nurturing tohi in body, mind, and spirit.

Some of these teachings are summarized by Cherokee traditionalist Benny Smith in his listing of "ᏍᎦᏚᎩ ᏗᎧᏃᏩᏛᏍᏗ Community Values" (Smith 2011, 320–22). They include *gadugi,* "People coming together as one and working to support one another," and *ulisgedi detsadayelvsesdi,* "Treat each other's existence as being sacred or important" (320–21). Values like *detsadaligenvdisgesdi,* "You all take responsibility for one another's well-being," are familiar in Cherokee tradition as they have been passed down through story. And so it is fitting that the names of the monsters in wahde's telling of "The Crooked-Faced Boy" are these very community values. When those monsters are reunited with the little boy's villagers, they return those shunned values back to community.

But just as "The Crooked-Faced Boy" shows, having knowledge does not matter unless one acts upon it. The traditional Cherokee teaching that Benny Smith shared, to "learn from all you observe," includes a responsibility to act upon what one learns (Chad Smith 2013, 19). Listen, watch, learn, and *do,* as Hastings said of traditional teachings.

It is in the doing, not just the knowing, that challenges arise as one seeks to stand in the middle. At least, that is my experience. But as many of the heroes of Cherokee oral tradition show, when one uses one's mind, body, and spirit to expand the reach of tohi, something powerful may occur.

And so this chapter on Elohi ends with a story about two boundary-crossing little creatures and those who welcomed them in. The Cherokee stickball game at the center of the story is called "the little brother of war" in the Cherokee language and was once used to settle disputes between towns and different peoples. It is played to reestablish tohi. In the story of "The Ball Game of the Birds and Animals," the game is not just between creatures but between worlds. As we transition to explore *Galvladi,* the Sky World, this story shows us how our interdependent relationships and unique characteristics are important not only to Elohi but to the vitality of other worlds as well.

THE BALL GAME OF THE BIRDS AND ANIMALS

by Noyi Teuton

Ilvhiyu tsigesv nigada inage anehi tsalagi itsaniwonisgv. In the great forever that was, all the forest dwellers spoke Cherokee. And just as Cherokees did many years later, the creatures of the worlds would gather for ball games between peoples to test their strength, stamina, and spirit. Once, the four-legged animals of the inage challenged the birds, *anitsisqua*, to a great ball game between their peoples. The anitsisqua accepted the challenge, and their leaders set the date and place. When the day for the game came, all the inage anehi and anitsisqua gathered at the place for their ball dances. The animals gathered down by the edge of the river, as was their custom, and the birds sat together in their treetops not far away. *Yona* (Bear) was the captain of the animals. His power was in his strength, and he could pull down and stand up to anyone who challenged him on the field. On the way to the ball grounds he swatted logs around like sticks with his great paws and said, "This is how I'll throw the birds about!" *Daksi* (Terrapin) also joined with the inage anehi, as it was a four-footed animal. Its name meant "lock," and for good reason, as its shell was so hard that even the heaviest blows could not harm or get to it once its limbs were tucked inside. Seeing Yona tossing around those logs got Daksi's blood racing. It rose up on its hind legs and crashed to the ground, saying, "This is how I'll squash any bird that tries to take the ball from me!" All the animals we know were crowded around, cheering each other on. Each animal had its ball skills, but the strong and fast ones like *Awi* (Deer) were the stars of their team.

The anitsisqua had the powerful *Awohali* (Eagle) as their leader. They also had *Tawod* (Hawk) and *Tlahnawa* (Falcon), both fierce hunters and fast and agile flyers. And yet, they say the anitsisqua were wary of the inage anehi. After all, their ball game was a match not only among themselves but also between the Sky World and Elohi. There was much at stake.

When the dance was over for the birds, they were preening themselves and making ready for the ball game when two little four-footeds climbed up Awohali's tree and approached the captain on his perch.

"Siyo Awohali," they said in unison. With his keen eyes the great bird had seen the two creatures no bigger than mice climbing his tree. But rather than pouncing on them for a pregame snack, he decided to let them approach. Perhaps they were messengers of the four-footeds.

"Siyo," he said. "The ball game is about to begin. Why have you members of the four-footeds come to the birds?"

"We come to ask if we may join your team," one of the little creatures said with his high voice.

Awohali was shocked at this surprising request. "You are creatures of Elohi. Why do you not play with the four-footeds?"

"We came and asked to join the animals' team, but they laughed at us and said we were too small to play," the other, dark-furred little creature said.

"They told us to go away," the lighter-colored creature said.

"I see," said Awohali. "I do not see how you can join the birds without wings. But since you have come here to help, let me talk to my fellow birds and consider your request."

Awohali, Tawod, and the other birds gathered together in the branches for a counsel. After some discussion the choice became clear: if the little creatures were to join the birds, they'd need wings. But what could they use for wings? They tried to think of what might work, but nothing came to mind. Finally, one of the birds noticed the drum they used for their dance. The drum was made of the skin of *Ogana* (Groundhog). There was just enough hanging over the sides of the drum to cut off and fashion some small wings. They cut the pieces of skin from the drum and stretched them with splits of cane so that they were taut. Then they tied them to the forelegs of the darker small creature.

Awi (deer)

"What is your name, little one," asked Awohali.

"*Dlameha dagwado'a,*" he said. "My name is Bat."

"Let's see if this will work," Tawod said. "Throw him the ball." One of the birds tossed the ball to Dlameha and Awohali said, "Now fly, Dlameha! And don't let us catch you."

Dlameha took to the air, and though its wings were not good for flying straight, they were terrific for cutting back and forth in crazy angles across the sky. The birds had never seen flying like that. Though they all tried to get the ball, none could match Dlameha's quick, unexpected turns and pivots.

"We've got a new team member!" Awohali announced.

"What about me?" asked the other little creature.

"We don't have any more ogana skin," said Awohali. "But let's see what we can do."

The birds preened themselves in thought for some time, then a voice from farther down the tree spoke up.

"Why don't we stretch his skin!" *Kawohaleni* (Pelican) said, and shook the skin under his large bill. The birds agreed to give it a try.

The little creature braced itself on a branch, and *Uguku* (Owl) and *Tsiyesdi* (Carolina Parakeet) each took a handful of skin on the little animal's sides and pulled. They flapped and pulled, and after several minutes the skin between the creature's fore and hind legs began to stretch out.

"That should do it," Tsiyesdi said. "Let's see you give it a try."

Awohali threw a ball to the little creature. It grabbed the ball out of the air and dove across to another tree, straight and true as an arrow.

"*Osda*!" the birds cheered.

"*Do detsado'a?*" Awohali called out to the little creature.

"I used to be called by another name. But now . . . *Dewi dagwado'a*. My name is Flying Squirrel."

"Birds, welcome Dewi, another new member of our ball team," said Awohali to hoots and calls from the anitsisqua.

The new members of the bird ball team showed their worth right from the start. When the signal was given and the game began, Dewi caught the ball and flew to a tree, tossing the ball to the other birds, who kept it away from the ground-bound four-footeds until it was dropped. Yona rushed in for the ball, but *Dludlu* (Purple Martin) swooped in and passed the ball to Dlameha, who flew in zigzags near the ground, so quickly and unpredictably that the speedy Awi could not keep up. With Awi almost running in circles, Dlameha rushed forward and threw the ball through the goalposts, winning the game for the birds.

In the celebrations that followed, Dludlu was given a gourd to build his nest as a reward for getting the ball when it dropped. And as they basked in their upset win over the animals, the birds all cheered for the newest members of their people, Dlameha and Dewi, who through their courage and willingness in spite of their size, brought unexpected gifts to the anitsisqua and a victory for the flyers of Galvladi over the four-footeds of Elohi.

As they took their ball and went home, Yona said to Daksi, "You know, the hardest part is we never even got a chance to carry the ball."

"There's always next time," Daksi said.

Jo'i ✦ Three

Galvladi

THE SKY WORLD

One winter day Loretta and I met with Sequoyah Guess at the chapel of the Cherokee Heritage Center to discuss teachings about *Galvladi,* the Cherokee Sky World. We had talked about standing in the middle and how our lives on Elohi are spent seeking balance and tohi while being influenced by forces of both the Sky World and Under World. I understood the Sky World in conceptual terms as our place of origin, a realm of form, structure, and regularity. I knew it as the home of Unetlvnv, to whom prayers are sent in words, songs, dance, and smoke. But I did not have a feel for how we relate to the creatures and forces of the Sky World on a daily basis and how they shape our life on Elohi.

Sequoyah pointed to the power and purpose of birds, which as flyers are of Sky World. "See, every animal and every bird has a purpose. Birds, they have a purpose in communicating with us. We use them in different ways. We relate to them in different ways. Now the blue jay, *dlaiga,* is the storyteller bird. Hastings used to tell me that blue jay and storytellers are the same way. The blue jay will always tell people when somebody's out there in the woods. They always warn the other animals and other birds, 'Hey, there's somebody out here!' They always get really vocal when people are around. Or danger. And Hastings said, 'We're kind of the same way.' We as storytellers and Cherokee language speakers. We're trying to get people the teachings and say, 'Hey, this is going on, this is going on!' Or, 'You should hear this because this is going to teach you something.' So, we're a little bit like the blue jays. Grandma used to say that was the storytelling bird."

Dlaiga
(blue jay)

"Hastings said it was the tattletale of birds," Loretta said, and we laughed. "He would say that if you didn't tell the blue jay you're going hunting, when he sees you out in the woods he'll tell everyone you're there. He'll follow you around all day hollering. So Hastings would always tell the blue jay, 'I'm going to be in the woods hunting.' Then they'd usually leave him alone."

"So, birds are talkers. They teach us about communication, about sharing story and teachings," I said.

"Like Hastings always said, nature talks to you. If you *listen*," Loretta said.

"That teaching is so important right now, with what we're doing to the environment," I said. Loretta's words made me think of how she told me once that humans can keep balance or destroy it. "People need to hear and return to these teachings to create tohi."

"I think so, too," Loretta replied, "but too often they're not willing to listen. In the summer I'll sit out on the porch in early mornin' and drink my coffee and listen to the birds. They say things. Sometimes warn me of things. Chickadees are bad news carriers most of the time. And the owl, you don't want to see the owl in the daytime. And if he's calling late in the evening it's gonna be bad weather coming sometime soon. So why do birds come to where you're sitting? It's to tell you something. But only if you're listening. It's the people that have changed, not the animals or birds."

Time and again in my conversations with Loretta and in my study of Hastings' work, the theme of listening—to nature, to the spirit, to each other—emerged as central to standing in the middle. Life is telling us things. It is communicating with us, they said, but we cannot engage with our relations and learn to live in tohi if we do not listen to one another. But what does it really mean to listen to nature? I knew the Cherokee word for "listen" is *atvgi'a*, a likely combination of the words *advliha*, he/she is breathing, and *agi'*a, he/she is picking up something. To "listen" to someone, the Cherokee linguist Ben Frey tells me, is to pick up the breath, the words, of another person. But listening with one's ears or observing with one's eyes is only one half of the process of communication. The other half is the act of speaking, performing, or recording one's ideas in writing or some other form to communicate one's thoughts, feelings, and imagination. When Loretta, Hastings, or other elders talked about how we needed to listen, I understood they were talking about a larger breakdown in communication as a whole. In a Cherokee cosmos where everything has its rightful place, this breakdown is telling. For whether through spoken words, the song of birds, or the drift of smoke, the act of communication originates as a gift from Creator in the Sky World.

Cherokee mythology tells that the cosmos began with two opposed but interconnected worlds, *Galvladi*, the Sky World in the air and space above us, and *Elohi Hawinadidla*, the Under World of waters and earth below us. The Under World is that source of roiling energy we name change and transformation: it is the Sky World that teaches us of form, predictability, and permanence. Composed of all creatures and forces that make their home in the sky and across space, the Sky World is truly vast and limitless. The sun, moon, planets, and countless stars are all of the Sky World. These light-bringers are whole and complete, their circularity offering a symbol and model of unity we humans use to this day. In spite of its vastness, from our vantage point the Sky World is a place of timeless order and regularity. Each day, the sun rises on Elohi in the east and sets in the west. Each month, the moon moves through its cycle of waxing and waning. Constellations rise and fall in the night sky over time, signaling the change of seasons, and fixed stars allow us to navigate by them, showing us the way home. On Elohi, where sky meets earth and water, Sky World's patterns become less regular as they interact with forces of Elohi and Elohi Hawinadidla. This is the realm of the ever-moving elements of wind, rain, thunder, lightning, ice, and snow. Here, Sky World is home to all flyers and the trees that provide them shelter. All creatures of Sky World—from birds to the planets—share something of the characteristics of this place, I was told. I wanted to learn more about these characteristics of Sky World and how our understanding of them and Sky World's creatures shapes Cherokee thought.

Loretta explained that the teachings of Galvladi tell of life's origins there and how to order and shape life on Elohi with Creator's gift of language. The original forms of the creatures we know on Elohi come from the Sky World. Though latecomers to Elohi, humans originated there as well. Elder teachings Hastings shared say that when we die, our bodies remain in the earth while our spirits seek a return to Sky World. When a spirit reaches the seventh height of Galvladi it will once again be at one with Unetlvnv. That cycle of return is dependent upon communion with Sky World and its teachings, which we learn and share through language.

Like atsila and tsola, elders say the Cherokee language, *tsalagi gawonihisdi*, is a direct gift from Unetlvnv. Cherokee language gave us the ability to speak and listen, but like other gifts of Creator, it only thrives if we use it to stay in relationship with each other and our fellow creatures. Though I understood that Cherokee language and the fire are two tools with which Cherokee people have sought communion with our source, I wondered what Cherokee teachings said about the nature of the Sky World. What forces shape it and those who live there? What are our responsibilities to Galvladi as human beings? And finally, what is Galvladi's relationship to the Under World?

This chapter on Galvladi presents names, stories, and reflections on the creatures and forces that inhabit the Cherokee Sky World. It tells of origins of life and models of order, form, and regularity in our experiences on Elohi. While its own origins are shrouded in mystery, patterns of the Sky World have shaped the measure of seasons, Cherokee understandings of law and morality, and views on our destiny and purpose as human beings. Today, Cherokees of different faiths have different names for this place—the Christians call it Heaven. But the power and mystery of the Sky World as a place of origin and place to which one's spirit returns continues to shape Cherokee views of the natural world.

Origins in the Stars

On a cold, clear, November night, look to the sky and find the Cherokee star constellation *Galaquogi Dinadalv*, the Seven Sisters, known to the Greeks as the Pleiades. It is from that system of hundreds of brightly shining stars, elders say, that we human beings originated. Our story begins with Star Woman, *Noquisi Agehya*, one of the Seven Sister stars. Elders say human beings lived on a planet somewhere among the Seven Sisters, but we were mistreated there—by whom, Hastings was not told. Star Woman witnessed our mistreatment and felt pity for us. And though it was forbidden for her to intervene, she decided to act. Star Woman gathered the human beings together, put us inside her terrapin-shaped body, and delivered us to Elohi, where upon her arrival her body opened up and we stepped out onto Turtle Island. When Star Woman returned to her sisters, Hastings said, she was punished by her family and hidden from view from those she saved by a cloud of dust. She is now called *Ulisigi*, the Dark One, the star that broke from her family and let compassion lead her to deliver human beings to Elohi. We still remember her as we look toward the night sky in winter, when the Galaquogi Dinadalv are their brightest and visible from dusk to dawn. When the Seven Sisters constellation disappears each spring, that marks the beginning of the planting season, a new beginning.

Human beings have other origins in the stars as well, Hastings said. There is a seven-pointed star, *Galaquogi Digosdayi Noquisi*, from which elders say sons of Unetlvnv came to live with women of Elohi. The children of these people were powerful, they say, as they had knowledge of how the forces of the cosmos worked. They became medicine people and are still remembered in the seven-pointed star of the Cherokee and the symbolic power of the number seven. When one looks toward the Seven Sisters constellation, there is a lone star that trails the sisters and is known in Arabic as *Aldebaran*, the follower. This may be Galaquogi Digosdayi Noquisi.

How powerful, I have thought, that the story of Cherokee origins begins with the salvation of the people by a female being who defied her family to show them compassion. Perhaps her sisters would have called Star Woman's act a crime, a willful act of disobedience to their code of noninterference. But maybe, when powerful emotions rose up in her like a tide from the Under World, they compelled Star Woman to do what was right even if it broke with her family and their rules. Perhaps she was called by a still higher law. Cherokees have understood the Sky World as a place of form, regularity, and order, but Star Woman's story teaches that order may become rigid, regularity may become static, and forms may become isolating. Star Woman's act of defiance to a celestial order gave us the ability to find our own paths toward tohi on Elohi. Though her sisters covered her in veils to obscure her view, our stories still remember Star Woman. She is still part of our sgadug.

ANITSUTSA ALE NOTSI (THE BOYS AND THE PINE) • *by Noyi Teuton*

Hastings and Sequoyah spoke of another story of the constellation known as the Pleiades. While the story of the Seven Sisters tells of the origin of human beings, the story of the Boys I retell here is about a return to the stars. In their similarities and differences, both stories speak to the importance of our relations, our connections to our ancestors, and the care that should be taken with each other.

Ilvhiyu tsigesv, in the great forever that was, there were seven boys who spent all their time at the village townhouse playing the *gatayusti* game and not helping out with their chores. Gatayusti, also known as chunkey, is a game played by bowling a stone disc with one hand and, in the other, throwing a spear toward where the disc eventually stops. The closer the spear lands to the far-off disc, the better the throw.

The mothers of these boys scolded them for playing games all day long and decided to play a trick on them. They gathered the chunkey stones together and boiled them with corn for dinner. When the hungry boys came home to eat, their mothers said, "Since you like the gatayusti game more than helping out in the cornfield, eat these stones for your meal."

The boys were hurt and offended. "If this is the way our mothers are going to treat us," they said, "let's go where we'll never trouble them again." And so they began a feather dance around the townhouse, praying for spirits to help them. After a little while, the mothers went to look for their boys to bring them home to dinner. But as they walked toward the village townhouse, they heard the sound of an *ahuli* (drum) in the air keeping rhythm, but could see no drum or drummer. Instead, they saw their boys dancing around the townhouse and were alarmed to see that their feet were not touching the earth. The mothers stood in amazement as their children danced and with each round they rose higher and higher as the drum sounded. Finally recognizing the danger, the mothers ran to grab their children before they lifted too far in the air, but by the time they reached them it was too late—they were already above the townhouse, dancing round and round. One mother grabbed a gatayusti stick, leaped up, and knocked her son out of the circle and onto the ground. But he hit the earth with such strange force that he sank into the dirt and it closed over him.

The other six boys rose higher and higher so quickly that they soon became just shining dots in the night sky. They stayed that way, and though their mothers could see them each night thereafter, they and the other villagers deeply grieved their loss. The mother of the seventh boy taken by the earth came every morning and evening and cried on the very spot where the dirt swallowed him. Soon, a green shoot came up from the tear-damp soil and grew to become the great tree we know as *notsi* (pine). It is said that notsi and *aninoquisi* (the stars) are of the same creation. They both hold within themselves the same brilliant light. Those dancing boys rose to Sky World and found their place among the *Galaquogi Dinadalv* (Seven Sisters). Their drum, they say, became a nearby nebula. Some people now call the Seven Sisters the *Anitsutsa* (the Boys) and others still call them Galaquogi Dinadalv. Sometimes the people danced the feather dance in honor of their relatives, the Anitsutsa, thanking them for the good growing weather the Boys would send to feed their Cherokee relatives on Elohi.

Nvdo Iga Ehi ale Nvdo Svnoyi Ehi (Sun and Moon)

Cherokee tradition says we are people of *atsila*, as fire was a direct gift to the people from Unetlvnv. But like all life on Elohi, whose original forms come from Sky World, fire on earth is related to that original fire that energizes our world and is known as *nvdo iga ehi* (the sun) or "celestial body, day dweller." In Cherokee tradition, the sun is a female being, and it is through her nurturing energy that we share life on Elohi. But just as all things in Cherokee worldview exist in complementary oppositions, our daylight sun has a nighttime counterpart, her brother moon, *nvdo svnoyi ehi*, or "celestial body, night, dweller."

Cherokee tradition understands our sky as a round vault that stretches to each horizon. Each morning, nvdo iga ehi comes out from under the eastern edge of the sky vault and makes her way across the sky until she sinks down in the west at the day's end. Her brother, nvdo svnoyi ehi, takes her place at night and charts his own east to west path across the sky. In their regular orbits, the sun and moon continue to give order to our lives through the cycles of seasons and growth. And we continue to depend on this order for life on earth.

Achieving and maintaining tohi in body, mind, and spirit depends upon understanding how the cosmos is ordered, Hastings taught, and the sun and moon play a central role in this ordering. Cherokee teachings say potent creatures and forces of the three worlds, like the sun and moon, should maintain their separation. This is because the ordered Sky World exists in natural opposition to the chaotic energy of the Under World. Birds, of the Sky World, and snakes, of the Under World, oppose each other for this reason. There are customs that trace back to an ideal of maintaining order by keeping opposed forces separate. Fire should never be extinguished with water; the mixing of these two elements of the Sky World and Under World may unleash unintended consequences. Instead, a fire should be extinguished with dirt from Elohi. Elohi is the balancing place, and so it is fitting that the forces of the Sky World and Under World reckon with each other in our midst.

It is cosmic irony that, while opposed, the forces of Sky World and Under World become most energetic and creative when they mix. The earth is renewed with thunder, rain, and the lightning that brings fire and new growth. The moon's pull brings the tides that move the waters around Elohi. In this interaction is rejuvenation, purification, and cleansing as understood in Cherokee custom.

I am reminded of this need for separation, renewal, and reconnection each year during the Green Corn ceremony. When the fire that has been burning all year is extinguished, one recognizes and releases all the feelings that have moved one away from tohi during the past yearly cycle of the sun. A new, pure fire is lit at the center of the square grounds and in ourselves. Cleansed with medicine and fire, we begin again.

DAUGHTER OF THE SUN • *by Noyi Teuton*

Just as humans are prone to powerful emotions that well up in us and that we are challenged to understand, much less control, the powers of Sky World are also subject to feelings. I retell this story from Ayu'ini as it reminds us that the forces we are subject to shape all life, big and small.

Ilvhiyu tsigesv, in the great forever that was, Sun lived on the other side of the sky vault. But as she made her way across the sky every day from east to west she'd visit her only daughter, who lived right in the center of the sky directly above Elohi. Sun would stop at her daughter's house for dinner each day.

Back then, they say, *Nvdo Iga Ehi* was angry with the people of the earth because no matter how brightly she shone for them, they'd squint when they tried to look straight at her. She found this disrespect offensive and told her brother, Moon, "My grandchildren are ugly creatures. Do you see the way they blink their eyes and twist up their faces when they look at us?" Moon said, "Well, I think they're beautiful. When I shine down on them each night they smile right back at me."

Moon's words made Sun jealous. She decided to rid the world of all the people for their disrespect toward her. Each day when she climbed high toward her daughter's house, Sun flooded the earth with sunshine. Soon, Sun's heat became so intense that people began to die of fever. People became afraid that if this kept up, nobody would survive Sun's intensity.

Messengers were sent to the Little Men, *Anisgaya Tsunvsdi*, also known as the Thunder Boys. They are the twin sons of *Kanadi* and *Selu*, First Man and Corn Woman. Their actions shaped life on Elohi during the ancient time. They live high in the sky far in the west now and can be heard as rolling thunder when they talk. As friends to human beings, they can be called on when help is needed with the Sky

World. After seeing what was happening to the humans the Little Men offered guidance. The only way to truly stop Sun, the Little Men said, was to kill her.

The Little Men made medicine and transformed two men into snakes, a copperhead (*tsowi*) and a spreading adder (*squanadeyo*). They then sent the snakes to Sun's daughter's house, where they were to wait by the door and bite Sun when she came to visit. The two snake men hid out and waited for Sun, but when she finally approached the door the next day, Squanadeyo was blinded by Sun's brilliance and could only spit slime, as he still does when he tries to bite. Sun saw both snakes and only wrinkled her nose in disgust as she walked into her daughter's house. Tsowi and Squanadeyo just slithered away.

The days got hotter and hotter, with more people dying from Sun's rays. And so humans asked the Little Men again for help. The Little Men used their medicine again and transformed one man into the powerful *Uk'tan* and another into *Ugasuti* (Rattlesnake). The plan stayed the same: hide by the door to Sun's daughter's house and strike when Sun approaches. The Little Men took no chances with the snakes this time. Uk'tan was huge, with a full rack of horns on its head. At the sight of it the people thought Sun surely would not get away this time. Smaller but fierce in its own way, Ugasuti rushed to the door to Sun's daughter's house and coiled up in anticipation. The plan was that they were both supposed to wait and strike together, but in its excitement Ugasuti sprang when the door suddenly opened, striking Sun's daughter just as she was looking for her mother's arrival. Sun's daughter fell dead.

"Wait! You were supposed to wait for Sun!" Uk'tan shouted in anger.

Ugasuti did not have the heart to kill again, and so it slithered back to the people. Uk'tan followed angrily. Thereafter it was said that the ugasuti should not be killed as it is kind and will not bite anyone unless it is disturbed, even warning you before it strikes.

When Uk'tan returned to the people, it just became angrier and angrier. Soon it turned on the very people it was supposed to protect. It was so dangerous that if it looked at a someone, the person's whole family would die. The people lived with the first uk'tan, but after a long time it was too dangerous for people and was sent to live in Sky World, where it remains today as, some say, the constellation known as Scorpio. Uk'tans are still among us and have been seen in recent memory. A sighting of one is said to portend changes for the Cherokee people. The other snakes who were once men are still with us always.

When Sun arrived at her daughter's house and found her dead, she went inside and grieved. Sun's heat no longer killed the people, but now there was another problem. The world was dark and cold because Sun did not leave her daughter's house. The people went to the Little Men again for their counsel and were told that if they wanted Sun to shine once more, they would have to bring Sun's daughter back from the realm of the dead beyond the Darkening Land in the west. Seven men were chosen. Each was given a sourwood stick as long as a hand. The Little Men said they needed to take a box with them. When they reached the realm of the dead, they would find the ghosts dancing. They were to stand outside the circle of dancers, and when the Sun's daughter passed them, they were to touch her with the sourwood sticks. She would fall to the ground, and they were to put her in the box and carry her back to her mother. But the Little Men warned the men: once the Sun's daughter was inside the box, do not open it.

So the men took the sourwood sticks and box with them, and they traveled seven days to the west when they reached the Darkening Land. There they saw a great dance of ghosts, just as the Little Men said they would see. Sun's daughter was there dancing around the circle. Each time she passed, one of the men would strike her lightly with his sourwood stick, and she would look at the man. Upon the seventh pass, she was struck and fell out of the ring onto the ground. The men put her in the box and left the ghosts dancing.

The men traveled east toward home with Sun's daughter in the box. But in a short while, she came to life and begged to be let out. The men looked at each other and did not answer, just kept going. But after a while she said she was hungry. And thirsty. She begged to be let out of the box. She pleaded with them to have mercy on her. But the men did not answer and kept on walking home. When they were getting close to their lands, the woman began to call out in a panicked voice, "I can't breathe! I'm smothering! I need air! Please just raise the lid a little bit!"

The men worried that Sun's daughter really was dying again, so against their better judgment they opened the lid just enough to let in some fresh mountain air. But as soon as they cracked the lid, there was a brisk fluttering sound and something flew past them into the bushes. They then heard the song of *totsuwa* (redbird) from deep in the brush.

The men closed the lid of the box and hurried to their village. But when they got there and opened up the box, it was empty. Sun's daughter was gone. We know now that the redbird was Sun's daughter. If the men had kept the box shut, as the Little Men told them to, she would have been brought home from the Darkening Land. It is said that if the Sun's daughter had been brought back safely, then others may also have been brought back from the realm of the dead. But now the dead cannot be brought back.

Sun saw the men trying to make things right when they headed off to the Darkening Land in search of her daughter. But when they came back empty-handed, she wept for her girl, and her tears flooded Elohi. Soon the people feared her grief would drown them. The people held another council and decided on their own to send men and women to dance and sing their best songs for Sun. She paid them no mind at first and hid her face, but when the drummer changed the rhythm to a new song, Sun looked up and was pleased at the sight of the smiling humans. It is said she let go of her grief then and shone once again.

Totsuwa (redbird)

"Where the Dog Ran" and the Path of Souls

Some traditional Cherokee teachings hold that each person has four *adanta*, or souls. Our consciousness as individual people with our own personalities, memories, and feelings is located in the soul that is in the head. The other adanta are located in the liver, heart, and our bones. These souls hold the physical life force of a person. Each organ has a different purpose and relationship with the energies that enliven a person. When the body dies, the conscious adanta in the head is released from the body. Once the body is buried, the energy from the other adanta seep back into the earth. Freed from its earthly constraints, the conscious, head soul begins its journey to the Sky World and the Path of Souls.

The soul travels to the Darkening Land at the western edge of Turtle Island where land meets sea. After that four-day journey, the soul must bide its time and wait for the right moment to make its trek onto the celestial body Cherokees call "Where the Dog Ran," but what other Indigenous peoples of Turtle Island call the Path of Souls. Today in the West, we call this phenomenon the Milky Way galaxy.

There is a legend that tells of the origin of the Cherokee name of our galaxy. Two hunters once lived in the sky, one in the north who hunted big game and one in the south who hunted small animals. The hunter in the north became jealous of the hunter in the south. One day he saw his rival's beautiful wife grinding corn into meal where selu is grown. He grabbed the woman and took her away across the sky to his northern home. The woman's loyal dog ate the cornmeal she had left behind and followed her north. But as he ran along after her, cornmeal fell from the dog's mouth and scattered a trail across the sky. Once in the north, the presence of the captive woman from the south made the weather warm until all the ice began to melt. After some time, the northern hunter could no longer endure the heat and released his captive. The woman returned once again to the south with her dog in tow, and the north cooled once again. This story is repeated each year in Galvladi and on Elohi as summer is taken by winter in the north after each fall harvest and returns to her home in the south when the weather warms.

When "Where the Dog Ran" just touches Elohi's horizon, the traveling soul ventures off into Sky World. A powerful river flows between earth and the Path of Souls, and one must cross this vast distance on a narrow pole. If out of balance, a soul may fall off into the river and be lost. But if a soul makes it across the river, it then follows the path eastward before turning west toward what is called the Land of Twilight. There the path forks, and the soul will face a guardian called *Gitli Noquisi*, the Dog Star, known in the West as Sirius (Lankford, 2007c, 190).

Gitli Noquisi must be fed in order to pass (Hagar 1906, 362). Knowing this, a soul's family will arrange provisions for its journey at the time of burial. Passing the first guardian, the soul continues its journey until another guardian dog star, this time Antares, must be offered food to pass. If the soul does not have enough gifts of food, it remains captive between the two dog guardians, unable to pass back toward Elohi or to move on. But once safely past these trials, the soul heads toward Galvladi to be with its ancestors.

Stories of the Milky Way as the Path of Souls exist among Indigenous peoples across Turtle Island (Lankford 2007c, 179). And while the details are sometimes different, the meaning of the soul's journey remains remarkably similar. Sky World is connected to Elohi, the stories tell, and upon physical death the soul will return to its source. On this journey it will face trials and will be judged, but a life well lived and assistance among the living may assure safe passage. As cycles of death and rebirth on Elohi are measured by seasonal patterns of the stars in Galvladi, we humans continue as well, changing but eternal.

GALAQUOGI DUYODATLV GALVLADI (*The Seven Levels of Heaven*)
by Hastings Shade

In Cherokee teachings, Hastings told me, the conscious soul does not die. Our physical bodies will age, become damaged, and eventually go back into the earth. But our lives as humans and as individuals follow a spiritual journey. This journey, Loretta said, is charted through seven levels. As humanity, we have moved through each level as we have come to experience, relate to, and understand the creatures and forces of Elohi and the cosmos. With each stage, we gain more experience, more knowledge, and a higher consciousness. The same path is followed by each of us as individuals. Our consciousness as an individual self continues to grow until, with enough learning, we come to dwell with our ancestors and Unetlvnv. "The spirit is not gone from here until we reach Creator at the seventh level," Hastings said.

LEVEL 1: The first level consisted of man, water, and everything that lived in the water. But every day he would look above him and see this hole. And every day he would see light shining through this hole that was above him. He was curious as to what it was. So man, in his infinite wisdom, figured out a way to get through the hole that was above him.

LEVEL 2: As he emerged through the hole that was above him, he found plants. He brought the water and things with him. Still there was this hole above him, and he could see the light shining through it. Again, in his wisdom, man figured out a way to get to the next level.

LEVEL 3: When he emerged through the third level, he found animals. Now he had water, everything that lived in the water, plants, and animals. But the hole was still above him, and he could still see this light every day.

LEVEL 4: Again, man figured out a way to get to the next level. Here he found insects. Now he had water, everything that lived in the water, plants, animals, and insects. But still the hole was above him.

LEVEL 5: Again, man figured out how to get to the next level. Here he found the birds. Now he had water, everything that lived in the water, plants, animals, insects, and birds. Still the hole was above him and he could see the light every day.

LEVEL 6: Now the hole that was above him is in the sky, and he has figured out a way to get to the level where the light that he sees every day is. He has developed planes, rockets, and has landed on the moon and landed machines on the planets. Man has learned what powers the sun.

LEVEL 7: But man still has one more level to get to, and that's where the Creator is. According to legend, we started at Level One to get to where we are today.

The Rabbit in the Moon

There is an old teaching Hastings once shared with me about how *Walosi* (Toad) swallows the moon. A long time ago, when folks would periodically see the moon slowly disappear from the night sky, they saw a giant toad swallowing it. The people were disturbed to see moon treated this way. They would beat on drums and make noise to scare off toad, and with the help of the people *nvdo svnoyi ehi* would slowly emerge from Walosi's mouth and the giant toad would leave. Balance was restored. Today we know this phenomenon as an eclipse, but it remains another example of the continuing tension between the beings of Sky World and Under World. Humans stepped in to maintain tohi, which has been our continuing role. Another time, Hastings, Sequoyah, and I were visiting at Ho-Chee-Nee Chapel on the Cherokee Heritage Center grounds when Sequoyah remembered a teaching and shared it with us. Like other stories of Galvladi, it reminds us to be particularly watchful for signs of change in the regular patterns of Sky World, as they may foretell changes to come for us.

"But, touching on something that Hastings said about the moon," Sequoyah said. "I don't remember the whole teaching; it wasn't really a story, but it was something that Grandma touched on now and then. She said if you look at the moon, especially a full moon, you'll see a rabbit up there. The shape of a rabbit. She was telling me that you'll know the world is about to end when the rabbit is upside down."

"Mmhm," Hastings nodded.

"So, slowly, even in my lifetime, I've noticed that rabbit is slowly turning, 'cause I remember back when I was a little boy that rabbit's ears weren't as far down as they are now. They were kind of drooping, but they weren't as far as they are now. I just remember that from Grandma. That teaching, that if you look at the moon you see the rabbit, and when it's upside down that's when the time is going to end."

"They say the moon around 1915, right before World War I, they said the elders were watching the moon and they say it shook, it rocked. The ones who pay attention to it. We can look at it and probably not see it, but the ones who are taught these things can see it," Hastings said. "They said that was a sign of turmoil. And right after that's when World War I started. They said that was a sign that there was going to be a lot of, you know, conflict or a lot of worried times. So, look at the moon." Hastings stopped and stared at part of the chapel's rock wall across the room. "Look at that rock, there's a face in that rock over there. See it?"

Sequoyah stopped and looked over his shoulder for a few moments. "Oh, yeah!" he said.

"But, the moon, they said the moon just rocked this way," Hastings continued. He shaped his hands as if he was holding a ball and rocked them back and forth.

Tlvdatsi Gigage (Red Lion)

One rainy afternoon years ago in Lost City, I sat under the roof of Hastings' open-air workshop with members of the Turtle Island Liars' Club. We were talking, as we sometimes did, about the mysteries of the Sky World and how Cherokee ancestors knew about these phenomena, when Hastings remembered a strange light in the sky he witnessed as a child.

"I was about seven or eight years old at that time. We lived at the old place. It was summertime, and we were lying out in that little old yard out there. We'd just sit out there. And I don't know what time it was, but when I woke up late in the night there was a light coming this way. I remember it coming this way. And behind it, it looked like a flame. But when it got over us it was pulsating. And you could hear it go, '*huunh—huunh*'—like a heavy breath every time it'd flame. And I looked back toward the house, and Grandma and Grandpa was standing on the porch looking at it. And it went on down past us. Just about that time, when I looked up there, they were standing there looking at it."

"You know, when you're little you don't think about stuff. Just accept what you see. But four or five days later I asked Grandma, 'What was that?' She told me it was called 'Red Lion,' *Tlvdatsi Gigage*. She says it passes every seventy-seven years. She said, 'You might see it again, but me and your grandpa will never see it again.' I was seven or eight years old. I'm getting pretty close to that seventy-seven years," Hastings said and laughed.

"What's it called again?" I asked.

"She called it 'Red Lion.' *Tlvdatsi Gigage*. And it looks like a man in the back, every time it breathed in '*huunh*'—just like it was breathing. It would just pulsate. From a distance it looked like fire. And when it got over us it was like something flowing, like that."

"Wow."

"And I asked her, and she said, 'Well, me and your grandpa will never see it again. But you might.' But I remember it was in the summer."

"How big was it?"

"It was pretty good-sized—about like that," Hastings said and spread his arms. "That tail was trailing it. That's what looked like it was pulsating. Just like, you know how hair in the water flows when you're swimming and somebody has long hair. That's what it was doing. It was just pulsating. And you could hear it when it got over us, you could hear it like it was breathing real hard, going '*huunh-hunnh*.' Every time it would do that, it would blow out. And it went on down there. I thought it was going to hit us, but it never did. But they knew it was coming. They knew what night. They were *looking* for it. They were both sitting on the porch looking at it.

"That's probably something that goes way, way back," Woody said.

"Yeah."

"Something from, maybe, migration times," Woody added.

"Yeah, because, how would they know it came every seventy-seven years? The story had to be passed down," Sequoyah said.

"Hundreds of years for that pattern to evolve," I said.

"Yeah. But she said every seventy-seven years. And I remember seeing it; I remember looking at it. I wasn't the only one, too. There were a bunch of us lying out there."

Years later I came across an article from 1906 that said Cherokees once called comets and meteors *Atsila Tlvdatsi*, or Fire Panther. I was reminded of the Red Lion Hastings had seen in his youth, and how his grandparents knew it would come every seventy-seven years. As Woody said, who knows how far back the memory of Tlvdatsi Gigage goes? But like all phenomena, it has meaning. In 1833, they say, when Cherokees lived in their traditional homelands, there was a meteor shower that some interpreted as a bad omen. The Trail of Tears soon followed.

AHYVDAGWALOSGI ALE UK'TAN (*Thunder and Uk'tan*)

by Noyi Teuton

Chroniclers of Cherokee oral tradition including Jack and Anna Kilpatrick, as well as James Mooney before them, recorded stories of how the Cherokee came to define themselves through their special friendship with the being Thunder, Ahyvdagwalosgi. Sometimes called Asgaya Gigage, or Red Man, because he is adorned in the bright red of lightning, Thunder has also been called Kanadi, the Lucky One. He is father to the Little Men, the Thunder Boys who live above in the Sky World in the west and can be heard talking during storms. Thunder is the husband of Selu and is now with her in the Sky World, having left Elohi when our world was new. The origin of the Cherokee friendship with Thunder begins with two boys witnessing a great battle between Sky World and Under World, order and chaos, in the forms of Thunder and Uk'tan. As in other Cherokee stories, the heroes of this foundational myth are not the strongest, fiercest, smartest, or most powerful. They are two children who, as the Kilpatricks note, act out of their innocence and pity, rather than a will to power. And their reward is love and friendship. I retell a version of this story told by Siquanid to the Kilpatricks, and by Sequoyah Guess to me, in the hope that others will pick it up, add to it other details they have heard, and continue to tell it.

Ilvhiyu tsigesv, in the great forever that was, two boys were hunting along a stream in a deep and rocky valley when they came across a large *inada* (snake) lying across a rock.

"*Osiyo*, you two fine hunters," the inada, lifting its head, said to the boys as they approached.

"*Siyo*," the two boys said, keeping their distance.

"I want to ask you something," the inada continued. "As you can see, I'm very thin and hungry. Would you two hunters find me some birds or squirrels to eat? When I get strong again, I'll help you in any way I can as long as we live."

The boys were good hunters, and so they decided to use their skills and help the weakened inada. The next day the boys walked back out to the rocky valley and found the inada in the same spot, lying on a large flat rock by a deep pool in the stream. They tossed the inada two birds and three squirrels. "*Wado*," he said, and within minutes had swallowed all the meat they had brought him.

The boys enjoyed helping the inada, so they walked up the rocky valley many times and brought the inada birds and squirrels to eat. Each time they came, they would toss the birds and squirrels on to the inada's flat rock and stand back and watch it eat. The inada was looking stronger and bigger, and it would wait eagerly at the edge of its rock for its meal.

A few days passed before the boys could come visit the inada again, but when they came at last with birds and squirrels, the inada had grown tremendously. It was now long and thick, hanging over the edges of the rock by the stream. The boys tossed the birds and squirrels to the inada and watched it eat. When it was finished, the snake nodded at the boys and they left.

"It should be strong enough to hunt for itself now," one boy said to the other. "Let's wait a while before we walk back out here and feed it."

A few weeks later, the boys walked up the rocky valley again to the inada's rock by the stream, but the snake was nowhere to be seen.

"Inada, your two hunter friends are here," one of the boys called out.

The boys saw movement from the crag next to the stream, and the inada slowly crawled out from between the rocks. Now the inada was truly enormous. Its body was the size of a large tree and covered with scales of blazingly bright colors. It had grown horns on its head like a deer and out of its forehead grew a large, clear crystal. As it crawled out of the darkness they could see lightning-like sparks shooting around and between the points of its horns.

"You are huge now!" one boy said and tossed the inada several birds and squirrels.

"You are all grown up," said the other boy.

"That's true," the inada said. "But remember what I said, we are to be friends for as long as we live. When you come again and feed me one last time, I will be at my full strength."

The next morning, the boys were hunting nearby when they heard deep crashing and rumbling sounds from the inada's valley. Several loud claps rang out as if the sky was cracking, but then the sounds became faint.

"What is that crashing sound?" one boy said. "Somebody may be in trouble over there! Let's go and see if we can help. That's where inada lives!"

The boys ran up the rocky valley along the narrow stream. When they arrived at the inada's home they saw their friend they had fed coiled around a man draped in a red glow, with white, blue, and yellow sparks flashing about his body. The boys could see inada and this man were fighting, and as the snake hissed and squeezed tighter, faint rumbles and cracks came from the red man. He could barely move.

"*Anichuja*! Boys! My grandchildren!" the man called out. "My name is *Ahyvdagwalosgi*. This inada coiled around me is *Uk'tan*. It is very fierce and kills people. I need your help. If you're able, shoot him in the seventh spot on his body. It will kill him!"

"*Tla*! *Tla*!" the Uk'tan cried. "No! Kill Thunder! He is more ferocious than me! His lightning will kill you! I am your friend!"

The boys did not know who to believe or what to do.

"You boys are my grandchildren and I am the helper of your people," Thunder said. "Uk'tan is not your friend, he only tricked you! He would kill you both, as he's killed other people. Shoot him on the seventh spot behind his head!"

Hearing these words, the boys believed Thunder. As Uk'tan cried out, they shot two arrows right in its seventh spot. Uk'tan died instantly and Thunder was free again.

"Wado, grandchildren," said Thunder and rose to his feet. As he stretched his body, a rumble echoed throughout the rocky valley and the smell of rain filled the air. "Now go back home the way you came here. Along the way, build seven fires. The Uk'tan can still kill you with its smell, but if you set those fires it will stop it. The smell will be stopped by the first fire, which will give you time to run ahead and start another. The smell will follow you, but once you build the seventh fire you will be safe. I will help you along the way."

"You and your people may always rely upon me," Thunder continued. "Until the end of the world, we must protect and help each other. I am *ugvwiyuhi* (chief) of all the fierce things in the world."

The boys did as they were told and escaped. They had decided to believe Thunder, and because of their trust Thunder will remain with the Cherokees as long as they exist. Some still fear Thunder, but Unetlvnv made it that human beings and Thunder should live together always as friends and protectors. When Thunder is called upon, he protects the Cherokee.

Doyadila Nusdidanv (Weather)

While our spirits come from the stars, Cherokee tradition traces life on Elohi back to the originating influences of Thunder and Corn Woman. When those two boys chose to help Thunder, a force of Sky World, and defeat Uk'tan, a force of the Under World, they aligned themselves and the Cherokee people thereafter with order over chaos, light over darkness, continuing life from temporary death. In Thunder, the Cherokee now had an ally with power over all weather, *doyadila nusdidanv*. Together with his wife *Selu*, the Cherokee people were provided with sustenance—corn from Selu's body and game from Kanadi's cave. But as is always the case in Cherokee thought, everything exists in delicate balances of tohi. While Thunder may control the weather, is it not *ama* (water) from the Under World that provides the conditions for life? A world without ama is lifeless. And did not Kanadi's game come from a cave, part of the Under World? Yes, Uk'tan was created by the Thunder Boys to kill Sun, but though it could not do so, the transformative powers of the Under World shape life on Elohi. And so the paradox is clear: though they have separate natures, the powers of Sky World and Under World are intermingled, both necessary for continuing life. We witness this dynamic relationship play out daily in what we call the weather.

In speaking of the weather, Hastings once explained to me to honor four forces: Fire, Wind, Earth, and Water. Each of these forces is alive. They can be listened to, if one is attentive, and a person may communicate with them as well. These forces are necessary for life, but they may also take life in an instant. Each force is also associated with a specific world. *Atsila* (fire) is a gift of the Sky World from Unetlvnv and exists with *gada* (earth) on Elohi. *Unole* (wind) is a force of Sky World. And *ama* comes from the Under World.

The transformational power of these forces of Sky World and Under World is expressed when they interact on Elohi. Roiling wind touches still water and creates waves. Water rises to the sky in dark clouds and comes back down to Elohi as *agasga* (rain) announced by thunder and *anagalisgi* (lightning), which in turn may bring fire. With the regular turn of the Sky World's seasons, *ama* is transformed into *unatsi* (snow) in the winter but becomes water once more in spring. Through the mediating power of the earth, the powerful opposing forces of Sky World and Under World become peaceful and generate life.

While it may appear that we human beings are powerless amidst these forces greater than ourselves, stories such as the battle between Thunder and Uk'tan teach that we do have a role to play in Sky World and Under World forces on Elohi. In a conversation Loretta Shade and I had with Cherokee elders Melvina King and Dorothy Ice, we discussed how Cherokees read patterns of the weather and speak to these powers.

"We didn't have radios a long time ago to tell us if a tornado was coming," Melvina said.

"Just our grandparents. They were our weather people," Dorothy said, and everyone laughed.

"Well, the weather wasn't so chaotic as it is now," Loretta said. We all agreed. "You know, our grandparents observed everything. They didn't use calendars or watch TV. When I was a child we'd hunt crawdads at night. Sometimes Grandpa would say, 'Tonight's not a good night.' And then we wouldn't go. Then when I was older, he told me why. 'We always hunt crawdads by the full of the moon,' he said. 'That's when their tails are fuller.'"

"My grandpa lived in an old log house," Melvina said. "Whenever there was a storm, all these people from Jay would stop at his house to take shelter. He said, 'All these people live in better houses than me. They could hide in their own houses,'" Melvina said, and we laughed. "But he knew how to use that axe, and that was why they came."

"Swing that axe around and talk to that cloud," Dorothy said. "Or bring the rain."

In speaking of her grandfather's use of an axe, Melvina was referring to the well-known tradition of speaking to an *aguluga* (twister) and swinging an axe into a stump to petition it to split and pass by. As passed down through family members, some people know the proper words to speak and actions to take to enter into relationship with forces of the weather. In such ways, the friendship of the Cherokee people and Thunder continues.

CONTROLLING THE ELEMENTS ✦ *by Hastings Shade*

Even during my short life I've seen the ones who could control the elements and change into different things.

My great uncle could make it rain. My aunt's husband could control the lightning. Some could control the storms. I've seen an old man cross a creek and not get wet. Someone will probably say, "So what? There's nothing amazing about that." There isn't. Except for the fact that there was a big water strider come across the water just before he appeared on the side of the creek we were on. The creek at that point was about eight to ten foot deep and about thirty yards across, with a steep bank on the side we were on. And he was close to eighty years old. One minute you see him on one side of the creek, the next he is standing next to you. It didn't bother me at the time, but as I got older I began to wonder how he had done that. When I asked Dad, he just said, the elders knew how to change into different things. That is all that was said about it.

My uncle, the one who could make it rain, told the people around him as he lay on his deathbed that if there ever came a drought, all they had to do was take a bucket of water and pour it on his grave. It would rain.

The dad of one of my cousins told him one time when we were in a drought to go pour water on my uncle's grave.

My cousin said he went and got a five-gallon bucket and filled it up and took it to the graveyard. He poured the whole bucketful on our uncle's grave. The next day it started raining—and it rained for three days straight! My cousin said he began to get scared. He thought he might have poured too much on the grave and it wouldn't quit raining.

Our uncle did say not to abuse the rain and to use his grave only when we really needed it.

ᎰᏍᏆ ᏗᎦᏎᏍᏙᏗ ᏓᏓᏁᏟᏴᏏᏙᎲ
ᏙᏯᏗᏢ ᏂᎦᎵᏍᏗᏙᎲ
(*Signs of Weather Change*)

ᎠᎯᎦᏴᎵ ᏣᏂᏜᏓ—ᎰᏍᏆ, ᏫᎾᏓᏃᎯᏏ ᏰᏓᎦᏎᏍᏔᏅ ᏙᏯᏗᏢ ᏂᎦᎵᏍᏗᏙᎲ ᏯᏅᏓᏁᏟᏴᏏ. ᏚᏢᎬ ᏣᎦᏅᏗᏴ ᏣᏏᎩᏔ ᏃᏉ ᎣᏍᏓ ᎨᏎᏍᏗ ᎢᎦ.

ᎠᏰᏟᎨᏍᏗᏍᎩᏂ ᏩᎾᎩᏔ ᏅᏓᏁᏟᏴᏏ.

ᎦᏙᎢ ᎾᏂᎨᏍᏗ ᏫᏗᏁᏙ ᏙᏅᏁᏤᏴᏝᏗ ᎠᎾᏗᏍᎪ.

ᏊᎾᏁᏍᎩ ᏗᎦᏍᏎᏍᏙᏗ ᏃᏉ ᏩᏏᏔᏅᎾ ᎦᏅᏔᏗ ᏯᎩ ᎤᏬᏚ ᎨᎮᏍᏗ ᏙᏫᏗᏢ ᎡᎳᏗ ᎾᎾᏁᎨᎢ ᏍᎩᏃᏩᏍᏗ ᎡᎳᏗ ᏓᏂᏏᏔᏅᏍᎪ—

ᎡᏚᏓ ᎩᎨᏒ ᎯᎠ ᏯᎦᏜᏍᏓ ᎨᏒ—ᎢᎦ ᎤᏳᏒᏍᏓ ᏗᏔ ᏯᏅᏜᏤ ᎤᏧᏧ ᏤᎾᎴᏍᏗᏬᏗᏔ ᏅᏓᏁᏟᏴᏏ ᏙᏫᏗᏔ ᏂᎦᎵᏍᏗᎲᎢ.

ᎡᎯᏰᎢᏗᏔ ᏅᏔᏏᎧᎾ ᏯᏅᏜᏤ. ᏤᎾᎴ ᎡᎯᏰ ᎠᎴ ᏤᎾᎴ ᎤᏒᎢ ᎩᏔ ᏫᏓᏁᏟᏴᎠ ᎦᏙᎾᏩᏍᏗ ᎠᎴ ᏯᏳᏚᎵ ᎢᏍᏙᏗ. ᎧᏓ ᎤᎵᏏᎬ ᏅᏍᏅ ᎦᎴᏴᏍᏗ, ᏗᎨᏅᏍᏗ ᎠᎴ ᏗᎫᎭᎵᏗ ᎠᎴ ᎦᏔᏳᏗ, ᏗᎪᏢᎢᏗ ᏲᏚᎵ.

ᏞᏯᏗᎬᏍᎷᏯ ᎤᎦ ᎡᎳᏗ ᏅᏍᏙᎢ ᎪᎯᏓ ᏯᏓᎴᎧᎦ. Ꮭ ᏯᎬᏳᎪᎯ.

SIGNS OF WEATHER CHANGE
by Hastings Shade

The elders say to watch the birds and you can tell if there is going to be a weather change.

If the birds were high in the tree, the weather would stay fair; and if they were about midway, the weather was due to change.

If the birds were close to the ground, there would be a cold spell.

Watch where the spider spins its web: high up means fair weather, lower down means weather change; this would drive the insects low.

Grandpa used to say to listen to the "old man," meaning the owl. If he hoots early in the afternoon, expect weather change before morning. If late in the day, you usually have the next day until the weather changes.

Anitsisqua (Birds)

Anitsisqua are of the Sky World. Though they may make their nests in trees and on land, they of all Elohi's creatures are most at home in the sky. And so it is natural, in Cherokee thought, that through observing their actions, behaviors, and teachings human beings may understand the patterns of Sky World as they relate to our life on Elohi. When one listens to the birds, as Loretta told me, they will teach you about your world.

Though flyers come in an incredible variety of shapes, forms, colors, and habits, they all share purpose, beauty, and economy in their unique expressions. They are industrious beings, always on the move. And they are curious creatures, forever attuned to changes in the weather and their environment. They are fierce hunters who cross boundaries between worlds, taking prey in the air, on land, and from the waters. And when the seasons change or their food disappears, birds migrate, flying incredible distances to their other homes.

In Cherokee tradition, anitsisqua are the messengers of Sky World. Through their song and behaviors they teach us of Sky World's regular patterns of seasons and weather on Elohi. And through their beauty, nobility, and free movement of their graceful bodies they remind us of the ordered cosmos. For these reasons and more, particular anitsisqua symbolize communication, eloquence, foresight, knowledge, and other important Cherokee values.

Birds

ᎠᏂᏥᏍᏆ ◆ anitsisqua (ah-nee-jee-squah) ◆ **birds**

ᏗᎦᏍᏆᏂ ◆ digasquani (dee-gah-sgwah-nee) ◆ **American coot, or mud hen** ◆ Name means: short-legged

ᎠᎵᏎ ◆ alise (ah-lee-seh) ◆ **American dipper** ◆ This is the bird that goes under water close to the edge when it is looking for something to eat.

ᎤᏦᏁᏓ ◆ utsoneda (oo-joh-neh-dah) ◆ **American redstart** ◆ Name means: tail shaking or tail spreading

ᏥᏯᏚᎢ ◆ tsiyadui (jee-yah-doo-ee) ◆ **American woodcock** ◆ Name means: looking for worms, or *utsayaduyoi*

ᏑᎵ ᎠᎦᏴᎵ ◆ suli agayvli (soo-lee ah-gah-yuh-lee) ◆ **ancient buzzard**

SULI AGAYVLI (*The Ancient Buzzard*) ◆ *by Hastings Shade*

Suli Agayvli, as our ancestors called him back then, means "the Ancient Buzzard." In the legend that tells of when all of the Cherokees were on the giant turtle's back floating around in the sky and the earth was still covered with soft mud, Suli Agayvli was huge. It began to get too crowded, and people were falling off the giant turtle. Suli Agayvli was told to go and try to find some land that was solid enough for people to live on. As he flew around the world he couldn't find any place that was solid enough to land. He began to tire and started to fly lower. As he did this, his wings dipped into the soft mud, and as he flapped his wings he began to create the mountains that we see. So he was called back, so that the whole earth wouldn't be nothing but mountains. This is how we know him and how mountains were formed.

ᎠᏂᎩᎾ • anigina (ah-nee-gee-nah) • **anhinga, or water turkey**

ᏝᎺᎭ • dlameha (dlah-meh-ha) • **bat** • "You have to include bat with the birds. One day when the animals and the birds had a stickball game, the animals didn't want the bat playing on their team because he was too little and they didn't know if he was an animal or a bird. It was with his help that the birds won the stickball game. Scientists say he is a mammal. But Indians say he is a bird for the reason mentioned above. The animals didn't want him, so the birds took him." H.S.

ᏗᏍᏚᎳᏂ • disdulani (dee-sdoo-lah-nee) • **bittern** • Name means: having big feet, or *disduleni*

ᏍᏆᎵᏍᏗ • squalisdi (sgwah-lee-sdee) • **blackbird** • "In the winter time," Larry Shade said, "you see blackbirds gather. Grandma would always say, 'Ni!' Look! It's gonna turn cold. And it holds true to this very day. When you see blackbirds gather or fly in groups, within a few days the weather turns cold."

Tsawolade (bluebird)

ᏣᏩᏳᎩ • tsawayugi (jah-wah-yoo-gee) • **blackbird, red-winged** • Used for a woman's name. Also known as *tsowasga*.

ᏝᎢᎦ • dlaiga (dlah-ee-gah) • **blue jay**

ᏗᏏ • disi (dee-see) • **blue-gray gnatcatcher**

ᏣᏬᎳᏕ • tsawolade (jah-wohl-deh) • **bluebird** • When you see the first bluebird in spring then the weather is going to change for the better. It will start getting warmer.

DLAIGA (*Blue Jay*) • *by Hastings Shade*

This is the tattletale of the birds. Grandpa said if you don't tell the blue jay you're going hunting, when he sees you out in the woods, he'll tell everyone out in the woods where you are at. He'll follow you around all day hollering. So, to this day, when I go hunting, I always tell the blue jay: "I'm going to be in the woods hunting." He usually leaves me alone. As the elders would say, "If you don't believe me . . . try it."

SULI (*Buzzard*) ✦ *by Hastings Shade*

The buzzard or vulture is mentioned more in Cherokee folklore than the eagle or the hawk. The buzzard is one of the birds that tried to get the fire for the Cherokees and burnt the feathers off his head. The smoke dulled his sense of smell—that's why, to this day, when he eats carrion he doesn't know that it's spoiled! He is also mentioned when the earth was still covered with water but was then known as the Ancient One.

TSIGALILI (*Chickadee*) ✦ *by Hastings Shade*

This is the bird that tells you when someone is coming to see you. If you watch him when you are outside, he will get real close to you. This is when he is telling you someone is coming to see you. But most of us have forgotten how to listen anymore. It is also known as the gossiper and the messenger.

ᎠᏓ ᎪᎷᏂ ✦ ada goluni (ah-dah goh-loo-nee) ✦ **brown creeper** ✦ Name means: wood trailer

ᏙᎴᏆ ✦ tolequa (toh-leh-gwa) ✦ **brown-headed cowbird**

ᏑᎵ ✦ suli (soo-lee) ✦ **buzzard, or vulture** ✦ Associated with nvwoti. Suli eats things others cannot.

ᏩᎵᏰᎵ ✦ waliyeli (wah-lee-yeh-lee) ✦ **canary** ✦ Name means: I am thinking

ᎤᏥᎹ ✦ utsima (oo-jee-mah) ✦ **catbird**

ᎦᏃᏢ ✦ ganotlv (gah-noh-tluh) ✦ **cedar waxwing** ✦ Name means: up against

Tsigalili (chickadee)

ᏥᎦᎵᎵ ✦ tsigalili (jee-gah-lee-lee) ✦ **chickadee** ✦ A messenger. ✦ *"In Cherokee tradition,* tsigalili *symbolizes communication—*diganotsalidi—ᏗᎦᏃᏣᎵᏗ." *H.S.*

ᏥᏔᎦ ✦ tsitaga (jee-tah-gah) ✦ **chicken** ✦ The chicken is much like the dog. The Indians had some, but they were a little different than the ones we see now. They were more of a wild variety.

KANATSEDALI ALE WALELI (*Crane and Hummingbird*)
by Hastings Shade

Kanatsedali is a catchall name for the crane species. There is a legend that tells of a race between Crane and Hummingbird. Once, the Crane and the Hummingbird both liked the same girl. But the girl liked Hummingbird because he was so handsome with his pretty colors. Crane was just plain white. Her mother had told her to marry the one that could provide her with the things that she would need. She knew that it would be the Crane, but she wanted to marry Hummingbird. So she came up with this plan. Hummingbird and Crane would race. The race would be around the world and she would marry the winner, which she thought would be Hummingbird because he flew so fast that you could hardly see him. On the day of the race they lined up, the girl said go, and with that Hummingbird was gone. He left Crane way behind. The Hummingbird flew all day, and when evening came he looked for a place to roost. The Crane just kept flying in the evening and passed where Hummingbird was roosting toward morning. At daylight he stopped to eat. He was eating when Hummingbird passed him. Hummingbird wondered how Crane had passed him. This went on for six days. On the evening of the sixth day, Crane passed where Hummingbird was roosting early in the evening. So he had a big lead on him by the time morning came. He stopped to preen himself, so he could look good when he passed the finish line, which he did right before noon on the seventh day. In the afternoon, Hummingbird came in. The Crane had won. This made the girl so mad she didn't marry either one. Just because something looks good doesn't always make it the best.

Kanatsedali
(crane)

ᏥᏔᎦ ᎤᏍᏗ • tsitaga usdi (jee-tah-gah oo-sdee) • **chicken, bantam** • Name means: small chicken

ᏥᏔᎩᎠ • tsitagia (jee-tah-gee-ah) • **chicken, prairie**

ᏗᎫᎵᏗᏍᎩ ᎪᏍᏓᏯ • digulidisgi gosdaya (dee-goo-lee-dee-sgee goh-sdah-yah) • **chimney swift** • Name means: keen dirt dauber

ᎠᏥᏓ • atsida (ah-jee-dah) • **cormorant** • Name means: short version of *atsadi diganiisgi*, or the one that catches fish.

ᎦᎾᏤᏓᎵ • kanatsedali (kah-nah-jeh-dah-lee) • **crane** • *"In Cherokee tradition,* kanatsedali *symbolizes eloquence*—ulilohi—ᎤᎵᎶᏂ*." H.S.*

ᎦᎾᏤᏓᎴ ᎡᏆ • kanatsedale equa (kah-nah-jeh-dah-leh ew-gwah) • **crane, whooping** • Name means: the big crane

ᎧᏴᏍᏆᎴᎾ • kayvsqualena (kah-yuh-sgwah-leh-nah) • **crossbill** • Name means: twisted nose

ᎪᎦ • koga (koh-gah) • **crow** • Named for the sound the crow makes. • "An old legend says that the crow was white at one time. As he tried to get the fire, the smoke turned him black. He has been black ever since." H.S.

ᏚᏘ • tuti (too-tee) • **dark-eyed junco, or snow bird**

ᏃᏈᏏ ᎠᏰᎵ • noquisi ayeli (noh-gwee-see ah-yeh-lee) • **dickcissel** • Name means: acts or looks like a meadowlark

ᎫᎴ ᏗᏍᎪᏂ • gule disgoni (goo-leh dee-sgoh-nee) • **dove, mourning**

ᏗᎦᏃᏣᏟ • diganotsatli (dee-gah-noh-jah-tlee) • **dove, rock, or rock pigeon** • Name means: message or news carrier. Same as homing pigeon.

ᎧᏬᏄ • kawonu (kah-woh-noo) • **duck** • A name used for the domesticated duck and when a duck cannot be identified.

ᎧᏬᎾᎭ • kawonaha (kah-woh-nah-hah) • **duck, canvasback** • Name means: all duck or principal duck

GULE DISGONI (*Mourning Dove*) • *by Hastings Shade*

The name means, "He Who Cries for Acorns." The elders say when you hear the first dove of spring, it means winter is over. They also say when you hear the first dove in the spring cooing to the west of you, toward where the sun goes down, you may not be living to hear him again the next spring.

AWOHALI UNEGA (*Bald Eagle*) ✦ *by Hastings Shade*

The bald eagle is used much like the golden eagle, but its feathers are not worn as much as the golden eagle's. Its feathers are made into fans and other things. It has beautiful white tail feathers. These are tied onto dancing sticks. Every part of the eagle is used; nothing is wasted. The claws are used for necklaces, the small feathers for decorations, and other parts of the body for different things.

AWOHALI (*Golden Eagle*) ✦ *by Hastings Shade*

To the Cherokees and many other tribes, the eagle is a bird that is revered above all others. The Indians believe that since he could fly the highest he was closest to the Creator and could see all things that were ahead for the Indians because of his superior eyesight. His feathers are worn with honor. The one who wore these feathers believed he had some of the same powers that the eagle had. To this day, the feathers are passed down to sons and other family members. The only time the feathers are buried is when the owner finds no one worthy enough to leave the feathers with. If the feathers are not buried with the owner for some reason, they will decay and fall apart. But if they are left with someone they will keep until the owner decides what to do with them.

To the Cherokee there are four ways you can get an eagle feather: through battle with a foe, or honoring a brave deed, or handed down to you, or as a gift from a medicine person. However you get one, eagle feathers are to be treated with respect. Respect to the giver, respect to the bird. This is how we Indians are.

The golden eagle is also known to the Indians as the war eagle. One way to get an eagle feather for young men was through battle. After battle, feathers were given in special dances. Some of the dancers were those who had earned the feathers by being a fierce fighter or doing something that was brave. The feather was worn during battle and special ceremonies; fashioned into elaborate headdresses or in the hair of the warrior; or made into a fan and carried in this manner or tied to a dance stick. However the feather is worn or carried, it is done in great honor. If a feather falls during a dance or ceremony, everyone stops, and the elders do a special ceremony before the feather is picked up and returned to the owner. Some say it's a bad omen for the wearer of the feather; this is why elders pray over it before it is picked up and given back.

ᎩᎦᎨ ᎠᏆᏍᏓᏗ • gigage aquasdadi (gee-gah-geh ah-gwa-sdah-dee) • **duck, redhead** • Name means: having a red head

ᎤᏯᏢ • uyatli (oo-yah-tlee) • **duck, ring-necked** • Name means: having something around its neck

ᎠᏬᎭᎵ ᎤᏁᎦ • awohali unega (ah-woh-hah-lee oo-neh-gah) • **eagle, bald** • *"In Cherokee tradition,* awohali unega *symbolizes foresight*—vdelohosgi—ᎥᏕᎶᎰᏍᎩ." *H.S.*

ᎠᏬᎭᎵ • awohali(ah-woh-hah-lee) • **eagle, golden, or war eagle** • Also known as *uwodu* tsugidatli, or beautiful feathers. • *"In Cherokee tradition,* awohali *symbolizes knowledge*—agatanai—ᎠᎦᏔᎾᎢ." *H.S.*

ᏣᏯᏂ • tsayani (jah-yah-nee) • **egret, American** • Name means: he is calling you

ᏩᎦ ᎠᏍᏓᏫᏗᏙ • waga asdawidido (wah-gah ah-sda-wee-dee-doh) • **egret, cattle** • Name means: follows cows around

ᏝᎿᏩ • tlahnawa (tlah-hnah-wah) • **falcon** • "Indians also wear the feathers of all the hawks, as they are related to the eagle, with similar qualities. They fly high and have great eyesight. These feathers are worn with honor also. The young men and boys get hawk feathers before they get eagle feathers." H.S.

ᎤᏦᏁᏓ • utsoneda (oo-joh-neh-dah) • **finch, purple** • Name means: tail spread out or tail shaking

ᎤᏘᎷᎩ • utilugi (oo-tee-loo-gee) • **flicker, northern** • Name means: head held up or looking up

ᏁᎦᏓ • negada (neh-gah-dah) • **flicker, yellow-shafted** • Name means: all as one

ᏧᎵᏍᏚᎵ • tsulisduli (joo-lee-sdoo-lee) • **flycatcher, great crested** • Name means: wearing caps

ᏕᏫ • dewi (deh-wee) • **flying squirrel** • "The flying squirrel has to be included with the birds for the same reason as the bat. The animals didn't want him on their team, so the birds let him play on their side during the stickball game. Scientists classify him as a mammal, but the Indians know different. How do I know this? The elders said so, and I believe them." H.S.

ᏌᏌ • sasa (sah-sah) • **goose** • The name used for the domesticated goose or any that cannot be identified. • *"In Cherokee tradition,* sasa *symbolizes fidelity*—gohiyuidi—ᎪᎯᏳᎢᏗ." *H.S.*

ᏓᎦᏢᎦ • dagatluga (dah-gah-tloo-gah) • **goose, blue**

ᏓᎦᎷᎦ • dagaluga (dah-gah-loo-gah) • **goose, snow** • "The elders say, when the geese begin to fly either north or south, as they come over, you are supposed to say, 'I'll be here when you all come back through again.' This way you will see them again. Don't ever mock what they're saying, otherwise you might not be around next time they come back." H.S.

ᎠᎦᏄᎦ • aganuga (ah-gah-noo-gah) • **goose, greater white-fronted**

ᏝᎾᏩ ᎤᏍᏗ • tlahnawa usdi (tlah-hnah-wah oo-sdee) • **goshawk** • The name in Cherokee means "little falcon." As it flies around, its silhouette looks like the larger falcon. So they named it the little falcon.

ᏥᏍᏆᏲᎦ • tsisquayoga (jee-sgwa-yoh-gah) • **grackle, common**

ᎤᎵᏂᏖᎩᏓ • ulinitegida (oo-lee-nee-teh-gee-dah) • **grosbeak** • Name means: twisted

ᎫᏊ ᎦᎾᏞᎢ • guque ganatlai (goo-gweh ga-nah-tlah-ee) • **guinea fowl** • Name means: tamed quail

ᎠᏚᏘ • aduti (ah-doo-tee) • **gull**

ᏔᏬᏗ • tawodi (tah-woh-dee) • **hawk** • This name covers all hawks. When one cannot be identified, it is called this name, *tawodi*. It's a catchall name for the hawk group. • *"In Cherokee tradition,* tawodi *symbolizes deliberation*—agasesdodi—ᎠᎦᏎᏍᏙᏗ.*" H.S.*

ᏥᎩᎵ • tsigili (jee-gee-lee) • **hawk, broad-winged**

ᏗᎦᏔᏅᎯᏓ • digatanvhida (dee-gah-tah-nuh-hee-dah) • **hawk, Cooper's** • Name means: the one with the long eyes

ᏝᏄᏩ • tlanuwa (tlah-noo-wah) • **hawk, mythical** • "The elders say at one time this hawk was big enough to carry off little children and often did this to feed its young. No one knows what happened to the hawk. One day it was gone. Could this have been one of the large birds that is now extinct? We can only wonder." H.S.

ᎩᏯ • giya (gee-yah) • **hawk, prairie, or rabbit hawk** • This hawk can be seen flying across a field. It is almost as large as the red-tailed hawk. The elders said it was hunting rabbits when they would see it flying around.

ᏗᎦᏘᏍᎩ • digatisgi (dee-gah-tee-sgee) • **hawk, red-shouldered** • Name means: the one that peeks. You can see it sitting in a tree on the edge of a field somewhere looking. Grandpa said, *agateno*, or "he is looking around."

ᏏᏄᏩ • sinuwa (see-noo-wah) • **hawk, red-tailed** • The hawk's feathers are still used in decorations and are worn in the hair. This is one of the bigger hawks.

Tsitsi (sparrow hawk)

ᏗᎦᏛᏅᎯᏓ ✦ digatvnvhida (dee-gah-tuh-nuh-hee-dah) ✦ **hawk, sharp-shinned** ✦ Name means: the long-shinned one

ᏥᏥ ✦ tsitsi (jee-jee) ✦ **hawk, sparrow** ✦ The small hawk has the same name as the dart for the blow gun. We do not know which got the name first, the hawk or the dart. They both fly fast. ✦ *"In Cherokee tradition,* tsitsi *symbolizes perseverance*—nigvyaisv—ᏂᎬᏯᎢᏒ." *H.S.*

ᎧᎾᏍᎪᏩ ✦ kanasgowa (kah-nah-sgoh-wah) ✦ **heron, great blue**

ᏍᏆᏯ ✦ squaya (sqwah-yah) ✦ **heron, green**

ᏅᏓ ᏗᎧᏂ ✦ nvda dikani (nuh-dah dee-kah-nee) ✦ **heron, little blue** ✦ Name means: looks at the sun

ᎧᎾᏍᎪᎦ ᎤᏍᏗᏟ ✦ kanasgoga usditli (kah-nah-sgoh-gah oo-sdee-tlee) ✦ **heron, yellow-crowned night** ✦ Name means: with a tuft or a crown on its head

ᏩᎴᎵ ✦ waleli (wah-leh-lee) ✦ **hummingbird** ✦ Also called *walela*. This is the one who had the race with the crane and lost. Known as the little bitty, wise, fast one.

ᎧᏴᏌᏅᎯᏓ ✦ kayvsanvhida (kah-yuh-sah-nuh-hee-dah) ✦ **ibis** ✦ Name means: long nose or long beak. Catchall name for ibis.

ᎠᎵ ᏣᏃᏍᎩ ✦ ali tsanosgi (ah-lee jah-noh-sgee) ✦ **indigo bunting** ✦ Also known as *tsowila*.

ᎫᏫᏍᎫᏫ ✦ guwisguwi (goo-wee-sgoo-wee) ✦ **killdeer** ✦ This name is still used as a boys' name among our people. It is also the name for one of the districts in the Cherokee Nation.

ᏓᎳᏆ ✦ dalaqua (dah-lah-gwah) ✦ **kingbird**

ᏣᏠᎢ ✦ tsatloi (jah-tloh-ee) ✦ **kingfisher**

TSATLOI (*Kingfisher*) ✦ *by Hastings Shade*

This is the bird to which the Creator gave the spear. But he couldn't use it like a regular spear. So he asked the Creator to give him something else he could use. The Creator said, "I can't do that, because the spear is yours. But I can fix it where you can use it." So the Creator put the spear on the kingfisher's beak. That's why now you can see him spearing fish along the creek or wherever there is water that has fish in it.

ᎠᏥᎳ ᎤᏍᏗᏟ • atsila usditli (ah-jee-lah oo-sdee-tlee) • **kinglet, golden-crowned** • Name means: fire on its head

ᏔᏣᎳᎩ • tatsalagi (tah-jah-lah-gee) • **kinglet, ruby-crowned**

ᏩᏔᏰᎵ • watayeli (wah-tah-yeh-lee) • **magpie**

ᏡᏡ • dludlu (dloo-dloo) • **martin, purple** • This name is still used to name boys in our tribe.

ᏃᏡᏏ • noquisi (noh-quee-see) • **meadowlark, eastern** • Name means: star

ᎧᏬᏂ ᎤᏍᏗᏟ • kawoni usditli (kah-woh-nee oo-sdee-tlee) • **merganser, hooded** • Name means: duck with a crown

ᏧᏍᎦ ᏗᎩᏍᎩ • tsusga digisgi (joo-sgah dee-gee-sgee) • **mockingbird**

TSUSGA DIGISGI (*Mockingbird*) • *by Hastings Shade*

Tsusga digisgi means "He Who Eats Heads." Legend tells that the mockingbird didn't have a voice, and he wanted one. He listened to the other birds singing and wished he could sing, too. One day, one of the smaller birds said, "Let me look into your throat. There may be something stuck in there that's keeping you from singing." Mockingbird opened his mouth and the little bird looked into it. The Mockingbird couldn't keep his mouth open any longer, so he shut his mouth. As he did this he bit the little bird's head off and swallowed it. Immediately, he had the smaller bird's voice. This gave him an idea. He thought, "If I can get some more bird heads, I can have their voices." So he began to ask anyone who would do it to look into his throat to see if anything was stuck in it. When one of them looked in, he would bite its head off. He continued to do this until one day the Creator found him and told him, "Since you have stolen all those voices, whenever you sing from now on, you will have to use all the voices that you have, even if you have to sing all night long." So that is why you can hear the mockingbird singing all night in the spring. I know it's true because the elders said so.

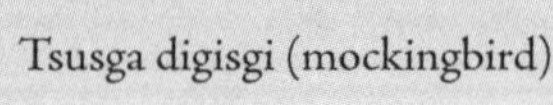

Tsusga digisgi (mockingbird)

ᎱᎱ • huhu (hoo-hoo) • **mockingbird, yellow, or yellow-breasted chat**

ᎦᎾᏍᏙᎦ • ganasdoga (gah-nah-sdoh-gah) • **nighthawk** • The nighthawk is also known as the bullbat. As it dives, the air rushing over its wings makes a roaring sound. This is where it gets the name of bull bat.

ᏧᎵᏰᎾ • tsuliyena (joo-lee-yeh-nah) • **nuthatch, brown-headed** • Name means: hard of hearing. Also called *dayaisgi*, or getting them out.

ᏕᏫ ᏓᎶᏂ • dewi daloni (deh-wee dah-loh-nee) • **nuthatch, red-breasted**

ᏕᏫ ᏯᎶᏂ • dewi yaloni (deh-wee yah-loh-nee) • **nuthatch, white-breasted** • If you don't watch how you say the names, you can get the red-breasted and the white-breasted nuthatches mixed up.

ᏩᏓᎦ • wadaga (wah-dah-gah) • **oriole, Baltimore**

ᏬᎴᏓ • woleda (woh-leh-dah) • **oriole, orchard**

ᎠᏣᏗ ᏗᎦᏂᏱᏍᎩ • atsadi diganiyisgi (ah-jah-dee dee-gah-nee-yee-sgee) • **osprey** • Name means: the one that catches fish. The fisherman of the birds. Also called *kanutsuwa*.

ᎠᏌᎷᎩ • asalugi (ah-sah-loo-gee) • **ovenbird** • Name means: tail shaking or tail wagging

ᎤᎫᎫ • uguku (oo-goo-koo) • **owl** • This owl has the same meaning to the Indian as the *sgili*. He is a messenger also. He rarely comes around a home.

ᏗᏍᏕᏥ • disdetsi (dee-sdeh-jee) • **owl, barn** • Name means: the one that hunts rats or mice, or *tsisdetsi tsuyohi*

ᏍᎩᎵ • sgili (sgee-lee) • **owl, great horned**

ᏗᎦᎵᏍᏆᎵ • digalisquali (dee-gah-lee-sgwa-lee) • **owl, long-eared** • Name means: having long ears

SGILI (*Great Horned Owl*) • *by Hastings Shade*

The name *sgili* means ghost, or sometimes witch. To Cherokees, he is a bad omen, the Death Messenger. He is a woodland creature. His place is in the forest. When he begins to come around a home, which is not his regular place to be, Cherokees think he is bringing a message of someone's death. Not always the people that live there, but it could be someone they know. That is why people don't like him to come to their home.

WAHU'I (*Screech Owl*) ✦ *by Hastings Shade*

This little owl is the one that the Indians believe is someone who comes to look in on them. The old saying is you can tell if it is a real owl if it starts hollering near your home. All you have to do is tie a corner of your bed sheet or your shirt tail in a knot. If it keeps hollering than it is real. If it quits after you do this, then it was someone. The elders say, "If you don't believe me . . . try it."

Wahu'i (screech owl)

ᏩᏁᎢ ✦ wahui (wah-hoo-ee) ✦ **owl, screech**

Ꮵ Ᏸ ᏍᏗ ✦ tsiyesdi (jee-yeh-sdee) ✦ **parakeet, Carolina** (extinct) ✦ Elders describe this bird—*ayelv itsiyusdi gigage askoli:* green body with a red head.

ᎬᎾ ᏧᎩᏓᏟ ✦ gvna tsugidatli (guh-nah joo-gee-dah-tlee) ✦ **peacock** ✦ "The elders say it's not good to have the feathers of the peacock in the house. Because of the shape on the feathers that looks like an eye. Because of this, people know what you are doing and what you are thinking." H.S.

ᎧᏬᎭᎴᏂ ✦ kawohaleni (kah-woh-hah-leh-nee) ✦ **pelican** ✦ Name means: duck with a big mouth or big mouth

ᏛᏗᏍᏗ ✦ tvdisdi (tuh-dee-sdee) ✦ **pheasant**

ᏬᏯ ✦ woya (woh-yah) ✦ **pigeon**

ᏬᏓᎶᏂ ✦ wodaloni (woh-dah-loh-nee) ✦ **pigeon, passenger** (extinct)

ᎠᎵᏟᏍᎩ ✦ alitlisgi (ah-lee-tlee-sgee) ✦ **pine siskin** ✦ Name means: boiling

ᎫᏇ ✦ guque (goo-gweh) ✦ **quail**

ᏓᎵᎢᎦ ✦ daliiga (dah-lee-ee-gah) ✦ **rain crow, or yellow-billed cuckoo** ✦ The elders say when the rain crow hollers, it will rain within one day.

ᏦᎳᎾ ✦ kolana (koh-lah-nah) ✦ **raven** ✦ The old people say that the mean medicine people turned themselves into the raven at night when they were looking for someone to feast on. They were then known as the "Raven Mockers." They were feared by all.

ᏙᏧᏩ ✦ totsuwa (toh-joo-wah) ✦ **redbird or cardinal**

ᏅᏃᎢ ᎤᏕᏘ ✦ nvnoi udeti (nuh-noh-ee oo-deh-tee) ✦ **roadrunner** ✦ Name means: going down the road

GUQUE *(Quail)* ✦ *by Hastings Shade*

The quail at one time did not have the whistle that he has today. The whistle belongs to the terrapin. One day Quail heard this whistle. He said, "I've got to have that whistle. It sounds better than the one I've got." He went where Terrapin was and asked, "Where did you get that whistle?" Terrapin said, "I've always had it. Why do you ask?" Quail said, "I just thought I might get me one like that." "You can't," said Terrapin. "Only we have this whistle." "Maybe I can borrow it just for a little while? I would give it back," said Quail. "I don't know. I better not," said Terrapin. "Just let me try it once. I'll just be right here," said Quail. "Okay. Just once," said Terrapin. When Quail got the whistle he backed up in the grass and tried the whistle. It sounded so beautiful. He told the Terrapin, "Let me get right over there and try it so you can tell better how it sounds." He did this until he got away with Terrapin's whistle. That's why to this day, you can hear the quail in the weeds but you can't see him. He is still hiding. He knows he stole the whistle that he has. The terrapin has no voice because he loaned it out. Never loan anything that you may need. You may not get it back.

TOTSUWA *(Redbird)* ✦ *by Hastings Shade*

There is a legend that says redbird, or cardinal, wasn't the color he is now. He was a drab green color. One day Wolf, known as the painter back then, came by where Redbird and his mate had their nest. And seeing Redbird sitting on a limb, Wolf said, "I found some red coloring that I could use today. But I couldn't get to it. It's in a hole in a rock and I can't get my paws into the hole, so I can't stir it up, because my paws are too big." He asked Redbird if he could help. Redbird asked, "How can I help?" The Wolf said, "You are small enough to get down into the hole and stir it up for me. Then all I'd have to do is dip my brush into the hole and continue painting." Redbird said, "I can do that. Show me where it is." So Wolf took him to the rock and showed him the hole. Wolf said, "You get down in there and I'll get some water and pour it down into the hole. Then you can stir it up." When Wolf brought the water back the Redbird was already in the hole. As Wolf began to pour the water into the hole, Redbird began to stir the water into the dye using his wings, just as you see birds taking a bath today. As he did this, the dye was getting all over him. When he had finished and came out of the hole, he looked at himself. He had turned red. He liked the color he had become. He flew back to the nest, all excited. He said to his mate, "Look at me! Isn't this color beautiful? Hurry and get to the rock and go paint yourself." She told him to watch the little ones while she went to paint herself. He said, "Okay," and she took off. But Redbird was so proud of his new color that he began to fly around showing everyone his new color and left the little ones unguarded. As the female got to the rock, she looked back and saw that their nest was unguarded as she went into the hole to paint herself. She kept worrying about the little ones. She didn't get as much coloring on her as her mate did. Just a red bill, and a little bit of red on her crest, wings, and tail. That's the color she is to this day. And that's why the redbird is the color he is today. The different colors that we see today were painted by Wolf. I know it's true because the elders told me so.

ᏥᏍᏉᏉ • tsisquoquo (jee-sgwoh-gwoh) • **robin** • The first bird of spring.

ᏍᏆᎷᏗ • squaludi (sgwa-loo-dee) • **sandpiper** • Name means: head bobbing up, or *alasqualudi*. Also known as *kanvsduwi*.

ᏣᏣ • tsatsa (jah-jah) • **sapsucker, yellow-bellied**

ᏧᏗᏇᏄᏣ • tsudiquenutsa (joo-dee-gweh-noo-jah) • **scissor-tailed flycatcher** • Also known as *anosdayi*, meaning sharp.

ᏌᏪᎩ • sawegi (sah-weh-gee) • **snipe**

ᏣᏍᏙᏩ • tsasdowa (jah-sdoh-wah) • **snipe, large, or Wilson's snipe**

ᏍᎪᏯ ᎠᎦᏙᏍᏗ • sgoya agatosdi (sgoh-yah ah-gah-toh-sdee) • **shrike, loggerhead** • Name means: looks at a bug. This is the bird that puts the bugs it catches on the barbs of fences, thorns, or anywhere it can impale them on something.

ᏩᎬᏔ • wagvta • wah-guh-tah • **sparrow, fox** • Name means: put into the fire. This was when the birds and animals were giving the humans diseases. The birds said they wanted to put us over the fire to burn our legs off, like we did to them.

ᏥᏍᏆᏯ • tsisquaya (jee-sgwah-yah) • **sparrow, house** • Name means: principal bird or all bird. House sparrow has been transplanted from another place and is widespread; he is not native.

ᏥᎦᏒ • tsigasv (jee-gah-suh) • **sparrow, song** • Name means: the whistler, or *tsigasvga*

ᏧᏂᎦᏙᎪᎯ • tsunigatogohi (joo-nee-gah-toh-goh-hee) • **sparrow, white-throated** • Name means: of the tail

ᏍᏆᎵᏍᏗᏯ • squalisdiya (sgwa-lee-sdee-yah) • **starling, European** • New bird introduced to North America in the 1890s.

ᏗᎦᎳᏯᏅᎯᏓ • digalayanvhida (dee-gah-lah-yah-nuh-hee-dah) • **stilt** • Name means: having long legs, a catchall name for stilt birds

ᏧᏆᏄᏣ • tsuquanutsa (joo-gwah-noo-jah) • **swallow**

ᏧᏗᏇᏄᎩ • tsudiquenugi (joo-dee-gweh-noo-gee) • **swallow, barn** • Name means: to pinch

ᏌᏌ ᎡᏆ • sasa equa (sah-sah eh-gwah) • **swan** • Name means: big goose • "*In Cherokee tradition,* sasa equa *symbolizes gracefulness*—ulisiidi—ᎤᎵᏏᎢᏗ." *H.S.*

ᏧᎢᏝᎢ • tsuitlai (joo-ee-tlah-ee) • **tanager, scarlet** • Name means: the nester

ᎧᏬᏄ ᎤᏍᏗ • kawonu usdi (kah-woh-noo oo-sdee) • **teal** • Name means: little duck

ᏩᏗᏰᎵ • wadiyeli (wah-dee-yeh-lee) • **thrasher, brown**

ᎧᏬᎬ • kawogv (kah-woh-guh) • **thrush, wood** • Name means: being cold, or *kanawogv*

ᏣᏫᏍᎩ • tsawisgi (jah-wee-sgee) • **towhee**

ᎤᏍᏗ ᎤᏍᏓᏘ • usdi usdati (oo-sdee oo-sdah-tee) • **tufted titmouse** • Name means: small tuft on its head

ᎬᎾ • gvna (guh-nah) • **turkey (domestic)**

Sasa equa
(swan)

ᎬᎾ ᎢᎾᎨ ᎡᎯ • gvna inage ehi (guh-nah ee-nah-geh eh-hee) • **turkey, wild** • The wild turkey was respected among the Cherokees. Its feathers were worn on headdresses and made into robes, fans, and other items, and it was a staple in the diet of the Cherokees.

ᎩᎦᎨ ᏗᎧᏂ • gigage dikani (gee-gah-geh dee-kah-nee) • **vireo, red-eyed** • Name means: red-eyed. Its eyes were not really red—they were more an orange color. There is no word in the Cherokee language for the color orange other than *gigage iyusdi*, or red-like.

ᏧᏍᎪᏍᏗ • tsusgosdi (joo-sgoh-sdee) • **vireo, white-eyed** • Name means: bright-eyed, or *tsusgosdi dikani*

ᏚᏩ • duwa (doo-wah) • **warbler**

ᏥᏯᎬᏚᏩ • tsiyagvduwa (jee-yah-guh-doo-wah) • **warbler, chestnut-sided**

ᏥᏯᏛᎦ • tsiyadvga (jee-yah-duh-gah) • **warbler, worm-eating** • Name means: he is going to eat the worm

ᎠᏚᏳᏂ • aduyini (a-doo-yee-nee) • **waterthrush, Louisiana** • Name means: wading, or *aduhini*

ᏍᏆᎴᏆᎵ • squalequali (sgwah-leh-gwah-lee) • **whip-poor-will**

ᏩᎫᎴ • wagule (wah-goo-leh) • **whip-poor-will, eastern** • Eastern Band of the Cherokees name for the whip-poor-will—and he does sound different from the one in the west.

Dalala (red-headed woodpecker)

ᏉᎦ • quoga (gwoh-gah • **woodpecker, pileated** • "This large woodpecker is also known as the 'wood hen.' The elders also called him 'the hammerer.' Late in the evening you could hear him pecking on a dead limb, and it sounded like someone hammering on a piece of wood. The elders would say, 'I guess he found something to fix. I hear him hammering.' *Diganvwaloido*, meaning 'he is hammering around.'" H.S.

ᏥᏍᏇᏄᏣ • tsiquenutsa (jee-sgweh-noo-jah) • **woodpecker, red-bellied**

ᏓᎳᎳ • dalala (dah-lah-lah) • **woodpecker, red-headed**

ᎬᏍᏆᎭ • gvsquaha (guh-sgwah-hah) • **woodpecker, sapsucker** • Name means: wash his face

ᎦᏄᎳᏣ • ganulatsa (gah-noo-lah-jah) • **wren, Carolina** • Name means: is in the grass, or *ganvla utsa*. This wren lives in the forest, not like the other two that like to live around a house. Also called *henili*.

Talitama (house wren)

ᏔᎵᏔᎹ • talitama (tah-lee-tah-mah) • **wren, house** • "This is the wren that the Indians say went around telling everyone when a baby was born and whether it was a basket weaver (girl) or a bow maker (boy). Usually seen making a nest on a porch or somewhere on a house. The elders say this way it could keep watch on what was going on." H.S.

ᎠᎵᏔᎻ • alitami (ah-lee-tah-mee) • **wren, winter** • Usually seen around the yard of a house. Not like the house wren.

ᏓᎶᏂᏯ • daloniya (dah-loh-nee-ya) • **common yellowthroat** • Name means: all yellow

DALALA (*Red-headed Woodpecker*) • *by Hastings Shade*

Dalala is the woodpecker that gave us the flute. Legend says there was a hunter in the forest who kept hearing this beautiful music. He began to search where the sound was coming from. He finally located the source. It was coming from a tree that had a dead limb way up on top. The hunter climbed the tree, and when he got to the limb he found something had made holes in the limb in such a way that when the wind blew across it, it made these beautiful notes. He wanted to know what had made this thing that made such beautiful music. He climbed down and waited. Soon, a woodpecker came back and began to peck on the limb. This is how he found out what made this thing that produced the music he was hearing. The hunter climbed back up and cut the limb off and took it to his village. This is how we got the flute. I know it is true because the elders said so.

Tree Relatives

Cherokee stories such as "The Boys and the Pine" have long associated *deligv* (trees) with Sky World. But in truth, like anitsisqua (birds), trees are mediating beings that cross borders between the three worlds of the Cherokee cosmos. With their crowns and branches in the sky, the green leaves and needles of trees take life from the sun, like other plants. But those branches and crowns also are home to birds and provide shelter for the other forest dwellers below. In this way, trees provide for creatures of the sky and Elohi. Under the surface of the earth, a tree's roots will spread out twice as wide as its crown, breaking rock and creating more earth as it searches for water and stability for future growth.

Cherokees have long held that, like other plants and all forms of life, trees communicate. Scientific studies have recently confirmed this. A tree's roots work symbiotically with vast networks of underground fungi to deliver not only food but communication between trees (Wohlleben 2015, 2). When one tree falters, another with better access to sunlight or water may learn of its neighbor's distress through their root systems and offer support. When a tree is under attack by insects, it releases scents to alert its neighbors to the threat, all the while sending toxins to its leaves to encourage the predators to leave (6). And when trees wish to reproduce, they coordinate with their neighbors and blossom at the same time in order to get the widest mix of genetic material and attract the most bees with their blossoms (12). In this way, forests are not made up of individual trees, but of families and communities of trees that live together socially, sharing with each other for their mutual support. Or, in other words, trees live in gadugi. These scientific breakthroughs on tree communication have led scientists to wonder if all plants communicate in similar ways. But as Loretta confirmed, Cherokee tradition has long held this to be true.

Adaya (red oak)

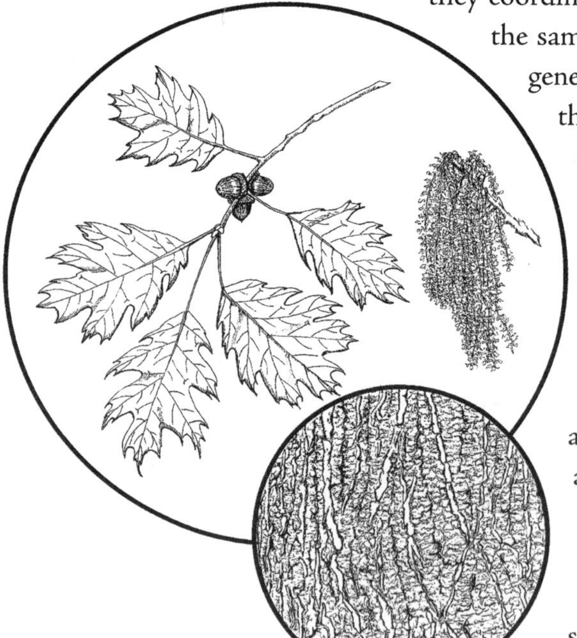

Like other plants, deligv each have a medicine to share, if they should wish to share that knowledge with a person. In addition to their medicinal use to establish tohi, trees are also associated with Sky World because it is through the burning of wood that fire comes into being on Elohi. In Cherokee tradition, seven types of wood are associated with the sacred fire brought to life at the stomp grounds. These woods may differ for various grounds but include red oak, post oak, hickory, blackjack, black gum, dogwood, and cherry.

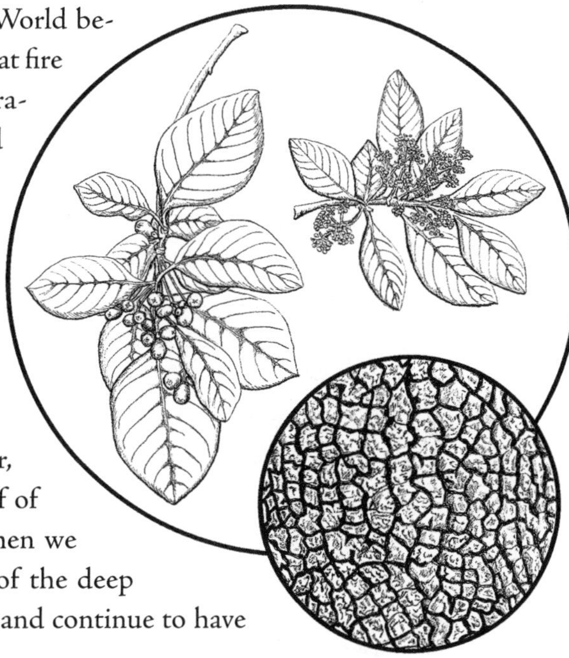

When considering the role of forests and trees in Cherokee tradition, Loretta suggested I speak with David Comingdeer, a long-time wildland firefighter and chief of Echota-Tanasi Ceremonial Ground. When we sat together at his home, David spoke of the deep relationships Cherokee people have had and continue to have with trees and their forests.

Uniqua
(black gum tree)

"Are there certain trees that stand out in Cherokee tradition that you can speak about?" I asked.

"Oh, yeah. There are certain trees that we use for ceremonial purposes. They have different meanings. Of course, any evergreen has a special meaning, and we have oral histories of what the evergreens mean. Everlasting life. Then other hardwoods, you know. Cedar is something that's widely used by Cherokees and lots of other tribes, too, to clean ourselves. Clean our home. Clean our area. There's a lot of uses for cedar, and we have other trees, too, that may not be an evergreen. In the hardwood categories the bark is used for medicine. The bark just under the outside bark, inside the tree. We used them to treat our blood or treat kidneys or some other diseases. Or it might be several different tree barks that you put together to make a tea. And so, you gotta know your trees. You gotta know your trees. You gotta know which ones go together, and there's even certain medicines that we have where it's not just picking the right tree, but it has to be a tree that has been struck by lightning and is *alive*. It's been struck by lightning but it's still alive."

"Do you think it's important for Cherokees today to have knowledge of the woods?"

"Absolutely. Absolutely. We are a people of the forest. Cherokees are a people of the forest, of the hardwood woodlands in this region of America. I mean, we're not exactly in our ancestral home here, but it's pretty close.

The same type of timber. When we were moved by force in 1839—when my family came here in 1839—and our communities relocated here after the Removal, we have stories of the men and the scouts who would go out and look for water sources in that first year we were here. There were no roads. There were no towns. There were no stores. There was no infrastructure here. So we moved into a total wilderness. So they sent the scouts out into the countryside looking for these freshwater streams and springs and rivers. And they recognized everything. They recognized everything. And so, to this day, a hundred and seventy-five, hundred eighty years after the Removal, you look at where our heaviest concentrations of Cherokees are and where our families have settled, and these old core families have settled in these little communities around here. We picked places, our great-grandparents picked places for us to live that looked very similar to our home in the east. We recognized it and we were of the forest, and so when we came here we didn't want to go and live out in the prairies over here west of us. We stayed here in the hills, where we found the hardwood timbers and the hickory and the oak, pine, cedar, that we recognized. And we recognized the fish that were here. The gar and the bass and the perch and the different fishes that live here. They were familiar to us."

Wane
(hickory tree)

"Are there any particular stories or teachings about the woods that you think would be good for others to hear or think about? Stories that are important to you?"

"One of the things that I remember learning was very interesting. I had a step-grandfather here. He was from this county. I call him 'Grandpa John,' and he was a war veteran. He told us one time, he said, 'You know, an Indian can always find water. Even in the driest of times. If you're in the mountains. Even if the springs are dry and the creeks are dried up.' And he said, 'One at a time, move the leaves from a creek bed. Find the lowest point where the leaves are all down there and pull the leaves back.' And he said, 'Underneath that there's gonna be water there.' He said that may be in a puddle in a leaf, or it may be a puddle in the bed of the creek. Or in the drainage. And there's certain trees you can look for. Sycamore. Willow. Cottonwood. They exist only where there's a water source. Like a spring or something. So even in the mountains here, in the timber, in the forest, if you are without water, you can get on a high point and look for those trees. The sycamore stands out. The bark looks like a bone. It's white and stands out from the forest. And even the leaves. You can hear sycamore leaves or the leaves of the cottonwood. Because the leaves are so big they sound different in the wind. So you can actually hear those certain trees even if you can't see 'em, and that leads you to water. And that's what I've taught my son. To recognize those sounds and the sights of those trees. And if you ever are in need of water, if you're out there and you need water, you can find it. And that's something that has come down through the line through the Cherokee story. Being able to locate water."

Tree Parts

ᎫᎴ • gule (goo-leh) • **acorn**

ᎤᏯᎷᎦ • uyaluga (oo-yah-loo-gah) • **bark** • Name means: the cover of a tree. Also called *uyalv*.

ᎭᏫᏂ ᎤᏯᎸ • hawini uyalv (hah-wee-nee oo-yah-luh) • **bark, inner**

ᎤᎳᏍᏚᏒ • ulasdusv (oo-lah-sdoo-suh) • **bud**

ᏚᎶᎢᏍᏛ • duloisdv (doo-loh-ee-sduh) • **fork**

ᎤᎦᎶᎦ • ugaloga (oo-gah-loh-gah) • **leaves**

ᎤᏩᏂᎦᏢ • uwanigatlv (oo-wah-nee-gah-tluh) • **limb**

ᎤᎾᏍᏕᏢ • unasdetlv (oo-nah-sdeh-tluh) • **root**

ᎤᏂᎵᎬ • uniligv (oo-nee-lee-guh) • **stump**

Trees

ᏠᎬ ᎠᎴ ᏕᎵᎬ • tlugv ale deligv (tloo-guh ah-leh de-lee-guh) • **trees**

ᏒᎦᏔ • svgata (suh-gah-tah) • **apple**

ᏧᏊᏃᎾ • tsukanona (joo-kah-noh-nah) • **ash**

ᎠᏓᎭ • adaha (ah-dah-hah) • **basswood** • Name means: all wood

ᎤᏙᎳᏂ • udolani (oo-doh-lah-nee) • **beech**

ᏧᏂᏁᏅᏗ • tsuninenvdi (joo-nee-neh-nuh-dee) • **birch**

ᎠᏣᎦ • atsaga (ah-jah-gah) • **birch, sweet**

ᎤᏂᏆ • uniqua (oo-nee-qwah) • **black gum**

ᎧᏂᎦ • kaniga (kah-nee-gah) • **blackhaw** • The small black fruit of this tree is good to eat.

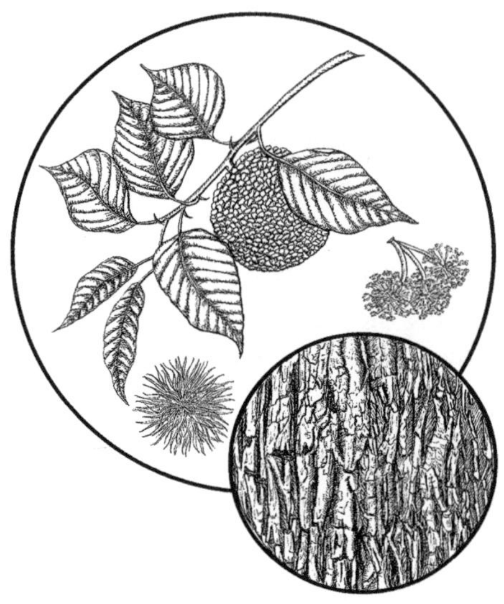

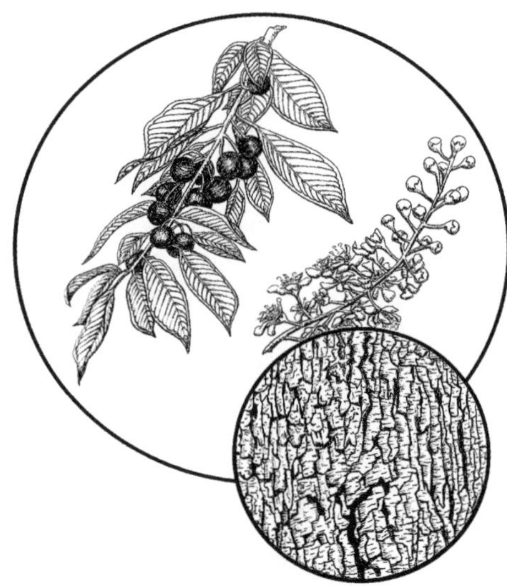

left
Kalowegati dalonige (bois d'arc tree, Osage orange)

right
Gitaya (cherry)

ᎧᎶᏪᎦᏗ ᏓᎶᏂᎨ ✦ kalowegati dalonige (kah-low-weh-gah-tee dah-loh-nee-gay) ✦ **bois d'arc, or Osage orange** ✦ This is the tree Cherokees use to make bows.

ᎠᏗᏰᏗᎪᏢᏙᏗ ✦ aditlodigotlvdodi (ah-dee-tloh-dee-goh-tluh-doh-dee) ✦ **boxelder**

ᎤᏍᏆᏓᎢ ✦ usquadai (oo-sqwah-dah-ee) ✦ **buckeye** ✦ Roots of this tree were used to poison and catch fish a long time ago.

ᎪᎰᎯ ✦ kohohi (koh-hoh-hee) ✦ **butternut, white walnut**

ᎠᏓᏧᏲ ✦ adatsuyo (ah-dah-joo-yoh) ✦ **buttonbush** ✦ Name means: bad wood or wood no good

ᏯᎾᏏ ᏧᏂᎩᏍᏗ ✦ yanasi tsunigisdi (yah-nah-see joo-nee-gee-sdee) ✦ **castor bean** ✦ Name means: what the buffalos eat

ᏧᎦᎶᎦ ᎡᏆ ✦ tsugaloga equa (joo-gah-loh-gah eh-qwah) ✦ **catalpa** ✦ Name means: big leaves

ᎠᏥᎾ ✦ atsina (ah-jee-nah) ✦ **cedar** ✦ *"In Cherokee tradition,* atsina *symbolizes purification*—asinvgalisgi—ᎠᏏᏅᎦᎵᏍᎩ." *H.S.*

ᎩᏔᏯ ✦ gitaya (gee-tah-yah) ✦ **cherry**

ᏓᏐᏓᏆᎵ ✦ dasodaquali (dah-soh-dah-qwah-lee) ✦ **chestnut**

ᎤᎾᎩᏂ ✦ unagini (oo-nah-gee-nee) ✦ **chinkapin** ✦ Nut from this tree is good to eat. Tastes like the hazelnut.

ᏥᏳ ᏳᏍᏗ ✦ tsiyu yusdi (jee-yoo yoo-sdee) ✦ **cottonwood** ✦ Name means: boat-like. There may have been canoes made from this tree. Also may resemble *tsiyu,* the tulip poplar, out of which boats were carved.

ᏒᎦᏔ ᎢᎾᎨ ᎡᎯ ✦ svgata inage ehi (suh-gah-tah ee-nah-geh eh-hee) ✦ **crabapple tree** ✦ Name means: wild apple tree

ATSINA (*Cedar*) AND THE EVERGREENS ✦ *by Noyi Teuton*

Sequoyah and I were speaking of plants and trees when he reminded me of the story of the evergreens staying awake for seven nights. "And so, they stayed awake to watch over us," Sequoyah said. "And the cedar, the pine, and the sage were the only ones that kept that promise to watch over us. And so, that's why most tribes believe in one of those. The sage, the pine, or the cedar. A lot of us use it for cleansing the body and soul. Spirit and mind. They're still watching over us. They're still holding on to that promise they made." Here is one version of the story.

Ilvhiyu tsigesv, in the great forever that was, when the plants and animals first came to Elohi, Creator gave them all a test. He asked them to take watch and stay awake for seven nights in a row, just as young men fast and stay awake during a ceremony. On the first night almost all the creatures stayed awake. On the second night some creatures fell asleep. On the third night many more fell asleep. The days and nights thereafter passed for the creatures in a gauzy haze, and by the time the seventh night arrived, only two inage anehi were awake, *Tlvdatsi* (Panther) and *Uguku* (Owl). Unetlvnv gifted both these beings the power to see in the dark and to hunt the birds and animals that sleep in the night.

Among the trees, *atsina* (cedar), *notsi* (pine), *nonu* (spruce), *usdasdi* (holly), and *dusugi* (laurel) all stayed awake through the seventh night. To these trees, Creator gave the gift of green leaves through all seasons. They also became keepers of powerful medicine. To the other trees that fell asleep, Unetlvnv made them lose their leaves each winter. To this day, the evergreens remain admired for their beauty and medicine. The smoke of the atsina is especially valued for its gift of purification.

Tlvdatsi (panther)

ᎧᏅᏏᏔ • kanvsita (kah-nuh-see-tah) • **dogwood**

ᎪᎧᏌᎩ • kokasagi (koh-kah-sah-gee) • **elderberry**

ᏓᏩᏥᎳ • dawatsila (dah-wah-jee-lah) • **elm**

ᏓᏩᏥᎳ ᎩᎦᎨ • dawatsila gigage (dah-wah-jee-lah gee-gah-geh) • **red elm, or slippery elm** • The inside bark of this tree is good for cuts and scratches. Also known as *dawatsilaha*.

ᎠᏓᏤ • adatse (ah-dah-jeh) • **fir** • Name means: new wood, or *adaitse*

ᎧᏃᏍᏓᏆᎵ • kanosdaquali (kah-noe-sdah-qwah-li) • **hackberry** • Make tea from this tree's bark in August. It is like nature's flu shot.

ᎢᏳᎩᏓ • iyugida (ee-yoo-gee-dah) • **hazelnut** • Nut looks like an acorn.

ᏃᏂ • noni (noh-nee) • **hemlock**

ᏩᏁ • wane (wah-nay) • **hickory** • A drink called kanutchie is made from the nut of this tree; very rich so don't have too much.

ᏩᎾᏚᏯ • wanaduya (wah-nah-doo-yah) • **hickory, pignut**

ᏐᎯ ᏧᏂᏍᏗ • sohi tsunisdi (soh-hee joo-nee-sdee) • **hickory, shagbark** • Name means: small hickory nuts

ᎤᏍᏓᏍᏗ • usdasdi (oo-sdah-sdee) • **holly**

ᏧᏘᎾ • tsutina (joo-tee-nah) • **ironwood**

ᎧᎶᏪᎦᏘ • kalowegati (kah-low-weh-gah-tee) • **locust** • Cherokees use this tree to make bows, spear handles, arrows, stickball sticks, and darts. A strong wood.

Kalowegati (locust)

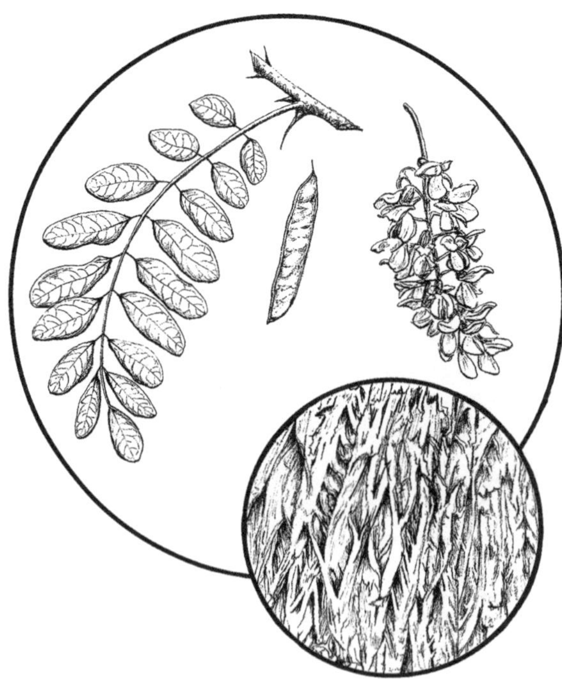

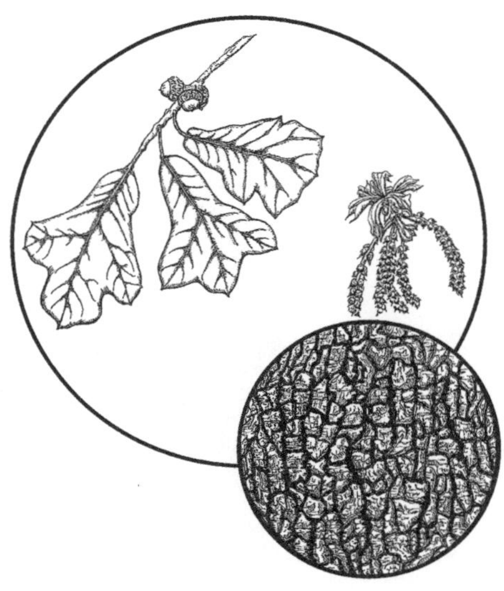

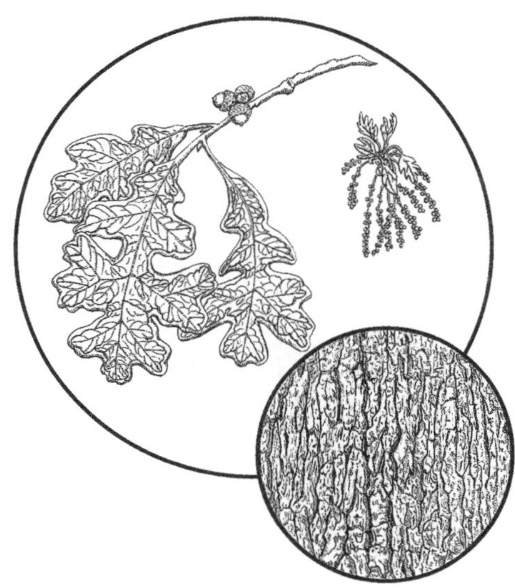

left
Noda
(blackjack oak)

right
Tsusga
(post oak)

ᎧᎳᏎᏥ • kalasetsi (kah-lah-seh-jee) • **locust, honey** • Name means: sugar or candy

ᎲᎾᎨᎢ • hvnagei (huh-nah-geh-ee) • **locust, honey** (small)

ᎫᏩ • kuwa (koo-wah) • **mulberry**

ᎠᏍᏔᎵᏥᎵ • astalitsili (ah-stah-lee-jeel) • **oak, bastard**

ᏃᏓ ᎠᎬᏂᎨ • noda agvnige (noh-dah ah-guh-nee-geh) • **oak, black**

ᏃᏓ • noda (noh-dah) • **oak, blackjack**

ᎫᎴ ᎠᎾᏆ • gule anaqua (goo-lay ah-nah-qwah) • **oak, burr**

ᏧᏍᎦ • tsusga (joo-sgah) • **oak, post**

ᎠᏓᏯ • adaya (ah-dah-yah) • **oak, red**

ᏙᎳᏥ • dolatsi (doh-lah-jee) • **oak, water**

ᏔᎵ • tali (tah-lee) • **oak, white**

ᏗᏒᎩ • disvgi (dee-suh-gee) • **pawpaw** • Name means: the ones that stink

ᏆᎾ • quanah (qwah-nah) • **peach**

ᏐᎯ ᎠᏂᏅᎯᏓ • sohi aninvhida (soe-hee ah-nee-nuh-hee-dah) • **pecan** • Name means: long hickory nut

ᏌᎵ • sali (sah-lee) • **persimmon** • The fruit is good to eat, but wait until it is ripe.

ᏃᏥ • notsi (noh-jee) • **pine**

ᏆᏄᏅᏍᏗ • quanunvsdi (qwa-noo-nuh-sdee) • **plum** • Name means: small peaches or like-a-peach

ᎠᏓ ᎬᏂᏓ • ada gvnida (ah-dah guh-nee-dah) • **poplar** • Name means: long life. Also called *noli*.

ᎦᎪᎩ • gagogi (gah-goh-gee) • **redbud** • Name means: liar. It's a liar because it tells you it's spring, but then it's not.

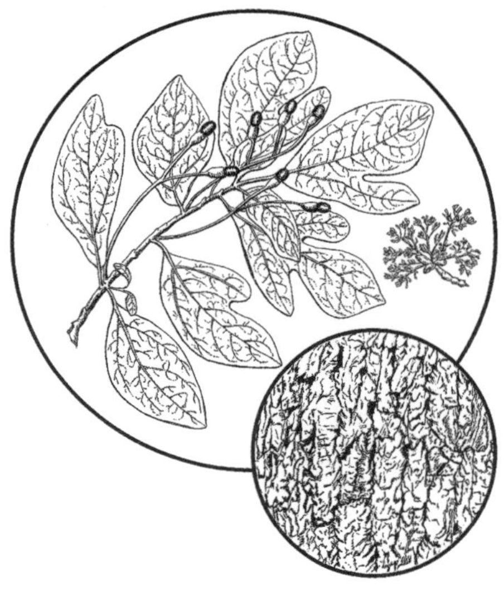

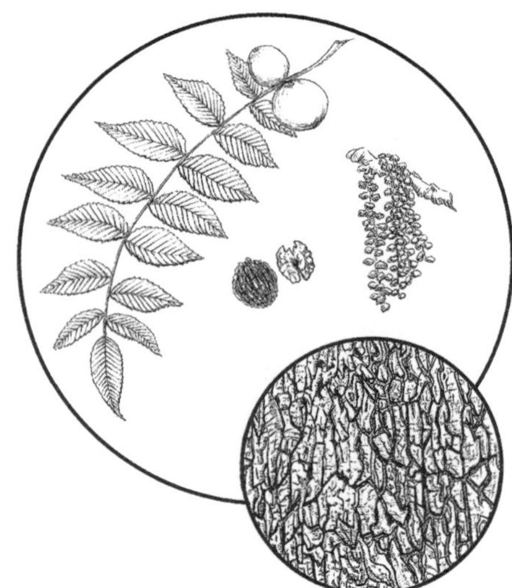

left
Kanasdatsi (sassafras)

right
Sedi (walnut)

ᎧᎾᏍᏓᏥ ✦ kanasdatsi (kah-nah-sdah-jee) ✦ **sassafras** ✦ The roots of this tree make a tea that you drink during the spring of the year. It's an energizer.

ᏅᏙᏇᏯ ✦ nvdoqueya (nuh-doh-qweh-yah) ✦ **sourwood**

ᏃᎦᏔᏟ ✦ nogatatli (noh-gah-tah-tlee) ✦ **spicewood** ✦ Sometimes a tea is made from this to break a fever.

ᏃᏄ ✦ nonu (noh-noo) ✦ **spruce**

ᏆᎶᏆ ✦ qualoqua (qwah-looh-qwah) ✦ **sumac, smooth**

ᎪᏧᎦ ✦ kotsunega (koh-joo-neh-gah) ✦ **sycamore**

ᏧᏣᏲᏍᏗ ✦ tsutsayosdi (joo-jah-yoh-sdee) ✦ **thorn** ✦ Name means: sharp or can prick you

ᏎᏗ ✦ sedi (seh-dee) ✦ **walnut**

ᏗᎳᎦᎵᏍᎩ ✦ dilagalisgi (dee-lah-gah-lee-sgee) ✦ **willow** ✦ Name means: limbs split

ᏗᎳᎦᎵᏍᎩ ᎤᏍᏗ ✦ dilagalisgi usdi (dee-lah-gah-lee-sgee oo-sdee) ✦ **willow, small** ✦ Name means: small limbs split

ᏗᏔᎵᏍᎩ ✦ ditalisgi (dee-tah-lee-sgee) ✦ **willow, weeping** ✦ Name means: seeping or sap coming out

Sky World to Under World

Cherokee tradition tells that we live in an ordered, ever-balancing cosmos. Sometime in the great forever that was, people recognized that the regularity of Sky World, with its revolving stars, planets, and seasons, gave form to our lives. People observed the patterns in Galvladi and the behavior of beings that inhabit the sky. People learned from those patterns and created order in their own lives on Elohi. Human beings cultivated and honored relationships with beings of Sky World. And as the story of the two boys who chose to help Thunder rather than Uk'tan shows, the Cherokee recognized the powerful, evenly matched forces of the Under World and Sky World. But it was Thunder's words that they trusted. With continuing faith in the power of communication, a hallmark of Sky World, we remain allies.

I carry in my pocket a medallion I etched that is a symbol of my relations and what it means to me to strive for tohi. The medallion is carved out of copper, a material Cherokees have long associated with the Under World. On one side I created an image of the three-tiered Cherokee cosmos based on the ancient Cox Mound–style gorget found along the Tennessee River Valley (Lankford 2007a, 10). A square with corners that loop and flow from one side to the other encloses an encircled cross outlined with sun rays. These loops, Hastings once told me, symbolize the cords—the teachings—that suspend Elohi from Galvladi. These are the tethers that keep Elohi from sinking into Elohi Hawinadidla—the Under World. On each side of the looped square is an image of a pileated woodpecker head, a symbol of the weather powers moving the seasons. Hastings told me that this symbol also represents our life cycle, each phase of our lives flowing from one season to the next, from birth to maturity, to old age, and to death. In the Cherokee view, there is no beginning to the journey and no end. We just keep going. If we missed one side of the square, the world would be out of balance. Similarly, each stage of our lives is inextricably tied to the worlds that give form to our existence and the gift of fire that enlivens us in body, mind, and spirit.

On the other side I etched the figure of *Kananesgi Amayi* (Water Spider). When I look at her and the symbol of fire on her back, I am reminded of the story of the gift of fire from Sky World. I am reminded that the Cherokee world did not begin with humans but with our plant and animal relatives. Like Star Woman, our animal relations risked their lives for human beings. They were transformed through their contact with fire, though they were not destined to carry and use fire as a tool. Only water spider had the skill, ingenuity, and courage to steal Thunder's gift from the Fire People and deliver it to us. Most of all, she had compassion.

Like the symbols on my medallion, the teachings that Hastings, Loretta, and other elders pass on through the generations form a pattern of understanding the world and an embodied practice, or way of life. There is a place for human beings in the world that Creator made. The gift of language from Unetlvnv and atsila from Kananesgi Amayi are the foundations of Cherokee peoplehood. But we have learned and may continue to learn from our plant and animal relatives.

With this acknowledgment of order, pattern, and communication, it is time to explore Elohi Hawinadidla, the mysterious Under World, whose transformative waters and fecund earth nurture all life on Elohi. Though Cherokee tradition tells that people came from the ordered Sky World above and it is to that place that one's spirit returns, it is in relating to the unpredictable and dynamic forces and beings of the Under World and inside ourselves that we may attain our full humanity.

Nvgi ✦ Four

Elohi Hawinadidla

THE UNDER WORLD

Larry Shade sat with Loretta and me at her home in Lost City reflecting on his experiences as a teacher taking students from the Cherokee Nation each summer on visits to the Cherokee homelands in the East. They stay for a time on the Qualla Boundary of the Eastern Band of Cherokee Indians, where they meet with community members and elders such as Tom Belt, who introduce them to important cultural sites. Larry told us that for many students the journey is life altering. Cherokee history comes alive for them. The topic turned to Larry's understanding of the Cherokee cosmos and his experience with students when they swam in Blue Hole at Red Clay Historic Park in Tennessee. Red Clay, known as Ela Wodi or "Earth Paint" to Cherokees, is a site that holds deep cultural meaning. The Cherokee Nation councils met at Red Clay in 1836 before Removal on the Trail of Tears. Still active today, Blue Hole is a natural spring that produces up to 400,000 gallons of 52-degree water each day at the site. In 1836 it provided fresh water to the 4,000 people who attended the tribal councils. Like other important natural springs throughout Cherokee country, Blue Hole is a gateway to Elohi Hawinadidla, the Under World.

"Yes, we are in the Middle World, Elohi," Larry said. "Then you have your Upper World with the stars, spirits, and all that existed. And then in the Under World is where the underwater creatures and mythical beings are. You know, I tell the kids the story of Blue Hole at Red Clay. I said, 'Guys, where you're standing, right to the left of you at the very bottom is a ledge. Underneath that ledge is an opening to the Under World where Uk'tan travels.' You're standing there, and you're looking, and you see the gravel, and you can see the bottom. And right at the edge of Blue Hole is a ledge. And this is where the Uk'tan travels from place to place and how he moves around in the Under World. And I told my story, and the students were all sitting in the water already. They all took a dive into the water earlier 'cause, you know, Cherokees are the only ones allowed in; they have free range in the park itself. And we counselors all looked at each other standing there—and we didn't want to jump in!" Larry laughed. I could empathize with their hesitation to enter a powerful gateway like Blue Hole.

"But those kids were egging us on, hollering, 'Come on, Coach Shade!'" Larry continued. "And so, well, you know, myself and a couple of other counselors that were there thought, 'Why not?' You know, there's your opportunity. If you don't do it now, you know . . . One of my sayings I teach my kids is that I never regret the things that I've done, I always regret the things that I didn't do when I had the opportunity to make a difference."

"Seize the day," I said. "So, what did you do? Did you dive in?"

"I went in," Larry said, and we laughed. "And when I dove down in there it's deep. I dove down there and, out of curiosity, I stuck my hand under that ledge to see if I could touch anything. But I didn't."

When I think about the Under World in Cherokee tradition, my mind comes back to stories like Larry's experience at Blue Hole. How fitting, I think, that those young people dove right into Blue Hole. Drawn by the cool, beautiful blue water on a warm summer day, they were attracted to the life-affirming properties of *ama* (water). But with the advantages of experience and understanding, Larry and his fellow counselors were aware of the other qualities of waters and of the Under World, symbolized in powerful sites like Blue Hole. Water is purifying and rejuvenating. It is life-giving. But water is also transformative and uncontrollable. Larry recognized a risk in diving into Blue Hole like his students, but on that day it was worth taking that risk to celebrate life together at Ela Wodi.

In my time spent with Hastings, members of the Turtle Island Liars' Club, and other elders, I have found that among the stories folks thrill at telling and reflecting on are those that arise out of our relationships with Elohi Hawinadidla. These stories are sometimes about the powers and creatures of the Under World, such as Uk'tan or snakes. Sometimes they are about the special powers people have shown. Sometimes they are about uncanny experiences at sites of *ulvsgedi* (the sacred), such as graveyards or old ceremonial grounds and churches. Or of waters and the underground. They are stories of *usgwanigodiyu*, or the wondrous. And part of their power, I was to learn, is that they may inspire us with a range of feelings—from awe to fear to love. In the process, we connect with the energies of Elohi Hawinadidla that unite us as creatures of Elohi.

The teachings of Hastings, Loretta, and other elders showed me that the Under World may reach us most strongly through our emotions. I understood that a sense of mystery in life and what acts upon us is coded within the Cherokee language. In Cherokee grammar there are twenty pronouns. One set of ten pronouns are used in about two-thirds of Cherokee verbs. These verbs, like *gawoniha* (I am speaking), are used to describe an action done to someone or something. The other set of ten pronouns are used when describing someone or something being acted upon. Verbs describing emotions use this set of pronouns because, in a very basic sense, feelings are not in our *control* (Standingdeer and Duncan 2016, 58). In Cherokee language and worldview, feelings are not something we may actively bring about in ourselves. A feeling or emotion is not an action, but a state of being that arises in us, like hunger, anger, or love. And so the source of feelings and emotions within ourselves is mysterious. Though we may cultivate the conditions for tohi and well states of being to emerge in us, they are not in our active control. We need to be careful with ourselves and with one another as our emotional states are created not only through our own actions but in relationships with others. These are among the teachings of the beings and forces of Elohi Hawinadidla.

While the Sky World is the world of light, consciousness, purity, boundaries, and control, the Under World is dark, creative, unbound, transformative, and unconscious. Cherokee mythology tells that our spirits come from Galvladi, but the physical life forces of human beings and other creatures of Elohi arise from the Under World. We are creatures of sky, earth, and water, and we need to be in relation to all these worlds to thrive in spirit, body, and mind. From Elohi's beginning when mud was drawn from the depths of the waters, our bodies and spirits have been nurtured from Under World's elemental forces that provide the ground for all life. But unlike the predictable Sky World, with its regular patterns of planets and stars that define our days and nights, Cherokee tradition holds that the waters and earth of Elohi Hawinadidla are in flux, unpredictable, and mysterious. Water and earth are living, Hastings said. One can witness how they change over time as they interact with the elements, plants, and other creatures. Staying in relationship with the Under World is fundamental to standing in the middle. Even though the depths and sources of earth and water are obscured from us, like our emotions, they shape our lives as human beings.

The power and mystery of Elohi Hawinadidla extends out through the creatures that live in its realm. In their forms and habits, snakes, fish, and insects reflect the boundary-crossing characteristics of this world, I was taught. Beings such as Uk'tan remind us of what may occur when destructive emotions like anger, jealousy, and greed overwhelm us. In dream or waking life, the Under World may visit us with spirit people or visions of the unexplainable. Whether dark and foreboding or purifying and nurturing, I wanted to learn more about the characteristics of Under World and how our understanding of them and of its creatures shape Cherokee thought and the process of standing in the middle.

This chapter on Elohi Hawinadidla presents names, stories, and reflections on the creatures and forces that inhabit the Cherokee Under World. It tells of sources of physical life and powers of generation, growth, and transformation in our experiences on Elohi. Embracing paradoxes, Elohi Hawinadidla is at once frightening and enticing, life-giving and life-taking, purifying and polluting, creative and destructive. Above all else, it is unavoidable in Cherokee thought as we are surely of Elohi Hawinadidla as much as we are of Galvladi and Elohi. We avoid the Under World at our peril. Learning to relate to its beings and forces without being overwhelmed by them, I was to find, is fundamental to living a balanced life on Elohi.

Deep Waters

Cherokee mythology tells that Elohi is suspended from Sky World by four cords, one at each cardinal direction. If the cords should ever break, Elohi will lose its anchors in the sky and sink into the deep waters from which our world of earth once emerged. The depths of the Under World remain. Always there, always waiting. But as long as Elohi remains tied to the heavens, the pull of gravity will not flood the earth and wash away the world of relations we have created with one another.

When talking about this story with friends and elders I find it fascinating that the Cherokee cosmos is understood to be literally hanging in the balance. Should we not maintain our relations—with Sky World, on Elohi, and with the Under World—the cords of our connection will break and Elohi will sink. Elohi is not actively drawn toward Sky World but pulled toward what Meskwaki poet Ray A. Young Bear calls that deep ocean of "forgetfulness." If we do nothing to cultivate tohi and stand in the middle, Elohi will be lost to the waters.

Relationships with waters are a cornerstone of Cherokee life. Long ago, villages were settled in fertile river valleys well suited for crops. Ideally, the river would be located on the east side of a village. As custom had it, each morning folks would go to the river for prayer and ablutions, to meet the coming day purified by communion with clean, living, running water. To this day, some people still go to water each new moon.

Water remains central to Cherokee ceremonial practice. Cherokee Nation elder Crosslin Fields Smith writes that the "sacred water treatment ritual that we do with our people is the blessing of all blessings" (Smith 2018, 2). In connecting to the spirit of all through song, prayer, and the medium of living water, the ritual "acknowledge[s] the sacredness of all life, and all that we depend on for health and well-being" (2). While we are all imbued with spirit, we are also made of water, Smith writes: "We are . . . connected to creation by water, as it sustains life and is a cleansing agent" (2). Going to water is a foundational ritual practice of Cherokee peoplehood. "That ritual goes beyond history," Smith writes. "It goes back to the beginning, and it remains unchanged today" (2).

Cherokee tradition holds that one should go to water at moving, fresh water. No doubt this custom has to do with moving water being cleaner than stagnant water, but it also reflects how tohi is associated with the free-flowing movement of water as a living symbol of a balanced world. Water in motion is healthy and nurturing. But stories tell of the dangerous power in deep pools and treacherous eddies in streams, rivers, and lakes. These pools are home to powerful forces, creatures, and spirits. A great leech is said to have lived where the Valley River meets the Hiwassee River in what is now the Eastern Band of Cherokee Indians territory. Long ago, a section of the Tennessee River several miles south of Chattanooga was home to a whirlpool called "the Suck." One unlucky man who was drawn into its current reported seeing people far down below the eye of the vortex. They called and reached up for him before he was whipped back to the surface and spat out. Near *Kuwahi*, or Clingman's Dome, there is said to exist a medicine lake whose waters heal animals wounded by hunters. Some say it cannot be seen by human eyes, while others say those who fast and pray may be granted the spiritual vision to view it. Natural springs are said to be portals to the Under World. Those who visit those places as guests have said the seasons are opposite of what they are on Elohi, and time moves more quickly. Moments spent in the Under World can pass as days on Elohi. A person who stays there too long, it is said, will die upon returning to the Middle World.

Just as in the east, life in western Cherokee territory has revolved around waters. Cherokee country is crisscrossed with waters. Stories abound of their power and mystery. Communities have lived amidst and through these waters. Cherokees live with the Illinois and the Neosho, the Verdigris and the mighty Arkansas. People know Clear Creek and Spring Creek, Greasy Creek, Baron Fork, Brushy Creek, Vian Creek, and Sallisaw Creek. My family knows Honey Creek, which flows through the lands we settled on after Removal. Back east, the Tuckaseegee and Tennessee continue to flow, though as with the Neosho and Illinois, humans have dammed them. And anyone who has spent time along the Oconaluftee knows it continues to speak.

Hastings told me one name for river in Cherokee is *Yvwi Ganvhida*, or Long Person, with its head in the mountains and feet in the lowlands. In recognition of the personhood of bodies of water they are to be respected and honored. He would often go to the creek to listen to the waters and be soothed by its voice. In that way and in continuing the tradition of Cherokee gigging and fishing he stayed in relation with waters and the creatures of the water.

"I think the most soothing and comfortable surrounding is a waterfall," Loretta told me. "Where you can hear the water coming off a branch into the stream or creek. And you're sitting there by the bank. That is relaxing. That makes you think of the art world. It makes you think of story. Ideas. It's where I do my thinking."

When flowing freely, I was taught, waters express and reflect tohi in the world. We can be lulled by their beauty and gentleness, even forgetting their power. But that is a mistake. As Hastings taught, water gives life but can also take it away. And though we are made from it, its sources and ways remain a mystery to us even as we maintain our relations.

RESTING WATER • *by Hastings Shade*

If you have ever been fishing or along a lake or stream at night and noticed that the water has calmed down so that no ripple showed on the surface, you'll understand. The old people say that at this time, the water is resting. For all things must rest.

At this time, if you enter the water very carefully, the old people say, when you go after fish, you will never fail to catch them.

AMA (*Water*) • *by Hastings Shade*

ᎠᎹ	ama	ah mah	Water
ᎠᎹᎢ	ama	ah mah yee	Creek
ᎤᏪᏴ	uweyv	oo weh yuh	Stream
ᎡᎬ	egv	eh guh	Flowing
ᎡᏉᏂ	equoni	eh gwoh nee	River
ᏴᏫ ᎦᏅᎯᏓ	yvwi ganvhida	yuh wee gah nuh hee dah	Long Person (River)
ᏦᎦᏗᎳ	tsogadila	joh gah dee lah	Up the River
ᎨᎢᏗᎳ	geidila	geh ee dee lah	Down the River
ᎠᎢᏍᏛᎬ	aistvgv	ah ee sduh guh	Deep Part
ᏗᎢᏍᏛᎬ	diisdvgv	dee ees duh guh	Deeper Part
ᏩᏍᏛᎩᏴ	wastvgiyv	wah sduh gee yuh	Deepest Part
ᎠᎹᎢ ᎤᏪᏓᏍᏗ	amai uwedasdi	ah mah ee oo weh dah sdee	Creek Bed
ᎠᎹ ᎦᏄᎪᎬ	ama gangogv	ah mah gah noo goh guh	Spring
ᎤᏴᏝ ᎠᎹ	uyvtla ama	oo yuh tlah ah mah	Cold Water

THE FLOOD • *by Hastings Shade*

There are many versions of the flood story. This is one of them.

At one time the Indigenous people could go anywhere they wanted to go. They hunted, fished, and gathered wherever they wanted to. Everything was there for them. The water was in the streams and lakes. They knew where the plants were. When they needed them they would go get them.

One day, they noticed the ground was damp. A few days later there was mud. Then water began to cover the ground. There wasn't much at first—they still could find the plants and other things they needed. Then the water got deeper.

When the earth got damp was when the Europeans first came to their homeland. A few at first, then more.

Then the water got to the calves of their legs. Then to their knees. At this time, more and more people came to their land.

It began to get harder to find things. The water was up to their thighs, making it harder to get around. The water had covered everything. This was when there were more and more people on their homeland.

Then the water got to their waists, making it even harder to do things. Still the water was rising. Up their chins, to their mouths. Then the Native person had to tilt his head to keep the water out of his nose. As he did this it covered his mouth, then his ears. Still the waters rose.

When the water covered his mouth was the time his language began to decline. When it covered his ears was the time when young people were sent to boarding schools where they couldn't hear the language. They were punished for speaking their own language, the language that the Creator had given them. Still the water rose.

Then it covered his eyes. The only thing that was sticking out was his nose. When it covered his eyes was the time the young people were sent on Relocation. Again, taking them from their homes where they couldn't see their families.

Then the water began to recede.

It's passing his eyes marked the time some of the ones who left returned home. Their elders were gone by now.

It went past his ears. He began to hear some of the language again, but most of the ones who knew the old ways were gone. Only some of the language was left.

As it passes his mouth, now he wants to learn the language again. He began to ask questions. In the 1970s the language was introduced in school, but it was being taught by some that weren't fluent in the language. That's why today some of the words sound different—they are not being pronounced correctly.

The water has never gone down completely. Because of fences, roads, dams, and people not wanting anyone on their land, Native people still have a hard time finding the things they need that Mother Nature had provided for them.

People will have to realize you can never own the earth. Man belongs to the earth. The earth does not belong to man.

If you don't believe this just remember man will be buried into Mother Earth. Mother Earth will not be buried into man.

How the White Man Was Made ✦ *by Hastings Shade*

An old Cherokee story says that White Man was made from the foam of the water. He used to float around on the water and let the wind push him around. One day he felt something solid. As he got to the edge, he finally stood up on his feet on something that was solid, which was Mother Earth to the Indians. He really liked this solid thing he was standing on. He began to move inland and away from the water. The farther inland he moved, the better he liked it. He wanted to make it his own. He didn't want to share it because he thought he might lose it again. So to this day, when White Man buys land, the first thing he does is put up "KEEP OUT" signs and fences. He doesn't want anyone else on the land that he has, and he's afraid he might have to go back to the water again.

Not realizing he will never own it; when he dies the land will still be here.

The Indians knew he would never own anything, and that's why they were willing to share the land, which wasn't his to take control over. The land was put here to provide everything the Indian needs.

Uk'tan

Of all creatures, *Uk'tan* is the being most associated with the transformative powers of the Under World. Created from forms of creatures found across the three-tiered Cherokee cosmos, Uk'tan's mixed nature marks it as both a being of the Under World and one of great power. Sequoyah Guess described the Uk'tan to me once. It is shaped like a giant rattlesnake draped in dazzling colors that shimmer and shift. The size of a large pine tree, Uk'tan's great head is crowned with a rack of antlers that glow and crack with micro bursts of lightning. In the center of its forehead, a transparent crystal juts out like a horn, split down the middle by a blood-red streak. Some say Uk'tan has wings and can fly. Others say it has only feathers behind its head. Its neck is patterned with seven rings, and its only vulnerability, legend says, is behind a scale on its seventh ring. This is the spot that was shot with arrows once by two boys, giving Thunder and Sky World the upper hand and win in his battle with Uk'tan and the Under World in the ancient time.

If one wishes to know of the Under World, I was told, then one should consider the story of Uk'tan. But folks do not often speak openly about such things. There are good reasons for this reserve. Though it is perhaps the most famous creature of Cherokee mythology, nobody would wish to encounter an Uk'tan. If one is seen, it must be kept a secret for seven years; one who reveals it risks death. The toxic smell of an Uk'tan can also kill a person. Perhaps most ominously, the sighting of an Uk'tan forecasts a great change soon to come for the Cherokee people. That change could be either good or bad, but if it is announced by an Uk'tan's presence once again in community, it will surely be world-altering.

Uk'tan has been a part of Cherokee life ever since the people asked the Thunder Boys for help to stop Sun from killing humans with her heat. Sun disliked the way people were not thankful for her light, squinting when they looked at her and complaining of her intensity. Instead, the people loved the Moon, her brother, and smiled up at him sweetly each evening. And so Sun became jealous of Moon and punished the people for their ingratitude, as even beings of the Sky World may be overcome by emotion. As friends to humans, the Thunder Boys offered to transform two humans into beings that could cross to Sky World and kill Sun as she visited her daughter's house at midday. One man became Uk'tan and the other became Rattlesnake. Fortunately for the creatures of Elohi, Sun was not killed in this ambush. Rattlesnake killed Sun's daughter by mistake and refused to continue to seek vengeance. But Uk'tan became bitter and vengeful upon its return to Elohi. It could not live with the people any longer and was banished to Sky World. But as with all beings in the cosmos, the spirit of Uk'tan remains.

Sequoyah Guess told me his father and a group of fellow churchmen saw an Uk'tan near Kenwood, Oklahoma, back in 1969. As in other stories of Uk'tan, they told of first hearing the sound of a cow or bull bellowing or crying from a nearby creek. When they went to investigate, they saw a giant snake with a crystal in its forehead swimming up the creek and bellowing. The snake entered a hole in the creek bank and continued to make its doleful sound until it eventually faded away. According to Sequoyah's thinking, the sighting of the Uk'tan foretold the return of the Cherokee Nation in full force and effect only a few years later.

According to tradition, the crystal horn in the center of an Uk'tan's head holds great medicinal power. There are stories of medicine people who have dived into the waters and wrestled with Uk'tan to attain pieces of its powerful horn. The living crystal must be kept hidden and fed regularly with blood, but if cared for it can assist greatly with foretelling the future.

In conversations with Sequoyah and others, I learned that Uk'tan is not evil. Instead, the story of Uk'tan offers teachings about the dangerous emotions that may arise in any of us when we lack gratitude or do not approach each other in tohi, as displayed in people's attitude toward Sun. Or lash out in vengeance, as Sun did toward the people. It offers warnings on what may occur if we try to manipulate or do not show care for the regular patterns that shape our world. Most of all, Uk'tan teaches us to respect and pay heed to Under World's tremendous powers of transformation.

Woody Hansen once told me that monsters remain among us, though they sometimes change forms. Greed and vengeance are still with us, and so in turn are things like colonialism, nuclear weapons, deforestation, pollution, and murder. Still, I wonder if deep inside, Uk'tan remembers it is kin to Cherokee. Perhaps that is why it continues to arise from time to time, forewarning us of the effects of our actions, reminding us of our relations, and signaling through its presence the continuing reality of the Under World.

Gada Hawinadidla (Under the Dirt)

Hastings, Loretta, Sequoyah, and other elders have often told me that the earth itself is alive. The very dirt under our feet changes and moves with the seasons, which bring sun, wind, rain, snow, and vegetation that shapes and moves soil across Elohi. We depend on *gada* (soil) for life. We are born from Mother Earth, Hastings said, and our bodies return to her when we die. But in that space when we live, one needs to use caution when digging into the earth and entering holes in the earth. At those times one is entering the body of Mother Earth. There is power there as well as danger. While one may find communion with ancestral spirits and life-giving forces in the earth, one may just as easily release to the surface energies and connections better left buried and alone.

Like other peoples of the Southeast, Hastings told me, Cherokees have had relationships with shaping earthworks. Cherokee village sites like the ancient mother town of *Kituwah* are designed around the four-sided, flat-topped earthen mounds upon which the council houses sat. In the center of the council house the village's fire burned. Rich in layered symbolism involving the Cherokee cosmos and steeped in spiritual significance, mounds are sacred sites. On visits back to Eastern Band of Cherokee Indians territory with his students, Larry Shade takes part in the tradition of continuing to build the Kituwah mound. "One of the traditions at Kituwah is for Cherokees from out west to bring dirt from their homeland and add it to the mound. You bring it in a turtle shell and add a little bit of your culture, your homeland, back to the mound. In that sense it's still being built." Some mounds, like *Nikwasi*, are well known for their continuing spiritual power. Located near Franklin, North Carolina, Nikwasi is home to spirit people who have emerged from the mound and come to the aid of Cherokees under duress in times of war. Relationships with ceremonial mounds continue in ceremonial practice as well. Today when a new fire is brought forth at the center of the square grounds during the Green Corn ceremony, a small four-sided, flat-topped mound is created. Around this mound the seven sacred woods are lit, and a new year begins.

Other types of earthworks exist across Cherokee territory. There are burial mounds as well as effigy mounds. Some of these were built by Cherokees, Hastings said, while many were already there when Cherokees arrived in the area. A great deal has been learned by archaeologists of the Southeast who have excavated these sites, but Hastings was disdainful of this practice and counted it as an act of desecration and spiritual endangerment. We spoke on this topic soon before his passing.

"An elder will tell you the spirit never leaves," Hastings said. "Only the form that you see here is going to be buried. The human body is what we put in the ground when we bury somebody. The *spirit*, that gray spirit, is always going to be around. And, if you'll look, if you lost a loved one or something, you can actually see 'em. That's why, around a mound, I won't get on it. Because you don't know what you're going to pick up. I hate to see people dig into 'em. I know archaeologists love it. But what are they causing? I had one tell me one time that he took a bowl home from a mound site. He said he took it home with him and the next day he took it back. He says, 'I couldn't sleep that night.' I said, 'Well, you took something home that you weren't supposed to take home.'"

In his work for the Cherokee Nation, Hastings visited old Cherokee village sites across the Southeast. The Cherokee Nation worked with the federal government in fulfillment of the Native American Graves Protection and Repatriation Act (NAGPRA) to identify human remains, gravesites, funerary objects, and sacred items. Investigation of sites like Kituwah show that Cherokee villages were scattered with graves. Long ago, it was often the custom to bury kin in the ground under one's dwelling, keeping them close.

"You could tell there were human remains there," Hastings told me. "Without even seeing it. There's just a feeling there. We went to a site in

Kentucky once and I wore my moccasins. I was looking for graves. And I could tell that official where every grave was. He said, 'Yeah that's where they're at.' 'Cause they had used that ground-penetrating radar. He said, 'How'd you know?' I said, 'You can feel 'em.' I mean, you can't describe what it feels like. I could sit here all day long and try to tell you what it feels like, but until you experience it yourself there's no way. Just like somebody getting in the water saying, 'Hey, this water's cold.' Take 'em two weeks to try to tell you what it feels like being cold. And you don't know it until you step in. That's the same way."

Natural caves are likewise a source of fascination and power. Ancient artwork is found on the walls of caves scattered across Cherokee territory in the Southeast, demonstrating the spiritual significance of these spaces. Cherokee writings in the Sequoyan script have even been found on cave walls. Inscriptions found nearly a mile into Manitou Cave in what is now Willstown, Alabama, offer a glimpse of the purification rituals performed by a stickball team in preparation for a game. The writings are dated April 30, 1828. Hastings wrote that the Choctaw called the Cherokee "Chu-loc," meaning people of the cave, which he speculated could be a reference to the relationships of Cherokees with these portals to the Under World. But just like fire, wind, and water, Hastings also said, gada can kill a person in an instant. And so, shaping the living earth and entering the living earth warrant respect and caution.

THEY DON'T KNOW WHAT THEY ARE DOING • *by Hastings Shade*

All the ones who are digging up graves or mounds, whether they are archaeologists, developers, artifact seekers, farmers, or curiosity seekers, they don't know what they are unleashing into the world.

According to the elders, some of the older ones who are buried in these places could control the weather, wind and rain, emotions, and diseases when they were living. They took these things with them when they died and were buried with them.

The elders tell of calling the spirits from these places to help defeat various enemies. But at some point in time it got to where these spirits were not there: they had been released. So now these things are loose in the world.

The weather is being so destructive, especially the wind. Also the heat. The world is warming up. Heat and fire were given to the Indians by the Creator.

Unruly emotions are affecting our young. Because they are not easy to control and have not been taught who they are, our young people are doing things that were unheard of not long ago.

Some people are using the things that were given to us to use for purposes other than their intended use. In other words, they are abusing the medicine to the point that they become addicted to it.

Diseases have come into the world and have no cure. The Native people had cures for these things at one time. And even we, as Native people, have come to forget who we are. If you don't believe this, all you have to do is look around and you can see these things.

ᎦᏙᏃ ᎠᏂᎦᏴᎵ ᏕᎦᏂᏌᏯ ᏗᎪᎯᏩᏍᏗ
(*Why We Respect Our Elders' Burial Grounds*)

ᏃᏊ ᏱᏗᎩᏲᎱᏏ—Ꮎ ᎥᏰᎸ ᏱᎦᏂᏌᎠᎾ ᏗᎦᏂᎩᎡ ᎡᎶᎯ ᎾᏗᎷᎪ ᎦᏓ ᎾᏂᏓᎳᏍᏗᏍᎪ—ᎠᏎᏍᎩᏃ ᎣᏓᏅᏙ Ꮭ ᎠᏲᎱᏍᎩ ᏱᎩ—ᏃᏊ ᎥᏰᎸᎢ ᏩᎴᏅ ᎤᎪᏍᎬ—ᎦᏙᎢ ᎣᏍᏓ ᏂᎬᏁᎨᎢ—Ꮎ ᎦᎸᎸ ᏥᏓᎪᏘᏍᎪ ᎠᎴ ᎤᏂᏥᎸᏍᎩ ᏥᏕᎩᎾᎡᎪ ᎠᎴ ᎤᏃᎴ ᏥᏕᏘᏬᎳᏕᏍᎪ, ᏕᎵᎬ ᎠᏃᎵᎯᏍᏗᎪᎢ—ᎥᏍᎩᏃ ᏗᎳ ᎠᏂᎷᎪ—Ꮭ ᏱᎬᏂᎦ ᎤᎾᏓᏅᏙᎩ.

ᎢᏩᏓᏘ ᎨᎦᎵᏃᎮᏙ—ᎢᎦᏚᎶᏆᏍᏗ ᎢᎦᏛᎪᏗᎢ—ᎠᏎᏍᎩᏂ ᎠᏤᏍᏓᏘ ᏥᏕᏘ ᏍᏓᏱ ᏂᎦᎳᏍᏗᏍᎪ ᎢᎦᏛᎪᏗᎢ ᎨᎦᏨᏃᎮᏛ—ᎢᏩᏓᏘ ᎠᎾᏁᎳᏍᏗᏍᎪ ᎢᎦᏛᎪᏗ ᎨᎩᏃᏎᎢᏗ ᎪᎱᏍᏗ ᏂᏓᎦᎳᏍᏴᏁᎡ—ᎥᏍᎩᏃᎢᏩᏍᏗ ᏅᎩ ᎢᎦ ᏙᏱᎦᏛᏗ—ᎠᎵᏍᏓᏗ ᎠᎴᎾᏍᏙᏗ—ᏃᏭ ᎢᎦᏛᏓᏍᏙᏗ—ᎪᎱᎴᏗ ᏩᏂᏘ ᎨᎩᏃᏎᎢᏗ ᏯᏂᎷᎩ.

WHY WE RESPECT OUR ELDERS' BURIAL GROUNDS • *by Hastings Shade*

Our bodies, once they are buried, return to the Mother Earth from which we came. But the Spirit lives on.

The bodies, when they begin to decay, nurture the ground and become the grass that we see and the flowers that we smell and the air that we breathe through the trees that produce oxygen. So this is how they come back to us.

Their Spirit is always with us. Sometimes they speak to us. We have to learn how to listen.

As long as we look to the modern-day world and the modern way of living, we will have a hard time hearing them. Sometimes they try to warn us of things that are going to happen.

So we need to fast for four days and go to a place where there will be no interruption—and listen—and if they have something to say to us—they will come.

ELDER TEACHING ON WHEN A YOUNG CHILD DIES

by Hastings Shade

Kids are only loaned to us to teach us—we do not
Teach them
They teach us—
How to raise them—
How to teach them things like the old way.
They choose us—we do not choose them.
Sometimes they only teach us for a short time
And then they choose to leave us.
It is not anything we have done
That causes children to leave us.
They chose to leave us on their own—
Their teaching is over for that family.
But their spirit is always with us.
Even though they are no longer here in the body, their
Teachings go on.
We will never forget what they taught us in the
Short time they were here.
We use this all our adult lives—
As do the kids that choose us—
When we are old enough to be taught.
By then something new will be here as well as the
Old ways—this is why there are new ones being
Born every day.

NA USDAGALV (*The Cave*) • *by Hastings Shade*

When we were young boys and used to hunt all the time, there was an old man who used to go hunting with us sometimes. One day we were hunting in a place we call Clear Creek. As we were walking along the hillside the old man said, "I'm going to show you all something, but I want you all to promise me one thing when I show this place to you: that you will never take anything out of there." We all said we promised not to.

We walked on a short way and we came to a hole in the side of the hill, which was big enough for a good-sized man to crawl into. It went straight down for about twelve feet. We didn't go into the cave that day because we didn't have any kind of light. He said, "There are some things down there you all can look at but don't bother anything." We said okay.

It was a week or two later we decided to go into the cave. We took some flashlights and a lantern with us. It was easy to crawl down into. There were hand- and footholds. When we got inside there was a room about eight by ten feet and just tall enough to walk upright if you were not a tall person. There was a small opening that led to another room that was about the same size as the first one. What we found in this cave was some old Civil War things. Pieces of old uniforms and buttons. Pieces of old leather bags and two old lanterns. As we continued to look around there was a feeling there was someone watching you. We didn't bother anything or touch anything. We didn't stay very long but came back out.

We never told anyone until we were older about the cave or what was in it. This was in the mid-1950s. I went back one other time and everything was like it was when we first went in it. I went into the service in 1958. Sometime during this period one of my friends took his cousin from Muskogee into the cave, and he told him not to take anything. As they came out, my friend came out first. What he didn't know was that his cousin had grabbed one of the lanterns and took it almost to the top of the opening and hid it among the rocks that were sticking out. My friend lived about three-quarters of a mile from the cave. Without my friend knowing it, his cousin sneaked back and got the lantern and took it home with him when they left. His cousin told him this later on.

When he got home, my friend's cousin put the lantern on his dresser. When his dad asked him where he got it, he said he found it. And that was all that was said. What happened the first night was that he had a dream of women and children crying like they were lost and hurt. But he couldn't find them.

The second night he dreamed of a young Rebel or Southern soldier who was wounded, bleeding, and bandaged up. He said that in his dream he tried to take care of the young man, but he couldn't help him.

The third night he dreamed he and some other people were running through the woods with soldiers shooting at them. He couldn't tell what color uniforms they were wearing, he just remembers them chasing the group. As he was running he fell down, and as he turned over on his back there was this soldier coming at him with a bayonet aimed at his chest. Just before he felt the bayonet go into his chest, he woke up. He said it was all too real. He couldn't sleep the rest of the night.

He was tired all day, and he said he was afraid to go to sleep that night. He hadn't got too much rest for three nights. He hated to lie down, but when he did he went to sleep. Sometimes during the night he woke up, and the way he was lying was facing the wall. He opened his eyes and noticed a light reflecting off the wall. He turned over to look for where the light was coming from. He saw that the lantern was lit. As he tried to focus his eyes, the lantern went out. Then he remembered what his cousin had told him: "Don't take anything out of the cave."

The next day he asked his dad to take him back to his cousin's house. When he got there, he told his cousin what had happened and what he had done. He and his cousin took the lantern back to the cave. He put it back close to the same place he had gotten it from. He said it still took him two to three months to feel better after he had taken the lantern back.

I got out of the service in the early sixties. I went back to the cave, but someone had thrown some large rocks into the hole and sealed it up. It's been close to forty years since I last went to the cave; I doubt that I could even find it today.

When the old man said to leave things alone, he never said what would happen, but now we know. There was something there.

ᎠᏕᎳ ᏧᏂᏍᏜᏛᏛ (*Buried Money*)

ᎠᏕᎳ ᎣᏙᎯᏜ—ᏦᎳᏧᏨᏫᏍᏗ ᏣᎳᏍᏙᏗ—ᎥᏍᎩ ᏂᎨᎡᎾ ᎣᎩ—ᏓᏰᎵ ᎪᎱᏍᏗ ᎣᎨᏑᏩᏔ—ᎣᏨᎸᎸᏬᏕ ᏣᏝᏔᏗᏍᏗ ᎤᏚᏁᏬ—ᎪᎱᏍᏗ ᎤᏂᎨᏝᏛ ᎤᎨᏎᏍᏗ ᎯᎨᏆᏝ—

BURIED MONEY ♦ *by Hastings Shade*

The elders say, "Any time you look for buried money, you need to be brave—or you would never find anything—because you wouldn't be able to concentrate on what you are supposed to be doing—and would probably get run off by whatever was left to guard the money."

GRANDPA AND THE BURIED MONEY ✦ *by Hastings Shade*

Grandpa told me this story.

"When I was a young man, an old man came to me and asked me if I would help him dig for some buried money. I told him I would help him whenever he got ready to dig for it. The old man told me he needed to find one more person to help us. He said, 'When I find him I'll come back and tell you what we need to do.' This was in the wintertime and it was later on into spring before he came back and told me he had found someone to help us.

"One evening, the old man and the one he had found to help us came to where I was staying with my uncle and began to tell us what we would have to do when we got ready to dig for the money. He told us once we got started we couldn't talk and to dig only when he started to dig and not to be afraid, 'cause if you are afraid then we will never get the money. Something will run us off. So we knew this and we waited until he got ready, which was when the corn was about thigh high. That was in the early part of May. It had been about five months since he first talked about doing this.

"The place where the money was buried was across the creek and just on the inside of a cornfield, right close to the fence line.

"The time came for us to dig, and we all met at the old man's house. Where the money was buried wasn't very far from this house, maybe a half-mile. He had told us we couldn't start digging until after midnight.

"It was about ten o'clock when we started off toward the creek. When we got to the creek we took our shoes off so we could wade the creek. We got to the other side, put our shoes back on, and went on to the cornfield. We crawled under the fence and got close to where the money was buried and sat down.

"We watched the old man as he lit his pipe and sat there and smoked. He had told us just watch him and do what he did. It seemed like we sat there for a long time. Then we seen him get up and grab his shovel. We did the same thing and started to dig. Up until that time we hadn't heard a thing. Back then it was open range. All the livestock roamed free, and the crops were under fence. Just when we started to dig we heard this bull begin to bellow and holler and paw the ground. This was the first time we had heard anything since we had been there. But we could tell he was outside the fence. We just kept digging. Pretty soon the bull was getting closer. You could hear him real good as he pawed the ground and kicked up dirt. You could hear the dirt and rocks hitting the leaves as he pawed the ground. Still, we kept digging, watching the old man. He didn't seem concerned about the bull bellowing and making all that noise.

"We had dug about three foot deep when we heard the bull inside the fence where the corn was planted. Now you could hear him breaking the corn stalks, and when he would paw the ground and kick up dirt you heard the dirt and rocks hitting the corn leaves. We just kept on digging.

"Pretty soon we heard him coming toward us running through the corn patch, breaking the stalks as he was coming. We watched the old man, and he just kept digging. The next thing we knew the bull was right there where we were, ready to run over us. We seen the old man throw down his shovel and crawl under the fence and run. We did the same thing, too, right behind him. This time when we got to the creek we didn't take our shoes off. We ran straight across the creek. When we got to the other side of the creek everything got real quiet again. No sound. The bull no longer making noise. Not even frogs or insects hollering.

"We didn't say a word to each other. We just went on back home."

Two or three days later, Grandpa said, he was real curious as to what kind of damage the bull had done to the cornfield. And he wanted to get his uncle's shovel back. So he went back to where they had dug. He said, "I looked at the cornfield and not a stalk was broken. Nothing was disturbed."

He said, "Something run us off that night. If we could have stayed and finished digging we would have found something. But we let our fears get the best of us."

He used to say, "If you want to hunt for buried money, you better be brave. Don't think about anything but what you are doing. What you are thinking might appear."

Atsadi (Fish)

Hastings Shade was renowned as a gig maker. I knew that fishing was an important part of his cultural practice. He was taught to make gigs and to fish with a gig and spear by his grandfather, Charley Smith. He fished with his grandfather and uncles and taught his children—Larry, Dondi, and Ron—to fish with gigs as well. He preferred to gig for fish in the winter, Loretta told me. By the light of the full moon they would fish the Illinois River, deep parts of nearby creeks, or other bodies of water by boat. Light from their gas lanterns would shine off the scales of the fish. They would gig carp, catfish, and suckers this way, asserting their sovereign fishing rights.

In warmer months, Hastings and his family members also noodled for catfish. Larry carries on this tradition of wading the creek and river banks in search of downed trees and other spots where catfish linger. Noodling, he explained to me, is not for the faint of heart. When noodling one time with family, Hastings dove underwater to search a hole with his hands. "He stayed under a long time," Larry said. "Finally, I see his leg kick, so I dove under water, too. He grabbed my hand and I found the fish. I knew he wanted me to grab the tail, so I ran my hand down its back and I thought, 'Oh, my god!' There was no end to that thing. I felt the fish start to move so I knew he was trying to pull us. So I just grabbed the tail and held on. I remember how heavy it was. Dad had his forearm underneath it and had one hand in its mouth and one in its gills. And when it landed on the ground it just flopped. That was the biggest flathead I've seen come out of that creek. Sixty-three pounds."

For many Cherokee families like the Shades, fishing is both a cultural pastime and an important source of food. Archaeological evidence suggests fish made up more than 25 percent of the meat diet of ancestral Cherokee communities in what is now eastern Tennessee (Altman 2006, 39). In addition to noodling and gigging, Cherokee ancestors fished rivers and creeks with weirs and nets (40). They also stunned fish with crushed black walnut hulls and other plants, then netting them (46). Hastings had used this method to fish, Loretta told me, but said it gave the meat a bad taste. Most folks today fish with hook and line. And fishing continues to be an important cultural practice, bringing people into relationship with the waters of Cherokee territory and the creatures that live within them.

Given the rich Cherokee tradition of fishing, I found it strange that fish are not prominent in Cherokee mythology. Loretta recalled the story that all fish descend from a giant fish, *daqua,* that lived in the Little Tennessee River. When that monstrous fish was killed and cut up, they say, all the smaller fish we know today were created. Fish are associated with the power and fertility of waters, Loretta said. But unlike many other creatures of the Under World, *atsadi* stay in their place. This is a surprising statement to make, given that any angler knows fish are ever on the move searching for food. But fish stick to the water. They do not cross over from the Under World and crawl on land, like snakes. Or fly, swim, and crawl, like insects. They are creatures of the water, and there they stay until caught for food by humans and other animals. This may be one reason there are few mythic stories exploring the behavior of fish and our relations with them. Though much of their world is inaccessible to us, Cherokees have relied on fish relatives for food. They continue to feed us, as they also continue to clean and nourish the waters of Elohi, which sustain us. Among other qualities, *anitsadi* symbolize breath and calmness in Cherokee thought.

Fish

ᎠᏣᏗ ✦ atsadi (ah-jah-dee) ✦ **fish**

ᎤᏃᎦ ✦ unoga (oo-noh-gah) ✦ **bass** ✦ Name given when the bass can't be identified.

ᎤᏃᎦ ᏧᎶᎢᏍᏗ ✦ unoga tsuloisdi (oo-noh-gah joo-loh-ee-sdee) ✦ **bass, largemouth, or black bass** ✦ Name means: bass with a stripe

ᎤᏃᎩᏯ ✦ unogiya (oo-noh-gee-yah) ✦ **bass, smallmouth** ✦ Name means: principal bass or all bass

ᎤᏃᎦ ᎤᏅᏥᏓ ✦ unoga unvtsida (oo-noh-gah oo-nuh-jee-dah) ✦ **bass, spotted** ✦ Name means: having spots or checkered

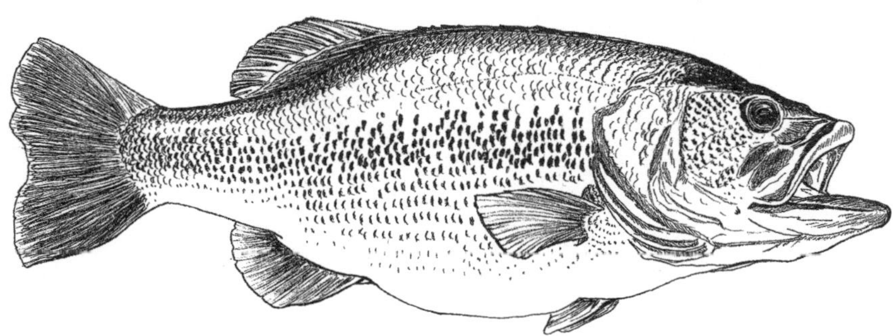

Unoga tsuloisdi (largemouth bass)

ᎤᏃᎦ ᎤᏁᎦ ✦ unoga unega (oo-noh-gah oo-neh-gah) ✦ **bass, sand** ✦ Name means: white bass

ᎤᎾᏥᏍᎬᎾᎨ ✦ unatsisgvnage (oo-nah-jee-sguh-nah-geh)✦ **carp** ✦ New name. This fish was transplanted from a different country.

ᎤᏍᏉᎳ ✦ usquola (oo-sqwoh-lah) ✦ **catfish** ✦ Name means: belly ✦ "A person can't go into a garden for four days after eating catfish," Loretta said. "It will make the garden die." ✦ *"In Cherokee tradition,* usquola *symbolizes breath*—nayadvv—ᎾᏯᏛᎥ." *H.S.*

ᏧᏥᏍᏓᎾᎵᏯ ✦ tsutsisdanaliya (joo-jee-sdah-nah-lee-yah) ✦ **catfish, blue channel** ✦ Name means: all shiny-side

ᏧᏥᏍᏓᎾᎳ ✦ tsutsisdanala (joo-jee-sdah-nah-lah) ✦ **catfish, channel** ✦ Name means: sides that shine when he turns

ᎤᏍᏉᎳ ᎡᏆ ✦ usquola equa (oo-sqwoh-lah eh-qwah) ✦ **catfish, flathead, or mud catfish** ✦ Name means: big-bellied cat fish. Also called *usquoliya,* or all belly.

ᏧᏥᏍᏓᎾᎳ ᎤᏁᎦ ✦ tsutsisdanala unega (joo-jee-sdah-nah-lah oo-neh-gah) ✦ **catfish, white channel** ✦ Name means: white shiny-side catfish

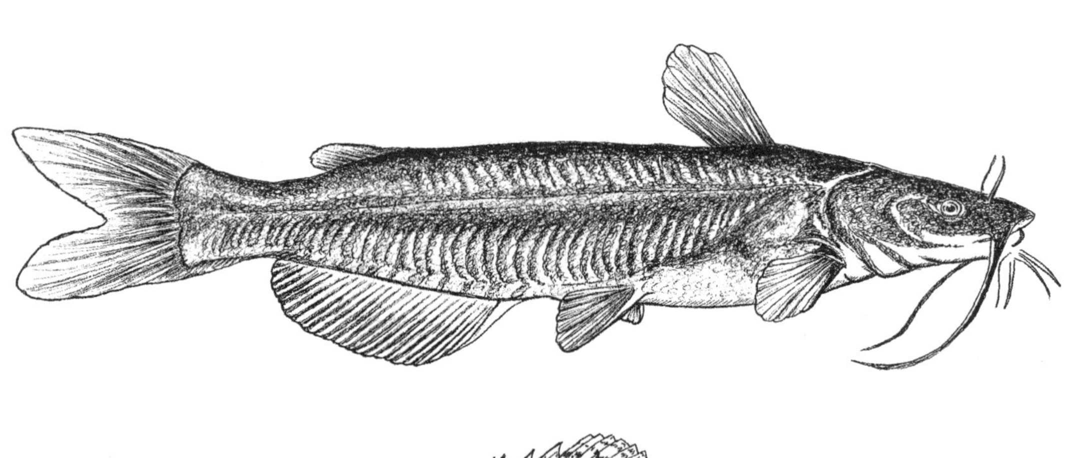

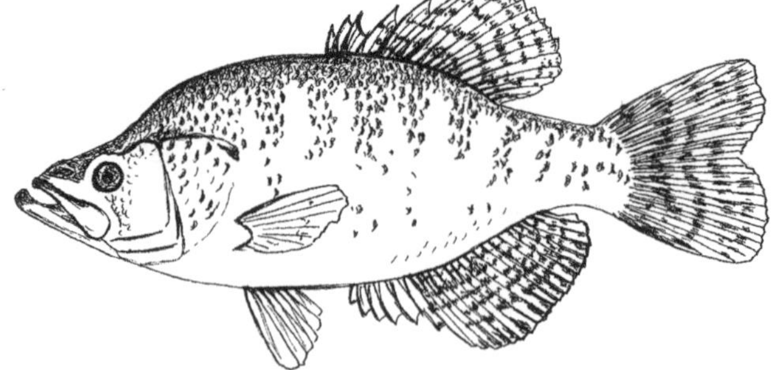

top
Usquola (catfish)

bottom
Agola unega (crappie)

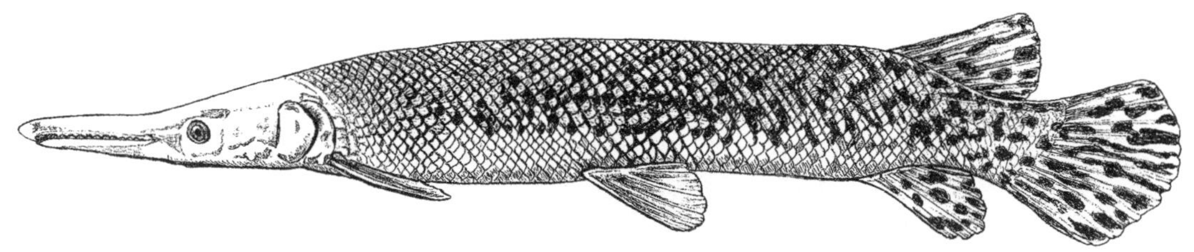

Danuga (alligator gar)

ᎠᎪᎳ ᎤᏁᎦ • agola unega (ah-goh-lah oo-neh-gah) • **crappie** • Name means: white perch. Same name for both white and black crappie. Good to catch after the dogwoods flower.

ᏥᏍᏓᏆᎸᏂ • tsisdaqualvni (jee-sdah-qwah-luh-nee) • **darter, johnny** • Name means: having a large head. Small fish but good eating.

ᏓᎦᎷᎾ • dagaluna (dah-gah-loo-nah) • **darter, rainbow** • This is the fish that has different colors on him.

ᎤᏐᏈᏘ • usoquiti (oo-so-quee-tee) • **drum** • Name means: hump on its back

ᏢᏕᏆ • tlvdequa (tluh-deh-qwah) • **eel** • Name means: wrap around

ᏓᏄᎦ • danuga (dah-noo-gah) • **gar, alligator** • The town of Gore, Oklahoma, has this name also.

ᎠᏣᏗᏯ • atsadiya (ah-jah-dee-yah) • **minnow** • Name means: all fish or principal fish

ᎠᏂᎩᏣᏗᏯ • anigitsadiya • ah-nee-gee-jah-dee-yah • **minnow, blackhead**

ᎤᏂᎩᏣᏓ • unigitsada (oo-nee-gee-jah-dah) • **minnow, hornyhead chub**

ᎠᎹᎠᎦᏘᏯ • amaagatiya (ah-mah-ah-gah-teeyah) • **minnow, topwater** • Name means: he guards the water or waits on the water. Also known as "mosquito fish."

ᎠᎪᎳ • agola (ah-goh-lah) • **perch** • Name for all perch.

ᎠᎪᎳ ᎬᎾᎨ • agola gvnage (ah-goh-lah guh-nah-geh) • **perch, black** • Name means: black perch

ᎠᎪᎵᏯ • agoliya (ah-goh-lee-yah) • **perch, bluegill** • Name means: principal perch or all perch

ᎠᎪᎳ ᏗᎦᏚᎳᎾ • agola digatulana (ah-goh-lah dee-gah-too-lah-nah) • **perch, goggle-eye** • Name means: bug-eyed or eyes sticking out

ᎠᎪᎳ ᎩᎦᎨ • agola gigage (ah-goh-lah gee-gah-geh) • **perch, sun, or red-ear sunfish** • Name means: red perch

ᎩᎦᎨ ᏧᎳᏡᏯᏛ • gigage tsulatluyadv (gee-gah-geh joo-lah-tloo-yah-duh) • **redfin shiner**

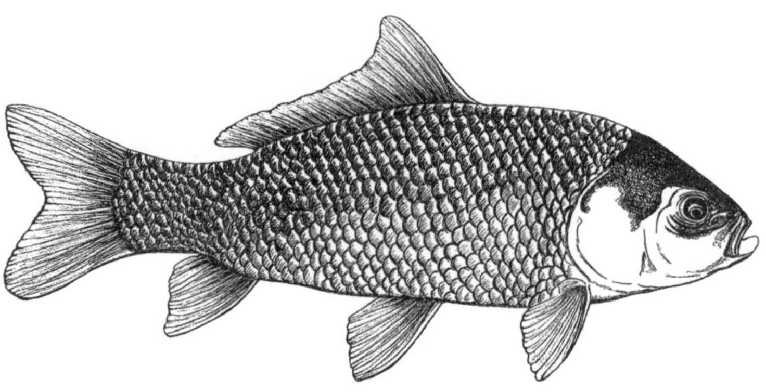

Gasada (buffalo fish, sucker)

ᎦᏌᏓ • gasada (gah-sah-dah) • **sucker, buffalo** • This name is still used to name boys—it's an old name. • *"In Cherokee tradition,* gasada *symbolizes calmness*—dohinusdv—ᏙᎯᏄᏍᏛ." *H.S.*

ᎠᏃᎵᎩᏯ • anoligiya (ah-noh-lee-gee-yah) • **sucker, mud**

ᎤᏩᏗᎵᎩ • uwadiligi (oo-wah-dee-lee-gee) • **sucker, quillback buffalo** • Name means: sticking out of the back

ᎠᏃᎵᎩ • anoligi (ah-noh-lee-gee) • **sucker, river redhorse**

ᏓᎶᎨ • daloge (dah-loh-geh) • **sucker, striped, or hog sucker** • One of the best-flavored fish around, but it has a lot of bones.

ᎣᎵᎦ ᎤᏁᎦ • oliga unega (oh-lee-gah oo-neh-gah) • **sucker, white**

ᎠᏓᏣ • adatsa (ah-dah-jah) • **trout**

ᏥᎵᏯ • tsiliya (jee-lee-yah) • **walleye**

ᏓᏆ • daqua (dah-gwah) • **whale or big fish**

Snake Relatives and Creatures That Live in the Water

If you look for *inada,* you will find the snake throughout Cherokee life. You might walk past a person in downtown Tahlequah wearing a T-shirt depicting an ancient Mississippian image of two rattlesnakes encircling a hand with an eye in its center. If in the summer you take a drive through the countryside you will likely see dead snakes along the highway. Warm weather may tempt you to take a dip in local waters, but watch for snakes. Walking through the woods to the water's edge, you could encounter a copperhead that strikes without warning. And once there, be mindful of water moccasins. They have approached me in the Il-

Ganequodi (cottonmouth, water moccasin)

GANOHALIDOHI ALE DAQUA (*The Hunter and the Big Fish*) ✦ *by Noyi Teuton*

As with Jonah in the Bible and Hercules from Greek mythology, Cherokee oral tradition tells of a man unexpectedly drawn into the Under World and swallowed by a monstrous creature from the deep. Loretta remembered this story, a version of which was told by Ayu'ini to James Mooney and that I retell here. Like others, with courage and ingenuity the hunter was able to emerge from the belly of the beast. But his trial marked him.

Long ago there was a *daqua* that lived in the Tennessee River. It was enormous, so large that it could swallow a person whole. Elders say a canoe of hunters were crossing the *Tvnasi* once when the daqua rose up from the depths and struck the bottom of the boat with such strength that the hunters were tossed into the air. As they came down, the daqua snatched one hunter in midair. It swallowed him whole and dove back down to the river bottom.

Once he recovered his senses and realized he was unharmed, the hunter later told, he found himself trapped in a dark, hot, and tight space. He fought for every breath. His hands pushed at the flesh around him and searched for an opening or anything to help him escape. He felt something sharp and knew it must be the shells of *dagvna* (mussels). He took hold of a shell and began to cut at the flesh of the great daqua's stomach. The fish thrashed about at the pain in its belly. Still, the hunter kept cutting. The daqua must have swum to the shallow waters for air, because when the hunter finally cut through the side of the fish, he could see the shallow water and shore nearby. The hunter squeezed through the hole and waded to shore. But it is said that the acid in the daqua's stomach had burned the hair from the hunter's head. He was bald thereafter.

A Cherokee village took its name from the great daqua. You can find the site of *Toqua* just south of Fort Loudon State Park in Tennessee.

linois River and are common in the Town Branch and other creeks.

Almost everyone has stories about snakes, if you ask. Whether they are feared, admired, or loathed, relationships with snakes are a part of Cherokee life. More than with any other class of creature, Cherokees have come to relate to the Under World through relationships with inada.

As birds express key characteristics of the Sky World, snakes embody the boundless, creative, life-giving powers of the underground and waters that energize Elohi. Cold-blooded, dependent on the Sky

World's sun for their warmth, inada nevertheless traverse the borders of the three-tiered Cherokee cosmos, shedding even their skins as they grow. Born from eggs like their nemeses, the birds, they are hatched underground. Then, with undulating locomotion that in its grace, beauty, and strangeness we cannot ignore, snakes are among us. While other creatures generally stay where they belong, snakes are explorers. They go where they please. They are just as likely to be found in a field as in one's own home. One of their kind, Uk'tan, took to the sky and became a constellation. They have even announced their presence across the chapters of this book, not waiting for their introduction in the Under World.

Our relationships with snakes unfold in dualities and paradoxes that have long captivated us. They evoke strong emotions in nearly all of us, but snakes themselves are often seen as emotionless. They excite our imaginations and slither through our artistic traditions, but they often seem driven by instinct, even lacking creativity. Yet a moment's reflection shows this is not so; snakes respond to their world as much as any of us do. Perhaps my own ambivalence toward them is because they are hard to read. Though ever-present in our world, they remain inscrutable and aloof.

Saliguga (snapping turtle)

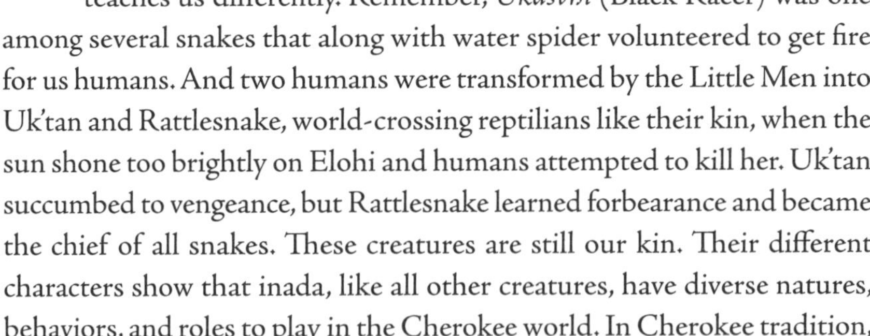

It is tempting to shun inada as wholly other to us, but Cherokee tradition teaches us differently. Remember, *Ukasvhi* (Black Racer) was one among several snakes that along with water spider volunteered to get fire for us humans. And two humans were transformed by the Little Men into Uk'tan and Rattlesnake, world-crossing reptilians like their kin, when the sun shone too brightly on Elohi and humans attempted to kill her. Uk'tan succumbed to vengeance, but Rattlesnake learned forbearance and became the chief of all snakes. These creatures are still our kin. Their different characters show that inada, like all other creatures, have diverse natures, behaviors, and roles to play in the Cherokee world. In Cherokee tradition, particular inada symbolize patience, willingness, being an emissary, and transformation.

Ever since Uk'tan battled with Thunder, snakes have been associated with lightning, rain, and waters. Perhaps it is for this reason that Hastings chose to list other reptiles and creatures of the water along with his list of snakes. Some of them, such as *Daksi* (Terrapin) and *Saliguga* (Snapping Turtle) are world-crossers as well. The teachings of life among these creatures, I came to learn, are vital to a living Cherokee world in which we strive toward tohi. Perhaps we see in them what we both fear and admire most inside ourselves.

Reptiles and Amphibians

ᎢᎾᏓ ᎠᎴ ᎠᎹᎢ ᎠᏁᎯ • inada ale amai anehi (ee-nah-dah ah-leh ah-mah-ee ah-neh-hee) • **reptiles and amphibians**

ᏍᏆᎾᏕᏲ • squanadeyo (sqwah-nah-deh-yoh) • **adder, spreading, or eastern hog-nosed snake** • Name means: low and wide

ᏧᎳᏍᎩ • tsulasgi (joo-lah-sgee) • **alligator** • Name means: having feet

ᏩᏥᎵ • watsili (wah-jee-lee) • **anole, green** • Name is similar to the Cherokee word for saliva.

ᎦᎴᎩ • galegi (gah-leh-gee) • **blacksnake, or rat snake** • Name means: the climber

HOW TO KEEP YOUR TEETH

Loretta and I sat with elders Dorothy Ice, Melvina King, and Rufus King, studying Hastings' book of reptile and amphibian names, when a Cherokee folk remedy came to Mr. King's mind.

"Have you heard how you can keep all your teeth?" the elder Rufus King asked me. Loretta and I were visiting with him and other elders about Hastings' creature name books.

"No, I haven't," I said.

"It's about a blacksnake," Rufus continued. "You catch a blacksnake out there. You catch him and you stretch him out. Then you start biting him on the back. You bite him all the way down his back. And then you turn him loose." After a pause we all laughed out loud.

"I think I'd rather just lose my teeth," Melvina King said.

"Me, too!" said Dorothy Ice.

"Her grandpa did that," Rufus told us.

"Yeah. My grandpa did," Melvina said.

"He did it?" I said.

"Mmhm," Melvina said. "I think he was about eighty years old before he lost a tooth. And it came back in."

"He got another tooth," Rufus confirmed.

"Straight as could be," Melvina said, and we all laughed again.

"Wow," I said. "He still lost a tooth, though."

"He lost a tooth but it came back in," Melvina said.

"Just like a copperhead or rattlesnake, they say if they lose a tooth it's gonna come back in. That's the way snakes are," Rufus said.

"But it's just a blacksnake you're supposed to bite?" I asked.

"Yeah," Rufus said.

"Do you have to keep biting the whole way down? Or can you skip parts?" I asked and we all laughed.

"All the way down!" Rufus said.

"I'd skip it all!" Dorothy said.

"I just skipped all of it," Melvina said.

ᎧᏄᎾ ✦ kanuna (kah-noo-nah) ✦ **bullfrog**

ᏐᎳᎨᎢ ✦ solagei (soh-lah-geh-ee) ✦ **bullsnake** ✦ The name is almost like flying snake.

ᏧᏘᏟ ᎠᏓᎸᏂ ✦ tsutitli adalvni (joo-tee-tlee ah-dah-luh-nee) ✦ **coachwhip snake** ✦ Name means: whip with a spike

ᏧᎦᏔᏥᏍᏓᏟ ✦ tsugatatsisdatli (joo-gah-tah-jee-stah-tlee) ✦ **copperhead** ✦ Names means: bright eyes. Also called *tsowi*. ✦ "In my relationship with copperheads," Woody Hansen said, "they remind me of our ancestor warrior men. Our skin color is similar. Our disposition is that we are not afraid of man. In combat we strike only when threatened. We climb, swim, and hunt. And as we age and grow in maturity, we change our ways as the copperhead sheds its skin."

ᎦᏁᏉᏗ ✦ ganequodi (gah-neh-qwoh-dee) ✦ **cottonmouth moccasin, or water moccasin** ✦ Real aggressive snake. Has a pure white color inside the mouth. Also called *newodi* and *ganadena*. ✦ "*In Cherokee tradition,* ganequodi *symbolizes willingness*—agatliya—ᎠᎦᏟᏯ." *H.S.*

Tsugatatsisdatli (copperhead)

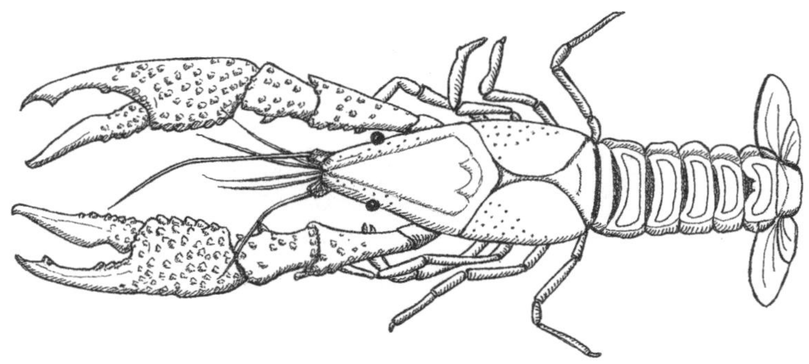

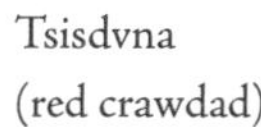

Tsisdvna
(red crawdad)

ᏄᏯ ✦ nvya (nuh-yah) ✦ **crawdad, blue** ✦ This was the color of all crawdads at one time. This is the one who did not leave the water and remained the color that he was.

ᏥᏍᎪᎩᎵ ✦ tsisgogili (jee-sgoh-gee-lee) ✦ **crawdad, prairie** ✦ "This crawdad found out too late that he was lured out by the Evil One and the sun cooked his flesh. So he dug into the ground where he was and this is where he lives to this day. The Indians do not eat him because his flesh is spoiled." H.S.

ᏥᏍᏛᎾ ✦ tsisdvna (jee-stuh-nah) ✦ **crawdad, red** ✦ "This crawdad was lured from the water by the Evil One and found out just in time to get back to the water before his flesh was cooked. He only scorched his outer shell and turned it red." H.S.

ᏖᎦ ✦ tega (teh-gah) ✦ **frog, leopard**

ᎠᎹ ᎠᏘᏲᎯᎯ ✦ ama atiyohihi (ah-mah ah-tee-yoh-hee-hee) ✦ **frog, rain** ✦ Name means: the one that asks for water

ᏓᎳ ✦ dala (dah-lah) ✦ **frog, tree** ✦ This is the one with the sticky feet. He can climb anything. ✦ *"In Cherokee tradition,* dala *symbolizes transformation*—adanetliyvsidohv—ᎠᏓᏁᏟᏴᏏᏙᎲ." *H.S.*

Dala
(tree frog)

ᎤᎦᏔᎾ ✦ ugatana (oo-gah-tah-nah) ✦ **flying dragon, or winged serpent** ✦ Name means: shiny eye or shining eyes. This is where the crystal comes from. ✦ Its name is written as Uk'tan or Uk'tena. It has a powerful ability to see anything that comes near it.

ᏐᎳᎩ ✦ solagi (soh-lah-gee) ✦ **flying snake** ✦ "Some people say this type of snake does or did not exist. There is a snake that will glide from a tree, but not this one. The Cherokee know that there is a snake that does fly. If the elders say that one exists, then I believe it. At least we have a name for one." H.S.

THE SNAKE THAT COULD FLY ✦ *by Hastings Shade*

Dad told me this story about what happened to him and his cousin when they were younger. They were helping bale some hay one time in an area we call prairie. There are some big fields there, and they still bale hay there to this day.

Dad said they had worked late that day trying to get finished, and it had gotten dark by the time they finished, which in the summer time is after 9:00 p.m. They started riding their horse across the field where they had just mowed. The field is about one hundred and fifty acres, and the grass where they had mowed was about two to three inches high. They heard something that sounded like someone swinging a rope around, and right then something wrapped around his cousin's neck. His cousin yelled, "*Inada*! Snake!" He grabbed it and threw it to the ground. Dad said he got off his horse and ran over to take a look. He wanted to see if it really was a snake. When he reached into his pocket he found only one match. When he struck the match and it lit, he only had a glimpse of the snake as it crawled off. He said it had wings, and as it crawled away they folded against its body. He had always heard that there were snakes that could fly. This was the first one that he had seen that had wings. He also said the wings looked like the ones bats have.

When you are riding a horse, your head is at least seven or eight feet above ground. And they encountered this snake in the middle of a big field. There was no way a snake could have glided from a tree. The trees around the field were small; the field he was talking about is in the middle of a mile section with fence rows that had small saplings.

Dad always said, "That snake came flying across that field."

This is one the elders called *solagi*.

ᎣᎦᏗᏯ ✦ ogatiya (oh-gah-tee-yah) ✦ **garter snake** ✦ Name means: waiting or the watchman

ᏎᎳᏉᎢ ✦ selaquoi (seh-lah-qwoh-ee) ✦ **green snake** ✦ Like blacksnake, green snakes are also used in doctoring teeth.

ᎤᏓᎵ ᎠᎦᏗᏯ ✦ odali agatiya (oh-dah-lee ah-gah-tee-yah) ✦ **guard snake** ✦ "This is the snake that only the Cherokees knew about. His name means 'Mountain Guard' or 'Guard Snake.' It was brought west but didn't survive here. There is no known cure for its bite. Some people may disagree that one even existed, but we know that it did." H.S.

ᎤᏍᏓᏟ ✦ usdatli (oo-sdah-tlee) ✦ **hoop snake** ✦ Name means: having a spike or stinger on his tail

ᏗᏔᏟᏍᎩ • ditatlisgi (dee-tah-tlee-sgee) • **joint snake** • Name means: comes apart

ᏗᏍᎬᏛᏂᏍᏗ • disgvdvnisdi (dee-sguh-duh-nee-sdee) • **kingsnake** • Name means: hit across the forehead

ᏜᏄᏏ • dlanusi (dlah-noo-see) • **leech** • Was and is used to treat ailments of the blood. Should be done by someone who knows what they are doing.

ᏘᏲᎭᎵ • tiyohali (tee-yoh-ha-lee) • **lizard**

ᎩᎦ ᏧᎭᏟ • giga tsuhatli (gee-gah joo-ha-tlee) • **lizard, collared, or mountain boomer** • Name means: blood around his mouth

ᏜᏁᎾ • dlanena (dlah-neh-nah) • **lizard, six-lined racerunner** • This is the green striped lizard that you see crossing the road or lying on it, especially a dirt road.

ᏚᏪᎦ • duwega (duh-weh-gah) • **lizard, spring**

ᏓᎬᎾ • dagvna (dah-guh-nah) • **mussel**

ᏓᎬᎾ ᎡᏆ • dagvna equa (dah-guh-nah eh-qwah) • **oyster**

ᎤᎧᏒᎯ • ukasvhi (oo-kah-suh-hee) • **racer, black** • Name means: smoke blinded. Like the blue racer, except he didn't fall into the fire, but the smoke blinded him and he crawled away as fast as he could.

ᏧᎳᏘᎢᏗ • tsulatiidi (joo-laa-tee-ee-dee) • **racer, blue** • Name means: trying to get away • "This is the snake that tried to get the fire for the Cherokees. As he looked into the tree where the fire was, he fell in and he started to crawl every which way trying to escape the fire, which he did. And to this day he still crawls this way." H.S.

ᎤᎦᏑᏘ • ugasuti (oo-gah-suh-tee) • **rattlesnake, diamondback** • *"In Cherokee tradition,* ugasuti *symbolizes patience*—nutsosedvna—ᏄᏦᏎᏛᎾ.*" H.S.*

ᎤᎦᏢᎩ ᎤᏣᎢ • ugalogi utsai (oo-gah-loh-gee oo-jah-ee) • **rattlesnake, pygmy** • Name means: lives in the leaves. "I was told by my ancestors that *ugalogi utsai* belongs to the Little People," Woody Hansen said. "It came out west with our medicine people."

ᎤᏦᎾᏘ • utsonati (oo-joh-nah-tee) • **rattlesnake, velvet-tail, or cane-brake** • Name means: makes noise with its tail or rattles

ᎪᎢ • goi (goh-ee) • **ringneck snake** • Name means: oil or grease. This is the one that you may find as you are working in the garden or flower bed or in the old decaying wood or leaves.

ᏚᏫᎦ • duwiga (doo-wee-gah) • **salamander**

ᏓᎦᎾᏓ • daganada (dah-gah-nah-dah) • **salamander, red** • Name means: licked something

One night back in 1994 Woody Hansen had a vision dream. The renowned Cherokee snake handler, educator, and storyteller of the Turtle Island Liars' Club recounted the dream to me, Hastings, and Sequoyah one afternoon at Hastings' house in Lost City. In his vision Woody gave chase to a little yellow rattlesnake that egged him on to follow, escaping each time Woody went to catch it with his snake catcher. The little yellow rattlesnake crawled into a hole in a rock wall, and when it poked its head out to laugh at him, he took his snake catcher and reached around in the hole. It was then that the hole fell in and opened up a cave.

Woody followed the little yellow rattlesnake into the cave and could hear all around him the echoing sound of snakes shaking their rattles. He wasn't afraid. He followed the little snake in and around a bend. The cave opened up into a large cavern. In the center of the space on a waist-high rock sat a big, old rattlesnake looking straight at Woody. "Why are you catching my kin?" the rattler asked him. "To educate people," Woody answered. "Not to kill or sell. To educate and learn more about you." The great rattlesnake nodded its head. "That is good," it said. And then Woody woke up. In the years that followed, Woody returned to his vision dream as confirmation of his chosen path to teach people how to live among snakes in peace.

In Cherokee tradition, *ugasuti* (rattlesnake) is considered chief among inada. Unlike other venomous snakes like *tsowi* (copperhead), who often strike without warning, rattlers will signal their presence by shaking their tails, letting whoever is near know they are there and want to avoid trouble. Killing a rattler was once considered a grave mistake that must be made right by asking its forgiveness before its spirit sought vengeance to balance the offense.

Woody shared stories of his journey as a snake educator in *Cherokee Stories of the Turtle Island Liars' Club*, including the story of how he was gravely injured when hit by a car after stopping to capture a copperhead near his home in Kenwood. He nearly lost his leg in that accident, but what he gained spiritually is a topic that Woody returns to often when speaking of his life's journey. An evangelical Christian, Woody finds inspiration both in the teachings of Christ and in Cherokee culture. As a close friend of Hastings, Loretta and I agreed Woody would be an ideal person to speak with about his relationship with snakes, his understanding of them as both a Cherokee and a Christian, and how his path has evolved since receiving his rattlesnake vision dream. And so I recorded a conversation with Woody, his wife, Joyce, and my brother Sean over breakfast one spring morning.

"Well, since I was hit by the car in 2007, I'm still in recovery," Woody said. "Today, I'm a student at Bacone College in Muscogee, studying Native American Christian ministry. March 9, 2019, I was ordained as a Baptist minister here at Ballou Baptist Church in Locust Grove. Just been very busy learning the path of what Christ wants me to be on, incorporating the Holy Spirit.

Ugasuti (diamondback rattlesnake)

In my walk as a snake handler, God's allowed me to have certain species of snakes when I needed one. If I needed a pygmy rattler one would appear within a couple days. Not all the time, but more than a lot. I've been blessed with his creation, and that's part of my story about sharing the education of snakes with humans. They're God's creatures."

"Mmhm," I said.

"He created them. They get a bad rap from the Devil and the Garden," Woody said, and we all laughed. "But you know, Moses and Aaron, God turned his staff into a snake when he was battling Pharoah. Out in the wilderness there was the bronze serpent that healed those who were sick. When the Israelites were disobedient, God sent serpents to bite them. And you look at Greek mythology. They talk about the star constellation Serpens named after serpents. They have the symbol of medicine, the caduceus staff with the entwined snakes. So, the snake really has a place of honor in creation. And I try to bring that to light to people who don't know, who just see snakes as an enemy just to be killed because they're a snake.

And some will accept it and others don't. Which is okay. Some people disagree with what I'm doing as a snake educator. They'll say things like, 'The only good snake is a dead snake.' That offends me. And I come back with, 'Well, you know, Brother, at one time the United States government had the same policy against Indians. The only good Indian was a dead Indian.' So. I disagree with their statement. But I say, 'It's your statement and you own it. I'm just here to educate.' But, you know, there are times like that when I've thought, 'Why do I get so offended when people act and think that way toward God's creation?' Well, you know, I'm a creature, *too*. Just like the snake."

Sean and I nodded.

"'There are times in my life where I've been hostile. And mad. And strike out like a copperhead or rattlesnake. You know?

It's just hard to explain. But God has allowed me to handle these snakes. I'm in my twenty-ninth year of snake handling and educating. I'm sixty-one. I can't imagine I was in my thirties when I started doing this. It's been enjoyable. Even being hit by that car, as hurtful physically as it was, it gave me a stronger spiritual value. A closeness to God for allowing me to live. And to keep my leg from being amputated.

Life is fragile. I've been buried alive. Thrown out of a car. Bitten by a rattlesnake. Bitten by a fiddleback spider when I was a kid. Lots of things.

So it all kind of adds up and channels me now to think, 'Well, Lord, you have taken care of me. And I didn't pay you the proper respect or honor.' Now the spiritual walk kind of directs me and my life," Woody continued. "And through the challenges I've had in my life, I didn't give up. Don't give up. That takes me back to the Trail of Tears. Don't give up, ancestors. You're forced to be removed. You're in a stockade for four or five months. Marched out west. They didn't give up. We've resettled here. No doubt the ancestors came to a strange land. A *dark* land. You know, what kept us going then? The stomp dance did. And mission work. Those two aspects in our lives."

"Mmhm."

"Our oral traditional ways. And the Christian ethics the missionaries brought over. So, all these things, when I look back and reflect on them, I was really blessed. Even though I've gone through a lot of bouts—some of my own doing. That's life. It's the response that we do. Any of these incidents could have put me in a tailspin. But now, I'm grateful for meeting Sequoyah and Sammy, because they taught me that for every life incident, there's a *story* to it. A story that comes out of it."

"Yes," I said.

"And God has given me these stories out of my own life events."

"Including your dream vision," I said.

"Yeah. My dream vision of the rattlesnake. That's right. The snake of my vision in 1994 was a yellow rattlesnake. There aren't any yellow rattlesnakes around here. But then about five or six years ago, Barbara Duncan of the Museum of the Cherokee Indian sends me an Eastern

Band book of Cherokee stories. In one of those stories of our eastern brothers . . . there's a story of a *yellow rattlesnake*," Woody said and laughed.

"Wow. Isn't that interesting?" I said. "That tieback."

"Yeah! That tieback. That particular yellow rattlesnake in the story lived in a cornfield and kind of protected it. But just the fact that there are yellow rattlesnakes and they appeared in my dream, a thousand miles away, many years later."

"That symbol of the snake," I said. "You were talking about how the experience of how people treat snakes is similar to the way people treated Native folks. Did you see that connection right away, or did it emerge over time?"

"It just happened. It just happened. I grew up reading a lot. Even as a sixth and seventh grader I read Dee Brown's *Bury My Heart at Wounded Knee* and learned about atrocities toward Indians. So I grew up with that kind of political attitude. I had a chip on my shoulder. But you combine that later in life with the Christian belief of forgiveness, of understanding, and that there's a bigger picture that Natives were persecuted as well as other people of the world, including God's chosen. So, we're all on the same planet experiencing persecution at different times. Great Spirit to me is Jesus. I grew with a lot of anger. It was hard to shed my militant ways. But I did once I reconciled in looking at God's purposes—for all peoples to find peace with him. And now I'm back in college at Bacone, where I know God has directed me. And I'm learning to go back to my Native spiritual ways and talk to Native people about Christ."

"People often speak of hating snakes," my brother Sean said. "But some say underlying hatred is fear. People hate what they fear. So in your belief system, does that enable you to encounter fear and know how to handle it?"

"Mmhm. It does. The snake can surprise you. He can come out of nowhere."

"That's what is scary," Sean agreed.

"Right. Just like life. It comes out of nowhere, an incident or something. It can strike you. You can get bit with no consequences, no venom. You might have a health scare. 'Oh, I thought I had cancer,' or 'I thought I had a bad heart.' But it was just a scare. Such as with the snake. I've been struck several times with no venom. Thank you, Lord!" Woody said and laughed. "'Cause it's not up to me—it's up to the creature if it wants to inject venom or not, you know? Just like life. It can strike. It can just lie there. Or it can just rattle. Just like things in our own lives. Sometimes we ignore the warnings. Could be one's health or finances. Or if we forget prayer. You know, those things happen.

Do I worship snakes? No. 'Cause people ask me that. They've bit me. Put me in the hospital twice. They don't respect me in that regard, but that's who they *are*. Like that story of the young Cherokee boy who finds a freezing rattler in the mountains. He puts it in his shirt to warm him up, knowing what he was. When he came back down and he warmed up, the snake bit him. The rattler said, 'You knew what I was when you put me in your shirt.' And I tell that to smaller kids. Know what's going to happen if you start drinking liquor. You start doing drugs. It's gonna bite you. Left untreated, it could kill you. Venom. Drugs. Alcohol. I said, 'Creator doesn't want you to live that way. You know what that is when you do it.'"

Listening to Woody, I was reminded of the importance of being in relationship with those parts of ourselves and our world that may frighten or seem foreign and mysterious to us. Respecting difference while acknowledging our interconnection and interdependence can be a challenge, but real dangers arise when we lose connection to aspects of *Unetlvnv uwotlvnv*, what Creator made. Nature.

DRY BITES

Hastings, Sequoyah Guess, Woody Hansen, and I were swapping lies in Hastings' outdoor workshop in Lost City. Woody had just finished telling us the story of the vision dream that led to his pact with rattlesnakes and the educational work he does with snakes now, teaching people how to live among snakes and appreciate them for their role in the world. The conversation turned to Hastings' reflections on his relationship with snakes and how, with maturity, their relationship has changed over time.

"I got hit the other night," Hastings said.

"By what?" Woody asked.

"A snake up there."

"Oh really?"

"I was coming home—"

"On your boots right there?"

"Nah, on my leg."

"It didn't hurt? No venom? Dry bite?"

"Nah, a dry hit," Hastings said. "Just had two spots. I put tobacco on 'em and they're gone. I was going to show you my scars but they're gone now." Everyone chuckled.

"We were coming back from the creek,

you know?" Hastings continued. "And the water was cold and my leg was numb. And I told my grandson, 'Something hit me.' And we looked. There wasn't nothin.' And when I got home I noticed I had two little old spots right there. I can't see them now. Oh, here they are. Hit me right there. Two little old fangs."

"Just got it in—" Woody said.

"Yeah."

"Just to let you know, 'I *could* have got you.'"

"Yeah. Well, I didn't feel it. I just felt it hit my leg. I felt something hit my leg 'cause I had shorts on."

After a pause, Hastings continued.

"We used to take gasoline and take a hose, stick it down their holes. My grandpa saw us do it and told me, 'How come you getting 'em out of their houses? You wouldn't want anybody coming in to your house to get you.'

"Yeah?" Woody said. "We never did that."

"He said, 'What you gonna do that for? You don't want nobody coming in to your house to get you.' So, I quit. The snakes made me sick. They started making me sick so I *had* to quit."

"Yeah, people ask me, 'Don't they make you sick?' I say, 'No. They used to before I started doing this.'"

"Sometimes you can smell one. I can be within thirty or forty yards of one and smell him. I can smell a rattlesnake. I don't have to see him to know he's there."

"And I've always got people asking me, 'Can I buy a rattle from you?' Or the bones," Woody said.

"I used to catch 'em and kill 'em. I used to sell the hides a long time ago," Hastings said. "Not anymore."

"Well, I got bit one time," Woody offered. "Sequoyah was with me. I was wearing gloves and—pow! 'Oh no! He got me!' This was probably about seven years after I first started my educational work with snakes. One was trying to get out and something was going on. I reached down there to close the lid or something and—a dry bite. He nailed me good, though. He was just telling me, 'I *could* have got you.'"

RATTLESNAKE CPR • *Told by Joyce Hansen and Woody Hansen*

Woody Hansen's experiences as a snake handler have run the gamut—from tragic and life-threatening to deeply spiritual or wildly humorous. Sometimes his stories of life among snakes touch on all these aspects at once. Woody and his wife, Joyce Hansen, took turns telling one such story with me and my brother, Sean, over breakfast at the Restaurant of the Cherokees in Tahlequah.

"What about your story?" Woody asked Joyce.

"Which one?"

"The resuscitation one."

"Oh, my *gosh*," Joyce said as she remembered.

"You know, I used to be an EMT. But I'm probably the only guy around that's given a rattlesnake CPR," Woody said, and we laughed. "It was her snake."

"Yes," Joyce said and sighed. "We were hunting on a plateau in Waynoka. That's where they have all the sand dunes. I went out with him one year, and he said, 'I'm going to go up over this ridge on the plateau. You can hunt around here.' And so as I was walking up the plateau I noticed this flat rock with a little bit of a shadow under it. And I looked. And there's a snake. And I thought, 'Oh, *great*. Now what am I going to do?" Joyce said, and we all laughed.

"She was new to snake hunting," Woody explained.

"I mean, I'd hunted with him but not really *hunted*. I'd just accompanied him. So, I had my snake catcher and I had this bag with me. And it was just an event backpack to carry stuff in."

"Plastic," Woody added.

"I didn't pay much attention to it. So, anyway, I pulled this snake out and just opened up the bag and just barely got it in. So. Snapped it up, put it together, and put it on the *end* of my snake catcher," Joyce said, and we all laughed as she made a gesture of holding the bag out as far as she could reach.

"That's how I would do it," I said.

"So, maybe fifteen minutes later I came up on Woody and said, 'I caught one!' And he said, 'You did? Let me see it!'"

"Oh, yeah. I was excited for her," Woody said.

"And so I opened it up, and he said, 'Here, let me get it.' And he opened up the bag and went to grab the snake . . . and the snake was just *lifeless*. He said, 'Oh, no! You killed the snake.'"

"I said, 'It's not rattling.' It couldn't breathe in that plastic bag."

"It wasn't a breathable backpack," Joyce said. "And so, anyway, it just flopped on the ground. And I thought, 'Oh, my gosh.' I just felt so bad because I thought I killed it. And so Woody got it and he said, 'Here. I've got some water.' He got that water out and he poured some water on that snake. And he picked the snake up, too."

"Right. I opened its mouth. Poured water in its mouth. And blew on it," Woody said and mimed as if he were blowing puffs of air into a snake's face. We all laughed at the thought of it.

"Poured more water on it," Joyce said. "And the snake started moving. It started moving."

"So we tied a little string on its tail then—not on the rattler," Woody said. "Let it sit there. And pretty soon it come totally alive and started crawling around."

"We sat on the side of the plateau in the shade resting and after a while he said, 'I revived a snake.'"

"You know, later, I said, 'I gave that rattler CPR,'" Woody said, and we laughed.

"He's the only person that would ever revive a rattlesnake," Joyce said.

"That's a delicate business," Sean said.

"Like kissing a cobra," Woody said.

ᏓᎴᏴᏍᎩ ✦ daleyvsgi (dah-leh-yuh-sgee) ✦ **salamander, spottted** ✦ Name means: burns you or will burn you

ᏣᏁᏴ ✦ tsaneyv (jah-neh-yuh) ✦ **skink**

ᏗᎩᏥ ✦ digitsi (dee-gee-jee) ✦ **tadpole**

ᏓᎦᏏ ✦ dagasi (dah-gah-see) ✦ **terrapin** ✦ "This is the one that said to the Creator he was getting tired of packing everything every time he moved. So the Creator gave him a house on his back. Now he takes everything with him whenever he moves. Name also means 'lock.'" H.S.

ᎠᏓᏢᎢ ✦ adatlvi (ah-dah-tluh-ee) ✦ **tiesnake** ✦ "This snake is like the flying snake. Some people will tell you there is no such thing. This snake has a line that goes from the corner of its mouth under the lower jaw, to the other corner. Usually a light color. Also known as the one that makes the water deeper. They have disappeared since the dams were put in." H.S.

ᏩᎶᏏ ✦ walosi (wah-loh-see) ✦ **toad** ✦ This is the small version of the one that the Indians claim swallows the moon during an eclipse.

HOW *WALOSI* GOT THE WARTS ON HIS SKIN ✦ *by Hastings Shade*

At one time, *Walosi*, or Toad, had smooth, beautiful skin. As he went here and there, all the other *inage anehi*—animals, birds, snakes, and insects—would tell him how smooth and beautiful his skin was.

One day the Cherokees began to migrate on their journey to their homelands in and around the Great Smoky Mountains. They had to cross an area that was damp, the place where Walosi lived.

When Walosi heard them coming, he dug a small depression in the ground like he always does when he wants to hide. If you have ever seen a place where Walosi hides, it isn't very deep, just enough where there is a thin layer of dirt to cover his back.

As he hid there the Cherokees walked over him. Not knowing he was there, some stepped where he was hidden and the dirt that was covering him worked its way into his skin. When the Cherokees had passed, he came out of his hiding place. He tried to wash off the dirt but it had worked its way into his skin. His skin became infected and scaly.

Ever since then, his skin looks like it does today. It has stayed that way. It looks like warts but is scales caused by infection the dirt caused where it worked its way into his skin.

Walosi was one of those that spoke up at the council of creatures when they all wanted to give the Cherokees diseases. And this was because Cherokees had stepped on him and made his smooth skin look like it does today.

ᏗᎦᏒᎩ • digasvgi (dee-gah-suh-gee) • **turtle, painted** • He complained about not having any color on his house. So the Creator gave him one that had some color.

ᏌᎵᎫᎦ • saliguga (sah-lee-goo-gah) • **turtle, snapping** • It was the Giant Snapping Turtle that the people were on before the earth became as we know it today. This is the small version. • *"In Cherokee tradition,* saliguga *symbolizes emissary*—ganvsida—ᎦᏅᏏᏓ." *H.S.*

ᎤᏝᏃᎢ • utlanoi (oo-tlah-noh-ee) • **turtle, softshell**

ᏧᏩ • tsuwa (joo-wah) • **waterdog**

ᎦᏙᎢ ᎤᎦᏎᏍᏗ • gadoi ugasesdi (gah-doh-ee oo-gah-seh-sdee) • **worm snake** • Name means: earth watcher or he who guards the earth

Sgoyi (Insects)

Cherokee tradition tells that insects as we know them were let loose in the world by *Kanadi*, also known as Red Man or Thunder. In the ancient time, his two sons born from Selu followed him into the mountains and spied on him as he carefully let a deer out of the cave of creation where all animals were kept. He quickly shut the stone door of the cave, killed the deer, and brought home the meat to his family. Being curious children, the boys sneaked back to the cave and slid aside the rock door that covered it to look inside. But before they could close it again, one after another in a flurry of fur and feathers, all the animals we know today spilled out and scattered to the four corners of the Cherokee cosmos. To teach them about the consequences of one's actions, Kanadi went inside the cave and kicked over the covered earthen jars that held the last creatures in the cave: *sgoyi*, or insects. It is said that swarms of biting flies, wasps, mosquitoes, and other insects covered the boys with stings and welts before Kanadi shooed the bugs away. Sgoyi are still with us today, sometimes biting us and sometimes bringing sickness, like the vengeful grubworm who wanted to bring humans disease for our treatment of his kind. Some say it is inevitable that certain sgoyi want to make us sick; bugs are so numerous that we often cannot avoid killing their kind, and thus bringing their eventual wrath. Still others, like *wadulisi* (honeybee), are important for the growth of our food plants and our very survival.

Wadulisi aninvsgi (honeybee)

In fact, some sgoyi are honored above nearly all other creatures in Cherokee tradition. It was *Doyunisi*, Water Beetle, after all, who dove from

Sky World down deep into the Under World to bring up the speck of mud that became Elohi. Like Doyunisi, Kananesgi Amayi has the power to cross the borders of worlds and carried fire on her back and under the water to deliver it as a gift to human beings. And so, though sometimes a nuisance and even dangerous to human beings, sgoyi hold an honored place among all life forms. The history of respecting sgoyi is at the heart of Cherokee tradition. Without them we would have neither Elohi nor Creator's gift of *atsila* (fire).

Sgoyi are found in the air, on the ground, underground, and in the water. There is power in being at home in each of the three worlds, but also danger, as they are food to birds, fish, snakes, and countless other animals of these places. Preyed on by many, sgoyi also give the gift of life. Without them, our world surely would not exist.

Insects

ᏍᎪᏱ ✦ sgoyi (sgoh-yee) ✦ **insects**

ᏙᏒᏓᎵ ✦ dosvdali (doh-suh-dah-lee) ✦ **ant** ✦ *"In Cherokee tradition,* dosvdali *symbolizes preservation—* alisidodi—ᎠᎵᏏᏙᏗ." *H.S.*

ᏅᏯ ᏧᏂᏫ ✦ nvya tsuniwi (nuh-yah joo-nee-wee) ✦ **ant, cow, or velvet ant** ✦ Name means: have a rock coat on

Dosvdali (ant)

ᏙᏒᏓᎵ ᎩᎦᎨ ✦ dosvdali gigage (doh-suh-dah-lee gee-gah-geh) ✦ **ant, fire** ✦ Name means: red ant

ᏩᎵᏩᎵ ✦ waliwali (wah-lee-wah-lee) ✦ **antlion** ✦ If you find his home and call his name, he will come out.

ᏩᏚᎵᏏ ᎪᏙᎡᎯ ✦ wadulisi godoehi (wah-doo-lee-see goh-doh-eh-hee) ✦ **bee, bumble**

ᏩᏚᎵᏏ ᎠᏂᏅᏍᎦ ✦ wadulisi aninvsgi (wah-doo-lee-see a-nee-nuh-sgee) ✦ **bee, honey**

ᎠᎪᏂ ✦ agoni (ah-goh-nee) ✦ **bee, news** ✦ Name means: starving

ᏝᏄᏣᏩ ✦ tlanutsawa (tlah-noo-jah-wah) ✦ **bee, sweat**

ᎦᎷᏍᏗ ✦ galusdi (gah-loo-sdee) ✦ **bedbug** ✦ Name means: axe, because of its shape. This one will live with you if you let it.

ᏍᎪᏯ ᎤᏯᏍᎦᏟ ✦ sgoya uyasgatli (skoh-yah oo-yah-skah-tlee) ✦ **beetle** ✦ Name means: bug that has a shell

ᏗᏓᏂᏏᏍᎩ ✦ didanisisgi (dee-dah-nee-see-sgee) ✦ **beetle, carrion** ✦ Name means: the one that buries

ᏔᎵᏍᎫᎩ • talisgugi (tah-lee-sgoo-gee) • **beetle, click** • Name means: the one that snaps his head

ᎠᏂᏤᎢ • anitsei (ah-nee-jeh-ee) • **beetle, green headed** • Name means: new ones or green ones

ᏥᏍᏛᏂ ᎠᏫ • tsisdvni awi (jee-sduh-nee ah-wee) • **beetle, horned**

ᏙᏯ ᎤᏍᏗ • doya usdi (doh-yah oo-sdee) • **beetle, water** • Name means: little beaver • This is the one that brought up the small piece of mud that started the land base that we have. Also known as *doyunisi,* beaver's grandma.

ᎠᏓ ᎠᏍᎪᎩᏍᎩ • ada asgogigisgi (ah-dah ah-sgoh-gee-sgee) • **beetle, wood sawyer** • Name means: the one that gnaws on wood

ᏧᏲᎾ ᏧᎵᎩ • tsuyona tsuligi (joo-yoh-nah joo-lee-gee) • **bull worm** • Name means: having horns

ᎧᎹᎹ • kamama (kah-mah-mah) • **butterfly** • Name also means elephant because of the way it flaps its wings—just like an elephant flaps its ears.

ᏍᎪᏯ ᎠᏂᏍᎩᎸᏍᎩ • sgoya anisgilvsgi (skoh-yah ah-nee-skee-luh-sgee) • **caterpillar** • Name means: bug that they used to sit on • "Loretta and I laughed about the name of this one. She didn't know why it was called this in Cherokee but said that elders read the furry back of the caterpillar to tell how strong the upcoming winter will be. The furrier the caterpillar's back, the harder the winter." C.T.

ᏧᎦᏃᏥ • tsuganotsi (joo-gah-noh-jee) • **centipede**

ᎤᏔᎾ ᏗᏓᏧᎢᏗᏍᎩ • utana didaleidisgi (oo-tah-nah dee-dah-leh-ee-dee-sgee) • **centipede, thousand legs** • Name means: the big one that will burn you

ᎶᎶ • lolo (loh-loh) • **cicada**

ᏔᎳᏚ • taladu (tah-lah-doo) • **cricket** • It is also known as the barber, *didastoyisgi.*

ᏔᎳᏉᎩ • talaquogi (tah-lah-qwoh-gee) • **cricket, mole** • Name means: a version of the number seven, *galaquogi*

ᎧᏅᏜᎢ • kanvdlai (kah-nuh-dlah-ee) • **cutworm, or moth caterpillar** • This one is the kind you find in your garden.

ᏛᏣᎦᎵ • dvtsagali (duh-jah-gah-lee) • **cutworm, green, or moth caterpillar**

ᏓᎦᏌᎵ • dagasali (dah-gah-sah-lee) • **daddy longlegs**

ᏗᎫᎵᏗᏍᎩ • digulidisgi (dee-goo-lee-dee-sgee) • **dirt dauber** • This is the insect that taught us how to build our homes using mud.

ᎦᏅᏃᏩ • ganvnowa (gah-nuh-noh-wah) • **dragonfly (small)** • Name means: pipe

WHY THE POSSUM'S TAIL IS BARE ✦ *by Noyi Teuton*

This is a story that Sequoyah Guess told me once. As he often reminded me, good-natured teasing is one of the surest signs of true friendship. Though some may consider Possum's lesson a bit harsh, this story expresses a teaching we all need to learn some time in our lives.

Ilvhiyu tsigesv nigada inage anehi tsalagi tsaniwonisgv. In the great forever that was, all the forest dwellers spoke Cherokee. *Siqua utseisdi* (Possum) is known as the "Grinning Hog" in Cherokee, and there's a good reason for that. At one time Siqua Utseisdi had a long, luxurious, silky, soft, and bushy tail. That tail was Possum's pride and joy. When he walked about he held his tail high for all the other animals to see. That tail would sway in the air like a flag. No animal had a tail that could match it. Each morning, Possum brought a comb with him and sat down near the center of the village and combed out that tail for all to see. And when the people had a dance, Possum would even sing about his tail. Now, *Tsisdu* (Rabbit) and Possum were best friends. But even so, Tsisdu was jealous of Possum's tail as he had just a little bitty one himself. "Something needs to be done about Possum and that tail," Rabbit thought to himself. "I've had just about enough of Possum showing off that tail." And so Tsisdu made up his mind to play a trick on Possum.

A big council and dance was planned, and all the animals were invited. It was Rabbit's job to go around and tell everyone this news. Rabbit walked over to Possum's house and peeked in the doorway. "*Siyo* Possum, there's going to be a big council and dance—will you go?" Rabbit asked in one breath. Possum sat next to his fire, lovingly combing his beautiful tail.

"*Siyo ginali,*" Possum said and slowly looked up. "That's good news about the dance. You know, I think I'll go if I can sit where everyone will see my beautiful tail. Wouldn't that make it better for everyone?"

"That's a wonderful idea," Rabbit said. "I'll be sure to make that happen. Tell you what, I'll even send over our friend *didastoyisgi* to comb and dress your tail before the dance."

Possum was very pleased with Rabbit's suggestion to send Cricket over to comb his tail. He agreed to come to the dance the next night. Rabbit went straight over to Cricket's house and told the one they call "the barber" exactly how to fix Possum's tail for the dance the following night.

The morning of the dance, Rabbit visited Possum again and said he was there to help Possum get ready. Possum laid out a mat near the warm fire. He stretched out on the mat in complete relaxation. Cricket arrived and began to comb out Possum's lovely tail. Possum just closed his eyes and enjoyed the pampering. Cricket then took a red string and wrapped Possum's tail tight to keep it smooth until the dance that night. But as she wound the string round and round, Cricket cut the hairs of Possum's tail right at the roots. Lulled by the fire and thoughts of how glorious his tail was going to look that evening, Possum had no idea his tail had been shaved.

Possum arrived late for the dance that night so that all could see his tail as he walked through the crowd. The best seat in the townhouse was reserved, just as Rabbit had promised. And when Possum's turn came to lead a dance, he loosened the string on his tail with a flourish and stepped to the center of the townhouse. A water drum struck a rhythm, and Possum called out "See my beautiful tail!" All the animals whooped and cheered in response. Possum danced around the fire and called out, "See what a fine color it has!" And the animals whooped and cheered even more loudly. "See how it sweeps the ground," Possum sang out and danced low and dramatically with bent knees, now really feeling the energy of the crowd. Possum was ecstatic and thought, "The people *really* love my tail!" Then Possum sang out with all its spirit, "See how fine the fur is!" And with those words a chorus of cheers, whoops, and laughter rang out so loud and long that the drummer could no longer drum. Possum turned to look at everyone. The animals were bent over laughing. Some were rolling on the ground in delight. They were holding each other up with their paws and hooves, their faces were red, their mouths were open, and their eyes were watering they were laughing so hard. It was the funniest thing most of them had ever seen. It was then that Possum looked back and down at his tail and saw that it was shaved completely bare. There was not one hair left on it. Possum was so shocked and embarrassed that he rolled over on the ground and grinned wide, just as possums do today when they are taken by surprise. Rabbit looked on and smiled. "Maybe that will teach him his lesson," he thought. And then he walked over and helped his friend up.

ᏩᎾᏚᎦ • wanaduga (wah-nah-doo-gah) • **dragonfly (blue, small)**

ᏩᏓᏚᎦ • wadaduga (wah-dah-doo-gah) • **dragonfly (green, large)**

ᎤᏥᏯ • utsiya (oo-jee-yah) • **earthworm**

ᏧᎦ • tsuga (joo-gah) • **flea**

ᏡᎩ • tvgi (tuh-gee) • **fly**

ᏗᎾᏓᏅᏍᎩ ᏡᎩ • dinadanvsgi tvgi (dee-nah-dah-nuh-sgee tuh-gee) • **fly, green** • Name means: it will lay eggs on you

ᎠᏓᎳᏚᏍᎩ • adalatusgi (ah-dah-lah-too-sgee) • **gnat**

ᏙᎳᎢᏍᏆ • tolaisqua (toh-lah-ee-sgwah) • **grasshopper**

ᏚᎵᏯᏛᎦ • duliyadvga (doo-lee-yah-duh-gah) • **grubworm** • Name means: he fell over • "The legend says when *inage anehi* were giving the Indians disease, he liked them so much and he was so happy that the Indians were going to be sick, he began to bounce up and down. He soon fell over and couldn't get back up. So to this day he crawls on his side or wiggles on his side. There is another grubworm named *daliyodagi* who is usually found in rotten logs." H.S.

ᎤᏍᏆᏚᎵ • usquaduli (oo-squa-doo-lee) • **hornet**

ᏓᎹᎦ • damaga (dah-mah-gah) • **horsefly**

ᎠᏟᎶᎢᏙ ᎤᏥᏯ • atliloido utsiya (ah-tlee-loh-ee-doh oo-jee-yah) • **inch-worm** • Name means: the worm that measures

ᏙᎯᎦ • tohiga (toh-hee-gah) • **June bug, or scarab beetle**

ᏏᎩᎩ • sigigi (see-gee-gee) • **katydid** • This is the one that sings babies to sleep.

ᎤᏥᏍᏓᎷᎩ • utsisdalugi (oo-jee-stah-loo-gee) • **lightning bug** • Name means: the one that shines

ᏘᎾ • tina (tee-nah) • **louse** • This is the one that will live with you if you let it.

ᏙᏯ ᎤᏂᏏ • doya unisi (doh-yah oo-nee-see) • **mellow bug**

ᏙᏌ • dosa (doh-sah) • **mosquito**

ᎠᏥ • atsi (ah-jee) • **moth**

ᎠᏓᏌ • adasa (ah-dah-sah) • **moth, large**

ᏩᏐᏝ • wasotla (wah-soh-tlah) • **moth, red**

ᏚᎾᏔᏭ • tunatawu (too-nah-tah-woo) • **moth, yellow**

ᏧᏓᎧᏂᏍᏗ • tsudakanisdi (joo-dah-kah-nee-sdee) • **praying mantis** • Names means: the one who looks at you or stares

ᎤᏂᎾᏌᎢ • uninasai (oo-nee-nah-sah-ee) • **roaches** • Name means: having something put up to eat

ᏥᏍᏡᎢ ᎢᏳᏍᏗ • tsistvi iyusdi (jee-sduh-ee ee-yoo-sdee) • **scorpion** • Name means: like a crawdad

Kananesgi amayi
(water spider)

ᎡᎶᏆ ✦ eloqua (eh-loh-qwah) ✦ **snail**

ᎧᎾᏁᏍᎩ ✦ kananesgi (kah-nah-neh-sgee) ✦ **spider** ✦ It was one of the spider's kind that got us the fire and showed us how to do pottery and fire it.

ᏗᎦᎯᏒᎩ ✦ digahisvgi (dee-gah-hee-suh-gee) ✦ **stinkbug**

ᎫᎫ ✦ gugu (goo-goo) ✦ **tick**

ᏦᎳ ᏥᏫᏍᎩ ✦ tsola tsiwisgi (joh-lah jee-wee-sgee) ✦ **tobacco worm** ✦ Name means: he spits tobacco juice. Also called *wasola*.

ᏍᎩᎾ ᎤᎩᎸᏙᎢᏗ ✦ sgina ukilvdoidi (sgee-nah oo-gee-luh-doh-ee-dee) ✦ **walking stick** ✦ Name means: devil's horse or devil's ride

ᎧᎾᏥᏍᏕᏥ ✦ kanatsisdetsi (kah-nah-jee-steh-jee) ✦ **wasp** ✦ The elders used to eat the larvae of the wasp. It makes you aggressive.

ᎧᎾᏥᏍᏕᏥ ᎩᎦᎨ ✦ kanatsisdetsi gigage (kah-nah-jee-sdeh-jee gee-gah-geh) ✦ **wasp, red**

ᎧᎾᏁᏍᎩ ᏗᎯ ✦ kananesgi dihi (kah-nah-neh-sgee dee-hee) ✦ **wasp, spider** ✦ Name means: spider killer

ᎠᏘᏥ ✦ atitsi (ah-tee-jee) ✦ **water bug**

ᏗᎳᏍᏙᎢᏗ ✦ dilasdoidi (dee-lah-sdoh-ee-dee) ✦ **water strider** ✦ Name means: scissors or to fight with

ᏓᏁᏍᏓᎳ ✦ danesdala (dah-neh-sdah-lah) ✦ **woolly worm, or moth caterpillar** ✦ Name means: bugs that are bunched together. Also called *unadatligi sgoya*.

ᏍᎦᏱ ✦ sgayi (sgah-yee) ✦ **yellowjacket**

ᎤᎳᎦ ✦ ulaga (oo-lah-gah) ✦ **yellowjacket (mythical)** ✦ "This is the one that killed the small animals and some children. The Cherokee found their nest in a large cave and smoked them out and killed them. To this day, you can still get rid of them this way: by using smoke." H.S.

Spirit People

There are other beings living among us besides the flesh and blood creatures with whom we share this world, Loretta explained to me. These spirit peoples are well known among the Cherokees, and stories are told of encountering them. But out of custom and respect, folks rarely speak of them publicly. And if they do tell of their experiences, they often leave out details that could identify where these beings live, where they were encountered, or other things of a personal nature that they experienced. There is great meaning to be found in experiences of the *anidawehi*, or those super with wisdom and abilities beyond we humans. Though some experiences, such as the sighting of an Uk'tan, may warrant sharing as they may have import for a community, others are meant only for the person who experienced the *ulvsgedi*, the wondrous. And so in both the experience and the telling of experiences of *ulvsgedi*, much is shrouded in mystery. Much is also left unsaid. As Hastings said, Cherokee knowledge is shared on a need-to-know basis. Perhaps the most important reason to tell these stories is to remind ourselves that these beings exist.

Over the years, Cherokees have told stories of their experiences and relationships with different types of spirit beings. In *tsalagi uweti*, the old Cherokee territory in the Smoky Mountains, people tell stories of the *Nvnehi*, spirit people who have their own villages deep inside the mountains and mounds like *Nikwasi*. Though they resemble Cherokees and speak the Cherokee language, the Nvnehi are invisible; they cannot be seen unless they want to be seen. There are stories of people hearing sounds of singing and a drum beating as if a dance were happening, but upon their following the sound to its supposed source, the sound shifted to come from another direction. The Nvnehi are said to be helpful to those who are lost in the woods, taking people to their underground villages before returning them home.

Perhaps the best-known anidawehi are the *Yvwi Tsunvsdi*, the Little People. Like the Nvnehi, Little People are invisible unless they wish to be seen. They are said to be handsome and resemble humans with long hair, but are very small—about knee-high. They love music and dance and have their own stomp grounds. They live in caves and prefer out-of-the-way places where they are left in peace. Though generally friendly, especially to children, they are known to be mischievous. They can be helpful to people, but if offended they have power to cause harm. They take special offense at having their homes disturbed by unwanted visitors. And they do not like to be talked about or to have much revealed about them. It is commonly known that if one finds an item in the woods and wishes to take it, something must be left in its place for the Little People. Hastings said, "Always leave scraps on the table for the Little People to eat after supper. If you don't, they won't let you sleep—until you get up and put something on the table for them to eat."

Loretta and I spoke of spirit beings and what might be said of them. She noted that Hastings included all creatures of the Cherokee world in

PREDATOR • *Told by Larry Shade*

In a conversation Loretta and I had with Larry about the ulvsgedi, he told me a story an elder once shared with him about a being he had encountered while collecting medicine. He spoke quietly and with the respect such an account of the wondrous deserves.

"There's a gentleman that we know. And we were looking for medicine one evening and I went with him. He said, '*Chuja,* you seen the movie *Predator?*" I said, 'Yeah.' He said, 'That alien.' He said, 'Just on that ridge over there, about three years ago, your Dad and I were looking for medicine. There was a plant that we were looking for.' And he said, 'I knew it grew on the edge of one of these hills, but I couldn't remember which.' He said, 'I came up to this ridge and it makes a steep drop and then back. It's one of those ridges where you're going down a hill then you take a jump and you're on the next hill."

And he said, 'It was in the wintertime. The leaves were down, and it was gettin' evening.' And he said, 'I knew we had to continue to look for the medicine, but I looked over and I saw something movin' with me.' And he said, 'I didn't think anything about it.' He said, 'The more I walked, the closer it got.' And he said, 'I forgot about it.' He said, 'I got to the edge of that ridge, and I thought, 'Well, I need to go over the edge of the ridge.' He said, 'I drop off that ridge and come up the other ridge. I walk to the top of that hill, and just about forty yards from me was this *thing* standing there. And it looked like 'predator.'"

Larry paused for a moment.

"And he said, 'You know, you don't run. You don't let it know that you're afraid of it. But you say in Cherokee: Go on. I'm not here to bother you. I'm looking for something.'" And he said, "I said that." And he said it was one of those situations where you hear something from one direction and get distracted. You look away and when you look back, it's gone. That's what happened. And, you know, you're out there and you get chills and your hair stands up on the back of your neck and you get goose bumps all over your arms and think, 'You know, these things exist.'

Grandpa used to tell us that when they moved into the area there were things out in the woods that are no longer there. As the areas became populated, the people moving into the areas pushed these things out. And you know, he'd always say, 'Where did they go? How do we see them again?' Because they were visible a long time ago."

his lists of beings. Everyday animals and plants are listed right alongside creatures such as Uk'tan, Tie Snake, and Tinuwa. While some consider these beings to be mythical, they continue to be real in Cherokee life. It is important to recognize these creatures as part of the Cherokee world, Loretta told me, but at the same time, decorum requires respecting the nature of our relationships with them.

"What about Bigfoot?" I asked Loretta. "I know folks are interested in sightings and stories of Bigfoot in eastern Oklahoma."

"That's *Utan Tsulasgi*. Bigfoot. There are lots of stories, but people hardly talk about 'em in public. An elder told me there are families of them. And there have been sightings of them in the area. Larry and Dondi went to Kenwood once to cut a walnut tree. A man who lived near there said an *utan tsulasgi* lived down the hill from there by the creek. If they don't want you to do something they'll make sure you won't. And they can make you sick. Dondi had a chainsaw that suddenly wouldn't work when he went down there to cut that tree."

DUQUESDI: THE FIRST BLOWGUN • *Told by Sammy Still*

The elder Sammy Still was a close friend of Hastings Shade and is a member of the Turtle Island Liars' Club. When the Liars' Club gathers, Sammy often tells stories and shares teachings about traditional crafts. The story that follows was told at a gathering of the Liars' Club some years ago, when the topic turned to the Yvwi Tsunvsdi, or the Little People. It is included in Cherokee Earth Dwellers in honor of Hastings and told in the spirit of teaching about the Cherokee world.

"Ahh, let's see. Well, there is one story that comes to mind. When we go out and do storytelling to people, a lot of them want to know about the Little People, *Yvwi Tsunvsdi*. A lot of times they told we're never to talk about the Little People. Never to say these things about the Little People. But then, you know, the way I feel about it is, if we're going to share our heritage and our culture and our stories as we were growing up, there needs to be a little bit told about the Little People. Maybe not getting into detail about it, but telling a little bit about the Little People in some of the stories that we tell. And so this way, it kind of answers the questions people ask by telling stories about Little People.

"So, this one is a story about *duquesdi*, the blowgun. This story hadn't been told in a while. No one really tells it. And how I got to know about this story was an elderly gentleman told me this story. And it's a story about the first blowgun that was ever made and how it came about.

"The story goes that there was this old man who used to live in this house. And he planted gardens and he used to go hunting, and he used to go fishing and would go out and gather his food. But as he got older—he was around maybe in his eighties—he couldn't get around much anymore. He sort of couldn't see too well. And he couldn't walk around in the woods like he used to. So he decided that he would plant a garden and plant his food there so he wouldn't have to go out and hunt, like he used to, and fish. Because when he was younger he could climb hills, walk over rocks, and walk through the woods with no problem because he was a young man. But, like I say, as he got older he couldn't do that anymore. He couldn't go out and do those things that he used to do because if he went out to go fishing out on the banks where it was rocky, he might trip and fall and break an arm or a leg. If he went hunting, he might trip over something in the leaves he didn't see. Fall and hurt himself. So he gave up going hunting and fishing. But this also meant he gave up his food. He gave up the meat that he would eat!

"So he couldn't go hunting anymore and get rabbits. Or hunt for squirrels or any other meat. He couldn't go fishing for meat. So what he did was, again, plant a garden right near his house. And everything that he planted in that garden, all that food, was right there that he needed.

"So that's what he did. He planted vegetables. Corn, beans, potatoes. He would gather that up and he would bring it into the house. He would have baskets sitting alongside the walls. There would be a basket of potatoes, basket of corn, basket of maybe turnips or whatever he'd grown. And then during the day, when he got hungry he would fix a bowl of vegetables to eat. He would fix that on his fireplace and he would put all his vegetables and things that he needed in there. And so, he would eat that and that's what he survived on. That was his food.

"But one day as he was sitting there eating his vegetable stew, he got to thinking. 'You know, I really do miss the taste of meat. I haven't had meat in *so* long. And me being as old as I am, I can't go out and hunt anymore. Or go fishing like I could. I really miss that taste of meat.' So he decided, 'Well, I'll pray to the Creator. I'll pray to God and ask him if there's any way that he could see fit that I may be able to taste meat one more time.'

"That evening, he sat down and he prayed to the Creator, and he asked him if there was any way he could maybe get the taste of meat again. If there was any way he could help him out and maybe get him a way to get meat so he could cook it and get that taste.

"Later that night, he got ready for bed. He went and made his bed and went in and lay down. And he prayed again to the Lord to find a way for him to have that taste of meat again. He missed it real bad. So bad. And then he went to sleep.

"That night, the Creator gave him a dream. And in that dream, the Creator answers his prayer.

"All of a sudden, as he's lying in bed, he hears this commotion in his room. The sound of little feet. And pretty soon the bed starts shaking a little bit. He wakes up, he turns around, and it's Little People.

"He looks at those Little People and says, 'What are you doing?' And one said, 'The Creator sent us to you. He sent us to you to show you how you can have the taste of meat one more time.'

"'Well how can that be?'

"'We're going to take you somewhere and show you where you can get a tool to make it so that you can go and hunt for this meat that you seek.'

Ahii (river cane)

"So the old man says, 'Okay.' He gets up, and he follows these Little People. They take him outside. They take him out to the edge of the riverbank and they find river cane, *ahii*. And these Little People tell him, 'You seek a tall, straight river cane. Cut that. Take it home with you. This is what you'll use to hunt for meat.' And he says, 'Well, I don't understand, but okay.' So he goes over there and he cuts that river cane. They come back home.

"When he comes back home the Little People show him how to clean out the inside of the river cane. And they show him how to make darts out of a piece of wood. They show him thistle to wrap around the ends of the dart so he can use that as ammunition to kill the animals that he's looking to hunt for meat. And he says, 'Well, that's good! I never did know that you could use river cane this way. I never did know that you could make a dart to shoot through this.'

"And the Little People say, 'This is what we call *duquesdi*, blowgun. And you can use this when you hunt for small game.'

"So he says, 'Well, how do you use it?'

"'You make this blowgun and you go out in your garden. And while you're sitting there you wait for the crows to come in. All these birds come in. When they come in to feed on your corn and your vegetables, you shoot them with your blowgun. And that way when you kill them that will be your meat that you can use to eat. You can finally get the taste of meat again.'

"He said, 'Okay.'

"They take him back to his house. They go in there, and he goes back and lies down in the bed. And he goes back to sleep.

"Well, the next morning, he wakes up and says, 'Hey!' He looks around and says, 'Was I dreaming? Or was that something that the Creator gave to me in my sleep?' And he looks up and he prays to the Creator, 'Thank you.' He gets up and remembers how those Little People came to him and showed him how to gather that river cane and how to make a blowgun. That morning, he goes out to the edge of the riverbank and he seeks the river cane. He finds it. He cuts up the river cane, comes back, and he fixes it and cleans it out. And he gets another piece of wood and carves out a dart. And he gets a thistle and ties that around his stick to make a dart out of it. He makes two or three.

"He goes out to the garden like the Little People instructed him to do, and at midday he's sitting out there real quiet. And sure enough, as he sits in that garden waiting, here come those crows, those birds that come up to feed on his vegetables and the corn that he planted. And he aims toward those birds—and he shoots! And he hits one of those birds. Bird falls. And he goes over there and says, 'Hey, that was pretty easy.' He sees another bird. He shoots again and kills that bird. They fall to the ground.

"Well, pretty soon he says, 'That should be enough meat.' So he goes over there and grabs those birds. He goes back home. He has a rock by the fireplace. It's a stone he uses to grind corn meal. And there's another stone he uses to beat that corn to make corn meal. So he decides, 'Hey, that will be good to use on these birds.' So he hangs the birds up on a string in front of the fireplace and he lets the bird dry out. And as it dries out and becomes hard, he gets those birds and crunches the meat into a powder form. And so he fixes his vegetable stew and adds that pounded meat that he has and pours it on that stew. And when he eats that stew he gets the taste of meat again. He says, 'Ohh, *thank you,* Lord. Thank you very much! You don't know how much I missed this taste of meat. Now I finally got the taste of meat back. And I didn't have to go out in the woods to hunt. It's right here in my garden.'

"So he has those birds hanging there and every time he cooks stew to eat, he would pound that meat and he would add that to his stew. And he would eat that.

"But then one day, a man comes walking down the road. And this man was known as a thief. He was known as a bad person. Everybody knew him as a real bad person. He's walking down the road, and he's homeless. Didn't have a place to stay. And he smells stew cooking. He smells food out there in the woods. The old man has been cooking his stew in his house. He says, 'Oh, that smells so good. That stew smells real good. I'm so hungry! I wonder if that person in that house will let me eat with him?'

"So he comes over there and he knocks on that door. Knock, knock, knock. The old man comes walking out, opens that door and says, 'Yes? Can I help you?' The man says, 'I was walking by and I don't know where I'm going, but I haven't eaten in days. And your food that I smelled cooking, oh, it smells so good. Is there any way I could come in and share a bowl of your food with you?' The old man says, 'Sure! Come on in!' He says, 'Come on in and sit down.'

"So the young man sits there, and the old man fixes him a bowl of stew. And while he's fixing a bowl of stew for that young man, that young man looks around. Against the wall he sees baskets of corn, baskets of lettuce and tomatoes. And he sees a string of birds sitting up there on that fireplace. He looks around and thinks to himself, he didn't see anybody else in the house. And so he says, 'Are you the only one that lives here?' The old man says, 'Yeah, I'm the only one that lives here.' And he says, 'Hunh.' And he thinks to himself, 'You know . . . ' And then he starts eating that soup. And when he starts eating that stew, oh, it tastes so good. He asks the old man, 'How do you fix that?' The old man says, 'Well, I have a garden out back and I have all these in the baskets. I cut 'em up and chop 'em up and put 'em in there. Boil 'em. And that's what I eat during the day.' So the young man says, 'Hunh.'

He thinks to himself, 'You know, I see all this food here. I see everything that's in here that I need. Nobody knows who this old man is. He lives here by himself. If I was to come over there and knock him in the head and kill him, I could have all this to myself. And nobody would know the difference.'

"So that's what he does. He goes over there and hits that old man on the head and kills him. And takes everything he has. He buries the old man out there in the back somewhere. And he thinks to himself, 'No one will know the difference. He lives here by himself. Nobody probably even knows he lives here.' So he starts to live there, enjoying the old man's property. He starts fixing his meal, he starts eating that stew that he fixes. But it doesn't taste right.

"He thinks, 'Something's wrong with this stew. It just doesn't taste like the way the old man cooked it. It just don't taste right.' So he looks at the food and says, 'Well, what needs to be done? I know! It tastes like there's no meat in there.' He sees those birds hanging up there.

"Well, these Little People that had come to the old man in his dream, the ones that had shown that old man how to make a blowgun and how to get the meat for his stew, they saw what this young man had done to this old man. And they didn't like that. They said he shouldn't have done that. So they cast a spell on him. And so this young man said, 'Okay, I see those birds over there, that's probably what he put in the stew!' So he gets that bird, and he gets ready to put it into the soup. But those Little People say to each other, 'No, we're going to cast a spell on those birds. When he dips the bird in to make the taste of the meat, they're going to come alive and fly away.'

"So, sure enough, he gets that meat and as soon as he dips it into the stew—that bird comes alive again and flies off. The young man was shocked. He said, 'I don't understand what's going on!' He says, 'Well, there's some more.' So he gets another bird and he starts getting ready to dip that in the soup and all of a sudden that bird just flies away. Comes alive and flies away. He's confused now. But still, he goes and gets another bird.

"Pretty soon there are no birds left. He says, 'I don't understand what's going on. Well, I'll just eat the stew that's there.' He goes and starts fixing stew again. Every day and every morning, noon, and night he eats that stew until pretty soon the food in the baskets is getting lower and lower till finally there's nothing left in those baskets.

"And, of course, this young man doesn't know how to plant a garden.

He doesn't know how to grow his own food. So he's sitting there, looking around, 'What am I going to do? There's no more food left.' Time passes slowly in the old man's house. And finally the young man dies of starvation.

"These Little People come back, and this is what they brought for this young man for doing harm to the old man. Because he had killed the old man, they put that spell on him that he would die from starvation and not have the taste of meat like the old man did. And so that's how the story goes with this young man passing away. This is the only time that I ever tell a story that has Little People in it."

We all sat quietly thinking about the teachings in the story.

"So, the moral of the story is . . . 'Let him eat crow!'" Sequoyah said with a chuckle, breaking the solemn mood.

"Yeah, 'Let him eat crow,'" Sammy said and smiled.

"He wound up eating crow," Sequoyah deadpanned.

"I don't know if you can make any sense out of that," Sammy said to me.

"Oh, yeah," I said. "It's a good one."

"Like Sequoyah and Hastings always say, we're all storytellers. But when we tell stories, he could tell the same story and tell it a different way. And Hastings could, too. So it's just the way the storyteller tells his story. And again, this is a story of the first blowgun that was ever made."

A Light at Half Moon and Tsegi-Utvsdodi (Jack-o-lantern)

Loretta, Larry, and I were talking about examples of *ulvsgedi*, the wondrous, that they had witnessed near their home in Lost City, near Hulbert. They and their kin have lived for generations in the area and have become attuned to mysterious phenomena that, while part of their experience, are unexplained. As with other things ulvsgedi, Loretta had shared with me, the most important questions do not necessarily have to do with explaining what a phenomenon is but with how it affected you and why it was revealed to you. These are questions of meaning.

"As an example, I remember one strange thing that happened to us,"

Larry said. "There's a place we call Half Moon Landing on Clear Creek, which flows into Fort Gibson Lake. As you drive in there's a bluff that's shaped like a half moon. There's a spring there. There are bluffs out there and there's a crack in one of them where it looks like the formation of them came together once. There's a crevice now there in the middle.

Well, Dad and I were fishing one evening and I was sitting in the back of the boat and he was up front. The inlet is a cove that goes out to the lake, and that's where Clear Creek runs in. We were fishing right in that area. I was sitting there, and here comes this red light in the distance. I thought, you know, at a distance it was a plane or something. And I'm casting. I'm looking. And all of a sudden, that light, it keeps coming. And I think, 'Well, maybe it's a helicopter or something.' I start listening. And there's no sound. And then it got close, and I knew it was small. And we were close to the bank, so I could judge its size. I said, 'Dad.' And he turned and said, 'What is it?' I said, 'Look.' And we turned around and watched that light. And we knew it was small because the light was between us and the bluff. And it came in and goes to that crevice, and it goes into the crevice. Well, I look at him and say, 'Well, what is that?' And he said, 'Uhm, I don't know.' And, you know, others have seen the same thing down there."

"Is that what he called Red Lion?" I asked.

"No, that's different," Loretta said. "That's called *Tlvadatsi Gigage*, and it only comes in certain years. But there was another being we called 'Jack-o-lantern' that Hastings used to talk about. We used to walk around, even late in the evening. That was always a ghosty place right there by the house. Across the ridge. And one time he said, '*Ni*! Look at that.' And I looked down there by the hill. And he said, 'Look at that.' It was an orange-looking light about as big as a medium-sized ball. You know how it looks whenever somebody's swinging a lantern that you carry? That's the way it was going. And he said, 'Man! Jack-o-*atsvysdi*.' You know, 'Jack-o-lantern.' And I said, 'Where?' I looked at it real good and that's what it looked like. It just went along and passed by."

"Grandpa whistled at it one time," Larry said.

"He said if you whistle at it it'll come toward you. So don't whistle at it, that's what he talked about," Loretta said and laughed.

"Yeah, well, we were with Grandpa that time and we saw what looked like one, me and Dondi. And he said, 'You boys wanna see it?' And, you know, fear says no and curiosity says yes. So Grandpa starts whistling at it like you'd whistle at a dog. And it stops. And it comes straight toward us. And Dondi says, "Uh, *Dudu?* No, *Dudu*. No." And so he stopped, and it goes right back to where it was coming from. And it gets in line where it was and continues. And as he got closer, you could see the light. But, you know, there was no figure or anything around it, but then in the shadow that it cast you could see the legs in the shadow or something that was there. There was something there. And I tell people what I've seen. And, you know, some people believe me, and some people don't. It's kind of harder to tell the story itself when you know you've got non-believers out there and they think you're crazy."

My discussion with Loretta and Larry reminded me of a story of Jack-o-lantern that Hastings told me years ago:

"We used to sit on the porch when we lived over here at Grandma's. They had a porch. It was pretty high. And when corn was about that high," Hastings said and leveled his hand to his waist, "oh, probably the last part of May, there used to be a Jack-o-lantern that'd come across that hill. It was down on the other side and it would come on up the hill. It looked like a—we used to swear up and down that somebody was carrying a lantern. 'Cause you could see the legs, you know? You know how you can carry a lantern and it casts a shadow across you? That's the way it looked. Dad and I would sit up there, and they'd whistle at it, just like you were calling a dog, you know? And that thing would stop and come straight across the cornfield. And it wouldn't be in the corn, it'd be on *top* of the corn. And you could see that light coming. And Grandma'd say, 'Ah, y'all leave it alone!' They'd quit, and that thing'd go back. It would go straight back to where it started, and it would start back up the hill. And then they'd call it back. They used to play with it. They call it "Jack-o-lantern." And I watched them do it a lot of times. Especially in the spring. There's so much traffic now and so many houses I don't know whether it even exists, but sometimes when I see the corn about that high I want to go up there and see if it's still there. I was planning on doing that this spring, but I didn't get to it. I'm going to go up there, sit down, and watch."

HOW THE INDIANS LEARNED TO DO EVIL THINGS

by Hastings Shade

Cherokee tradition deals with the world as it is, and so it recognizes that malignant forces exist that actively move against tohi and Elohi's natural rhythms. Few are so naïve as to think such forces do not exist. When elements of the earth are manipulated without due concern for what they unleash, we end up with the atomic bomb and nuclear weapons that threaten the existence of all life. There are stories about known, malignant, powerful beings that actively move against the flow of nature for their own selfish gain or hatred. One such being is Utluga. In extending her life by stealing the life force of others, Utluga models our worst fears of others and in ourselves. She could only be killed by the life-affirming cycles of women. Some versions of this story say that Cherokees learned healthful medicine from the dying Utluga. But Hastings says that is not the case. Bad medicine was learned from her.

Many, many years ago there was only one evil thing in this place, a witch who was called *Utluga*, Sharp Finger. One finger on her hand had a long, sharp fingernail, and this is what she used to get to the liver of her victims—especially the ones who were sick and weak.

This is how she prolonged her life.

Everyone feared her.

One day the people got together and asked one of the elders how or what they could do to get the best of the witch. The elders told them to watch which way the witch came from and to get seven women who were on their moons and to line them up. The elders said that as the witch passed by each one, the witch would begin to get weak.

They did this, and when the witch came, she began to pass by the women and she began to get weak. By the time she got to the seventh one she was so weak that she couldn't defend herself. So they tied her to a stake and started to burn her. As she started to burn she began to say evil chants, and she said these all night long until daylight when she finally died. Some people learned some of the chants.

This is where the evil came to be that some of the people know now.

LEGEND OF THE WHITE SNAKE • *by Hastings Shade*

Many, many years ago a small boy was playing around the stomp grounds and he found a small white snake. Instead of killing it, he took it home with him and began to feed it. The snake began to grow.

This represents the time that the Europeans first came to Indian Country—when the Indians fed them or they would have perished in their first winter here.

The snake began to grow and needed more food and room. He got bigger and bigger, and the boy started to feed him small animals such as rabbits, squirrels, coons, and birds.

This represents the time more Europeans began to arrive—and needed more food and land. They began to kill most of the small game around their area and clear more land.

Still the snake grew bigger and bigger, requiring more food and area to grow. And the boy's grandson was feeding him now—and he was eating deer, bear, elk, and woodland bison.

This represents the time that more and more Europeans began to arrive—thus requiring more food and land, and began sending animal hides back to their homeland.

The snake grew larger and larger, requiring more and more food and area to grow. And he began to eat the Indians.

This represents the time the Europeans began to kill the Indian for his land.

It was at this time the great-great grandson of the boy who found the snake decided he would have to kill the snake.

So he took his bow and arrow and went to where the snake's upper body was—and aimed at the seventh rib, for this is where the snake's heart is.

But as he shot, the arrow glanced and fell short.

This represents the time the Indians tried to come to an understanding with the Europeans that there was enough land for everyone—the arrow falling short meant the Europeans wouldn't listen because they thought the Indians had the best part of the land.

Still the snake grew and grew, requiring more food, more land, eating more and more Indians, and taking the land.

And the grandson of the boy who had tried to kill the snake the first time decided he was to kill the snake. So he also took his bow and arrow and went to the place where the snake's heart was and he shot the arrow, and again it glanced. This time it hit the snake but did not penetrate the skin.

This represents the time the Europeans began to realize the Indians were gaining more and more knowledge of the Europeans' culture and language.

Still the snake grew, requiring more food and area to grow—still eating the Indians and taking their hunting ground.

So another grandson decided he would have to be the one to kill the white snake. So he took his bow and arrow and went to where the snake's heart was located and shot his arrow. Again, the arrow glanced, but this time when it hit the snake, it penetrated the skin. The snake began to thrash around and coil up. And as it does this, the arrow is penetrating deeper and deeper into the snake's body.

This represents the present time.

The arrow penetrating the body is when the Indian began to get educated in the European school. The snake wiggling around represents the Europeans beginning to realize and recognize the Indian ability to learn their ways. And when the arrow reaches the heart of the snake, the European will know the Indians are their equals.

Also, as the blood comes out of the snake—

This represents the European blood being scattered and thinning out.

In the end, the legend says only Indian blood will be left, and people will be lining up to prove they have Indian blood.

THREE RAVEN MOCKERS ✦ *by Hastings Shade*

Ever since bad medicine was learned, there have been people who use it to further their own selfish ends. Among the most loathsome and feared of these practitioners are the Raven Mockers. Raven was once a war title given to a respected protector of the people, a person who would sacrifice his life so that others might live. The Raven Mocker is just the opposite. When a person is sick and close to death, a Raven Mocker will visit the bedside in disguise and feed on the life force found in the person's liver and heart. The remaining life of the victim is added to Raven Mocker's own. In this way, the Raven Mocker's life is extended. Sequoyah Guess once remarked to me that during training a medicine person needs to learn both good and bad medicine. Stories of the Raven Mocker teach us about the choices we all make in seeking tohi or not. And to remain vigilant for those who would disrupt its flow.

This is a story my aunt would tell. She said she remembered when she was a little girl about eight years old, there was an elderly lady who was sick, and people would take care of her and sit up with her at night.

One night, she, her mom, and her dad went to help the people. Women were taking care of the elderly lady inside the house. They would feed and bathe her while the men visited and children played outside. They wouldn't let them make noise in the house.

Later on into the night, as the children got tired and sleepy, she remembered going in and sitting on her mother's lap. It wasn't too long after she sat down that the elderly lady began to stir about and have a hard time breathing. One of the ladies went outside to get an elderly gentleman. He came in and walked around the old lady's bed, and the elderly woman who was ill settled down, so the elderly gentleman went back outside.

Not long after that, the sick lady began to stir around and her breathing became labored again. Once more, they went and got the old man, but this time when he came in, he was smoking a pipe. Just as he got close to the bed, he blew smoke toward the sick lady on the bed. As the smoke got close to the old lady it revealed three people standing by her bed that no one in the room had seen.

My aunt said she could see these people real plain. There were two women and a man, and when the smoke disappeared so did the people. Then the old sickly lady settled down again.

The old lady died about three days later.

My aunt said that sometime later, she asked her father who those people she had seen in the smoke were. He told her those were mean people. When someone was sick they would come and eat on their heart and liver—this made them live longer. They are known as the *Kolvn Aniyelisgi*, or Raven Mockers.

Grandpa used to say if you hear a crow cawing at night, it's probably not a crow but a Raven Mocker going to dine somewhere.

THE SPOTTED PIG • *by Hastings Shade*

It started one evening. As the family sat down for supper, they heard a noise that sounded as if someone or something was trying to get under the house. When they went outside to check what it was, they saw this big spotted pig backing out from under the floor of the house. When it saw them it started to run around the house. One of the younger boys ran around the other side of the house to head it off. When he came around the house he saw an old man going through the gate. He had on a pair of overalls that had patches on the seat of them. Dark patches. And he remembered that when he looked at the pig that was backing out from under the house, it had dark spots on its rump.

He told the others what he had seen. Their grandpa said, "If it's what I think it is, it will be back." Nothing happened the rest of the night.

The next evening they heard the same noise again. As the rest of the family went out one door, the boy grabbed the shotgun and ran out the other door to the other side of the house. It was the same pig again. It ran around the house again, and as it went through the gate the boy noticed the dark spots on the pig's rump. This time it didn't change into the old man.

The boy aimed at the rump of the pig and pulled the trigger. The pig began to squeal as it ran down the road. Their grandpa said, "Well, if it was someone, we will hear who it was tomorrow."

The next day someone told them they had found the old man that lived down the road from them in his house. He could hardly walk. So they took him to the doctor, and he had buckshot in his buttocks. He was in the hospital. They couldn't figure out how he got shot.

Their grandpa just laughed and said, "Well, that serves him right for trying to bother other people at their home."

Someone later told their grandpa that the old man had gotten jealous of him. Their grandpa had gotten a good crop of potatoes, and when the old man had asked for some, Grandpa didn't give him many. Grandpa said, "I gave him all that he could carry. If that wasn't enough he will just have to grow his own."

Sometimes we expect too much from other people when they are trying to help us all that they can. We are never satisfied.

ᏅᏬᏭᏔ ᏌᏚᏬᏭᏞ (*Old Saying*)

ᎡᎵᏏ ᏂᎨᎡ, ᏦᎩᏃᏎᏬ—ᏓᏍᏗ ᏫᎳᏦᏕ ᏕᎳᏉᎩ ᏩᏝᎩᏗ ᎢᏣᏕᏂᏄ ᏅᎡᎢ ᏌᎩ—ᎪᎱᏍᏗᏍ ᏌᏣᏞᏔᏗᏍᎢ ᏓᏍᏗᏍ ᏰᏕᏂᏁᏉᏞ ᏌᏂᎪᎯ.

OLD SAYING

by Hastings Shade

My grandmother used to tell us, "Never run around the house more than seven times at night. If you do, something will join you—and you probably wouldn't like what you see."

DEER WOMAN ✦ *by Hastings Shade*

The elders talked of a woman who was half deer. They said that one time they were having their Green Corn ceremony and were dancing. The dance was at night, and after midnight a pretty young woman joined them. No one knew her. All the young men tried to get close to her when they would dance.

This went on until just before daybreak, when she disappeared. Nobody knew where she had gone. When it became daylight, they found deer tracks around where they had been dancing and where she had been. They knew that the Deer Woman had joined them.

The elders say if she ever got a young man alone, she would draw the life out of him. The elders would tell us to be careful about whom we went out with when we go to a place where people are dancing.

Asgisvsgv (Dream)

A peculiar quality of Under World is to shroud in mystery not only its creatures and forces but also its manifestations inside each of us. The Cherokee cosmos comprises a unity of light and dark, order and change, that we may navigate to stand in the middle in tohi. This much I have learned through the years. But sometimes the clarity of this conceptual model has lulled me into assuming I really *do* understand the Under World. It is then when something happens to remind me that mystery and unknowability are part of the fabric of life on Elohi. One such event occurred when Sequoyah Guess and I took a drive one day and the discussion turned to dream, *asgisvsgv*.

I had known Sequoyah for many years and we were close friends, but it occurred to me we had never talked about the role of dreams in Cherokee traditional thought.

"What do you think of dreams?" I asked. "Are they important in Cherokee tradition?"

"Oh, yeah," Sequoyah said. "My grandma, Maggie Turtle, used to read dreams for folks. They'd come over to the house and tell her their dreams. And then she'd sit with the dream for a while by herself, and they'd come back and they'd talk about the dream images."

I was taken aback by Sequoyah's comments. How could we never have talked about the importance of dreams? He had talked often about his grandma, Maggie Turtle. She was the one who taught him stories and set him on the path to being a storyteller. But he had never mentioned that she helped people with their dreams. Or that he considered dreams important to Cherokee ways of knowing. It was almost as if this important part of our mutual experience had kept itself hidden in shadow.

"Are your dreams important to you?"

"They've always been important to me," Sequoyah said. "I think about my dreams and what they tell me. I've learned a lot from my dreams. Just like the wind. Sometimes I'll go out at night and listen to the wind through the trees. It tells me things."

Some time later, I thought about Sequoyah's words when Loretta and I discussed the power and meaning of dreams. Our dream life is the flip side of our waking life and is associated with those parts of ourselves that arise out of the Under World. A dream of water, Loretta told me, means that something good will happen to you. A dream of snakes, insects, or rotting fish may mean someone is angry with you, and something bad may happen soon. Regardless of the images, a dream is just as important as the events in one's waking life. Though their source is mysterious, they are meaningful and as much a part of our human experience as anything else.

Though I did not intend it, throughout my work on *Cherokee Earth Dwellers* my dreams became an important part of my reflective and creative process. The teachings Hastings, Loretta, and other elders and knowledge keepers shared reach across the whole breadth of our experience as human beings, from our everyday experiences with the natural world to philosophical concepts concerning a life well lived. I thought about those ideas in the daylight, and at night they spoke to me in the images of dream. Time and again, teachings tell us to listen, to observe, to pay attention to what is around us without letting another way of knowing determine what is true, real, or worth considering. Unfortunately, most folks today ignore the way we connect with Elohi Hawinadidla each night when we sleep. But welcoming that connection, I found myself at peace with the mysteries and contingent truths the Under World offers. And I learned a great deal about myself.

Soon after Sequoyah passed on, he visited me in a dream. We were at a storytelling, and he urged me to go ahead and tell a story. I told a Snoqualmie story I had learned in the Pacific Northwest. And then I told Sequoyah's classic story, "Wolf Wears Shoes." This was Hastings' favorite story that Sequoyah told. As folks who have heard him tell it can confirm, it is a rich and humorous lie made all the more lively by the voices Sequoyah gave to each animal character. He told it just as his grandma did. And in my dream, I did my best to tell it that way, too. He smiled on, bemused and, I think, proud of his friend for trying. Maybe someday I will tell it that way in waking life.

Because They're Gonna Have Kids, Too

One of the last times I saw Hastings, we spoke of Cherokee tradition, standing in the middle, and of the perpetuation of Cherokee language.

"What do you think it's going to take to make the language really come back?" I asked.

"Dedication," Hastings replied.

"But how can you get people to use it more?"

"They're gonna see it. They're gonna see it, one of these days," Hastings said and gestured to the world around us. "And they're gonna say, 'Hey. *This* is what I've been hearing.' And it's gonna take a rude awakening."

"About what?" I asked.

"About what's *happening*," Hastings said emphatically. "And it may not happen this year or next year. But there's going to be an awakening for some people. They'll say, 'If I don't learn our language and our traditions, then I'm not going to be who I *am*. Or who I *want* to be.'"

Hastings was fortunate to have elders who shared with him their teachings of the Cherokee natural world and of the creatures of the Cherokee cosmos. He grew up among storytellers who shared the gayegogesdi tradition that offers lessons on how to stand in the middle. In turn, Hastings spent his life sharing these teachings with future generations. Loretta told me that Hastings taught Cherokee language, culture, and history not simply out of an obligation to his ancestors and the past, but to continue the relationships that Cherokees have cultivated with the other beings that share our world. It is through these relationships that we find joy, purpose, and meaning in life. It is through these relationships that we learn to live well in peace, in tohi.

Cultivating a life lived in tohi of body, mind, and spirit is a challenge. Our lives on Elohi are shaped by so many forces pulling at us, including many of which we are often not aware. But if we remind ourselves to listen not just with our ears, but with our whole being, we may become open to new relationships with our relatives and deepen those we already have. Learning the names and stories of the creatures of the Cherokee cosmos is part of this continuing process.

Sequoyah once told me that his grandma said, "White people invented writing because they didn't know how to listen. But we listen to the stories of our elders." But if it is true that writing may lead to forgetfulness, it may also lead to remembering and imagining. It is our hope that in sharing the names, teachings, and stories in *Cherokee Earth Dwellers*, folks will learn the names and stories of the creatures with whom they share existence. They will teach them to their children. They will share them. They will breathe new life into them and grow the web of connections that tie us all together as family.

Early on in our work together on *Cherokee Earth Dwellers*, I asked Loretta a question.

"Why should children be curious about Cherokee traditions?"

"Why should they be *curious*?" Loretta said in surprise. "Because they're gonna have kids, too, some day!" she said, and we laughed. "And their kids are gonna have kids. And if they don't learn our traditions they won't be able to say, 'Well, this is the way I was brought up. This is what I was taught.' And there's just so many things to learn."

"Yes," Sequoyah said. "And there's one thing that Hastings used to say that I always remember. 'Everything in this world can do without people. But, if you take just one thing out of the world, people would die out.'"

And so may we always remember our relations so that we may stand in the middle together. *Ayetli ididogesdi.*

Afterword

Like other books, *Cherokee Earth Dwellers* has a backstory. Behind the words on the page, relationships among people and the more-than-human world came together to create the text you hold. When Loretta Shade, Larry Shade, and I began working together on the publication of Hastings' collection of creature names, I had little sense of how deep and complex our exploration of the Cherokee natural world would become. But from our initial conversations it quickly became clear that in order to depict the natural world as understood in Cherokee tradition, we would need to enlist the help of many others. I would ask Loretta a question and she would respond, "I don't know. I'll need to ask an elder about that." Of course, Loretta was an elder herself, but being humble, she never referred to herself that way. She would call or text a fellow elder with our questions. Sometimes that elder would need to reach out to another elder for an answer. But eventually an answer would return to Loretta, and she would share it with me to include in *Cherokee Earth Dwellers*. In this way the book itself represents living Cherokee knowledge distributed throughout Cherokee community. In the spirit of sharing and in honor of Hastings, many folks contributed their knowledge to this book.

While Loretta and I had four years on the project, over the final two years of its writing our time together intensified. I called her several times a week as we made our way through the creature names, stories, and characteristics of the Cherokee natural world. Over time it became clear to me that much of the knowledge Hastings shared in his writings was also known by Loretta. And though she wished to honor her late husband for his work, *Cherokee Earth Dwellers* is very much Loretta's book as well.

When the COVID-19 pandemic was unleashed on our world, Loretta and I focused our work on *Cherokee Earth Dwellers*. The global context of climate change and environmental degradation made us both feel that the teachings the book shares are all the more urgent. By this time, health concerns made Loretta housebound. Still, whenever I called, she would answer, and we would continue our work. In this way Loretta reviewed full drafts of the *Cherokee Earth Dwellers* manuscript and we discussed each creature name.

I knew Loretta's health was fragile. There were days I would call and she'd say, "Let's talk tomorrow." I would call back the next day, she would be in good spirits, and we would talk about Cherokee language and the natural world as the OU basketball game played in the background. We spoke just a couple of days before her passing. Larry later told me that while she was in the hospital Loretta said she owed me a phone call. The teachings shared in this book were on her mind right until she made her transition.

At her memorial, former principal chief of the Cherokee Nation Bill John Baker offered a fitting tribute for Loretta. Chief Baker said that if the Cherokee Nation bestowed the title of Beloved Woman, as the Eastern Band of Cherokee Indians still does, Loretta Shade would be our Beloved Woman. Dating back to at least the 1700s, the title of Beloved Woman is given in honor of public service, heroism, honesty, and wisdom. With her decades of commitment to Cherokee language and cultural revitalization, Loretta surely personified what it means to be a Beloved Woman to the Cherokee community.

In honor of Loretta Shade, Hastings Shade, Sequoyah Guess, and all the elders and knowledge keepers who contributed to this book, we humbly offer *Cherokee Earth Dwellers*.

Acknowledgments

On behalf of the family of Hastings and Loretta Shade, Larry Shade would like to thank his family, friends, elders, and members of the Cherokee community for their love, wisdom, strength, and guidance. Larry wishes to recognize these elders in particular for sharing their knowledge with his family over the years and for their contributions to the Cherokee teachings Hastings recorded: Tom Shade, Aunt Maxine Neugin, Carl Shade, Leonard Shade, Martin Welch, John Marble, Sam Mellowbug, Sam Carey, Charlie Carey, George Bigfeather, Aggie Bigfeather, Felix Bird, Bob Crittenden, Buck Neugin, Charley Smith, Mack Vann, Ruby Gifford, and Totem Hair. Larry and the Shade family wish to thank the Creator for the blessings they have received throughout their lives.

Chris Teuton would like to recognize the many people and organizations that afforded him the time and means to work on *Cherokee Earth Dwellers*. Generous support across the University of Washington system provided research funding, leave time, scholarly support, and an ideal space to write. Funding and research leave from the College of Arts and Sciences made the completion of this book possible. Thanks go to divisional deans Judith A. Howard and George Lovell for their support. The Walter Chapin Simpson Center for the Humanities at UW provided research assistance and a vibrant scholarly community with whom to discuss the project through its Society of Scholars program. Thank you to director Kathleen Woodward and her team. The Center for American Indian and Indigenous Studies (CAIIS) at UW provided funding for the illustrations in *Cherokee Earth Dwellers*. Thank you to CAIIS co-directors Jean Dennison and

Chadwick Allen and the CAIIS board. The faculty and staff of the UW Department of American Indian Studies have been supportive throughout this project. Many thanks to all these fine colleagues, and in particular to AIS administrator Marcia Feinstein-Tobey. The Helen Riaboff Whiteley Center at Friday Harbor Laboratories on San Juan Island, Washington, provided a scholarly refuge to write and reflect. Much of *Cherokee Earth Dwellers* was written at a kitchen table in a Whiteley Center cabin looking out onto beautiful Friday Harbor. Many thanks to the Whiteley Center community and staff.

Chris Teuton and the Shades also wish to thank the staff of the University of Washington Press for their dedication to bringing the vision of this book into reality. Editorial director Larin McLaughlin and UW Press shepherded this complex project through every stage of development with attention to detail, with concern for the reader, and with the vision for the book at the center of each decision. Many thanks to the excellent readers and editors of the manuscript, each of whom took significant time to offer useful feedback on how to improve the book.

Chris Teuton offers thanks to Hastings Shade, Loretta Shade, Larry Shade, and the Shade family for their friendship, guidance, and trust in working with the teachings and knowledge passed down in their family. He thanks other members of the Turtle Island Liars' Club, including Sequoyah Guess, Sammy Still, Woody Hansen, and their families, for their friendship, stories, and teachings. He thanks artist MaryBeth Timothy for the care, patience, and dedication she showed in beautifully illustrating the Cherokee natural world. Cherokee scholars Ben Frey and Clint Carroll each read the full manuscript and offered crucial assistance with plant knowledge and Cherokee language. Cherokee Nation community member Billy Shotpouch offered insightful feedback on early drafts of the manuscript. Heartfelt gratitude goes out to all these folks, as well as to all contributors to *Cherokee Earth Dwellers*, a sgadug that includes family, friends, elders, and mentors, both those who remain with us and those who have passed on. All of Chris's family, but especially his wife Melissa, his children Markus and Azalea, his brother Sean, and his mentor, Craig Werner, have brought love, joy, and counsel throughout his journey with *Cherokee Earth Dwellers*. Much love and thanks to all. Finally, he wishes to thank Unetlvnv and the other living beings of Unetlvnv uwotlvnv for the blessings and teachings of this life. ᏩᏙ ᏂᎦᏓ!

Glossary of Cherokee Terms

Cherokee words as used in *Cherokee Earth Dwellers* but not presented in the lists of creature names. For an excellent Cherokee-English resource, visit www.cherokeedictionary.net.

adadvnidiyadodi ✦ endurance
adalenisgv ✦ beginning
adanetliyvsidohv ✦ transformation
adanohedi ✦ "what is told," an accounting of an event
adanta ✦ spirit or soul
adawehi ✦ magical
adayvsdesdisgi ✦ drugs, or things that harm your mind
advliha ✦ he/she is breathing
agasesdodi ✦ deliberation
agasga ✦ rain
agatanai ✦ knowledge
agatliya ✦ willingness
agayulage ✦ old woman
agi'a ✦ he/she is picking up something
aguluga ✦ twister, or tornado
ahuli ✦ drum
ahyvdagwalosgi ✦ thunder
alisidodi ✦ preservation
ama ✦ water
amayetli ✦ between the waters, an island
anagalisgi ✦ lightning
anehi ✦ they live
anehi tsalagi tsaniwonisgv ✦ dwellers spoke Cherokee
Aniatsila ✦ Fire People
anichuja ✦ boys
anidawehi ✦ beings super with wisdom
anigehya, agehya ✦ women, woman
Anigidui ✦ Coming to the Top or Coming Out People
Anikituwagi ✦ the people of Kituwah, a Cherokee name for themselves
aninohalidohi ✦ hunters
aninoquisi ✦ stars
Anisgaya Tsunvsdi ✦ Little Men, or the Thunder Boys
anisgaya, asgaya ✦ men, man
Anitsaguhi ✦ Bear Clan
Anitsalagi ✦ the Cherokee people
Anitsutsa ✦ the Boys, or Pleiades constellation
Aniwasasi ✦ Cherokee name for the Osage people
aniyegogi ✦ storytellers, or liars
aniyvwi ✦ human beings
aniyvwiya ✦ American Indians, the Real or Principal People, the Cherokee
anvskvti ✦ May
anvyi ✦ March
Asgaya Gigage ✦ Red Man
asgisvsgv ✦ dream

asinvgalisgi ✦ purification
asvtlv ✦ bridge
atsila ✦ fire
atvgi'a ✦ listen
ayetli ✦ middle or center
ayetli gadoga ✦ He/she stands in the middle or center
ayetli hidogesdi ✦ You will stand in the middle or center
ayetli ididogesdi ✦ You all and I will stand in the middle or center
ayetli tsidoga ✦ I stand in the middle or center
Ayu'ini ✦ Swimmer, Eastern Band of Cherokee Indians medicine man and knowledge keeper, primary informant to ethnologist James Mooney
Ayv Elohi gehi ✦ I am an earth dweller
ayvdagwalosgi ✦ thunder

dagwado'a ✦ I am called
Daksiyi ✦ Turtle or Terrapin's Place, Tuckaseegee River, also known as *Daksigi*
Dehaluya ✦ June
dideyohvsdi ✦ teachings
Digadatseli'i ✦ We Belong to Each Other, the Cherokee Citizen-Scholars Society
diganatla'i ✦ domesticated animals
diganotsalidi ✦ communication
digugotanv ✦ judgment
dikalvgv ✦ east
dikanowadvsdi ✦ law
dodalv ✦ mountains
dohinusdv ✦ calmness
doyadila nusdidanv ✦ weather
dulisdi ✦ September
dunidi ✦ October
duquesdi ✦ blowgun
duyodatlv ✦ levels
duyukdv ✦ straight or true

eduda ✦ grandfather
eladidla ✦ below
Ela Wodi ✦ Earth Paint, or Red Clay, Tennessee
eliyadvdi ✦ resourcefulness
Elohi ✦ Middle World, or Earth
Elohi digegv ✦ I am from Elohi
Elohi gedoha ✦ I am on Elohi
Elohi Hawinadidla ✦ Under World

gada ✦ soil, dirt, earth, land
Gado usdi detsado'a? ✦ What is your name?
gadugi ✦ people working together for the benefit of all
gadvgv'i ✦ purpose, or "it's sticking to the center"
galaquogi ✦ seven
Galaquogi Digosdayi Noquisi ✦ Seven-pointed Star, origin of sons of Unetlvnv
Galaquogi Dinadalv ✦ the Seven Sisters, or Pleiades constellation
galoni ✦ August
Galvladi ✦ Sky World
galvladidla ✦ above
ganvnowa ✦ pipe
ganvsida ✦ emissary
gatayusti ✦ chunkey, a betting game
gawoniha ✦ I am speaking
gayegoga ✦ teachings shared through story
gayegogesdi ✦ storytelling
gayegogi ✦ liar, storyteller
geyatahi ✦ prudence
giduninugo ✦ coming out like the bud of a plant
Gitli Noquisi ✦ the Dog Star, Sirius
gohiyuidi ✦ fidelity

Hadlv gedoha? ✦ Where am I?
Hadlv tegv? ✦ Where are you from?
hawa ✦ okay or alright
hawiya ✦ meat
hisgi ✦ five

Ilvhiyu tsigesv nigada inage ✦ In the great forever that was, all the forest
inage anehi ✦ forest dwellers or those who live in the wild

Inage Utasvhi ✦ He-Who-Grew-Up-Wild
inage'i ✦ the wild
Itagunahi ✦ John Ax, Eastern Band of Cherokee Indians elder, storyteller, artist, and informant to ethnologist James Mooney

jo'i ✦ three

kagali ✦ February
Kanadi ✦ the Lucky Hunter, or First Man
Kananesgi Amayi ✦ Water Spider
kanoheda ✦ an account, or story
kanohesgi ✦ one who gives an account of an occurrence, storyteller
kanvtsi ✦ traditional drink made from hickory nuts
kawoni ✦ April
kayegwoni ✦ July
Keetoowah ✦ Cherokee name for themselves
Kituwah ✦ name of Cherokee mother village near Cherokee, North Carolina
Kuwahi ✦ Mulberry Place, or Clingman's Dome mountain

nayadvv ✦ breath
nigvyaisv ✦ perseverance
Nikwasi ✦ Cherokee village and mound site located in Franklin, North Carolina
Noquisi Agehya ✦ Star Woman
nutsosedvna ✦ patience
nvdadegwa ✦ November
nvdo iga ehi ✦ sun, "celestial body, day, dweller"
nvdo svnoyi ehi ✦ moon, or "celestial body, night, dweller"
nvgi ✦ four
Nvnehi ✦ spirit people
nvwoti ✦ medicine
nvya ✦ rock

oginali ✦ friend
osda ✦ good, or things are normal presently
osdv iyunvnehi ✦ According to Cherokee scholar Julie Reed, "continual act of perpetuating positive well-being for the community"
osi ✦ normal state or neutral state of being
Osigwutsu? ✦ "Are you still good?" or "Do things remain normal presently?"
osiyo, siyo ✦ hello, or all is normal presently

sagwu ✦ one
sahoni ✦ saber-tooth tiger
saluyi ✦ the woods
Selu ✦ Corn Woman, First Woman
sgadudv dvhdatlesv ✦ community helping one another
sgadug ✦ community
sgili ✦ witch or ghost
siniqua ✦ pterodactyl
sogwili ✦ horse

tali ✦ two
talugisgi ✦ metal
tlanuwa ✦ giant hawk
tloges ✦ field
Tlvdatsi gigage ✦ Red Lion
tohi ✦ peace, flow, harmony, wellness
tohi oyelv ✦ peaceful body, or well body
tsalag uweti ✦ the old Cherokee lands, or original Cherokee territory in east
tsalagi gawonihisdi ✦ Cherokee language
tsiyukdi ✦ straight
tsuganawv ✦ south
tsulitsvyasdi ✦ courage
tsunadeloquasdi ✦ school
tsunilosv ✦ culture, or "what they have passed on"
tsuyvtlv ✦ north

udohiyu ✦ true or truly
ugasesdidega ✦ guardianship
ugvwiyuhi ✦ chief
Uk'tan ✦ Flying Dragon, winged serpent, "shiny-eyed" one
ulilohi ✦ eloquence
Ulisigi ✦ the Dark One
ulisiidi ✦ gracefulness

ulsuwid ✦ colors
ulvsgedi ✦ sacred, wondrous
unatsi ✦ snow
Unetlvnv ✦ Creator, "the one who provides or gives"
Unetlvnv uwotlvnv ✦ what Creator made, or nature
unole ✦ wind
unolvtanv ✦ January
usdagalv ✦ cave
usgwanigodiyu ✦ the wondrous
usonv'i ✦ evil
Utan Tsulasgi ✦ Bigfoot
utlinigidi ✦ strength
Utluga ✦ Sharp Finger
utugi igvsv ✦ hope for us all
utvsonv ✦ old man

vdelohosgi ✦ foresight
vhyugi ✦ disease
vsgiyi ✦ December

wado ✦ thank you
winiduyugodv ✦ directions
wudeligv ✦ west

yvwi ganvhida ✦ long person, or river
Yvwi Tsunvsdi ✦ the Little People

Works Cited

Altman, Heidi M. 2006. *Eastern Cherokee Fishing*. Tuscaloosa: University of Alabama Press.

Altman, Heidi M., and Thomas N. Belt. 2009. "*Tōhi*: The Cherokee Concept of Well-Being." In *Under the Rattlesnake: Cherokee Health and Resiliency*, edited by Lisa J. Lefler, 9–22. Tuscaloosa: University of Alabama Press.

Aveni, Anthony. 2019. *Star Stories: Constellations and People*. New Haven: Yale University Press.

Brings Plenty, Scott M. 2019. "Tri-Council Declares State of Emergency for Cherokee Language." *Cherokee One Feather*. June 27, 2019. www.theonefeather.com/2019/06/tri-council-declares-state-of-emergency-for-cherokee-language.

Carroll, Clint. 2015. *Roots of Our Renewal: Ethnobotany and Cherokee Environmental Governance*. Minneapolis: University of Minnesota Press.

———. 2020. "Cherokee Relationships to Land: Reflections on a Historic Plant Gathering Agreement between Buffalo National River and the Cherokee Nation." *Park Stewardship Forum* 36, no. 1 (January 6): 154–58.

"Chief Hoskin Announces $16M Cherokee Language Initiative." 2019. *Cherokee Phoenix*, October 1, 2019. www.cherokeephoenix.org/Article/index/10359.

Corntassel, Jeff, Taiaiake Alfred, Noelani Goodyear-Ka'ōpua, Noenoe K. Silva, Hokulani Aikau, Devi Mucina, eds. 2018. *Everyday Acts of Resurgence: People, Places, Practices*. Olympia, WA: Daykeeper Press.

Feeling, Durbin, William Pulte, and Gregory Pulte. 2018. *Cherokee Narratives: A Linguistic Study*. Norman: University of Oklahoma Press.

Fogelson, Raymond D. 1982. "Cherokee Little People Reconsidered." *Journal of Cherokee Studies* 7 (Fall): 92–97.

"Great Smoky Mountains National Park." 2020. *United Nations Educational, Scientific, and Cultural Organization*. whc.unesco.org/en/list/259. Accessed Sept. 1, 2020.

Hagar, Stansbury. 1906. "Cherokee Star-Lore." In *Boas Anniversary Volume: Anthropological Papers Written in Honor of Franz Boas*, 354–66. New York: G. E. Stechert and Company.

Hudson, Charles. 1976. *The Southeastern Indians*. Knoxville: University of Tennessee Press.

———. 1978. "Uktena: A Cherokee Anomalous Monster." *Journal of Cherokee Studies* 3 (Spring): 62–75.

Kilpatrick, Jack F., and Anna G. Kilpatrick. 1964. *Friends of Thunder: Folktales of the Oklahoma Cherokees*. Norman: University of Oklahoma Press.

Lankford, George E. 2007a. "Some Cosmological Motifs in the Southeastern Ceremonial Complex." In *Ancient Objects and Sacred Realms: Interpretations of Mississippian Iconography*, edited by F. Kent Reilly III and James F. Garber, 8–38. Austin: University of Texas Press.

———. 2007b. "The Great Serpent in Eastern North America." In *Ancient Objects and Sacred Realms: Interpretations of Mississippian Iconography*, edited by F. Kent Reilly III and James F. Garber, 107–35. Austin: University of Texas Press.

———. 2007c. "The 'Path of Souls': Some Death Imagery in the Southeastern Ceremonial Complex." In *Ancient Objects and Sacred Realms: Interpretations of Mississippian Iconography*, edited by F. Kent Reilly III and James F. Garber, 174–212. Austin: University of Texas Press.

Lefler, Lisa J., and Thomas N. Belt. 2022. *Sounds of* Tohi: *Cherokee Health and Well-Being in Southern Appalachia*. Tuscaloosa: University of Alabama Press.

Martyn, Marial. 2018. Back cover in Crosslin Fields Smith's *Stand as One: Spiritual Teachings of Keetoowah, Awakening to the Original Truths*. Taos, NM: Dog Soldier Press.

Mooney, James. 1900. *Myths of the Cherokee*. New York: Dover.

Reed, Julie. 2016. *Serving the Nation: Cherokee Sovereignty and Social Welfare, 1800–1907*. Norman: University of Oklahoma Press.

Risling Baldy, Cutcha. 2018. *We Are Dancing for You: Native Feminisms and the Revitalization of Women's Coming of Age Ceremonies*. Seattle: University of Washington Press.

Smith, Benny. 2011. "ᏯᏕᏚᎩ ᏗᏫᏃᎶᏯᏗ Community Values." In *Cherokee Writers from the Flint Hills of Oklahoma: An Anthology*, edited by Roy Hamilton and Karen Coody Cooper, 320–22. Stilwell, OK: INDIGITRONIC.

Smith, Chad "Corntassel." 2013. *Leadership Lessons from the Cherokee Nation: Learn from All I Observe*. New York: McGraw Hill.

Smith, Crosslin Fields. 2018. *Stand as One: Spiritual Teachings of Keetoowah, Awakening to the Original Truths*. Taos, NM: Dog Soldier Press.

Smith, Linda Tuhiwai. 2012. *Decolonizing Methodologies: Research and Indigenous Peoples*. 2nd ed. London: Zed Books.

Standingdeer, John C., Jr., and Barbara R. Duncan. 2016. *Your Grandmother's Cherokee: Level 1 Course*. Asheville, NC: Flying Lizard Languages.

Teuton, Christopher B. 2012. *Cherokee Stories of the Turtle Island Liars' Club*. Chapel Hill: University of North Carolina Press.

Wohlleben, Peter. 2015. *The Hidden Life of Trees: What They Feel, How They Communicate*. Vancouver: Greystone Books.

Yoon, Carol Kaesuk. 2009. *Naming Nature: The Clash between Instinct and Science*. New York: W. W. Norton.

Index

fig. after a page number indicates an illustration